JEDEDIAH SMITH

JEDEDIAH STRONG SMITH

JEDEDIAH SMITH

And the Opening of the West

by

DALE L. MORGAN

UNIVERSITY OF NEBRASKA PRESS • LINCOLN/LONDON

Library of Congress catalog card number 53-10550
ISBN 0-8032-5138-6
Manufactured in the United States of America

First Bison Book printing: June, 1964

Bison Book edition reprinted from the 1953 edition by arrangement with the Bobbs-Merrill Company.

To My Mother

EMILY HOLMES MORGAN

PREFACE

In the exploration of the American West, Jedediah Strong Smith is overshadowed only by Meriwether Lewis and William Clark. During his eight years in the West Jedediah Smith made the effective discovery of South Pass; he was the first man to reach California overland from the American frontier, the first to cross the Sierra Nevada, the first to travel the length and width of the Great Basin, the first to reach Oregon by a journey up the California coast. He saw more of the West than any man of his time, and was familiar with it from the Missouri River to the Pacific, from Mexico to Canada. He survived the three worst disasters of the American fur trade, the Arikara defeat of 1823, the Mojave massacre of 1827, and the Umpqua massacre of 1828, in which no less than forty men fell around him, only to die a lonely death on the Santa Fe Trail under the lances of the Comanches.

Jedediah Smith is an authentic American hero, a man who packed a staggering amount of achievement into the time between his twenty-third and thirty-third years, yet his is a story with a strange aftermath, for Jedediah Smith dead has had to fight for survival in the American memory with the same tenacity he brought to the struggle for physical survival during the years he ranged the West. His countrymen did their best to forget him entirely, but the integrity and magnitude of his accomplishment, the energy and the passion which infused his life and work, have finally brought him out upon the sunlit plateau for all to see.

He went to the Rockies in 1822 as one of the rawest of the green hands recruited by William H. Ashley and Andrew Henry for their fur-trading venture on the upper Missouri and the Yellowstone. That decade is seen now as a golden age in the history of the West, and some enduring reputations were made. The roll call of the Ashley men would include William L. Sublette, Thomas Fitzpatrick, James Bridger, Hugh Glass, Mike Fink,

James Kirker, Antoine Leroux, "Black" Harris, Robert Campbell and James P. Beckwourth, to say nothing of such rivals as Antoine Robidoux, Etienne Provost, Joshua Pilcher, William Henry Van derbuıgh Lucien Fontenelle and the brothers Bent. Yet Jedediah Smith rose head and shoulders above them all. Within a year he was at the head of an Ashley party; in two years he was Ashley's partner; in one year more he was senior partner in a firm which dominated the mountain fur trade until he quit the Rockies. He was "old Jed," but he was also "Mr. Smith," and the distinction is meaningful.

Jedediah Smith was an unlikely sort of hero for the brawling West of his time, that West about which it has been said that God took care to stay on his own side of the Missouri River. For Jedediah was a young man modest and unassuming, quiet and mild of manner, one who never smoked or chewed tobacco, never uttered a profane word, and partook of wine or brandy only sparingly on formal occasions. He took his religion with him into the wilderness and let nothing corrode it. That would have made him merely curious, except that he took with him also indifference to privation and personal suffering, endurance beyond the point where other men died, courage and coolness under fire, intelligence that impressed everyone, leadership of a high order, and energy and drive enough for three men.

In many respects he exemplified the American genius. Jedediah Smith entered the West owning his rifle, his Bible, the clothes on his back and very little else. He returned to the States eight years later having sustained himself and a large business operation through all that time by his proficiency as a trapper and his adeptness as a trader. Exploration was not a primary purpose with him; it was incidental to the pursuit of a business. In consequence, as an explorer he was a distinguished amateur in comparison with those two professionals, Lewis and Clark. He saw more of the West than they did and sustained himself through greater difficulties, but his education was not equal to his opportunities; he fixed the latitude and longitude of no geographical feature in the West, and he brought home no scientific collections. Yet this may be said too: Lewis and Clark were provided with a force of men under military discipline; they were outfitted relatively well; and nothing was asked of them except that they reach the Pacific by way of the sources of the Missouri and come home rich in information. Superbly they did their job; the Lewis and Clark Expedition will always remain our national epic of exploration. In contrast, everywhere Jedediah Smith traveled, the travel had to pay its way in beaver.

Like Lewis, Jedediah died in tragic circumstances while still a young man, before he had been able to do anything about publishing his journal or his map, and he had no William Clark to be his literary executor. The disasters which attended his odyssey left gaps in his journals no one was competent to fill, least of all the farmers, tradesmen and artisans who were his brothers. Fire pursued even such papers as survived—fire in Missouri, fire in Illinois, fire in Iowa, fire in Texas—and it was not until 1934 that a brilliant young scholar found and published the surviving fragments of his journals.

Jedediah Smith's place in history has been established by the labors of modern students who have had the patience and the energy to search out the record, disregarding a folk belief which has persisted since the presidential campaign of 1856, that nothing of importance happened in the West before Frémont's time. This latter-day reputation is in no sense a manufactured thing, for the solid accomplishment has always been there. It is not merely the slow emergence of the facts but improved perspective on the forces that have shaped our national life which has finally revealed Jedediah Smith's true stature.

He entered the West when it was still largely an unknown land; when he left the mountains, the whole country had been printed on the living maps of his trappers' minds. Scarcely a stream, a valley, a pass or a mountain range but had been named and become known for good or ill. A new kind of American, the mountain man, had come into existence during those eight years, and Jedediah Smith and his associates had had the shaping of him. They showed that the West would have to be conceived on American terms, that no parallel with the steppes of Asia would hold; they effectively carried the energies of American life beyond the temporary boundaries that had pent them, and initiated vortexes of force which made their country finally one nation.

Something of this, I hope, emerges from my book. Jedediah Smith's life in the West was a sustained adventure, yet it always added up to a great deal more than a simple adventure, and this biography is written with an eye to the symbols. It also attempts —for the first time, and that is curious in view of how much has been written about Jedediah Smith's decade—to tie together the events and personalities which make this so colorful an age, showing how the divergent happenings proceeded out of central energies. Even the story of Hugh Glass hitherto has been told merely as a folk epic, and I shall be satisfied if those who read my book gain from it an organic sense of the West, the play of cause and effect marvelously intricate on occasion, but always a whole.

Thanks to the generosity of libraries and librarians the length and breadth of the land—a generosity which spills over into England and Mexico—and to the steady emergence of new source materials, I am able to extend the record in ways my fellow scholars will appreciate. Nevertheless I owe much to those who have labored in the field before me, who have helped to organize my ideas and suggest lines for research, and I should like to make special acknowledgment to them: To J. J. Warner and Joe Meek, who kept Jedediah Smith's memory alive during the first two generations after his death. To H. H. Bancroft, who opened up the riches of the California archives and otherwise created a foundation in solid fact. To Hiram M. Chittenden, whose classic study of the American fur trade has influenced all modern scholarship. To E. D. Smith, who was instrumental in preserving most of the known personal letters by his grand-uncle, and whose research for a biography he was never able to complete beat out trails for all later students. To Harrison C. Dale, whose brilliant monograph on the Ashley-Smith explorations, first published in 1918, opened new vistas in fur-trade history. To John G. Neihardt, who published the first biography of Jedediah Smith in 1920 and later published an epic poem, "The Song of Jed Smith," which contributed largely to a revaluation of a neglected American hero. To Charles L. Camp, whose historical and bibliographical labors, in all directions around Jedediah Smith, have helped enormously to extend the record. To Maurice S. Sullivan, who by an extraordinary feat of scholarship found and published the fragmentary Smith journals, and who also wrote a posthumously published biography which exhibited in new perspective Jedediah Smith's experiences in California. To Francis A. Wiley, whose unpublished Ph.D. thesis on Jedediah Smith vigorously spaded the same field. To Frederick Merk, whose studies in the dynamics of the British and American fur trade have shaped all modern thinking about the fur trade. And finally to three great archives, the Hudson's Bay Company in London, the Missouri Historical Society in St. Louis, and the National Archives in Washington.

This book has used all the known source materials, including a number of documents which are here for the first time shown to exist. But I hope that the end has not yet come in the steady emergence of records. The principal hope for fresh discoveries centers on the various archives in Mexico City; as work continues in these archives, the lost journal of 1826 and letters of 1826-1827 may yet be found. Jedediah's final map appears to be irretrievably lost, known only in the form of David H. Burr's borrowings from it. An earlier map, which Jedediah apparently drew for his hosts of the Hudson's Bay Company while at Fort Vancouver in 1828-1829, a map which remained in Oregon for more than twenty years and seems finally to have been carried off to Washington, is a find which may yet be made, though I have haa no luck with it. Letters, accounts, maps, every kind of document to illuminate and extend the record of Jedediah Smith's life, may await discovery. Perhaps this book will provide some incentive for search in attics, old desks and elsewhere. I should be happy to learn of anything that may be found.

DALE L. MORGAN

Salt Lake City, Utah

CONTENTS

LIST OF ILLUSTRATIONS

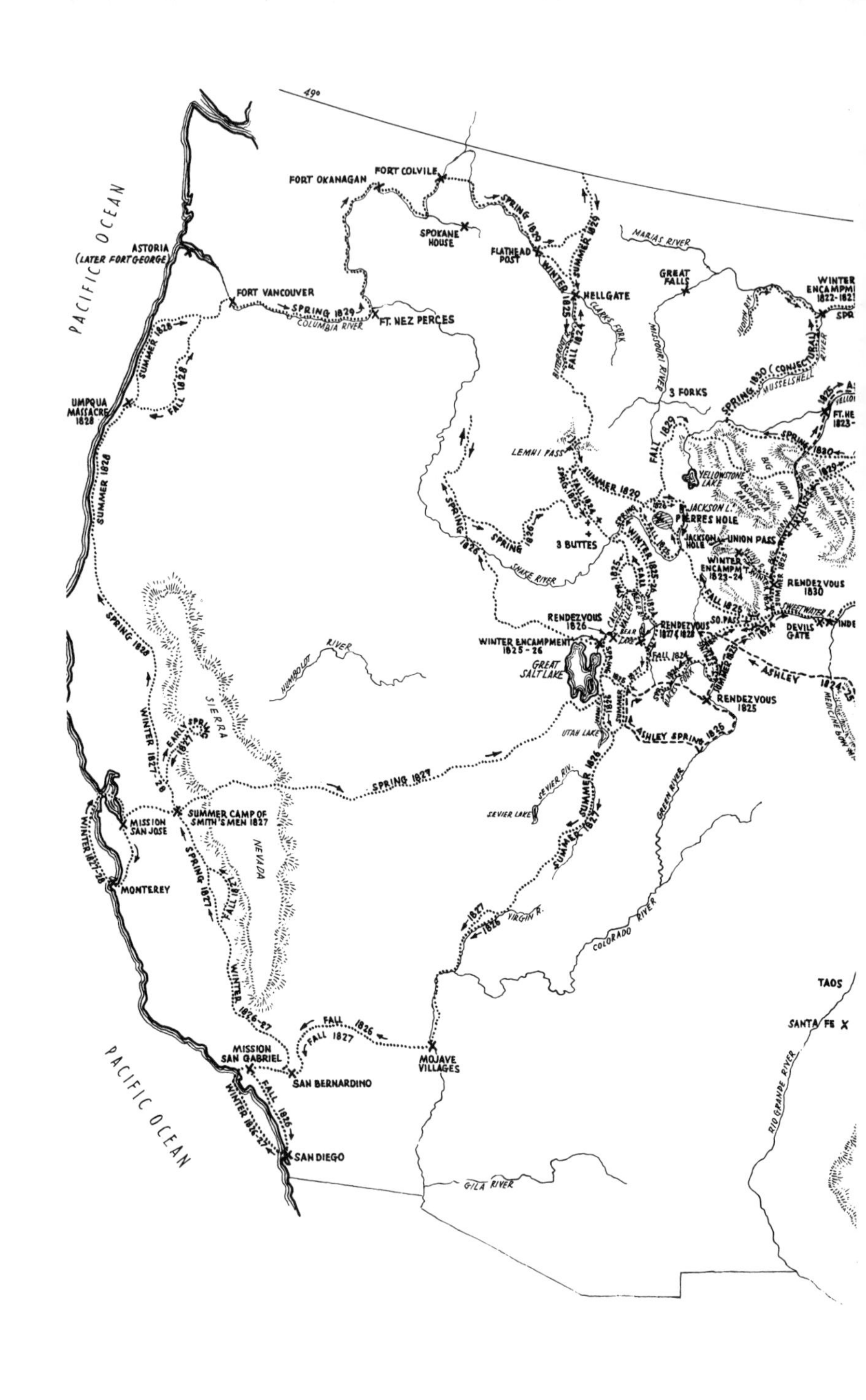

49°
PACIFIC OCEAN
ASTORIA (LATER FORT GEORGE)
FORT OKANAGAN
FORT COLVILE
SPOKANE HOUSE
FLATHEAD POST
HELLGATE
CLARKS FORK
MARIAS RIVER
GREAT FALLS
MISSOURI RIVER
3 FORKS
FORT VANCOUVER
SPRING 1829
COLUMBIA RIVER
FT. NEZ PERCES
SUMMER 1828
FALL 1828
UMPQUA MASSACRE 1828
SPRING 1828
LEMHI PASS
SUMMER 1829
FALL 1829
YELLOWSTONE LAKE
JACKSON L.
PIERRES HOLE
JACKSON HOLE
UNION PASS
ABSAROKA RANGE
BIG HORN MTS.
WINTER ENCAMPM'T 1823-24
RENDEZVOUS 1830
SPRING 1830 (CONJECTURAL)
MUSSELSHELL RIVER
3 BUTTES
SPRING 1826
SNAKE RIVER
RENDEZVOUS 1826
WINTER ENCAMPMENT 1825-26
GREAT SALT LAKE
BEAR LAKE
RENDEZVOUS 1827 & 1828
SO. PASS
SWEETWATER R.
DEVILS GATE
ASHLEY
RENDEZVOUS 1825
ASHLEY SPRING 1825
UTAH LAKE
GREEN RIVER
HUMBOLDT RIVER
SIERRA NEVADA
SPRING 1827
SEVIER RIV.
SEVIER LAKE
SUMMER 1826
SUMMER 1827
SUMMER CAMP OF SMITH'S MEN 1827
MISSION SAN JOSE
WINTER 1827-28
MONTEREY
VIRGIN R.
COLORADO RIVER
FALL 1826
FALL 1827
WINTER 1826-27
MOJAVE VILLAGES
MISSION SAN GABRIEL
SAN BERNARDINO
SAN DIEGO
GILA RIVER
TAOS
SANTA FE
RIO GRANDE RIVER

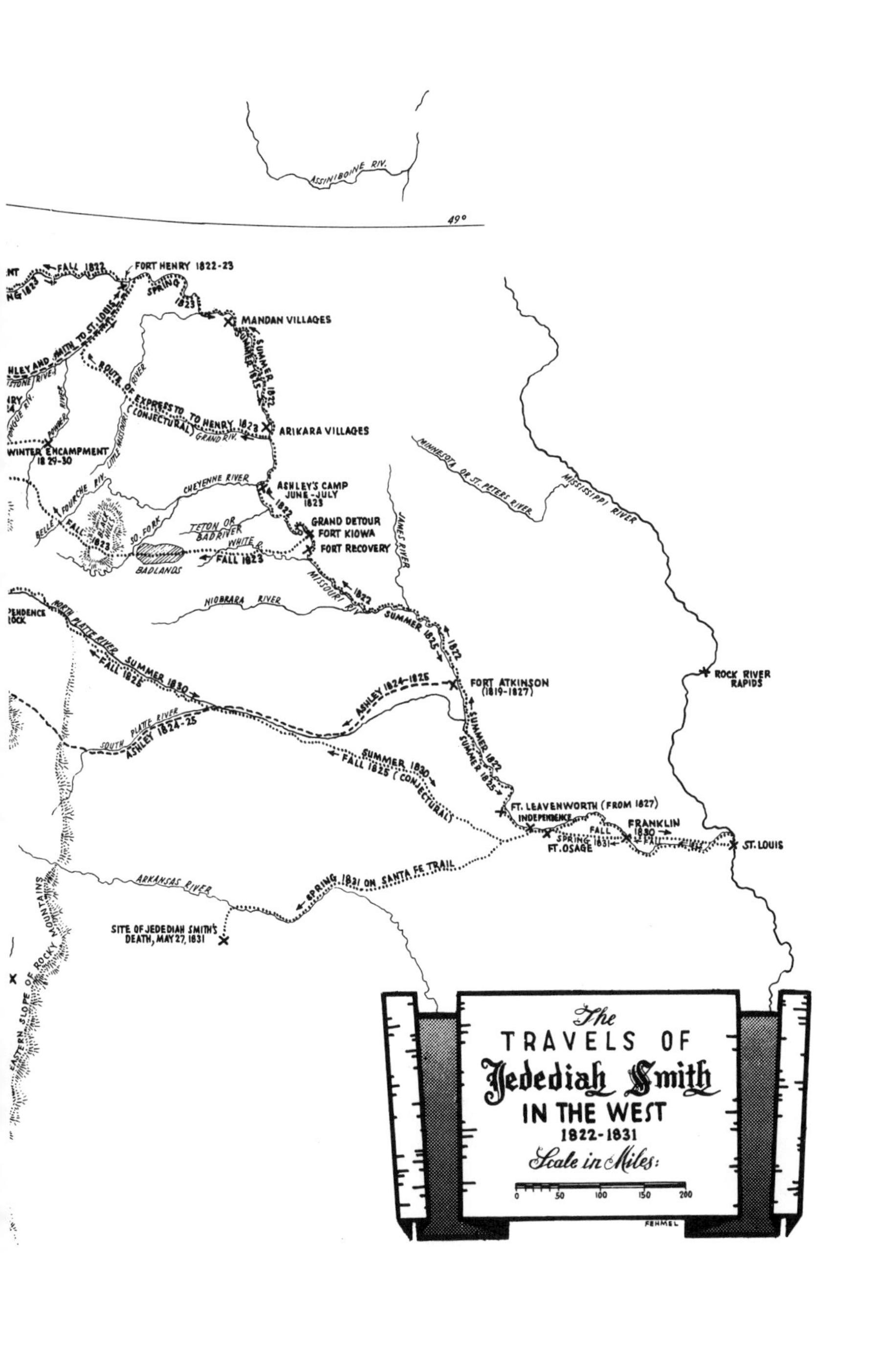
The TRAVELS OF Jedediah Smith IN THE WEST
1822-1831
Scale in Miles:
0 50 100 150 200
FEHMEL
ASSINIBOINE RIV.
49°
FALL 1822
FORT HENRY 1822-23
SPRING 1823
MANDAN VILLAGES
SUMMER 1822
SUMMER 1823
ROUTE OF EXPRESS TO HENRY 1823 (CONJECTURAL)
ARIKARA VILLAGES
GRAND RIV.
LITTLE MISSOURI RIVER
POWDER RIVER
WINTER ENCAMPMENT 1829-30
BELLE FOURCHE RIV.
CHEYENNE RIVER
ASHLEY'S CAMP JUNE-JULY 1823
BLACK HILLS
FALL 1823
SO. FORK
TETON OR BAD RIVER
WHITE R.
GRAND DETOUR
FORT KIOWA
FORT RECOVERY
BADLANDS
JAMES RIVER
MINNESOTA OR ST. PETERS RIVER
MISSISSIPPI RIVER
MISSOURI RIV.
NIOBRARA RIVER
NORTH PLATTE RIVER
SUMMER 1830
FALL 1825
SUMMER 1825
FORT ATKINSON (1819-1827)
ASHLEY 1824-1825
SOUTH PLATTE RIVER
ASHLEY 1824-25
ROCK RIVER RAPIDS
FALL 1825 (CONJECTURAL)
FT. LEAVENWORTH (FROM 1827)
INDEPENDENCE
FALL
FRANKLIN
SPRING 1831
FT. OSAGE
ST. LOUIS
ARKANSAS RIVER
SPRING 1831 ON SANTA FE TRAIL
SITE OF JEDEDIAH SMITH'S DEATH, MAY 27, 1831
EASTERN SLOPE OF ROCKY MOUNTAINS

JEDEDIAH SMITH

1. YOUNG MAN OF ENTERPRISE

The advertisements laid before the public by the St. Louis *Missouri Gazette & Public Advertiser* on Wednesday morning, Feb. 13, 1822, were more enlightening and far more entertaining than the news. The usual outrages were in progress in Ireland, trouble remained the staple diet of South America, and here was the grist Congress had ground out on a day in January five weeks since. But no information as to what was new in town. The advertisements told more about that.

Here, for example, was Mr. Paulet Dejardin cautioning all persons against trusting or selling on credit to Emily his wife, who had left his bed and board without just cause. And Mr. W. E. D. Wines singing much the same tune; Mrs. Wines also had quit the marital bed, "through the persuasions of her mother." Down the page Mr. John Shackford was moved to speak of mackerel; he had just acquired fifteen barrels. There was more of poetry in the souls of Messrs. Tracy & Wahrendorff, who offered to a discriminating clientele an assortment of Madeira, Teneriffe, Lisbon Port, Claret and Malaga Wine, Cognac Brandy, Rum, Gin and Cordials, though as practical storekeepers they had also laid in a supply of dye stuffs, shoes and boots, bar iron, plough moulds, Indian goods, pork, Glassware and Spanish Segars.

This of course was the merest beginning. But the big news in St. Louis this week was an advertisement at the foot of page 3. Signed by the lieutenant governor of the state, the advertisement made a fact of what had been tavern gossip for five months.

TO

Enterprising Young Men

The subscriber wishes to engage ONE HUNDRED MEN, to ascend the river Missouri to its source, there to be employed for one, two or three years.—For particulars enquire of Major Andrew Henry, near the Lead Mines, in the County of Washington, (who will ascend with, and command the party) or to the subscriber at St. Louis.

Wm. H. Ashley[1]

Enterprising young men, as General Ashley well knew, were a specialty of St. Louis. The ad did not specify how the hundred young men were to occupy themselves on the sources of the river Missouri, nor did it have to. One thing only had made St. Louis the largest and most thriving town on the frontier: the fur trade of the Far West. That trade had made fortunes for some and ruined others, but there were few in St. Louis whose well-being did not in some way depend on what was happening up the great rivers.

Sprawled over a hillside along the western bank of the Mississippi five miles below its confluence with the Missouri, St. Louis lived by the wealth borne to it on the swirling yellow waters. From above, flatboats, keelboats, pirogues, canoes and rafts floated down with cargoes of lead, lumber, wheat, whisky, pork, and the staple furs and buffalo robes. Up the river from below came the slim keelboats, propelled against the current by powerfully muscled boatmen or by clumsy square sails; and among the keelboats in increasing numbers splashed the new steamboats, a sight to which none upon the western waters had grown entirely accustomed. Both were laden with the varied wealth of the outside world for which St. Louis exchanged its furs. From these boats, and from the ferries that plied between the city and the green Illinois shore, thronged boatmen, trappers and traders, Yankee peddlers, miners, farmers, soldiers of the Republic and, not least conspicuous on the streets, gaily blanketed Indians come to Red Head's Town to confer with General William Clark.

The streets along the water front were narrow and crowded, cluttered with warehouses and stores, but those on the heights were spacious, and adorned with finely built houses which gave the town a pleasing and substantial appearance. Some of the streets had lately been paved, which was progress to those appalled by St. Louis' dust and mud, but something less to the old

French habitants who complained of the "rocks put in the streets," on which the rude wooden wheels of their carts were forever shattering.

With a population edging past five thousand, St. Louis was experiencing the growing pains that mark the transformation of a village into a city. Only six years ago there had not been a single brick house in the town, but more than a third of its dwelling places were now wholly or partly built of brick. Many frame and some log houses were yet to be seen, the old French dwellings apparent at sight, built with their hewn logs planted perpendicularly in the ground.

St. Louis "under the Hill" was only less notorious than Natchez. On the Hill itself the townspeople were having their troubles learning to live together with ever less elbow room. Many families had the medieval habit of disposing of slops and worse by throwing them into the streets from any handy window; and passers-by had to reckon with the prevailing conviction that the way to dispose of a defunct dog, cat or rat was to take it by the tail and hurl it into the street, to remain till rain, wind, sun and passing cart wheels should return it unto the dust.

St. Louis streets were a continuous spectacle. Fine broadcloth rubbed elbows with coarse homespun, greasy buckskin and greasier blankets. Boatmen from the Mississippi and Ohio, like the *voyageurs* from the Missouri, swarmed ashore, spoiling for whisky, whores and a fight. Hoosiers and Suckers bound for the rich farmlands of the Boonslick country and beyond, like the more numerous Kentuckians, strolled the streets of the metropolis, their wide-eyed, sun-bonneted women on their arms. St. Louis was a Southern town with an abundance of Negroes, but they answered more readily to French than to English. The old French heritage of St. Louis was, in fact, always on show. The crude carts had clumsy wooden wheels innocent of iron tires, and they were drawn by little Canadian horses. Just as striking was the St. Louis manner of gearing ox teams, for the French had no truck with the ox yokes and bows of the Americans; they fastened five-foot stakes with leather straps to the horns of their animals and required their teams to pull with their heads.

This was a town adventurous in its spirit, too quarrelsome

and short of temper; gentlemen were always taking themselves at dawn to Bloody Island in the Mississippi, while the unwashed worked off their grievances in tavern brawls. Beyond that it was possessed of a certain graciousness and a feeling for the good things of this world. One could walk the streets and never be out of hearing of the fiddles pouring forth on the soft night air the gaiety and the sadness of life. It was a rare evening when a public party was not in progress somewhere in the town, and the newly established theater was the pride of St. Louis.

Catholic in its origins, St. Louis took pride in the new Cathedral on Church Street, adorned as it was with paintings by Rubens, Raphael and Veronese, and with ancient and delicately wrought gold embroideries donated by wealthy Catholics in Europe. The Baptists and the Episcopalians had church buildings too, but the Presbyterians held their meetings in the circuit court room, and the Methodists in the old courthouse. Otherwise the show places of the city were the imposing residences of the brothers Auguste and Pierre Chouteau, on the hill overlooking the town; the council chamber of General Clark, containing "the most complete museum of Indian curiosities to be met with anywhere in the United States"; and the Indian mounds and other remains of antiquity north of town, where also was situated the Mound Garden, kept by Mr. James Gray as a place of entertainment and recreation.[3]

In this city, primarily, General Ashley must recruit the men for his expedition to the Rocky Mountains. They would be a mixture of the good with the bad. The Creoles of St. Louis, skilled watermen all, and some of them the best woodsmen in the world, were passionately fond of the whisky barrel, and too mercurial to be depended on in a fight. For leavening Ashley needed a goodly number of Kentuckians or Virginians, with their long rifles, sharpshooter's eye and unwillingness to yield an inch under fire. If the kind of man he was looking for happened to hail from Pennsylvania, New York or even New England, why, all were fish which came to his net.

Of the circumstance which swept him into the tide of Ashley's great enterprise, Jedediah Smith wrote in after years with directness and economy of phrase:

I had passed the summer and fall of 1821 in the northern part of Illinois, and the winter of 21 & 22 at or near the Rock River rapids of the Mississippi. In the spring I came down to St Louis and hearing of an expedition that was fiting out for the prosecution of the fur trade on the head of the Missouri by Genl Wm H Ashley and Major Henry I called on Genl Ashley to make an engagement to go with him as a hunter. I found no difficulty in making a bargain on as good terms as I had reason to expect.[3]

Nothing of how he came to be in the West, nothing of his family or circumstances. Jedediah's reticence has become a silence of American history itself, and not much will ever be known of him before the spring day in 1822 he sought out General Ashley's residence on South B Street.

By family tradition Jedediah Smith's ancestors on his father's side came to America not long after the Plymouth colony was founded, and thereafter raised successive generations in Massachusetts and New Hampshire. Jedediah Smith, Sr., was born in New Hampshire April 21, 1767, and with him began the long westering which ended for the Smith family at the shore of the Pacific. The Smiths were a tall breed, brown-haired and blue-eyed, farmers and artisans who led sober, God-fearing lives and were typical of a strain which has flowed steadily in all the tides of western migration. At the close of the Revolution the West lay alluringly open to land-hungry New England, and the elder Jedediah Smith was one of those who deserted the rock-bound hills to seek out the green land over the horizon. But first, on October 21, 1790, perhaps at Easthampton, Connecticut, Jedediah Smith married Sally Strong.

Like the Smiths, the Strongs were of old American stock, their progenitor having come to Massachusetts from England in 1630. They were a folk adventurous, practical and pious; one of them, it is recorded, was paid eighteen shillings a year for blowing the trumpet on Sundays to summon the townsfolk to church; another was killed by Indians in New York in 1709; yet another was one of the first to go over Niagara Falls and live to tell of it. Sally Strong, born March 3, 1771, was four years younger than her husband. It was the duty of women in this generation to work hard, fear God and bear their husbands many sons. The children made their appearance soon enough, but the first-born was a daughter. Sally was born October 8, 1791. Next came a son, Cyrus, born April 6, 1793, but he died young.

The move to the Susquehanna Valley of southern New York was the first great adventure of the Smith family. The valley had been opened to settlement in 1786, and the farms were still being cleared when the elder Jedediah Smith, in company with his brother-in-law Cyrus Strong, opened a general store in the new village of Jericho in Chenango County. Bartering lumber for merchandise, they floated great rafts down the Susquehanna and resupplied themselves from wholesalers in the river towns below. It was a livelihood, and the Smiths made their home at Jericho (now Bainbridge) in the lovely green valley until shortly before the War of 1812.

Jedediah Strong Smith was the fourth child born at Jericho. The eldest son, Ralph, issued into the world September 11, 1794, followed by Betsey on February 12, 1796, and Eunice on October 7, 1797. Jedediah was born January 6, 1799. Other children, Maria, Almira and Alman, died young, but then came sons more resistant to infant ills. Born at Jericho were Austin, June 4, 1808, and Peter, March 10, 1810. Three more sons—Ira Gilbert, October 18, 1811; Benjamin Greene Paddock, January 12, 1813; and Nelson Jones, December 22, 1814—came along after the family had moved on to the shores of Lake Erie.

The Susquehanna during the Revolution had been a preserve of the Iroquois, and the recent past still brooded on the long green valley. The artist George Catlin, whose boyhood was spent along the Susquehanna a few miles farther down the river, remembered an Iroquois who as a child had participated in a great retreat up the valley; the red man's father had buried a golden pot, and these many years later he had come back hoping to find it. The golden pot had been found already by the white man's plow—a small utensil of brass which had been magnified by a child's eyes into a treasure. . . . Catlin's Iroquois was killed in the night by some white man in whom the vengeful passions of the old wars still burned.[4] This was not a safe country for Iroquois, and the child Jedediah saw few of them, but he hunted deer and squirrels amid the tall oaks, basswood and sweet-smelling sassafras which covered the rolling hills.

Apparently in late 1810 or early 1811 some unpleasantness started the Smiths again on the long trail west. What the trouble was it is difficult now to ascertain, but according to the memory preserved in the community, the elder Jedediah was detected passing counterfeit coin. Perhaps he was merely a victim of circumstances, for he reared a family of unassailable reputation. The elder Jedediah's partner, Cyrus Strong, stayed on at Bainbridge, and there and at Binghamton, a little farther down the valley, became a pillar of the community. But Jedediah, Sr., with his wife and the family which now numbered four sons and three daughters, set out to make a new life in the West. They settled just beyond the New York border in North East Township, Erie County, Pennsylvania. Here, perhaps, the Smith family became involved with the Simons family, with lasting effect on the life of Jedediah Strong Smith.

"Diah" was now a tall, slender youth of twelve, with a restless interest in the world and a thirst for knowledge. He found a mentor in Dr. Titus Gordon Vespasian Simons, whose memory as a pioneer physician lingers in several Pennsylvania counties. Dr. Simons' son Solomon married Jedediah's favorite sister, Eunice, and his daughter Louisa married Jedediah's eldest brother, Ralph, so there were family ties. But Dr. Simons won Jedediah's love and respect for what he was himself, and Jedediah's letters are never so glowing as when they speak of the old doctor.

It is said that Dr. Simons presented the youth with a copy of the book published in 1814 which at last gave to the world the narrative of the journey Meriwether Lewis and William Clark had made to the Pacific, and that Jedediah carried this book on all his travels. Perhaps that is legend only, for the tides of American history were strong enough to pick Jedediah up and fling him westward. The local movement of those tides swept the Smith and Simons families west along the shores of Lake Erie and on into the Western Reserve of Ohio; they were there by 1817. Members of both families settled in and around Ashtabula, but others, including Jedediah's father and eldest brother, moved on south and west, to Green Township in what is now Ashland County.[5]

The family had little money, and that, as much as the pull of the West, may have taken Jedediah finally from home in the spring of 1821. Perhaps by one of the lake boats, perhaps overland, he made his way to northern Illinois, where his journal takes up his story.

The young man who came knocking on General Ashley's door received a warm welcome, for reliable men were hard to find this spring. The General's caller was a lean young fellow, brown of hair and blue of eye, perhaps six feet tall, who talked with a self-possession that belied his twenty-three years. Serious of mind if not entirely humorless, there was a quiet passion in him which would emerge in the course of an hour's conversation. He proposed going to the mountains to make himself a first-rate hunter, thoroughly acquainting himself with the character and habits of the Indians, tracing out the sources of the Columbia and following the great river to the sea. But also, practically, seeing to it that all this was profitable to himself.[6]

Here was a man after Ashley's heart, for he too was capable of a vision infused with the sternest understanding of his own interest. Virginia-born, he had come to Missouri as early as 1805, settling in the Ste. Genevieve district below St. Louis. There he had become the neighbor and friend of Andrew Henry, acting as one of the witnesses to Henry's marriage in December 1805, and doubtless condoling with the bridegroom when the marriage grated asunder after only eighteen days. Ashley was slight of frame and of medium height, with a thin face, prominent nose and jutting chin, not especially striking in his appearance yet a man of distinguished presence. Intelligent and forceful, he inspired confidence and respect, and was early made a captain in the Ste. Genevieve militia and a justice of the peace for his district. During the war with Britain, he and Henry had removed to Washington County, attracted by the possibilities of Missouri's infant lead-mining industry. Henry had embarked on mining operations while Ashley, seeing so much shot issuing from the smelters, commenced a powder manufactory. The business had prospered during the war and for a time thereafter. He then turned his attention to surveying and real-estate promotion, and by 1819 had established himself in St. Louis.

Throughout this period Ashley advanced steadily in the territorial militia. In 1814 he was commissioned lieutenant colonel of the Sixth Regiment of Washington County, with Andrew Henry major of his First Battalion; by 1819 he had become a full colonel, and in 1822 he was a brigadier general. Although he lacked the fire of his friend young Tom Benton, he had won the lieutenant governorship in Missouri's first state election, and he had just finished presiding over the first session of the Missouri Senate. Ashley wanted wealth and its perquisites, and was willing to gamble for them. But above all he wanted political preferment, and whatever wilderness adventures he might embark on, he understood them to be a means to this end.[7]

General Ashley had the aspect of a man able to pay his bills. If he lacked experience in the fur trade, this could not be said of his partner. Andrew Henry had gone to the mountains as early as 1808 as a partner in the old Missouri Fur Company. During the next three years he had penetrated to the remotest sources of the Missouri and even crossed the continental divide to the South Branch of the Columbia—Lewis' River, the Snake—to build a post. Starvation and the Blackfeet had finally driven everyone out of that country. Henry had come down the Missouri in 1811 with the expectation of returning to the rich fur country beyond the mountains, but dissension disrupted the Company, and later the war with Britain stopped all trading and trapping in the upper country.[8] If anyone was capable of re-establishing the American fur trade on the fabulously rich waters of the high Missouri, Andrew Henry appeared to be the man.

A four-way competition was shaping up for the wealth of the upper Missouri, and since the previous summer it had been an exciting question who would get there first. The Missouri Fur Company, revitalized by a reorganization in 1820, for a year had been preparing an expedition under two of its ablest partisans, Robert Jones and Michael Immell, with the intention of reoccupying the country from which it had been driven ten years before. Simultaneously the formidable firm of Berthold, Pratte and Chouteau, "the French Fur Company" to its rivals, was getting together an expedition of sixty men which would establish a post in the Sioux country and then go on up the river to the Mandans. An international complexion was given the rivalry by the Columbia Fur Company. In the wake of the consolidation of the North West Company with the Hudson's Bay Company, some of the Nor'Westers who had been cut adrift had come down from Canada and found American partners; now they were preparing to penetrate to the Mandans by a different route, via the sources of the Mississippi and the St. Peters.[9]

At the same time traders who had gone out to New Mexico the previous summer had received a warm welcome, unprecedented for American traders, explained by the news of the revolution in Mexico which had broken the Spanish grip on the lower reaches of the continent. William Becknell had come back to Missouri in February with the news that the gates of Santa Fe had been flung wide open, and he and others were preparing a trading venture which among other novelties would take out the first wagons ever to depart for the Rocky Mountains.[10] Competition made men suited to the fur and Santa Fe trade scarce and valuable and contributed to the generally roseate aura that enveloped St. Louis this spring.

Ashley and Henry showed imagination and enterprise throughout their years in the fur trade, and the terms to which they came with their men gave the competition a rude surprise. Our information comes from Thomas Hempstead, the Missouri Fur Company's acting partner at St. Louis. On April 3, 1822, the day Henry got off for the mountains with Ashley's advance party, Hempstead wrote Joshua Pilcher, the acting partner on the Missouri:

> Genl Ashley's company starts this day with one boat and one hundred & fifty men by land and water they ascend the Missouri river to the Yellow Stone where they build a Fort the men are all generally speaking untried and of evry description and nation, when you see them you will judge for yourself, the Company will be conducted by honourable men I think, but I expect they will wish nothing more of us than to unite in case of difficulty. my opinion as regards the manner that those men are employed might differ with yours, but I

think it will not, they are engaged in three different ways I am told the hunters and trapers are to have one half of the furs &c they make the Company furnish them with Gun Powder Lead &c &c, they only are to help to build the fort & defend it in case of necessity, the boat hands are engaged as we engage ours, the Clerks are also the same but of those are the fewest number. I do think when men are engaged upon the principals of the above, that regularity, subordination, system, which is highly necessary to have on that river should be the first object of any company to establish but pray let me ask you in what way it can be done under those circumstances Should the hunters wish after they get above to leave them in a mass in what way will they prevent them, this kind of business of making hunters will take some time and much trouble.[11]

The point was well taken, but the hunters Ashley and Henry were going to make would revolutionize the Western fur trade. The companies would always require hired servants, *engagés*, but the free trapper became the rock on which the fur trade of the Far West was built.

Henry's departure was noted by the press as well as by the competition; the *St. Louis Enquirer* observed that the Three Forks of the Missouri was a region said to possess a wealth in furs not surpassed by the mines of Peru, and if that did not suffice, the party might go as far beyond as the mouth of the Columbia: they would be absent three years.[12]

Jedediah did not leave St. Louis with the first boat; perhaps he arrived too late in the spring, or perhaps it was the part of wisdom to retain a few good men for the second boat. Another letter by Hempstead written from St. Louis May 5 gives an oblique glimpse into the General's problems; he mentions the great shortage of men, the country cleared of them, and adds, "Gen[l] Ashleys boat is now awaiting for Some guns for his expedition which Bostwick had brought acrost the mountains." It was hard even to find keelboats; the various companies had scoured the rivers for them as far down as the mouth of the Ohio.[13] But under the command of one Daniel S. D. Moore, Ashley's second boat, the *Enterprize*, sailed from St. Louis May 8, 1822, with Jedediah Smith on board as a hunter.[14]

Nothing young Diah had seen during his boyhood in New

York, or later in Ohio and the Illinois, had prepared him for the country he now entered. West of the Mississippi America became another land.

The keelboat no sooner penetrated the turbulent mouth of the Missouri than its true clumsiness became apparent. Perhaps one hundred feet long and twenty feet wide, a ribbed craft built on a keel covered with plank, it had a very shallow draft, from two to three feet. Most of the deck was covered by a long, boxlike structure in which the cargo was stowed; only enough space was left for a narrow path from bow to stern on each side of the boat. When the wind was right—which was seldom, in consequence of the writhing course of the river—a tall, square sail could be hoisted from the mast which stood a third of the way down from the bow. At such moments the life of the *voyageur* seemed worth while. In deep water it might be necessary to propel the boat by the twelve oars which projected from the forward part of the cargo box; that was work enough, but it was in shallow water that the *voyageurs'* skill and strength were most truly brought into play. Divided equally on either side of the keelboat, the men would "set" their poles at the head of the boat, settle the sockets into their shoulders, then push with all their might. With heads suspended nearly to the track of the running board, they would walk painfully to the stern, then at the patroon's command trot back to the stem for a new "set." He was a powerful man who could endure this labor for very long; it is no wonder that on the Western waters the boatmen were regarded as a breed apart.

In swift water or in other unlucky circumstances none of these means of attacking the current might suffice, and the crew must resort to the cordelle. A stout cable was stretched from the mast to the *voyageurs* on shore, who inch by inch and foot by foot, tearing their way through underbrush, along the sides of rocky bluffs and through the clinging muck of marshy banks, dragged the boat upward against the current. It was incredible that keelboats ascended the Missouri at all, and Jedediah must have shared the wonder of everyone who saw the operation for the first time.[15]

His privileged status as a hunter spared Jedediah most of this grueling labor, but no man was delivered from the savagery of

A MANDAN VILLAGE ON THE MISSOURI

Charles Bodmer, 1834. From Maximilian, Prince of Wied-Neuwied, *Travels in the Interior of North America,* Tab. 16.

THE INTERIOR OF THE HUT OF A MANDAN CHIEF

Charles Bodmer, 1834. From Maximilian, Tab. 19.

HORSE RACING OF SIOUX INDIANS NEAR FORT PIERRE
Charles Bodmer, 1833. From Maximilian, Vig. XXX.

FUNERAL SCAFFOLD OF A SIOUX CHIEF NEAR FORT PIERRE
Charles Bodmer, 1833. From Maximilian, Tab. 11.

the country. The terrain lying back from either bank of the river bore small resemblance to the serene forest lands of the East. The low banks of the river were covered by tall timber, sometimes so interlaced with wild grapevines and tangled brush that a hunter could not penetrate it. Fallen trees of enormous size often piled up one on another, overgrown with nettles as tall as a man. No buckskin parried the whiplash sting of these nettles, nor blunted the sharp thorns of the climbing roses and buckthorn. The insects were bloodthirsty. Woodticks burrowed into the skin, and though they might be cleared away by a bloody swipe of the hand, their heads remained in the wounds, burning and festering. Mosquitoes swarmed in numbers beyond belief, and their bites left burning welts which lasted for days.

It was surprising how few the flowering plants were, and the sweet-singing birds. In this country one might go for days without hearing a bird other than the harsh hammering of a woodpecker or the screeches of green parakeets flinging themselves across the river. This was a lonesome land. The scattered villages lay back from the river, and it was only infrequently that a ramshackle cabin was seen. Occasionally Jedediah got a shot at a turkey, a deer or hogs run wild, and packed his kill to the river bank for the boat to pick up as it passed.

At night Jedediah might lie awake too tired to sleep, listening to the long turbulence of the river. In this month of flood stage, the waters roared continually out of the wrath and agony of their seaward passage. Somewhere in the darkness a riverbank, undermined by the voracious current, would cave in with a sound like distant cannonading. Nearer at hand and unending was the remorseless crunch of driftwood ground together by the seething waters. Stiff and sore, he could lie the whole night through, listening to the tormented river, gasping in the warm, humid air and slapping at the swarming insects until the sun again glared in the sky.

At great intervals a pirogue would appear on the shining water, arrow-thin, swift and graceful as a boat was on this river only when headed downstream. Sometimes it was manned by Indians—Iowas, Sauks or Kaws en route to Red Head's Town for a visit of state or complaint; sometimes the boat, a hollowed-out cottonwood, rode low in the water, freighted with a trader's furs and dressed hides. For the most part, however, the upriver passage was an experience of loneliness, heat, exhaustion, muscle soreness, rushing water and the raw, exposed face of wilderness.[16]

The monotony of the voyage was broken briefly when the boat reached Franklin, westernmost town of any pretensions in the United States, but still not imposing; the town was a clutter of wooden shacks which the Missouri was making up its mind to sweep away. Opposite Franklin, a few scattered cabins clinging to a bluff on the right bank laid claim to the name Boonville. The plain lying back on either side of the river was the Boonslick country, named for its first settler, whose long pursuit of the setting sun had ended here. The aged Daniel was less than two years dead.

At Franklin there was news of Major Henry's party, which had passed up the river April 25, thus far safe. Ezekiel Williams, who had been in the mountains with Henry before the war, shook his head. The Blackfeet, he predicted, would attack, rob and kill his hunting parties, and Henry need not be surprised if he were driven from the mountains as he had been eleven years before.[17] Prophets of doom, however, are never wanting, and Jedediah was not prepared to concede the same authority to village seers that he accorded to the prophets of his Bible. The *Enterprize* pulled on up the river.

The yellowish gray color of the water made it difficult to recognize shoal places, and when the boat grounded the labors of the whole crew were required to float it again. It was necessary continually to move the boat from one bank to the other, for no power on earth was capable of moving it upstream in mid-current. Time after time the boat would get into a precarious situation among drifting logs, in danger of stranding and being burst wide open. Most dreaded by the crew were sawyers, trees washed into the river and bobbing up and down in the current. Great branches could thrash up out of the water, capable of overturning a boat or ripping out its bottom. Snags were another hazard, and "planters" yet another, trees which had become fixed to the bottom of the river. But the Missouri had an infinite capacity for making trouble, and it was none of these that put an end to the *Enterprize.*

Late in May on a windy day twenty miles below Fort Osage, the present Sibley, Missouri, the boat had to turn a point full of sawyers. An unexpected yawing brought the top of the mast against an overhanging tree. Wheeling around broadside to the powerful current, the *Enterprize* was swept under. In a few seconds boat and $10,000 cargo were gone. Only a few articles that floated were saved.

All that could be done was to get the news down to Ashley. Daniel Moore set off for St. Louis while his men, including Jedediah, set up a makeshift camp on the riverbank, to wait.[18]

The wait may have been wearisome, but it need not have been. This was a storied river. It was a century and more since the first *voyageurs* had dug their paddles into these murky waters. Some of the men encamped on the riverbank might be descendants of those early adventurers, given to great tales told in the firelight. Others may have recalled that it was up the Missouri that the first adventurers to Santa Fe had gone, the brothers Mallet in 1739, a quarter of a century before the founding of St. Louis. As late as 1792 Jacques d'Eglise had gone up the river to become the first white man to reach the Mandan villages from below. Two years later the alarmed Spanish reaction to the intrusion of British traders southward out of Canada had brought about the first formal expedition to the upper Missouri, sent out by the Company of Commerce, which proposed to build a chain of forts all the way from St. Louis to the South Sea. Not forgotten was the impetuous Welshman, John Evans, who had come to America seeking proof that America had been discovered in the year 1170 by the Welsh prince, Madoc. Evans had gone up the river in 1795 with James Mackay of the Company of Commerce, intending to combine his search for the white Indians with a tour of exploration beyond the Rockies. He got only as high as the Mandans before turning back, a skeptic.[19]

There had been others on the river, but none so exalting to the imagination as the two captains who between 1804 and 1806 made their way to the Pacific and back. Lewis and Clark's map and the journal were a guidebook to this vast wilderness, the only one there was. Jedediah admired profoundly the achievement of the two captains, and would listen to any story of them or their men.

If Ashley was dismayed by Daniel Moore's arrival in St. Louis June 3,[20] he did not permit the news to paralyze him; to this crisis he reacted with energy and decision. In eighteen days he had another boat and forty-six men off for the mountains. Either Moore was unwilling to trust his luck a second time or Ashley could not risk another miscarriage of his plans—the General himself came with the boat.

Contrary to the usual custom of the traders, Ashley laid in a plentiful supply of provisions, mainly sea bread and bacon, so that the boat and its crew were not dependent on the fortunes of the hunters. Notwithstanding, as Jedediah relates in his journal, after the General picked up his stranded men he kept a few good and active hunters out on the bank hunting for such game as the country afforded—

. . . which consisted of Black Bear, Deer, Elk, Raccoon, and Turkeys in abundance. And as the Country was well stocked with Bees we frequently had a plentiful supply of honey. For some distan[c]e up the Missouri the country is verry fine, and as the Genl kept me constantly hunting to which I was by no means averse I was enabled to enjoy the full novelty of the scene in which I was placed and . . . avoid the dull monotony of following along the bank of the river entirely dependent on the motions of the boat.

The Platte was an important point of passage. Here, in times gone by, the upper Missouri was considered to begin, and *voyageurs* laying eyes on the Platte for the first time were given all the delicate attentions that new hands at sea enjoyed on crossing the equator. The Platte was a strange, challenging, useless river, too shallow to be navigated for any distance with boats, not even the skin boats of the Indians. Fur hunters had been to its sources, and in 1820 Long's expedition had ascended its south fork all the way to the mountains, returning by way of the Arkansas. Neither had much good to report of it.

Forty miles above the mouth of the Platte, at Council Bluffs, Fort Atkinson's whitewashed walls bespoke in somewhat mixed fashion the power and prestige of the United States. Here had petered out the great military enterprise of 1818-1819 which had been designed to establish a military fort at the mouth of the Yellowstone. The troops had got no higher the first summer than the Bluffs, and their wintering post had become a permanent cantonment. Yet the fort impressed all who passed this way, for the garrison made it a populous place, and it was substantially built. The locality was the more important for its trading posts—both the Missouri Fur Company and the French Company had principal establishments here.

Beyond Council Bluffs were two of the most famous landmarks on the river. Blackbird's Hill, a cone of yellow sandstone rising three hundred feet above the river, was the tomb of a celebrated chief of the Omahas. As fearsome a personality as the Missouri tribes ever knew, he had become a great magician after obtaining from the white traders a supply of arsenic; he was said to have poisoned twoscore tribesmen to establish a reputation as one who could foretell death. No chief on the river had been more dreaded. In 1800 he and a large part of his tribe had been carried off by smallpox. He was buried, sitting upright on a live horse, on this yellow hill.

A little higher up, and on the opposite side of the river, was Floyd's Bluff. Here was buried the only man lost on the Lewis and Clark Expedition. Sergeant Floyd had been seized with a bilious cholic and died, as the book of the two captains attested, "with a composure which justified the high opinion we had formed of his firmness and good conduct." On August 20, 1804, the Corps of Volunteers for North Western Discovery had buried him on top of the bluff; the place of his interment was marked by a cedar post on which his name and the day of his death were inscribed. All travelers up the river visited the grave; the stake marking it had often been destroyed by prairie fires, and just as often replaced. Many of those who passed this way would have no graves finally save the hungry bellies of prairie wolves, and this was their cenotaph.

The country was now much altered—in Jedediah's phrase it

had become "one extensive prairae interrupted only by the narrow fringes of timber along the rivers, the surface gently undulating and covered with grass. No mountains. In some parts immense herds of Buffalo. Antelope in abundance. Some Deer, Bear and Elk and some Deer of the Blk tail kind." They were approaching the Grand Detour of the Missouri, the fantastic bend where the river flowed a loop thirty miles around to make a distance of a mile and a half.

This was Sioux country, and here was located the newest outpost of the Missouri Fur Company, Cedar Fort or Fort Recovery. Notwithstanding determined efforts, Joshua Pilcher and Thomas Hempstead had not been able to get their mountain expedition off ahead of Ashley; though now on the river, it was some distance downstream. The Sioux lands below the Grand Detour were the objective of the French Fur Company this summer, and while Ashley was on the upper waters, they would be busy building a post a dozen miles above Cedar Fort. The man in charge for Berthold, Pratte and Chouteau was Joseph Brazeau, "Young Cayewa," as the French called him. The post he built, a famous one, was officially named Fort Lookout, but as long as Brazeau remained on the Missouri it was called Brazeau's Fort or Fort Kiowa.[22]

Cedar Fort exemplified the type of post Major Henry by now was building at the mouth of the Yellowstone. Such a fort consisted primarily of a square stockade made of cottonwood pickets, with a blockhouse in one corner and a wooden tower diagonally opposite, each boasting a small cannon and between them able to sweep all four sides of the fort.[23] An example was yet wanting when such a post had fallen to Indian assault—it was vulnerable only to the cutthroat competition of rival traders.

More interesting than the fort were the Sioux. These were the first Indians Jedediah had seen who had not been corrupted by white civilization. In the early days no Indians along the Missouri had been more feared or detested, for they were a powerful people and knew it. Historically the Sioux had been the middlemen in trading to the Plains tribes the goods that French, English and Spanish fur traders brought into the valley of the Mississippi, and they did not take kindly to loss of their function.

The passage of white men through their country meant, moreover, that guns and ammunition would be traded to their enemies, and the Sioux disliked the thought of it unless they controlled the supply. It was a minor miracle that black-browed Manuel Lisa of the old Missouri Fur Company not only reconciled the Sioux to the necessities of commerce, but bound them to the American interest in the process. They had stood steadfast with the Americans through the recent war with Britain, and trouble with the Sioux was now of rare occurrence. Jedediah thought the Sioux generally above the common stature, with a complexion lighter than most Indians; they had intelligent countenances and in general were fine-looking men. In the moral scale, Jedediah added in his journal (and this might indicate that no brave had offered the strait-laced young man his wife or sister for a bedfellow—a gesture of hospitality not uncommon), "they rank above the mass of Indians."

It was policy to establish good relations with the Sioux, and Ashley gladly smoked the calumet with them while distributing the presents all Indians expected, but with as little delay as possible the General took his boat on up the river. By September 8 he had reached the Ree Villages in northern South Dakota, a few miles above the Grand River.

The Arikaras ("Rees" to the French *voyageurs*, who reduced all tribal names to a convenient syllable) were Indians of notoriously unstable disposition, and Ashley approached them with caution. They had behaved like the curse of God toward the Spanish traders on the Missouri before Lewis and Clark, but received the two captains with much cordiality. A chief Lewis sent down the river in 1805 died before he could be returned to the tribe, and for this reason or out of a natural bent for raising hell, in 1807 they attacked the party of Ensign Nathaniel Pryor, driving it down the river in confusion. Four years later they received the Astorians amiably and traded to them the horses which made possible that great journey overland to the Columbia, but they had been in a bad mood for several years now and some fresh hell-raising was about due.

Constant harassment by the Sioux had made it necessary for the Rees to fortify their villages. Their stockades were fashioned merely from pieces of driftwood, poles of different sizes, willows, brush and other odds and ends,[24] but they were an effective protection from the Sioux, and had it been possible to defend their cornfields as effectively the Rees would have had little fear of the powerful enemies who intermittently besieged them. In contrast to the roving Sioux, the Arikaras lived on fixed sites, only moving from time to time when they had exhausted the fertility of their cornfields or, as travelers were sometimes persuaded, could no longer endure their own stench.

Like most of the Indian villages of the upper Missouri, the Ree towns swarmed with dogs and children. Of the former every family appeared to have thirty or forty, of every imaginable size and color, as savage of aspect as any wolf. Most of the western tribes had used dogs as pack animals during the centuries before horses were known on the Plains; they were still so employed. But dogs were fattened for the kettle too, one of the choicest viands the Indians could place before a guest, and men who traveled to the mountains had to learn to quiet their stomachs and partake with epicurean detachment. Before the rounded earth lodges, the Ree women were at work dressing buffalo robes stretched on frames. The lodges and the women seemed to Jedediah about the only things that stayed put, for the braves appeared to be as excitable as the children and the dogs, continually chasing this way and that.[25]

Gravely the General counciled with the chiefs, giving them the customary presents, promising that when he came up the river next year he would bring such articles as they desired. And meanwhile trading for some horses, for it was late in the season, and Ashley thought it expedient to take a few men and proceed by land to the Yellowstone, the boat to come along behind as rapidly as her patroon could move her.

General Ashley, Jedediah says, "took charge of the party that went by land . . . and to this party I was attached. He moved with great care, being somewhat apprehensive of danger from the Arickara indians." This last stage of the journey was memorable chiefly for Jedediah's dawning conception of the vastness of the numbers in which the buffalo roamed the West. During the summer he had seen and killed buffalo, but these were occasional cows or a bull. When they came on a herd the second day after leaving the Ree Villages, it seemed to Jedediah's unaccustomed eyes "that all the buffalo in the world were running in those plains. . . . over the hills and plains they moved in deep dense and dark bodies resembling the idea I have formed of the heavy columns of a great army. As they took the wind of the party they ran making the ground tremble with the moving weight of animal life."

Continuing on, over a prairie gently undulating and so well grassed that Jedediah could begin to understand how such vast herds could subsist, the General's party arrived at the Mandan Villages on the Missouri near the mouth of the Knife River. No place in the West surpassed the Mandan towns in historic interest. As long ago as 1738 the Sieur de la Vérendrye, exploring south and west from the Assiniboine River in search of Indians said to be whiter than any known, had reached the Missouri here. Four years later his sons explored yet farther to the south and west, as far as the Black Hills, before turning back into Canada. The English and the Spanish had come to the Mandan country in turn, beginning in the 1780s, and it was from here that Lewis and Clark had set out on the last stage of the journey that brought them to the rain-swept Pacific. Since white men had known them, the Mandans and their neighbors, the Minnetarees, had lived in fixed villages here where the Missouri tired of its long eastward passage from the Rockies and turned southeast to find the Mississippi.

Like the Sioux and the Arikaras, the Mandans were notably openhanded with their women, a complaisance which made their towns a topic of interesting reminiscence the entire length of the Missouri; they were given also to certain ceremonies of fertility scarcely imagined by the Methodist circuit riders from whom Jedediah had received instruction. To the ways of the western Indians the young man still required to be hardened, and it was just as well that no opportunity offered for a more intimate acquaintance. Of their reception by the Mandans, Jedediah says only that the General and his party "were invited into a large Lodge and some of the principal chiefs being invited, the pipe of peace was smoked according to the usual ceremonies. A council was held and the Gen[l] said such things to them as he thought most likely to secure and continue their friendship."

The safety of the boat looked to, Ashley and his men set out again for the Yellowstone. They crossed the Little Missouri, remarkable even in comparison with its namesake for the turbidity of its waters. The ground was more broken, but still gently undulating, watered by creeks and springs and well clothed with grass—fine buffalo country.

The Yellowstone at last. They arrived October 1, two weeks in advance of the boat, to find a fort awaiting them. The cannon barked a welcome and Major Henry received them joyfully. Fort Henry was a picketed enclosure on the right bank of the Missouri, a quarter of a mile above its confluence with the Yellowstone. A log structure had been built at each of the four corners, and these, joined together by pickets, enclosed a space which could serve as a corral if the fort were invested by Indians. The fort stood on a narrow tongue of land between the two rivers which was sufficiently elevated to be above high water. A heavily timbered bottom along the far shore of both rivers pleasingly hinted at the forested regions above.[26]

Henry's party had reached Fort Atkinson without event early in May, and paused only briefly before continuing up the river. An old hand on the Missouri, Henry had scorned carrying with him much in the way of provisions, but by the time he reached Cedar Fort he rued the decision, for with provisions exhausted, and no prospect of game, his men by twos, threes and half dozens began making their way back. This dribbling away of his man power may have continued all the way to the Yellowstone, though Ashley picked up some of the stragglers.[27] The cost to the partners had been high, but here they were in the fur country, their fort built and a year's outfit on hand.[28] New to the business they might be, but they had beaten the opposition to the Yellowstone. Ashley must now turn back to make arrangements for the second year's outfit. Henry would remain in the mountains and whip the trapping force into shape.

When Ashley in his pirogue was gone, Jedediah must have taken a long look around—the dark growth of timber on either hand, the wide rivers so curiously discolored, the October sun hot overhead, the smell of the raw wood of which the fort was built strong in his nostrils, newness gripping the world. No hills lifted anywhere on the wide circle of the horizon, but he had reached the mountains. Here at the junction of the Missouri and the Yellowstone, by agreement, the Rocky Mountains began.

2. *THE HUNTERS AND THE HUNTED*

Major Henry equipped two parties for the fall hunt. One was to go up the Missouri, the other up the Yellowstone. He himself intended to see the Missouri detachment as far on its journey as Milk River.[1] Who took charge of the Yellowstone operation history has been slow to reveal, but there is good reason to think that the head of this party was John H. Weber, a one-time Danish sea captain, who had come to Missouri not long after Ashley and Henry and had known them since Ste. Genevieve days.

Captain Weber has remained a hidden figure in the annals of the fur trade. Born in 1779 in the town of Altona near Hamburg, then part of the Kingdom of Denmark, Weber received a fairly good education but at an early age ran away to sea, soon becoming master of a sailing vessel. The Napoleonic wars seriously complicated the life of Danish seafarers, and young Weber made his way to America.

> Nature had done well by him [a contemporary says]; he was a man of large and powerful frame, of erect carriage and graceful manner, his face indicated the superior intelligence behind it, he had a nose like a Roman Emperor and an eye as regal and piercing as that of an American eagle, the courage of a hero, and the staying qualities of a martyr . . . but he was impetuous and peculiar in many ways and at times disagreeable and unhappy. His was a mercurial nature that went up in hope and down with despair.[2]

Captain Weber enters Jedediah's life from unexpected tangents at intervals for four years, but they scarcely had time to get acquainted this fall, for the Major had a job for the young man. Jedediah and another hunter, one A. Chapman, were sent up the

Yellowstone with a few men to make some meat for the fort. They were also, Jedediah says, "to take what Beaver we could conveniently."

The number of beaver that could be taken in the near vicinity of the fort was not large, for the real beaver country lay higher up, but probably Jedediah now for the first time practiced the operation on which the fur trade and his own fortunes ultimately depended. Along a big river, beaver were ordinarily trapped with the aid of dugouts, which left no scent and provided easy access to the shore. Here the beaver customarily lived in burrows dug in the banks, the entrances to which were several feet below the September low-water mark. The traps, which were heavy iron affairs weighing five pounds or more, were placed in the water where a path or slide entered it. The purpose was to catch a beaver by one of his paws and drown him before he could gnaw the paw off; to prevent the beaver from dragging the trap out on the ground, a long, stout pole was driven through the trap ring and anchored to the bank by a five-foot length of steel chain. Usually the trap was baited with a twig smeared with castor, the musky secretion of the beaver's perineal glands (which, pound for pound, were valued as highly as the beaver pelt itself). Visiting his traps, the beaver hunter would be able to locate his catch by the trap pole, or if the trap had been pulled free from the bank, by a small "float stick." In high country, or on streams small enough for the beaver to dam, trappers would work from the shore, wading into the water from above or below to place their traps at the favored locations; since furs were prime only in the cold seasons of the year, this meant much wading in icy streams and a rheumatic old age—should the trapper live to old age, which was unlikely if he did not keep on the move and give due attention to what was going on around him. Ordinarily the traps, which might average from five to ten to the man, were placed in the semiobscurity of dusk and raised in the gray light of dawn. The beaver would be skinned on the spot, and with the castor glands and tail (one of the supreme delicacies of the mountain larder) would be brought into camp, where the pelt would be stretched on a frame, scraped and, after being dried, folded fur side in for convenient packing. The presence of beaver was always apparent at sight: if not from their dams, then from cuttings. An experienced trapper could gauge the probabilities of finding beaver by the character of the vegetation, for they fed on the bark of such trees as cottonwood, willow, birch, alder and aspen; rarely they might subsist on the roots of plants like the water hemlock.[3]

Beaver was the universal quarry, and had been since there was a fur trade in America. Skins of average grade were used for the tall-crowned hats which had been the fashion in England and Europe for centuries, while the finer skins were sold to furriers and the discriminating markets of Russia and China. Otters —"land otters" as they were known in the trade, to distinguish them from the most valuable of all furs, the sea otter of the Pacific—were occasionally caught in the traps and had the same value as beaver. Other furs were rarely taken, more commonly traded from Indians. Individual beaver pelts—"*plus,*" the French-Canadians called them, "plews" to the Americans—would weigh from a pound and a half to two pounds in the case of full-grown animals, half that for pups, and, depending on the market, might be worth from four to six dollars a pound in St. Louis. Ashley's innovation was that he had undertaken to deal with the trappers as independent operators, paying for beaver delivered in the mountains half their value in St. Louis; prices quickly became standardized at three dollars a pound, from five to six dollars the plew. The profit per beaver might be less than if all the men of a trapping force were *engagés,* but under the new arrangement the trappers had far more incentive to increase their catch; at the same time, the overhead was reduced, for it was necessary to fund wages only for the heads of parties, the bourgeois (the "booshways") and the clerks ("the little booshways"). This was the essential background to Jedediah Smith's first trapping venture, and it held for all that he afterward did in the West, though local stringencies forced adaptations in the relations of Company and men.

The meat-making and trapping mission out of Fort Henry did not occupy Jedediah long, and he was soon back at the post. The Major with twenty-one men already had set out for the

Missouri in boat and canoes, and Weber's Yellowstone party had got off in canoes for the mouth of the Powder, which they were instructed to ascend as far as possible.[4] Although Jedediah says nothing of their passage, during October the Missouri Fur Company's belated "mountain expedition" under Immell and Jones briefly visited the new post and then moved on up the Yellowstone, intending to winter at the mouth of the Big Horn, where as far back as 1807 Lisa had had a fort. Forty-three men made up the opposition, and Henry would have to look sharp lest the wealth of the Three Forks country be skimmed off under his nose.[5]

Never in his life was Jedediah Smith disposed to laze about a fort eating salt pork, or even hump-rib and beaver tail, and shortly he set out up the Missouri on Henry's track, traveling along the bank of the river. Other than Chapman, Jedediah does not call the roll of the party, and the unfulfilled promise of his journal, that he would list their names in the margin, is tantalizing in view of the possibility that the men included three friends whose names were about to be immortalized—Mike Fink and his boon companions Carpenter and Talbot.

In the course of their journey Jedediah and his fellow trappers encountered Henry, who with eight men was returning to the fort. Learning from the Major that the advance party had gone on as far as the Musselshell and would winter there, Jedediah himself pushed on to the Musselshell, arriving about November 1. He got there none too soon, for the river was already filling with ice; these were latitudes of furious cold.

We were generally good hunters [Jedediah's journal says] but at that time unacquainted with the habits of the Buffalo and seeing none in the vicinity we supposed they had abandoned the country for the winter. We therefore became somewhat apprehensive that we should suffer for want of provisions. While a Part of the company were engaged in preparing houses for the winter I took some of the best of the hunters and made every exertion to procure a supply of meat sufficient for our suport. And we were indeed verry successful, for we killed all the small game of the vicinity particularly Antelope and deer Laying up a supply of meat that drove the apprehension of want entirely from our minds. Our houses being finished we were well prepared for the increasing cold. When the weather had at length become extremely cold and the ice strong and firm across the River we were astonished to see the buffalo come pouring from all sides into the valley of the Missouri and particularly the vast Bands that came from the north and crossed over to the south side on the ice. We there fore had them in thousands around us and nothing more required of us than to select and kill the best for our use whenever we might choose. . . . In our little encampment shut out from those enjoyments most valued by the world we were as happy as we could be made by leisure and opportunity for unlimited indulgence in the pleasure of the Buffalo hunt and the several kinds of sport which the severity of the winter could not debar us from.[6]

So ends Jedediah Smith's account of his journey to the mountains. It is three and a half years before he reappears with letter or journal. During that time his life must be pieced together from the impression he made on his contemporaries, and there were many men to take note of Jedediah Smith's passage and remember him above his comrades. A mild man and a Christian, they called him, and this alone would have set him apart in the mountains.[7] But the mildness of his manner and his troubled sense of unworthiness in the sight of God only brought out in stronger relief his other qualities. Jedediah had intelligence he was able to apply under pressure, toughness of spirit, a capacity for endurance beyond that of most men, and above all the courage and grace in the face of adversity that men call gallantry. Wherever he went, these qualities made their impression, and for a time we may follow Jedediah through the eyes of other men.

Something of his life during this period may be recovered, too, from the tales told of his companions. This was a golden age in the history of the West, and all the Ashley men have something of the stature of culture heroes. That Jedediah Smith emerged head and shoulders above them all is in itself a measure of greatness.

Mike Fink, Jedediah's comrade of the winter camp on the Musselshell, was of the breed, half horse, half alligator, which for a generation had been the glory and the scourge of the inland waterways. Barrooms the length of the Ohio and the Mississippi had seen Mike bound into the air, clapping his heels together and crying his vainglory: "I am a Salt River roarer, and I love the wimming, and as how I am chock full of fight!" In his hat he wore the cocky red feather emblematic of his supremacy among all the brawling boatmen, and the stories about him were legion.

They were not, alas, tales of the skill, strength and courage he brought to his calling as a keelboatman; the stories had to do with Mike the ring-tailed screamer, the man who could outrun, outjump, outshoot, outbrag, outdrink and outfight ary man on the rivers, and in no way behindhand with the wimming either.

Perhaps it was the novelty of the thing that induced Mike Fink to join Ashley's expedition. The lure of new country, the far land never yet seen, the buffler and the grizzly just born to be shot by Mike Fink—these must have brought Mike to the mountains.

He had two bosom friends, Carpenter and Talbot. A common sport of these friends was to fill a tin cup with whisky and shoot it from one another's heads at seventy paces. The chronicle says that Mike and his friends, having taken service with Ashley in the threefold character of boatmen, trappers and hunters, ascended as far as the mouth of the Yellowstone, and after building the fort "with nine others, went to the Muscleshell River where they found a warm and commodious habitation for the winter." [8]

During this winter Mike and Carpenter fell into a deadly quarrel. The quarrel is said to have been over a girl; if so, she was a girl back in the settlements, for no Indians set up a winter camp with Jedediah and his companions, and Americans newly come to the mountains did not outfit themselves with a squaw in their passage up the Missouri. The quarrel was patched up for the time being, and only Carpenter guessed at the bitterness Mike Fink hugged to himself.

That winter the Missouri froze to a depth of four feet, and it was April 4 before the river discharged itself. Next day the company on the Musselshell was visited by a party of Indians, and on the sixth they embarked in canoes for the Judith River. So says Daniel Potts, another member of the camp, who adds that in about one day's travel the whites discovered where a party of hostile Indians had wintered, and felt that they had reason to congratulate themselves on having gone undiscovered. On April 11 Potts was severely wounded by the accidental discharge of a rifle; he had to be taken down to the Yellowstone.[9] Potts remained at Fort Henry all summer, recovering from his wounds, and if the party that ascended the Missouri has any other historian, he has not come forth.

Not all those who had wintered on the Musselshell joined in the spring hunt. Potts had to be taken down the river and others may have turned back on their own account. Fink, Carpenter and Talbot were three who made their way back to the fort. Only eleven were left to push on up the river into the Blackfoot country,[10] and Jedediah Smith was not among them.

On reaching the Yellowstone, the quarrel between Fink and Carpenter broke out afresh. Again it was patched up, and by way of evidencing the sincerity of the reconciliation, Mike proposed that he and Carpenter shoot the whisky cup from each other's heads as they had done so many times before. A copper spun on high, and when it came down, Mike had the first shot.

Carpenter's pride would not let him back out. He told Talbot that Mike intended to kill him, but dying was something all men came to sooner or later, and he strode out to where Mike waited. He filled the cup with whisky, placed it on his head, then stood to await the shot. Mike paced off the usual range and leveled his rifle, then lowered it to say with a smile, "Hold your noddle steady, Carpenter, and don't spill the whisky, as I shall want some presently."

Again he raised his rifle. With the sound of the shot, Carpenter pitched forward on his face. The onlookers ran to him and turned him over. He had been shot in the center of his forehead, an inch and a half above the eyes. Mike set the breech of his gun on the ground and, putting his lips to the muzzle, blew the smoke out of the barrel. Finally he said, "Carpenter, you have spilled the whisky!"

The sequel is variously related. The earliest account, published within two months of the tragedy, says, "Another man of the expedition (whose name we have not yet heard) remonstrated against Fink's conduct, to which he (Fink) replied that he would kill him likewise, upon which the other drew a pistol and shot Fink dead on the spot." The account we have followed, which was published six years after and hangs together well, relates that among a party who had an exaggerated dread of Mike's prowess, the crime was permitted to pass for an accident, and Mike was allowed to go at large.

But Talbot, who was Carpenter's fast friend, was convinced of Mike's treacherous intent, and resolved upon revenge whenever an opportunity should offer. Some months afterward [some weeks afterward, more probably], Mike, in a fit of gasconading, declared that he had killed Carpenter and was glad of it. Talbot instantly drew his pistol, the same which Carpenter had bequeathed to him, and shot Mike through the heart. Mike fell and expired without a word.[11]

There is a macabre touch to what follows. Later in the year, after Henry had abandoned his fort on the Yellowstone, a Blackfoot war party visited the deserted post and found the two graves. The Blackfeet dug up the bodies to strip them of clothing, but finding them in a putrid state, left without further molestation.[12] Thus the man Mike Fink came to his mortal end, beginning a legend which has never ceased to grow.

Talbot was not called to account for killing Fink; nobody had any authority to do so, and as the chronicle says:

. . . few doubtless felt any inclination, as it was probably considered a just penalty for the killing of Carpenter. Moreover Talbot was a terrible enemy, ferocious and dangerous as a grizzly of the prairies. About three months later he was present in the Aricara battle under Colonel Leavenworth, where he displayed a coolness which would have done honor to a better man. He came out of the battle unharmed, but about ten days later while attempting to swim the Teton River he was drowned.[13]

Major Henry had to get a message downriver to Ashley. The drift of that message is certain even though some of the details have to be guessed. Henry had to have horses. He had not been able to acquire enough on the Yellowstone, and it was urgent that Ashley, coming up the river this spring, should buy some from the Indians. That meant the Sioux or the Rees.

The farther one got toward the mountains, the harder it was to buy horses and the more they cost. Horses purchased from the Sioux might cost double their price in Missouri, and Jedediah found later that a good horse in the Rockies might cost as much again, up to $150 apiece. The Crows were generally happier to acquire than to dispose of horseflesh, and Henry, who had reached only the outer limits of the Crow country, had had no success in buying from them. None of the Yellowstone's rich southern tributaries, the Powder, the Tongue, the Big Horn, was accessible by water very far up, and to trap their sources pack animals were required. The same was true if Henry followed the example of the Missouri Fur Company and undertook to trap the Three Forks of the Missouri from the Yellowstone, for that involved crossing the mountains west of the bend of the Yellowstone.

Henry's message was entrusted to Jedediah Smith. Downstream the Missouri was a highroad, and there is little question that Jedediah set out by dugout or pirogue. Of his adventures along the way nothing is known, nor where he fell in with Ashley, but Ashley knew what Henry desired of him when he arrived at the Ree Villages on May 30, 1823.

With two keelboats, the *Yellow Stone Packet* and *The Rocky Mountains,* the General had left St. Louis for the mountains on March 10.[14] Good men had been hard to find; they were not forthcoming even when Ashley advertised a wage of two hundred dollars a year.[15] One of the few good recruits, the calm Virginian James Clyman, had completed a crew by combing out every grogshop and brothel under the Hill, and Clyman was not the more impressed with the result for having assembled the men himself; Falstaff's Battalion, he remarked dryly, was genteel in comparison.[16] In all, Ashley had a force of about ninety men aboard his keelboats when Jedediah reached him.

The commission Henry had sent his partner was a ticklish one. In March a party of Arikaras had come down to Cedar Fort and robbed and beaten six Missouri Fur Company *engagés* who were out collecting furs and robes that had been traded from the Sioux. A few days later another party had attacked the post itself in broad daylight, and Angus McDonald with his clerks and eight or ten *voyageurs* had beaten off the attack, killing two Rees and wounding several others.[17] The Arikaras would be in a mood to settle scores.

Ashley approached the two Ree Villages with considerable care. They were about three hundred yards apart, situated on the right bank of the Missouri on ground sloping gently up from the water. In front of the towns was a large sand bar, around which the river, here very narrow and with the channel close to the right bank, flowed a horseshoe course. This was an exposed and dangerous expanse of water, and the Rees had built a breastwork of dry timber at the upper part of the bar. Moreover, their towns looked to have been freshly picketed. On the opposite side of the river the ground was high and somewhat broken, affording cover for an enemy while rendering difficult the use of a cordelle.[18]

Ashley anchored his boats in mid-channel and went ashore in a skiff to open negotiations. He was met on the beach by two of the principal chiefs, Little Soldier and Grey Eyes, whom he invited to board his boat. Little Soldier refused, but Grey Eyes clambered into the skiff. That was a favorable sign, for the chief had been known for nearly twenty years as a very tough customer, and one of the Rees killed at Cedar Fort was Grey Eyes' son. Ashley made the chief some presents and informed him that he had nothing to do with the company that had injured the Rees. He could not be held accountable for the actions of every white man on the river, but the Great Father at Washington would inquire into the circumstances, and justice would be done.

The Ree chief said that it would be necessary to hold a council, and advised Ashley to remain where he was until then. That night Grey Eyes came out on the beach bringing word that the Rees had decided to remain friendly and would be willing to trade. Much relieved, the General told the chief that he wished to send about forty men by land and would like to trade horses enough to outfit them, say forty to fifty. Grey Eyes replied that

Ashley might pitch his tent on the beach in the morning, when the horses would be forthcoming. All angry feelings occasioned by the affray down the river were now allayed; the Rees considered the Americans friends.

Trading began on the morning of May 31. The wary Ashley kept his boats anchored in the river and ferried his trading goods to the beach in the skiffs. During the day he succeeded in purchasing about nineteen horses and over two hundred buffalo robes,[19] but in the early evening the trade was suddenly broken off when one of the chiefs wanted to trade for guns and ammunition. The business had gone well to this point, but now things took an ugly turn. Ashley's men remained under arms all night.

Toward morning a severe windstorm blew up, accompanied by violent rain and lightning. It was impossible to move the boats, nor would it have been advisable, for the horses that had been traded from the Rees could not be taken over the river until the storm subsided. Until then, horses and the men who had them in charge must remain on the rain-swept sand bar directly under the guns of the lower village. For the boats to leave was to invite an assault on the shore party, of which Jedediah Smith is understood to have had the command.[20]

Late in the afternoon, the Bear, principal chief of one of the villages, sent Ashley an invitation to visit him at his lodge. The General accepted, not wishing the Rees to think he had the slightest fear of them. Taking with him his interpreter, the redoubtable Edward Rose, Ashley went to the lodge of the Bear, where he was treated with every appearance of friendship. One of the chiefs, Little Soldier, was so markedly friendly as to tell Ashley that the Rees would attack him before his departure, or, failing that, assault the shore party as soon as they separated. He advised Ashley to swim the horses across the river.

The General thought it likely that this was a stratagem to get the horses out from under the guns of the boats; Indians had been seen on the opposite shore during the day. The whole situation was confused. Although a good many of Ashley's company, after his return to his boat, must have crawled into their buffalo robes to sleep only by fits and starts, others were so scornful of danger or in such need of a woman as to slip out of camp and go into the Ree Villages.

Sometime after midnight an uproar broke out in the Ree towns, and Edward Rose burst down the slope with the news that Aaron Stephens had been killed. The men were immediately ordered under arms, and it was debated whether an attempt should be made to get the horses over the river. The wind had lulled, but nothing resembling military discipline existed among Ashley's men. Some were sure they were safest where they were; others would be damned before they yielded an inch to so mean a set of villains; yet others demanded that the Rees be made to give up the body of Stephens for decent burial.

The furor in the Ree towns continued till dawn. Just before daybreak one of the Rees approached near enough to call out that if they would let him have a horse, he would bring out the body of Stephens. The men on the beach refused to move until the horse was given the Indian, but in a few moments the man returned to call out that Stephens' eyes had been put out, his head cut off, and his body otherwise mangled. The sun was now rising, and its appearance was the signal for a fusillade to break out from the lower town. Some of the balls whistled past the boats or thudded into the cargo boxes, but most showered around the shore party.

Jedediah and those with him on the beach dived behind the horses. So severe was the fire that within a few moments most of the animals were killed or wounded, and a number of the men. Seeing how destructive the Indian fire was, Ashley ordered his *voyageurs* to weigh anchor and lay to shore. But this was the kind of crisis for which the Creoles were notoriously unfitted. Incredibly valiant and ready to meet the emergencies of river travel, they went to pieces under fire. James Clyman, who was on shore with Jedediah Smith amid the rain of balls, says that there were many calls "for the boats to come ashore and take us on board but no prayers or threats had the [slightest] effect the Boats men being completely Parylized." All that Ashley could manage was to get the two skiffs started inshore. One was large enough for twenty men, the other half that size. When they got to the beach, the infuriated shore party would not budge. The large skiff went back with only four men, two of them wounded, and when it would have pulled a second time to the beach, one of the oarsmen was shot down, the craft being set adrift.

By then the position of the shore party had become untenable. The Rees were advancing at right angles to their stockade and had reached the point of the sand beach. The men leaped into the river to swim to the boats, ninety feet out. Some of them made it. Others were shot down before they got well into the water. Some who appeared to be badly wounded sank while attempting to swim. The anchor of one of the keelboats was weighed, the cable of the other was cut, and the boats dropped down the river. The Rees gave them a last volley as they went. The entire action lasted scarcely a quarter of an hour.

A single glimpse is afforded us of Jedediah Smith on the sand bar in the moment it was realized that the battle must be abandoned as lost. One who had known Jedediah wrote nine years later: "When his party was in danger, Mr. Smith was always among the foremost to meet it, and the last to fly; those who saw him on shore, at the Riccaree fight, in 1823, can attest to the truth of this assertion." [21] We can picture him ramming one last ball home and firing at the Rees spilling down on him while the men of his party splash into the water toward the boats. Then himself abandoning the beach, thrusting the muzzle of his rifle into his belt, and running into the river, swimming for it with the balls from the Ree fusils reaching angrily after him. . . . This day Jedediah Smith made his reputation. Yet in all honesty he might have agreed with Jim Clyman, who said afterward, "Before meeting with this defeat, I think few men had Stronger Ideas of their bravery and disregard of fear than I had but standing on a bear and open sand barr to be shot at from bihind a picketed Indian village was more than I had contacted for and some what cooled my courage."

Clyman's escape from the sand beach is an epic in itself. He was a strong swimmer but the powerful current swept him down past the keelboats. There was nothing for it but to try to swim the river, which meant getting rid of rifle, pistols, ball pouch and hunting shirt, which was buckskin "and held an immence weight of water." Nearly strangled, he heard a voice crying, "Hold on, Clyman, I will soon relieve you." This was Reed Gibson, who had swum in and retrieved the skiff which had got adrift; Clyman was so exhausted that Gibson had to haul him into the skiff, but as he lay gasping in the bottom of the boat, Gibson groaned, "Oh, God, I am shot," and fell forward in the skiff. "I encouraged him," Clyman says, "and [said] Perhaps not fatally give a few pulls more and we will be out of reach." Gibson rose up and took a few more strokes with the only remaining oar, using it as a paddle, then complained of feeling faint and fell forward again. Clyman took his place in the stern and shoved the boat across to the eastern bank. There he hauled the skiff up on shore, telling Gibson to remain in the boat while he climbed to high ground to see how they stood. Almost immediately he discovered several Indians swimming across the river after them. Gibson said, "Save yourself, Clyman, and pay no attention to me as I am a dead man, and they can get nothing of me but my scalp." Clyman considered getting in the skiff again, meeting the Indians in the water and braining them with the oar. But there were too many, and they were too near shore. He looked for a place to hide, but there was only a thin line of brush along the bank.

"I concluded," Clyman says, "to take to the open Pararie and run for life by this time Gibson had scrambled up the bank and stood by my side and said run Clyman but if you escape write to my friends in Virginia and tell them what has become of me." So Clyman ran for the open prairie, and Gibson for the brush. In a moment three Indians mounted the bank and started in headlong pursuit of Clyman. There was no possibility of hiding. The ground was smooth and level for perhaps three miles. Clyman held his lead the whole way, and had just enough strength to gain the rising ground beyond. There he shook off his pursuers, "made them a low bow with both my hand and thanked god for my present Safety and diliveranc."

Clyman now turned south across a rolling plain.

But what ware my reflection being at least Three Hundred miles from any assistanc unarmed and u[n]provided with any sort of means of precureing a subsistance, not even a pocket Knife I began to feel after passing So many dangers that my pro[s]pects ware still verry slim, mounting some high land I saw ahed of me the river and Quite a grove of timber and being verry thirsty I made for the water intending to take a good rest in the timber I took one drink of water and here came the boats floating down the stream the [men] watc[h]ing along the shores saw me about as soon as I saw them the boat was laid in and I got aboard.

Gibson was on board also, but he did not recognize Clyman, "being in the agonies of Death the shot having passed through his bowels I could not refrain from weeping over him who lost his lifee but saved mine he did not live but an hour or so and we buried him that evening."

This was the worst disaster in the history of the Western fur trade. Painfully Ashley could consider its magnitude. There was Aaron Stephens, cut to pieces in the Ree Village, and the number of the dead after him was twelve altogether. Eleven more were wounded (and two were going to die).[22] The number of killed alone comprised a sixth of Ashley's force. Most of the killed and wounded had been with Jedediah Smith on the beach; never had men acted with more coolness and bravery, but this was a total defeat. So well shielded had the Rees been from the return fire that it could not be supposed any real execution had been done.

Once the survivors were embarked and the boats out of range of the Rees, Ashley had restored some vestige of control. He ordered the boats to drop down to the first timber, where he could place men and vessels in a better state of defense, and keep a sharp eye out for survivors. The dying Gibson had been taken on board, and Clyman's luck had led him to the very refuge the boats were seeking.

They were still too close to the Rees; six or seven hundred warriors armed with London fusils were a formidable enemy. It was expedient to drop farther down the river. When the boats stopped again, it was on an island where they could defend themselves. Here also they could bury Reed Gibson and John S. Gardner.

The men who had accompanied Ashley to the mountains were a varied lot, but the variety did not extend so far as to include an ordained minister. Jedediah Smith stepped forward, and while the men stood silent around, with bowed head he prayed to that God in whose sternness all were prepared to believe, in whose compassion at this moment they much needed to believe; the prayer was a powerful one.[23] The bodies of the two men were then laid in their graves. The only marker they could place was a log, lest the graves be opened by the Indians.

While his men slept, Ashley paced the shore. The men of his shore party had distinguished themselves even in defeat, but his boatmen had behaved as cowards. It was not likely they were even ashamed, but their morale was destroyed. Somehow he must put the pieces together again. At sunup he paraded his men and outlined his plan to get them past the Ree Villages. (This would have involved timbering up the exposed side of each boat and making the passage by night.) But the *voyageurs* were panicked by the mere suggestion that they face the Rees again.

Ashley asked how many men would agree to remain with him until reinforcements could be obtained from the Yellowstone. Only thirty men spoke up, and six or seven of them were wounded. The boatmen were determined to go back down the river, by desertion if not by arrangement.

There was no point to remaining here unless help could be summoned from above. Ashley asked for a volunteer to carry an express to Major Henry.

If any single moment in Jedediah Smith's life was decisive in the making of his career, it was this. He stepped forward.[24] Jedediah may have been shrewd enough to realize what the gratitude of the General could mean to him, but he also understood the responsibilities of courage and the necessity of accepting duty.

Ashley found a man to go along—a French-Canadian, it is said. With this one companion, Jedediah set out for the Yellowstone. Ashley fortified the smaller of his two keelboats, *The Rocky Mountains*, and took on board those who were willing to stay, with needed supplies. The rest of the goods he loaded into the large boat and started it downriver with the boatmen and the wounded. The goods would be left at Fort Kiowa, and the boat would go on to Fort Atkinson, carrying the news of his defeat.

Ashley moved down the river as far as the mouth of the Cheyenne.[25] Thereabouts he would remain till reinforced.

3. THE MISSOURI LEGION

The *Yellow Stone Packet* reached Fort Atkinson June 18, 1823, ten days from Ashley's camp at the mouth of the Cheyenne. Ashley's letter and the eyewitness accounts of the boatmen shocked and horrified Henry Leavenworth, colonel commanding at the fort, and Benjamin O'Fallon, the peppery agent in charge of Indian Affairs.

> I have thought proper [Ashley's letter said] to communicate this affair to you as early as opportunity offered, believing that you would feel disposed to make these people account to the government for the outrage committed. Should that be the case and a force sent for that purpose in a short time, you will oblige me much if you will send me an express at my expence, if one can be procured that I may meet and cooperate with you. . . . I expect to hear from Major Henry, to whom I sent an express, in twelve or fifteen days, during that time I shall remain between this place and Aurickaree towns, not remaining any length of time in one place as my force is small, not more than twenty three effective men.

Any action taken would have to be on Leavenworth's own authority, for it would require weeks to get orders from below. The Colonel decided to assume the responsibility and ordered six companies of the Sixth Infantry to prepare to march.[1]

Leavenworth was a brave and energetic officer who had distinguished himself in 1814 at the battles of Chippewa and Niagara Falls, but he had little practical experience of the Indian character, and his own officers, to say nothing of O'Fallon and the Indian traders, tended to regard him as a politician who in an Indian campaign might become blind to the necessities of the situation. Easterners who had killed off all their own Indians had developed tender feelings for the red men other people had to live with, and at an inconvenient moment Leavenworth's thoughts might stray eastward.

Major O'Fallon called in Joshua Pilcher to see what could be done. As acting partner of the Missouri Fur Company on the Missouri, Pilcher was pleased to find that the opportunity had arisen to deal with the Arikaras, albeit it had taken an outrage on the lieutenant governor of Missouri to arouse the military to this pitch of righteous wrath.[2] The previous summer Pilcher had accompanied his Mountain Expedition as high up as the Mandans, where he established a post called Fort Vanderburgh. At the Ree Villages, like Ashley, he had been well received. On their promise to commit no further depredations, he had left a clerk and merchandise. Notwithstanding, the Arikaras had attempted to waylay his boat when he came down the river again; during the winter they had attempted to rob the clerk; and in March had come the nasty business in the Sioux country.[3] Pilcher was agreed with O'Fallon on the necessity of teaching the Indians a lesson, and he was prepared to back up a punitive expedition with the whole disposable force of his company.

As O'Fallon saw it, the behavior of the Arikaras was symptomatic of a general evil. No respect was entertained by any of the upper tribes for the military prowess of the Americans, who were regarded as a people contemptibly few in numbers, a roving band without a settled home. Although chiefs of the upper Missouri tribes from time to time had been brought down the river to visit the Great White Father, the tales of the returning dignitaries always were dismissed by their people as big lies. Ashley's defeat had created the opportunity to administer a lesson that would make a lasting impression on all the upper tribes.

Leavenworth had refused to move at all unless O'Fallon stayed behind to keep the local Indians tranquil, so Pilcher was being asked to represent the Indian Office. Since Leavenworth's force was infantry, it was important to round up some Sioux auxiliaries to scour the country ahead of the whites; if the Arikaras were warned of the oncoming troops, they might retire up the river or into the plains, keeping their distance until the advancing season or the exhaustion of his supplies should force Leavenworth to go back down the river.

Should the Rees think they had nothing to contend with but the Sioux, they might well suppose, in O'Fallon's phrase, "that the bleeding traders, afraid to return themselves, [had] employed and sent them to avenge their blood, and return to their Villages either to receive or avoid them." Once the Rees had been invested in their villages, Leavenworth's troops could come up with artillery and pound them into submission. The Sioux would get some plunder and prisoners and the Ree Villages would be burned. "The news," O'Fallon assured Pilcher, "will fly like lightning to the most distant Tribes. The *Blackfeet* will hear & tremble when they think peace and tranquility will be restored to the land, and although great will be your sacrifice in a pecuniary point of view (danger privation and fatigue of no consideration) you will soon be amply compensated in the bosom of the richest fur country in the world."

Leavenworth had sworn that he would not think of peace till the blood of the traders had been avenged; still, Pilcher must be on his guard, for the Colonel was a mere sojourner in this country.

> A great deal depends on you and Gen[l]. Ashley [O'Fallon concluded] always bear in mind that it is not only an individual but the whole A'rickara nation that owes us blood and I am in hopes that no true American will tamely stand by and witness the reception or even recognize a white flag, so long as the brow of an A'rickara is decorated with the scalp of our people.[4]

O'Fallon now addressed himself to the "Forty three men who deserted Gen[l]. Ashley after his defeat by the A'Rickara nation of Indians." Their unexpected arrival from above, he told them, had mortified his national pride and distressed his heart greatly.

> I deplore the death of those of my brave Countrymen, who fell victims to the sculping knife of the A'rickaras—I feel most sensible the disappointment, the mortification and pecuniary loss of your employer Gen[l]. Ashly—he is my friend, he is your friend, he is the peoples friend—The most enterprising—the most energetic, and amongst the greatest military chieftians of the State of Missouri.

Deeply O'Fallon felt their shame in having abandoned their employer in the savage wilderness, far from home, friends and country. A great military expedition was about to ascend the Missouri, and Colonel Leavenworth had need of boatmen. Here was their opportunity to return to the relief of their friends—"to avenge your wrongs—to revenge the death, and bury the bones [of] your more than brave comrads whose spirits have pursued, sheding tears in your tracks." [5]

Moved by this eloquence or by Leavenworth's proffered wage, something like twenty boatmen agreed to return. Next day, June 20, O'Fallon wrote Ashley by express that military aid was on the way, and that a final end would now be put "to the repeated and most shocking outrages of the A'rickaras." Some 230 officers and men of the Sixth Regiment and another 40 or 50 men of the Missouri Fur Company would join Ashley with this end in view.[6]

Leavenworth's command embarked June 22. Three keelboats, including Ashley's *Yellow Stone Packet*, transported the supplies, two six-pounders, and part of the force, the rest of the troops proceeding by land. Pilcher was slower getting off, but on June 27 overtook the U. S. force, having aboard his two boats sixty men of his company and Leavenworth's 5½-inch howitzer. The river was high and turbulent, and the passage was rough. On July 3, about 150 miles above Council Bluffs, one of the boats was wrecked on a snag, a sergeant and six men being drowned. The loss included fifty-seven muskets and bayonets and a quantity of salt pork, but as proof that this was an efficient force, part of the flour was saved and all the whisky. Five nights later, in a tremendous storm, the *Yellow Stone Packet* was driven violently upon a sand bar, losing mast and deck. Both boat and cargo were near being lost, which would have forced the inglorious return of the expedition. Battered by wind and wave, Leavenworth was glad, on reaching the Missouri Fur Company's Fort Recovery (on the west bank of the Missouri, ten miles above the mouth of the White River), to halt three days to refit.[7]

For Pilcher the violence of the elements was the least distracting feature of the upstream voyage, for a succession of expresses with appalling news had reached him from above. Ashley had had another party slaughtered, high on the Missouri above the Great Falls; and his own Immell and Jones had been cut down on the Yellowstone. The Mountain Expedition into which had gone the supreme effort of the Missouri Fur Company was a shambles. The men lost were the flower of his force, and the loss in money, $15,000 at the lowest estimate, placed in jeopardy the existence of the Company.

What had befallen the Ashley men can be set forth in a few words. This was the party with which Jedediah Smith had wintered on the Musselshell, and which, to the number of eleven, in two canoes had paddled up the river in April. By mid-May they had reached Smiths River, above the Great Falls, but here the Blackfeet pounced on them, slaughtering four (their names remembered as C. Mayo, Iyo and Lemai, and one "not recollected") and driving the rest in confusion down the river.[8] A full stop was thereby put to operations on the high Missouri; it was six years before American trappers risked themselves in that country again.

The Immell-Jones Massacre is a longer story. In October 1822 the Missouri Fur Company's partisans had voyaged up the Yellowstone to winter at the mouth of the Big Horn at a temporary post they called Fort Benton. They made a good fall hunt, better than Henry's, amounting to thirty packs—1,500 beaver. Leaving these in cache, early in the spring they crossed over to the Missouri.

The party by this time was reduced to thirty men, for during the winter thirteen *engagés* had deserted, striking north toward Jedediah's winter camp (they were slashed at by the Blackfeet; four were killed and the rest lost their outfit).[9] They were the only Americans to reach the Three Forks in 1823, but Immell and Jones found the fabled wealth cleaned out already; the Blackfeet had trapped the streams. Nevertheless, the Missouri Fur Company men moved up the Jefferson as high as its forks, making a respectable twenty-pack hunt before wheeling about on May 16 to return to the Big Horn.

Two days later, while still on the Jefferson, forty miles above the Three Forks, Immell and Jones encountered a party of thirty-eight Blackfeet, who came boldly up and smoked. These turned out to be Piegans, a division of the Blackfeet somewhat less murderous than the rest.[10] The two parties camped together overnight. When they separated, the Piegan chief Iron Shirt was given a certificate of good conduct and some small presents. Immell was an old partisan of the Missouri Fur Company who had been chased out of this country by Blackfeet thirteen years before, and knew something of their ways; from here on the fur hunters stood not on the order of their going. The headlong flight brought the company into the path of a far more formidable war party—and this time the Blackfeet were Bloods.

When Immell and Jones ran into the Blood ambush, they had nearly reached safety, having got back across the mountains to the Yellowstone, within a few miles of a Crow camp with which they had wintered. The trail the scattered party was following wound along a steep hill, the base of which was washed by the river. The Bloods rushed on the whites with lance, battle-ax and scalping knife, and Immell and Jones fell among the first. Five others were killed and four wounded; the wonder was that any got away. The party lost its horses, equipage, traps, beaver, everything. Those who escaped crossed the Yellowstone on rafts to reach the refuge of the Crow camp. One of the clerks, William Gordon, immediately set out by land for Fort Vanderburgh to get word of the disaster to Pilcher. The other clerk, Charles Keemle, built skin canoes, raised the thirty packs of the fall hunt and arrived at the Mandans shortly after Gordon. The men who carried the express down to Fort Recovery were fired on as they passed the Ree towns; the Rees kept up a fusillade until the canoe was out of sight.[11]

The same day Leavenworth and Pilcher reached Fort Recovery, July 19, Ashley comes back into view, through a letter written at Fort Kiowa, thirteen miles above. He had had a long and lonesome wait, uncertain whether Jedediah Smith had got through to Fort Henry. . . . Of that journey nothing is known save the fact that Jedediah accomplished it. With his lone companion he must have veered away from the Missouri up the valley of the Grand, and from its head crossed over to the Yellowstone; as all of Ashley's horses were lost in the battle with the Rees, the mission necessarily was performed on foot.

Henry reacted with decision to the news. Leaving twenty men to garrison the post, he embarked his men in canoes and set out down the Missouri. The unpredictable Rees, instead of greeting him with a shower of balls, came out on the beach waving buffalo robes, the time-honored invitation to a parley. Henry paid no attention, the river swept his canoes past, and a day or so later he joined Ashley a hundred miles below. This may have been about the first week of July, a month from the time Jedediah Smith left with the express.[12]

During all this time Ashley and his men had remained near the mouth of the Cheyenne, mostly on an island opposite. Jim Clyman, one of the party, says they lived "on Scant and frquentle no rations allthough game was plenty on the main Shore." This hard living was Clyman's fault in part, for when on one occasion he was allowed to go ashore and had to be left there overnight, he killed a buck and found himself "in town"—plenty of wood, plenty of water, plenty of fat venison, "nothing to do but cook and eat." Thereafter he was not allowed to go ashore for fear he might never return.

Ashley's original idea had been, as soon as he should be reinforced by Henry, to fortify *The Rocky Mountains* and take it up past the Ree towns in defiance of the enemy. At the same time he had permitted himself to hope for help from below—if not troops, men from the other companies trading on the river. Now that Henry had joined him, it was possible to look at the situation more realistically. If troops did ascend the river this year, it was unlikely they would put in their appearance until fall, and it was imperative that he and Henry get parties into the field for a fall hunt. They needed a showing for their creditors; the furs Henry had brought down with him as the proceeds of the first year's hunt were disappointingly few in number.

They had to have horses, of course; this critical lack still existed. If they could get horses, it might be just as well to forget about the river for the present. Henry could return to his post with animals enough to fit out two parties, one to trap the southern tributaries of the Yellowstone, the other to go up the

Big Horn and on across the mountains to Columbia waters. Meanwhile Ashley would outfit a third party, also destined for the Columbia, which would strike directly overland from the Missouri. They had at hand just the man to command such a party, a young man who had been making himself a reputation all spring. But nothing was possible without horses. It was decided to drop down the Missouri to the vicinity of the Teton or Bad River. If they could fall in with a Sioux band willing to trade a sufficient supply of horses, all the rest would follow.

Again no horses. Leaving Henry and the men encamped at the Teton, Ashley dropped down the river another 120 miles to the posts below the Grand Detour, hoping to find Sioux possessed of that wealth which just now he prized above any other. On his arrival at Fort Kiowa Ashley received O'Fallon's letter of June 20. This put a different face on affairs, and on the afternoon of July 19 the General hastily set out to rejoin Henry. But first he wrote a letter to one of his creditors in St. Louis, to be taken down with the furs Henry had collected. (The boat, which reached St. Louis August 15, was placed in charge of one Samuel M. Smith, whose first name has not heretofore been known; historians who have concluded that the man Smith could be nobody but Jedediah have had a lamentable time explaining how Jedediah could be in two places at once.) This letter has provided most of our information as to what Ashley had done and proposed doing since his defeat. It also had an implied plea: "If we are successful in our expedition against the Aricaras we can in all probability put our business above in a short time, on a good footing." [13]

When Leavenworth and Pilcher reached Fort Recovery, they found at hand only a few Yanktons and Tetons. Pilcher sent out runners to the various bands, and they hoped to bring the cavalry up to six or seven hundred. Leavenworth had grown in wisdom; the force he had embarked at Fort Atkinson seemed less than imposing now. To O'Fallon he wrote:

If the Aracaras and Mandans unite, I shall proceed to the Mandans; and if they keep the Aracaras in their village, I shall attack them.

We shall do our best to obtain a victory. The honor of the American arms must be supported at all events. But I can plainly perceive that our force is not sufficient to inspire that degree of awe and respect amongst the Indians which I would wish. We make but a small show on a large prairie by the side of four or five hundred mounted Indians. If we can obtain a fair fight, our superiority will probably be more apparent.[14]

On July 23 the advance was resumed. Leavenworth had reduced his six companies of infantry to five, arming one with rifles, and also forming a small corps of artillerists. The expedition grew in size as Saones and Hunkpapas joined up. This promised the most fun the Sioux had had in years; the extermination of the Arikaras was a project they had worked at desultorily for a generation, and now the whites were going to do the job for them.

Leavenworth joined Ashley on July 30[15] and paused for two days to give the Sioux time to come up, meanwhile effecting a final organization of his command. "The Missouri Legion," as he styled it, had as its core Leavenworth's own regulars. The combined force of Ashley and Henry consisted of some eighty men, including the fainthearts who had come back up the river as boatmen. The two leaders, brigadier general and major respectively of the Missouri state militia, had rank enough for any army. Their men were divided into two companies of forty men each. Jedediah Smith was named captain of one company, Hiram Scott of the other, and their subordinates were men of quality: Hiram Allen and George C. Jackson were lieutenants; Charles Cunningham and Edward Rose, ensigns; one Fleming, surgeon; Thomas Fitzpatrick, quartermaster; William L. Sublette, sergeant major. The men of the Missouri Fur Company, including the survivors of the Immell-Jones Massacre and the clerks and servants of the now-abandoned post at the Mandans, were organized as a separate company under Joshua Pilcher (who was given the nominal rank of major and retained it the rest of his life). The roll of Pilcher's officers was as distinguished as Ashley's, with the former West Pointer, William Henry Vanderburgh, as captain, Moses B. Carson first lieutenant, and William Gordon second lieutenant. Angus McDonald was appointed captain in nominal command of the Indian auxiliaries. These auxiliaries were estimated to have totaled 750 mounted warriors, of which perhaps a third had guns.

On August 8, having reached a point twenty-five miles below the Arikara Villages, Leavenworth disembarked his men. That night they camped fifteen or sixteen miles below the Ree towns. Arms were examined, ammunition distributed and strips of white muslin given the Sioux to wrap around their heads, that friends might be distinguished from foes.[16]

Next morning, August 9, Major Woolley, with a crew of ten for each boat, was directed to continue up the river. Pilcher's command was assigned to this detail, the Missouri Fur Company men being the most reliable *voyageurs* in Leavenworth's command. The rest of the Legion marched on the enemy.

After crossing Grand River, five or six miles below the villages, Leavenworth ordered a small force of the Sioux to precede the troops and give battle to the Rees if they should come out from their villages, and at all events to prevent them from running away. Leavenworth had long experience in handling regular troops, but his education in the ways of Indian auxiliaries was just beginning, and he had already begun to worry over the peculiar behavior of Fire Heart and his Saones, who it was reported were determined to join the Rees if the whites should be defeated. However, the Yanktons, the Tetons and some of the Saones set out for the battle with great enthusiasm, and the whites followed on the double-quick. Captain Bennet Riley with the company of riflemen moved out in front, followed by Ashley and his mountain men. The four companies of infantry followed, with the remaining Sioux on the flanks and in the rear.

The Sioux galloped ahead impetuously, and were well ahead of the foot troops when they burst on the plain on which the Ree Villages stood. Not at all averse to battle with these accustomed marauders, the Arikaras met the Sioux at the edge of the plain, half a mile from their towns, with a ferocity and valor that matched their own.

So far had the Sioux outdistanced the rest of the Legion that they had sustained the action alone for a full hour when the whites reached the battlefield. The fight was showing signs of going against them when Jedediah arrived on the scene. It was an amazing spectacle that opened to view, for Indian warfare on the Missouri was a thing peculiar to itself; as Clyman says, "the plain was covered with Indians which looked more like a swarm [of] bees than a battle field they going in all possible directions." Leavenworth quickly formed his line, placing the mountain men on the extreme right, the four companies of infantry in the center and Riley's riflemen on the extreme left, but the Sioux were so much scattered in front of the troops that to fire would have produced an indiscriminate slaughter of Sioux and Rees. The opportunity to fight an immediately decisive action promptly vanished, for the Arikaras broke and ran for their villages, hotly pursued by the Sioux. Leavenworth's men advanced to within three or four hundred yards of the stockaded villages and halted just out of gunshot. It had all gone according to plan. They had treed the coon. All that remained was for the artillery to come up and shoot the coon out of the tree.

From ten to fifteen Rees lay dead on the plain, which made this a victory for the Sioux, though they had two killed and seven wounded. Waiting on the artillery (the boats were having hard work of it against adverse winds), Jedediah had opportunity to reflect on the singularity of savage warfare. Scattered over the late battlefield, the Sioux were busily engaged in cutting up the bodies of the dead, after which they attached cords to the dismembered arms, legs, hands and feet, and dragged them triumphantly over the ground. Nearer the Ree Village, within long gunshot of it, lay a dead brave. An old Sioux chief brought up one of his wives, who with a war club began raining blows on the corpse, the chief taunting the Rees the while for their cowardice in allowing his squaws to strike their braves in gunshot of their village. But the most arresting spectacle was afforded by what Clyman describes as a "large middle aged Sioux" belonging to "the grizzle Bear medicine," who came on hands and feet to the body of a dead Ree, "snorting and mimican the bear in all his most vicious attitudes and with his teeth tore out mouth fulls of flesh from the breast of the dead body of the Ree." The Sioux averted their eyes, and begged the whites not to watch, for that would impair the power of the medicine.[17]

It was sundown when the boats arrived, too late in the day to press the action to a finish. Jedediah tightened his belt on his empty belly and lay down under the stars. Not, perhaps, to sleep, for the night, by Clyman's vivid account, was

> a lively picture of pandimonium the wa[il]ing of squaws and children the Screams and yelling of men the fireing of guns the awful howling of dogs the neighing and braying of hosses and mules with the hooting of owls of which thy [were] a number all intermingled with the stench of dead men and horses made the place the most disagreeable that immaginnation could fix Short of the bottomless pit.

At sunup Leavenworth set about the reduction of the Arikara towns. Captain Riley with his riflemen and Lieutenant Bradley with a company of infantry were ordered to invest the upper village, and one of the six-pounders was sent to support them. The rest of his force Leavenworth reserved for the assault on the lower village, the one overlooking the sand beach on which Jedediah had fought the desperate action of June 2. Ashley's men were still on the extreme right, resting on the river, next to them Lieutenant Morris with the other six-pounder and the howitzer, then the remainder of the infantry, with the Indians scattered and in the rear.

The thinking that had been done back at Fort Atkinson now had to be equated with military reality. The six-pounder detailed to labor with the upper village turned out to have been posted at too high an elevation, so that the shot passed harmlessly over its target to splash into the river beyond, and though this was presently rectified, the effect on the Rees was not remarkable. The battery under Lieutenant Morris kept up a brisk fire with just as little apparent effect.

For the Sioux the novelty of this kind of warfare soon wore off; besides, they were hungry. They wandered off to the Ree cornfields, where ripening corn, squash, pumpkins and beans made the war seem more worth while. The example was one that Jedediah and his companions must have been tempted to follow, for they had eaten nothing since the previous morning. They waited for the steady pounding of the artillery to bring the

Rees out to be shot at, meantime whistling a few rifle balls into the Ree stockade.

Toward noon Leavenworth began inquiring into what it would involve to carry the villages by storm. The stockades were said to be very strong, and it was reported that a five-foot trench had been dug inside the stockade since the battle with Ashley. Angus McDonald was of the opinion that the defenses could be carried only by "sapping and mining." And once inside, the Rees must be expected to fight like demons, the women with the men. Leavenworth began to be conscious that he had entered on this Indian war without orders. What would become of him if any considerable part of his command was butchered did not bear thinking about.

Still, something had to be done. He decided to test the real strength of the defenses by an attack on the upper village. Riley and his riflemen would make the assault, covered by the rest of the regulars, while Ashley's men kept the lower village occupied. Gladly Jedediah and the other mountain men scrambled into a ravine within twenty yards of the enemy and began spattering lead against the stockade.

Riley was delighted with his orders, but as the moment for action approached, Leavenworth grew apprehensive. Fire Heart's Saones had retired altogether from the battle, and were believed to be in the hills waiting on the issue. The rest of the Sioux were scattered literally from hell to breakfast, from the field of battle to the Ree cornfields.

Riley's job was to reach the stockade and breach it so they could get a look inside. He was then to withdraw, and if it seemed advisable to storm the village, that would be done by the entire command. But if the Sioux saw Riley withdrawing, they might conclude that the whites were beaten. The more Leavenworth considered his situation, the less he liked it, and he countermanded his orders for the assault. Riley, as Jim Clyman relates, "became allmost furious and swore that he demande the priviledge stating that they had been laying at garison at Council Bluffs for 8 or 10 years doeing nothing but eating pumpkins and now a small chance for promotion occured and it was denied him and might not occurr again for the next 10 yeares." Opposition only confirmed Leavenworth in his determination, and the charge was abandoned.

Unable to decide on any course that did not also finally commit him, Leavenworth did not rejoice in the disagreeable news Pilcher now brought him. The Sioux had lost interest in the battle and were wandering off in every direction. Unless some decisive turn was given affairs, Leavenworth would be stranded without allies.

Leavenworth agreed to a general assault on the lower town. But when he returned to the lower village, he found that Lieutenant Morris had virtually exhausted his round shot. Leavenworth directed him to cease firing and ordered his forces to withdraw from the upper village, Ashley's men meanwhile being moved back out of their ravine. The Sioux were still industriously engaged in stripping the Arikara cornfields, and it was incumbent on Leavenworth to warn them. The message he sent could not have been more unfortunately phrased, for the Sioux were advised to leave the cornfields "to save their stragglers from the tomahawks of the Aricaras." The Sioux disappeared altogether, and after nightfall Leavenworth saw no more of them.

By the time his disgusted officers completed their retirement it was well after 3:00 P.M. During the entire day's action, the Legion had suffered only two slight wounds, which did not say much for the way the battle had been pressed. If the Arikara War ended as it had begun, the Sixth Regiment was going to be the laughingstock of the army; thus far the Sioux had done the only fighting worth mentioning.

Subsistence was short, and Leavenworth was preparing to send a foraging party off to the cornfields when he observed a few Rees and Sioux holding a parley in front of the villages. This was the first opportunity to talk with the enemy, and Leavenworth hastened to improve it. He and Pilcher went out to join the conference.

At sight of the Colonel, an imposing figure in his blue and buff uniform, one of the Rees advanced, begging him to have pity on their women and children. The man who had caused all the mischief, the chief Grey Eyes, had been killed, he said. Peace was the wish of the whole tribe, for a great many people and horses had been killed. Leavenworth replied that the whites had come here not to fight but to make peace; the white men's hearts were good. The Ree disappeared behind the stockade with this news, and Pilcher returned to the boats scarcely willing to speak to the Colonel; the discussion he had had at Fort Atkinson with O'Fallon was rising to haunt him.

Several Rees emerged from the lower village, including the chief Little Soldier. Leavenworth and Pilcher went forward to meet them, and the cordiality with which Leavenworth greeted Little Soldier added to Pilcher's bile; as he told the Colonel afterward, "the affectionate manner in which you embraced him, done credit to the goodness of your heart; but did not in my humble opinion, comport with the dignity of the *Legion's chief.*" [18] Another six or seven Indians and several of Leavenworth's officers joined the parley, all sitting on buffalo robes spread ceremoniously on the ground. Leavenworth then laid down his terms for peace. The Arikaras must restore Ashley's property, promise to behave well in future, and as immediate evidence of good faith, deliver into his hands five hostages to be taken down to Fort Atkinson.

The Rees agreed to restore such property as they still had, but declared that the horses had been killed or stolen by the Sioux. Leavenworth favored the delegation with an oration on the great power of the Americans, with which the Rees might have been more impressed had they witnessed some striking evidence of it. Still, the Rees promised fair, and taking into consideration the smallness of his force, "the strange and unaccountable conduct of the Sioux, and even the great probability of their joining the Aricaras against us—and also considering the importance of saving to our country the expense and trouble of a long Indian warfare, and the importance of securing the Indian trade," Leavenworth agreed to make peace.

Now the calumet was brought forth. The glowering Pilcher refused not only to smoke but even to shake hands, getting up and pacing back and forth while telling the Rees they should look out for him hereafter. At Leavenworth's insistence, he agreed to smoke, but obstinately refused his assent to the rest of the proceedings. Since the Rees regarded Pilcher more than Leavenworth as the real head of the expedition, the effect on them was not happy.

During the day Leavenworth had lost all faith in the Sioux, and thought it not unlikely that they would join the Arikaras in a night attack on him. He ordered his forces to entrench, and they slept uncomfortably on their arms. When the sun came up on the eleventh, the Sioux had vanished, as also six army mules and seven horses belonging to Ashley. This would involve tedious explanations to the Quartermaster's Department, but Leavenworth was glad to have seen the last of such allies.

Negotiations with the Rees were resumed. It was agreed that other chiefs should come out for the parleys, and that some of the whites should visit the village to allay the fears of the Indians. Edward Rose volunteered to go alone within the Ree stockade to size things up. Deeds of bravado were the foundation on which Rose's reputation rested; he was known among the Crows as "The Five Scalps" because he had once singlehanded stormed a fortified position held by a beleaguered war party of Minnetarees, killing five and driving the rest out to be slaughtered.[19] Any Indian would think twice about provoking trouble with Rose, and the Rees were even a little fond of him. He disappeared inside the stockade, returning to report that the Rees were indeed humbled and had suffered considerably from the bombardment. Several of Leavenworth's officers then visited the Ree town, to find the pickets very frail and the ditches of the most shallow description; in short, they should have been able to take the place before supper the first afternoon.

Anxious to distribute the responsibility, Leavenworth ordered Pilcher to draft a treaty. The Major refused. Andrew Henry was next appealed to, since he had a subagent's commission of sorts, but Henry politely declined too. Leavenworth drafted the instrument himself. It was a simple document, providing that the Rees should restore the arms taken from Ashley's party in June, along with "such other articles of property as may remain in their hands, which were obtained of gen. Ashley in exchange for horses"; that free navigation of the Missouri should be guaranteed; and that American citizens entering their country should hereafter be received in friendship. In return the Arikaras would become friends of the United States, bound in a firm and inviolable peace.

This was all very well, but nothing of Ashley's property was forthcoming save three rifles, a horse and eighteen robes. On the afternoon of the twelfth Little Soldier informed Leavenworth that nothing more could be done. The upper village, which had taken no part in the attack on Ashley, declined to contribute anything; and, as Little Soldier pointed out, the principal villain of the piece, Grey Eyes, was dead. Leavenworth threatened an immediate attack on the village if the first article of the treaty were not complied with, for this was the only gauge he had for the good faith of the Rees. Alarmed, Little Soldier begged to be allowed to come over to the side of the whites; by way of demonstrating his good faith, he pointed out where the village might best be attacked, and even advised that more execution would be done if the cannon fired low.

The point about Ashley's property had to be abandoned or the battle resumed. Leavenworth called a council of his officers and the heads of the fur companies. After some discussion it was agreed to attack the villages next morning.

Rose came in with word that the Rees were preparing to abandon their villages during the night. Nothing in his experience had prepared Leavenworth for the kind of responsibility he had had to take on himself in this campaign. With each crisis he had temporized, hoping for some development that would take him off the hook, and he reacted in characteristic fashion to Rose's news. Calling in his officers, he announced a decision: "The Little Soldier has used every effort to induce his people to comply with the treaty, but all he has done, will avail nothing; he says he is unable to make good the property himself, and I have therefore determined to abandon the charge and dispense with that article of the treaty." He sent Rose to inform the Rees he had waived the principal article of the treaty. There was no need for them to flee their towns.

In fairness, Leavenworth's own explanation should be given:

I felt that my situation was a disagreeable and unpleasant one. It appeared to me that my reputation and the honor and brilliancy of the expedition required that I should gratify my troops and make a charge; but I also thought that sound policy, and the interests of my country required that I should not. . . . For my own part I felt confident that the Indians had been sufficiently humbled, fully to convince them of our ability to punish any injury which they might do us, and that they would behave well in future if we left them undisturbed in their villages.

The smell of the battlefield had not improved during the three days Leavenworth's command had been bivouacked on it, but Jedediah could mark one striking difference from the first night: the preternatural quiet that prevailed. The reason became evident at dawn on the fourteenth. During the night the Rees had evacuated both villages without attracting the attention of Leavenworth's sentries.

The entire campaign had had a comic-opera character, and this final development was of a piece with the rest. Leavenworth dispatched his interpreter with a few men to find the Rees and bring them back. While waiting for their return, the Colonel went into the villages to inspect the damage done by his artillery. He observed that the towns were

. . . completely riddled. We found thirty-one new graves, and we found that several old ones had been opened, and the surface set thick with prickly pears to conceal the new dirt. We know that 10 men, who were killed by the Sioux in the skirmish on the 9th, were buried in five graves; and we know, also, that more than one was buried in several of the other graves. From the best evidence that we could collect, it is supposed that more than 50 of their people were killed, and a great number wounded.

Pilcher, however, conceived that very little damage had been done by the cannonade, and he doubted that the number of Rees killed, including squaws and children, exceeded thirty.[20] The only living things found in the two villages were the aged and infirm mother of the dead Grey Eyes, forty or fifty dogs and a lone rooster.

Late on the fourteenth the men sent to find and reason with

the Rees returned from a profitless mission. Next morning the troops and the men of the fur companies were embarked for the return voyage. The mother of Grey Eyes was given plenty of provisions and water, and left in possession of the towns. The boats were scarcely out of sight of the villages, however, when a great column of smoke billowed up behind. Infuriated, Leavenworth scratched off a note to Pilcher: "The Colonel commanding, is extremely mortified to say, that he has too much reason to believe, that the Riccaras towns, have been set on fire by [your] company, contrary to the most positive orders, and in violation of their word of honor to obey orders; with such men he will have no further intercourse." [21]

Pilcher had a better command of invective:

> You came to restore peace and tranquility to the country, & leave an impression which would insure its continuance, your operations have been such as to produce the contrary effect, and to impress the different Indian tribes with the greatest possible contempt for the American character. You came (to use your own language) to "open and make good this great road"; instead of which, you have by the imbecility of your conduct and operations, created and left impassable barriers.

The acrimony would boil over into the newspapers, the War Department, the Indian Office, the halls of Congress, the nation's statutes—the military blaming the traders and the traders blaming the military. The Arikaras now would live in a permanent state of hostility toward all fur traders. . . . Jedediah Smith had been rarely privileged to participate in the Arikara campaign. It had been granted him to witness at close range a demonstration of the power and majesty of the United States.

4. SOUTH PASS

The Missouri Legion broke up at the Grand River. Leavenworth gave the Ashley men an honorable, and the Missouri Fur Company men a dishonorable discharge and shoved off for home.

Ashley and Henry had the satisfaction of having made the general suffering on the Missouri still more universal, but whether that was a net gain depended on where the Rees had gone and in what temper. Ashley estimated his losses in the disaster of June at $2,265. What had been recovered from the Rees did not even reimburse him for his further losses from the Sioux; the seven horses run off were another $420 gone. Moreover, the firm had lost $1,540 in the rout of its upper Missouri party.[1] With all this, the only way of determining whether free navigation had been restored to the Missouri was by putting the thing to the test.

It was in every way better to go back to the situation that existed before the cymbals and the drums of the Missouri Legion were heard in the land. If they could trade horses from the Sioux, Henry could pack in to the Yellowstone such goods as he imperatively required, and simultaneously they could get Jedediah Smith off to the mountains. More broadly, affairs at the end of their first year in the mountains stacked up like this: The Missouri Fur Company had been driven from the Yellowstone and had abandoned their post at the Mandans; it was unlikely they would be a factor hereafter in the upper country. The French Fur Company had got no higher up the river than Fort Kiowa, and in the present state of things probably would not venture above the Sioux. The Columbia Fur Company had reached the Missouri overland from their main bases on the Mississippi and the St. Peters, but their establishment at the Mandans was a mere outpost.[2] Ashley and Henry were left in sole possession of the mountains, and their luck should be due to turn.

Meanwhile they must look sharp lest they starve. They had been on short rations while with Leavenworth, and this was the reason for separating from him, to give them a chance to subsist by hunting. In convenient stages, as they could find game, they would drop down to Fort Kiowa, where their goods were stored.[3]

An incident of the downward voyage was the drowning of Talbot, the slayer of Mike Fink, at the Teton River. The tradition is that this drowning occurred ten days after Leavenworth's battle with the Rees, say August 25. Pilcher was back at Fort Recovery by August 20, but it was the end of the month before Jedediah Smith reached Fort Kiowa in Ashley's company.[4]

The Sioux had returned from the wars too, and were mourning their dead—in Indian warfare no victory was altogether a victory if any were lost. From the conical leather lodges, in all directions around the post, rose the ceaseless howling. The Tetons had suffered most, and it was from their lodges especially that the high keening came. The lament was appropriate otherwise, for the post was out of provisions and the Indians were suffering from hunger. Perhaps because of the movement of such large bodies of men up and down the river this summer, game had disappeared into the hinterland, and the Sioux were being compelled to follow. By so much were Ashley's difficulties increased, for the departing Sioux were taking their horses with them. . . . One person at the fort would have attracted Jedediah's interest, the aging Toussaint Charbonneau, once interpreter for Lewis and Clark and now in the service of the French Company.[5]

The first horses that could be bought were used to get Henry off to the Yellowstone. He had a long hike ahead of him, for animals were procurable in numbers barely sufficient for pack purposes. Jim Clyman, who records this melancholy circumstance, recalled that Henry's party amounted to about thirteen men, but it must have been larger than that, for the partners had mustered eighty men for the Missouri Legion, and even with the constant erosion still had at their disposal a considerable force of hunters and *voyageurs*. It was possibly about September 1 that Henry launched on his journey, one forever famous in the annals of the West because his party happened to include Hugh Glass.[6]

There remained the problem of outfitting Jedediah Smith. Of goods there was no lack, but transport was another matter. It was late September before Ashley had Jedediah in shape to leave Fort Kiowa, and then only by courtesy of the French Fur Company, whose factor lent horses to supplement the few Ashley was able to trade;[7] these Jedediah must send back as soon as he could obtain others. As in Henry's case, there was no question of the men riding; all the horses were required for the baggage.

This first party led by Jedediah Smith was a small one. Jim Clyman remembered many years later that it totaled only eleven men, and while this may have been too low for the first stage of the journey, it is doubtful if the number exceeded sixteen.[8] The company assayed extraordinarily high in quality. Most of the men had been with Jedediah Smith on the beach under the Ree towns, and they had that confidence in themselves and one another that men feel who have stood fire together.

There was the Kentucky-born William L. Sublette, tall, whip-thin, long and gaunt of face like another Andrew Jackson, and possessed of Jackson's resilient energy and iron resolution. Bill Sublette had been able to come to the mountains this spring only because friends in St. Charles had outfitted him with a good rifle and a suit of buckskin, but already he had made a name for himself. There was the lank Virginian, Clyman, grave of manner, slow spoken, of a reflective cast of mind but unbelievably enduring. There was the ruddy-cheeked young man from County Cavan, Thomas Fitzpatrick, born the same year as Jedediah, of medium height and somewhat slender but sinewy and strong-willed, possessed of the same intelligence, drive and capacity for leadership that had made Jedediah a booshway at twenty-four. The daredevil Thomas Eddie was another. Only the names of Branch and Stone are preserved. Perhaps the most striking personality was Rose, whose ferocious temper, stunning readiness for battle and savage humor had already made him a legend. The others are anonymous.[9]

The route Jedediah adopted had not been used hitherto for trapping incursions into the West. Furnished with a guide by the French Company, Jedediah proposed to strike for the Black Hills by a route as direct as possible, expecting to fall in with some of the remoter Sioux bands and from them obtain horses. He would then cross the Black Hills, again by a route as direct as the nature of the country permitted, and go on across the valleys of the Powder and the Tongue to strike the Big Horn somewhere above its lower canyon. There he might fall in with the party under Captain Weber that Andrew Henry was sending up from the Yellowstone, after which the spring hunt of both parties would be made beyond the continental divide.

The first day's march from Fort Kiowa was over a dry, rolling desolate highland. That night Jedediah dropped down into the valley of what Clyman calls White Clay Creek, probably the White River,[10] "running thick with a white sediment and resembling cream in appearance but of a sweetish pu[n]gent taste." Their guide warned them against using this water too freely, as it caused "excessive costiveness." They gulped it down regardless.

A little the worse for wear, next day and part of the next they proceeded up the narrow valley of the White before leaving it to cut across a wide bend. It would be twenty-four hours before they saw water again, but their means of taking water was small. The party trudged on until dark, making a dry camp on a ridge where the needle-pointed prickly pear grew so profusely the thirsty company could scarcely find room to spread their blankets. At dawn they got under way, and just before noon reached the water hole on which they had relied. It was dry. There was not even a little damp mud to suggest it might be worth their while to dig. It was another fifteen miles to the river.

Clyman says that they set out again, urging and hauling along their dejected horses as fast as possible. The guide got far ahead and at last disappeared. The rest of the party straggled over a distance of a mile or more, with Jedediah Smith bringing up the rear. Clyman's pack horse was more tractable than the others, and he got some distance ahead. His companions veered off to right and left in search of water, so that "we ware not onley long but wide and it appeared like we might never all collect togather again."

Following as nearly as he could on the course where the guide had last been seen, but deviating a little to the right, an hour before sunset Clyman had the luck to stumble on a water hole. He paused long enough to fire his gun before plunging into the pool. A moment of soaking up the life-giving wetness, and Clyman waded out to fire his gun again. A man and horse made their appearance, running for the water. The horse outran the man, plunging in with a resounding splash. Each man as he came fired his gun and shouted—"as soon as he could moisten his mouth Sufficienty to mak a noise."

By dark all but three had reached the water. Jedediah was one of the missing, but he came up at last. When he could speak, he said that the other two had given out. To conserve body moisture and give them a chance at survival, he had buried them in sand up to their necks, then had gone on, hoping to return in time to save their lives. Jedediah started back on one of the horses, returning later in the night with the two men.

Next morning the little company resumed the journey. It was still four or five miles to the river, where their guide awaited them. The river where they came back to it was a beautiful, clear stream running over a gravelly bottom, with some timber along its course. Refreshed, they continued upstream to an encampment of Bois Brule Sioux, where they paused for several days to trade for horses, obtaining enough to give them two animals apiece and several extras. It was then possible to send their guide and the borrowed horses back to Fort Kiowa.

We packed up [Clyman says] and crossed the White Clay river and proceeded north westernly over a dry roling Country for several days meeting with a Buffaloe now and then which furnished us with provision for at least one meal each day our luck was to fall in with the Oglela tiribe of Sioux[8] whare [we] traded a few more horses and swaped of[f] some of our more ordina[r]y.

The country continued nearly the same, the grass short, and more than a sufficiency of the prickly pear, until they struck the South Fork of the Cheyenne a few miles below the place where it emerged from the Black Hills. After crossing the Cheyenne, they rode into a badlands such as none of them had ever seen—

a tract of country [Clyman describes it] whare no vegetation of any kind existed beeing worn into knobs and gullies and extremely uneven [composed of] a loose grayish coloured soil verry soluble in water running thick as it could move of a pale whitish coular and remarkably adhesive there [came] on a misty rain while we were in this pile of ashes and it loded down our horses feet in great lumps it looked a little remarkable that not a foot of level land could be found the narrow revines going in all manner of directions and the cobble mound[s] of a regular taper from top to bottom all of them of the percise same angle and the tops sharp the whole of this region is moveing to the Misourie River as fast as rain and thawing of Snow can carry it.

Inclining more to the west, Jedediah and his men reached better going. They were approaching the Black Hills, which rose at first only slightly above the rolling plains, but presently became a pleasant, undulating region of pointed dark pines, refreshingly different from the hot and dusty land they had thus far seen. The hills grew higher and near the dividing ridge were more brushy, with scrubby pine and juniper.[11] Beyond the divide the ravines were steeper, rugged and rocky. The western slope of the Black Hills was undiscovered country, and Jedediah thought it probable he was on the eastern heads of the Powder. But this was singular terrain, the beginnings of his education in mountain travel. One evening late, Clyman says:

. . . gowing d[o]wn a small stream we came into a Kenyon and pushed ourselves down so far that our horses had no room to turn while looking for a way out it became dark by unpacking and leading our animals down over Slipery rocks three of us got down to a n[i]ce open glade whare we killed a Buffaloe and fared Sumpiously that night while the rest of the Company remained in the Kenyon without room to lie down.

It would not do to follow the streams. Jedediah climbed a ridge and was lucky enough to emerge upon a main divide, which he followed a considerable distance before descending again. But the ridges yielded no feed for the horses, which became weak and emaciated. Five of the animals had to be given a chance to recruit, and Jedediah left three men to look after them while he took the rest of the company on; the young captain hoped to find beaver in numbers sufficient to justify the whole party in stopping.[12] At the same time he ordered Edward Rose to go ahead and find the Crows. If they were really on the waters of the Powder, they had reached Crow country, and Rose might be able to get fresh horses.

Five days later, toward evening, the little company was threading its way through a brushy bottom, the men on foot leading the horses. A large grizzly came down the valley. He struck the line nearly in the center, turned and ran parallel with it. Jedediah, being in advance, ran to the open ground, and as he emerged from the thicket met the bear face to face.

Jim Clyman tells the story:

Grissly did not hesitate a moment but sprang on the capt taking him by the head first pitc[h]ing sprawling on the earth he gave him a grab by the middle fortunately cat[c]hing by the ball pouch and Butcher K[n]ife which he broke but breaking several of his ribs and cutting his head badly none of us having any sugical Knowledge what was to be done one Said come take hold and he wuld say why not you so it went around I asked the Capt what was best he said one or 2 [go] for water and if you have a needle and thread git it out and sew up my wounds around my head which was bleeding freely I got a pair of scissors and cut off his hair and then began my first Job of d[r]essing wounds upon examination I [found] the bear had taken nearly all his head in his capcious mouth close to his left eye on one side and clos to his right ear on the other and laid the skull bare to near the crown of the head leaving a white streak whare his teeth passed one of his ears was torn from his head out to the outer rim after stitching all the other wounds in the best way I was capabl and according to the captains directions the ear being the last I told him I could do nothing for his Eare O you must try to stitch up some way or other said he then I put in my needle stiching it through and through and over and over laying the lacerated parts togather as nice as I could with my hands water was found in about ame mille when we all moved down and encamped the captain being able to mount his horse and ride to camp whare we pitched a tent the onley one we had and made him as comfortable as circumstances would permit this gave us a lisson on the charcter of the grissly Baare which we did not forget.

Lying torn and bleeding at the feet of his men, Jedediah retained a power of decision and a clarity of mind which illustrated clearly why he was their captain. Tradition has persisted in the Smith family that Jedediah killed his bear, but it seems unlikely. Mountain tradition was that Arthur Black, Jedediah's later companion in the adventures on the Pacific slope, once saved him from the attack of a bear,[13] and, if so, this may have been the occasion, though Black's presence in the party of 1823 has not been proved. Jedediah bore the marks of this encounter to the end of his life, eyebrow ripped away, ear scarred and torn. These were honorable scars, but of a kind to give men pause when they looked at him, and Jedediah wore his hair long thereafter, hanging down over his ears.

In the clean western air a man's wounds heal fast, and within ten days Jedediah was able to mount his horse and ride a few miles. With winter approaching, his party needed all the westing it could get; even a couple of miles a day added up. While he was down, his men had scouted the country, and Jedediah had a clearer conception of where he was. It developed that the Cheyenne drained the western as well as the eastern slope of the Black Hills: Clyman had followed the South Fork back to where it cut through the southern base of the hills, and had returned to camp with this intelligence and a wonderful tale of a canyon he had found, walled in by cliffs of black and shining slate, the very place doubtless where Moses obtained the tablets on which the Decalogue was inscribed. (Clyman was full of other tales too, having chanced on a grove of petrified trees. A sizable portion of the West's folklore dates from this autumn, for in between bear stories and Injun doins, the campfires were soon hearing about the peetrified forests with trees, branches and leaves all turned to stone, wild cherries peetrified into rubies of reddest hue, and peetrified birds a-sittin' on the branches a-singin' peetrified songs.)

The party had not gone far when they struck the trail of a large band of Cheyennes. The Cheyennes received them kindly, and also another company of whites which to Jedediah's surprise came up behind. This was a Missouri Fur Company party under Charles Keemle and William Gordon.[14] Pilcher had declared that the Missouri Fur Company would go no more to the mountains, but Jedediah's foray west from Fort Kiowa changed his mind. Fort Recovery was only a dozen miles below Kiowa, and just as good a base. If he was not prepared to lift his sights beyond the Rockies, Pilcher was at any rate willing to compete for the Crow trade. As hastily as he could make the arrangements, he got Keemle and Gordon off on the trail of Jedediah Smith; en route they had picked up the three men and the horses Jedediah had left to recruit, and now all could go on to the Big Horn together.

Two days after they parted from the Cheyennes, definitely on the Powder now, Edward Rose brought into camp fifteen or sixteen Crows, big, handsome men with a large streak of fun in them. The Crows had several spare horses, which greatly relieved Jedediah's broken-down animals and gave his men a chance to ride. However, the Crows were of a mind to travel faster than Jedediah's horses could endure, "so," Clyman relates, "Capt Smith gave them what they could pack sending Rose with them and we followed at our own gait stoping and Traping for beaver occasionly Crossing several steep and high ridges which in any other country would be called mountains."

The hills west of the Powder River were bewildering; they seemed to run in all directions. But they were better supplied with game than any region Jedediah had yet seen. It was now November and the nights were frosty, though the days continued warm and pleasant. The trail Jedediah was following wound up over the Owl Creek Mountains—the Littlehorns, the mountain men called them—and came down to the Big Horn, which above the Littlehorns had been known to the fur traders for years as Wind River. Here the men of the two fur companies fell on hard times, for the Crows had recently passed up the river, killing or driving off all the game. It was necessary to press on and overtake the village, a disagreeable business because the weather had turned cold and blustery, with a dust of snow blowing continually on the bitter north wind. Horses and men were exhausted by the time they reached the Crow encampment.[15]

The winter camp of the Crows was high up Wind River, probably in the vicinity of modern Dubois. Gratifyingly, Jedediah here made contact with the party Henry had outfitted for the Big Horn. It has to be supposed that the party was led by the moody Captain Weber.

Henry's adventures getting back to his fort and after must wait for the next chapter. But he had acquired some horses from the River Crows, as the band along the Yellowstone was called to distinguish it from the Mountain Crows,[16] and with these he got Weber off to the mountains. Daniel Potts, now recovered from his wounds, was one of the party and has left the only account of its adventures. They moved up the Big Horn, taking a few beaver en route, to reach the Big Horn Basin probably by late October, then crossed the "second range of mountains," the Littlehorns, to the Wind River Valley. The party had lingered in trapping the Big Horn Basin or an early storm howled down upon them, for Potts adds, "In crossing this mountain I unfortunately froze my feet and was unable to travel from the loss of two toes." The Crows carried him to their village and installed him in the lodge of their chief, "who regularly twice a day divested himself of all his clothing except his bre[e]ch clout, and dressed my wounds until I left them." [17]

Clyman does not mention Weber's party, nor does Potts mention Jedediah's, yet what the two have to say about the locality of the camp and about life with the Crows this winter makes it manifest they were together. The Crows had always been friendly to the whites, though they were continually at war with their neighbors the Blackfeet, the Sioux and the Cheyennes; in this respect they were more intelligent than the Arikaras, who had picked a fight with the only people who might have enabled them to maintain themselves against the Sioux. It is true the Crows had run off the horses of William Clark in 1805 and of Robert Stuart in 1812, but thieving was the Crow pride; it became an accepted mode of livelihood for them to steal the trappers' horses and restore them for a reward—an operation, said Bill Gordon of Pilcher's company, "so common that it hardly interrupts friendship." Although in the next decade the first fine fervor wore off the Crow affection for the whites, they took pains only to rob the trappers, never to kill them. "This," Gordon said in 1831, "they frankly explain by telling us that if they killed, we would not come back, & they would lose the chance of stealing from us. They have no shame about stealing and will talk over their past thefts to you with all possible frankness and indifference." [18]

The Crows were a remarkable people. Their children were taught to ride at the earliest possible age. Infants were put on a cradleboard, which was hung from the saddle and the horse turned loose to follow the village. As soon as the baby could sit up, it was tied on a saddle. By the time they reached the age of four, Crow children could ride alone and guide a horse. Raised in the saddle, they were matchless riders and their physical hardihood was amazing. This winter Clyman observed dozens of them running buffalo on horseback for hours at a time, naked above the waist. Many took a bath every morning, even when "the hoar frost was flying thick in the air and it was necessary to cut holes in the ice to get at the water." He adds, "the whole employment of the males being hunting and war . . . at the time we ware there at least one third of the warriors ware out in war parties in different directions they being in a state of warfare with all the neighbouring tribes."

"Crow beaver" was already favorably known to the market, much superior to "ordinary Missouri beaver." Besides having the natural advantages common to mountain beaver, the fur much longer and thicker, Crow beaver was scraped and rubbed to make it pliable and fit for transportation.[19] This reflected the superior industry of the Crow women, which was notable in many other respects. No one outdid them in the domestic arts. Their lodges were the largest, the best constructed and the most handsomely ornamented the mountain men saw anywhere, and the shirts, leggings and robes they produced found a ready market in all the surrounding tribes. Another positive merit in the eyes of the whites, the Crow women were extremely fond of white men. As the tribal rites which required the participation of a single woman of proved chastity were in constant danger of being abandoned, this must have been a big winter for Jedediah's men. Tough, courageous, active, sensual and ribald, the Crows were the best of mentors for men adapting themselves to mountain life.[20]

The cold weeks of the winter encampment on Wind River were one of the great epochs in Edward Rose's life, for he alone among the whites could understand the Crow tongue, and from his exploit of the five scalps the Crows were disposed to regard him as the greatest man alive. It was not merely that he alone could serve as interpreter; the Crows would do nothing without him. He was consulted on all occasions; his word was law, and none knew better how to give it an elevated tone, meanwhile handing out Jedediah's goods with a lavish hand. By the time the winter camp broke up, Jedediah was well satisfied to leave Rose among a people who held him in such high esteem.[21]

What Jedediah wanted from the Crows more than their beaver was information about the country west. The idea was difficult to get over, perhaps because the Crows could scarcely conceive that a man should look for anything beyond the limits of their own land. The Crow country, they said, was a good country. The Great Spirit had put it exactly in the right place; while you were in it, you fared well; whenever you left it, whichever way you traveled, you fared worse. To the south were great, barren plains, the water warm and bad. To the north the winters were long and bitter, without grass—you could not keep horses there and must travel with dogs; what was a country without horses? On the Columbia the people were poor and dirty, paddled about in canoes and ate fish; they were forever taking fishbones out of their mouths. On the Missouri the people lived well in their villages, but they had to drink the muddy river water, such water as a Crow's dog would not drink. Everything good was to be found in the Crow country, all kinds of climates and good things for every season. There was no country like the Crow country.[22]

Still, the Crows added, just across the Wind River Mountains was a country with streams so rich in beaver a man did not require traps to take them. He had only to walk along the banks with a club.[23]

That was the sort of country Jedediah was anxious to see, and sometime in February 1824 he started his little company up Wind River to learn whether he could cross the mountains by Union Pass, the way the Astorians had gone in September 1811. From the summit of Union Pass it was possible to see, far to the west, three immensely high, snow-covered peaks, veritable breasts of the world, which indeed the French-Canadians called the Tetons. Those peaks were encircled by the great South Branch of the Columbia and were a momentous landmark. But Jedediah's party had to turn back; they could not force a passage through the snow. Down to the winter camp and another round of conferences with the Crows. "I spread out a buffalo Robe," Clyman says, "and covered it with sand, and made it in heaps to represent the different mountains . . . from our sand map with the help of the Crows, [we] finally got the idea that we could go to Green River, called by them Seeds-ka-day." [24]

The recommended route was south up the Popo Agie to the southern extremity of the Wind River Mountains, then west to a wide gap. The gap was South Pass, and that its existence should not have been known to Jedediah Smith or any of his party is strange, for the returning Astorians had come through it in October 1812.[25] In American exploration, discoveries have had to be made and remade, and it was Jedediah's destiny to walk unknowing in the footsteps of many great wilderness adventurers, French, Spanish, British and American.

It was late February when Jedediah set out again, up the southern branch of the Wind. This had been a hard winter, with heavy snow and galelike winds, and travel was difficult and dangerous. Jim Clyman and Bill Sublette nearly froze to death while hunting, and things did not improve when the party crossed the ridge at the head of the Popo Agie and came down to the Sweetwater. The furious winds had swept the south slopes clear of snow, but they had also scoured the buffalo out of the country. The evening Jedediah reached the Sweetwater the wind blew with such violence that the men had to stay awake the whole night hanging onto their blankets and robes. Next morning they gathered a pile of dry pine logs and sought to build a fire. Impossible; the wind blew the fire away.

They cleared off the snow in the lee of a clump of willows and huddled in their blankets. The wind raged all that day and the next night without the slightest letup. The second morning Clyman and Branch wrapped themselves in their buffalo robes and moved down the stream a way. Not far below camp the river entered a narrow canyon afterward famous as the Three Crossings on the Oregon Trail, and here, under the rocks, the two men found shelter from the wind. Branch saw a mountain sheep on the cliffs overhead and fired. The animal obligingly tumbled down at their feet. "we soon prepared him," Clyman remarks, "and packed him to camp whare efforts were made to broil small pieces but soon gave it up the wind still keeping such a continual blast as to prevent even a starving mounteneer from satisfying his hunger." They took to their blankets again, the only way to keep from freezing. Late in the night, finally, the wind lulled. Clyman rose shivering from his blankets, made a fire and began to broil thin slices of meat. The savory odor aroused his companions, and the rest of the night they cooked, ate and told one another lies.

That was their arrival on the Sweetwater, a foretaste of what Jedediah must expect of this violent land. He had to wait for the weather to break, and fortunately Clyman found a sheltered valley below the canyon with an abundance of dry aspen and plenty of mountain sheep. Next day they moved down to Clyman's aspen grove, struck en route by a cloudburst of snow, a downfall sufficient to have buried them alive had it long continued. They were ready after two such experiences to cultivate patience, and they remained in the camp on the Sweetwater until the mountain sheep were well thinned out.

It was about the second week of March 1824 when scarcity of game and the compulsion of the spring hunt started them up the Sweetwater again.[26] Jedediah cached powder, lead and other supplies, and instructed his men to rendezvous at this point if circumstances should separate them. At all events, the party was to reassemble here or at some navigable point on the stream below by the first of June.

If spring had touched any part of this country, it was still a stranger to the chill valley of the Sweetwater. Jedediah climbed into a high land of rolling plains and rounded hills, choked with snow in the hollows, bare where the wind had a fair sweep. Winds just short of gale force ripped continually out of the north and west, driving powder snow in furious ground blizzards, mantling men and animals with white that turned to ice. In lulls the sky was blue overhead, the sun brilliant, but both dissolved into fiery mist under the assault of the wind.

On the sixth morning of this hard journey Sublette and Clyman brought down a buffalo just as Jedediah came up with the company. The men shouted their delight, for some had eaten nothing for four days. To cook the meat appeared a needless refinement, and the smoking red flesh was wolfed down as fast as it could be cut from the carcass. Afterward they traveled till sundown in the hope of finding water, but settled for a sagebrush fire. This had been a cold, miserable day, with no water save melted snow, but it had brought them a buffalo. As an incident of the day's march, the party had crossed South Pass, the first known westward passage by Americans.[27]

In retrospect this crossing of South Pass is a high moment in American history. Others had traversed South Pass before him, but Jedediah Smith's was the effective discovery, the linking of the pass in the lines of force along which the American people were sweeping to the Pacific. The North Pass of Lewis and Clark had been more barrier than portal. Andrew Henry in 1810 had crossed the continental divide at the head of the Madison, and briefly the maps showed a "Southern Pass" where he had gone, but once South Pass itself was known, both were forgotten. To this wide depression along the continent's spine, missionaries followed the mountain men, settlers and gold seekers coming in their turn, thousands on thousands pursuing the vision or driven by the need. Much was to come of Jedediah Smith's discovery of a way west, but he crossed the divide shaking with cold, anxious about the condition of his horses, hopeful the streams would yield him beaver, knowing or soon to know that many men had come before him into the valley of the Green. Sublette's buffalo made the day memorable, and perhaps this homely reality places history in truest perspective.

It was not until the following day that Jedediah could be sure, from the gentle inclination of the land, the way the gullies ran, that he had indeed crossed the fundamental divide. No man was unmoved, ever, in passing from Atlantic to Pacific waters; but Jedediah and his men wanted warmth in their bones, running water, buffalo and beaver. Continuing west, inclining a little to the north, they struck upon the Big Sandy. Some of the men, Clyman says, "went immediately to cutting the ice with their Tomahauks called out frose to the bottom. . . . they had got down the length of thier arms and was about to give it up I pulled out one of my pistols and fired in to the hole up came the water plentifull for man & horse." There were also willows for a fire, over which they roasted the remains of their buffalo. Next day the party moved on down the Sandy. At nightfall they killed another buffalo.

March 19 brought them to the Green itself, the Seeds-kee-dee Agie of which the Crows had told them, Prairie Chicken River. Spanish traders before this time had reached the river far to the south and called it the Verde for the thin ribbon of green its banks flaunted through a waste of rock,[28] and this name won out finally, the more appropriate because in the river's upper course where Jedediah first reached it, the water itself takes on a greenish tinge from the shales which compose its bed. But for Jedediah the Green ever afterward was the Seedskeeder or Siskadee. That Jedediah was not the first to reach this river in its upper valley we have remarked already. John Colter may have traversed its remote headwaters as early as 1807 on the great circuit he made into the wilderness south and west from Manuel Lisa's post on the Big Horn.[29] Andrew Henry's men almost certainly saw something of the upper valley in the spring of 1811, and the Astorians crossed and recrossed it that year and the next. Donald Mackenzie trapped the valley from the west at the head of a brigade of Nor'Westers in 1820-1821, and another British brigade made a rich haul on the Green as late as the summer of 1823. The Green River Valley was as fine a beaver country as the mountain men ever found in the West, and if beaver did not now exist in such numbers as to justify the tall talk of the Crows, there was plenty of sign to gladden Jedediah's eye.

The little company reached the Green probably near the mouth of the Big Sandy. Small as the party was, numbering only eleven men, Jedediah divided it for the spring hunt. Six of the men he took to trap farther south; the other three he left under Fitzpatrick[30] to trap the head branches of the river. Clyman went with Fitzpatrick, so that we have no firsthand account of Jedediah's adventures, but it is a substantial certainty that he followed the Green down as far as Blacks Fork, and made his spring hunt on that stream and its tributaries. The name of Blacks Fork may date from this year; and it is significant that one of the head branches of Blacks Fork has always been known as Smiths Fork.

Fitzpatrick's party remained in camp on the Green till the ice gave way, then left to trap the upstream tributaries. They found beaver in abundance, and a family of Indians who called themselves Shoshoni or Snakes. These were glad to feast on the overplus of beaver the trappers gave them, but one morning after the snow had disappeared the Snakes disappeared too, and with them all the horses. The whites could not even determine in what direction they had gone. The name of the stream has ever since preserved the memory—Horse Creek.[31]

Making the best of his misfortune, Fitzpatrick continued trapping on foot with fair success. When time for rendezvous drew near, he cached his traps and furs, hung his saddles and other equipment on trees, and set out for the Sweetwater. To his great satisfaction, about noon the first day, on turning the point of a ridge, he met face to face five or six Indians mounted on his horses. He and his men sprang to seize the lariats, then ordered these good friends to dismount, half minded to make an example of them on the spot. The Snakes led the whites to their camp, a mile up a steep mountainside, where they found six lodges housing eighteen men, a plentiful supply of squaws and children, and what Clyman describes as "our old acquaintences that we had fed with the fat of Beaver while the earth was thickly covered with snow." All the horses were given up but one. Fitzpatrick was bound to have that one too. He seized one of the Snakes, tied him fast and informed the rest that the man would be killed if the horse were not given back. When the animal was forthcoming, Fitzpatrick gave the Snakes a few presents and departed for his caches. After digging up his furs and traps and cutting down his saddles, he set out anew for the Sweetwater, traveling night and day until he was out of reach of the Snakes.

At the rendezvous, where they arrived about the middle of June, there was no sign of the booshway. Fitzpatrick decided while waiting to reconnoiter the Sweetwater and establish whether the stream was navigable. He had no idea how this stream fitted into western geography, whether it was a branch of the Platte or of the Arkansas, but if there was any chance of getting their furs down by water, he wanted to know it. With Clyman he rode some fifteen miles downstream, finding the river broad and shallow in all that distance. Instructing Clyman to go on and halt at the first likely point, Fitzpatrick turned back with the horses to fetch the rest of the party.

Preliminary to moving, he opened the cache made in March. The powder was damp, so he spread it out to dry and was on the point of packing up when Jedediah made his belated appearance, laden with the proceeds of a fine spring hunt. The snow meanwhile had been melting in the mountains, swelling the size of the Sweetwater so much that it seemed likely the river could be made to serve their purpose after all. Jedediah decided to build a bullboat of buffalo hides and in this unwieldy craft try to get their furs down to Ashley, a job he delegated to Fitzpatrick, Stone and Branch.[32] The other seven men and all of the horses he would retain for a fall hunt farther west than any of them had yet gone.

While Fitzpatrick set to work on the framework of the boat, Jedediah rode down the Sweetwater to pick up Clyman. He followed the stream all the way to its junction with a large river that flowed from the south, a river he could guess to be the North Platte. There was no sign of Clyman, but in a thick clump of willows Jedediah found evidence that his man had come this far down—a shelter built, driftwood gathered for a fire. There was also Indian sign about, which Jedediah's eye was now experienced enough to appraise. A war party had been through here, a score or more, with half again as many horses. It did not require a vivid imagination to picture what had become of Clyman. Dispirited, Jedediah turned back up the Sweetwater to rejoin his company. It would be a year before he learned that Clyman, by the thinnest of margins, was still alive.

5. *THE ADVENTURES OF HUGH GLASS–AND OTHERS*

While Jedediah Smith was finding his way to South Pass and beyond, Andrew Henry was struggling to keep Ashley and Henry afloat on an ocean of troubles. The experiences of the Major and his men en route to the Yellowstone are one of the most striking chapters in the history of the West, and their subsequent adventures on the Yellowstone had an important bearing on Jedediah's future. The story revolves about the misadventures of just one of the Major's men.

Hugh Glass had come up the river with Ashley in the spring of 1823, had participated in the first battle with the Rees and had been wounded in the leg. In the literature he is called "old Glass," which would ordinarily mean that his companions had grown fond of him or got used to his eccentricities; but there is some indication that he was literally an old man in 1823. Little enough is known about him otherwise. George Yount, who knew Glass in the mountains a few years later, gives a fabulous account of the hero's earlier life, including his experiences as a sailor, his capture by pirates, his extraordinary escape and his still more extraordinary wanderings among the Indians. That the account is fabulous does not mean that it is not also veracious, but none of it can be proved. It is enough that he was a member of the party with which Andrew Henry set out from Fort Kiowa in September 1823.[1]

Henry's horses were too few and too heavily laden, and with the Rees dispersed no one knew where, the journey would be hazardous. Mindful of the danger, Henry ascended the Missouri no higher than the Grand, then, as Jedediah Smith had done in June, veered off to the west. On a day in September as the com-

Courtesy, Library of Congress.

SOUTH DAKOTA BADLANDS

Photo by Arthur Rothstein, Farm Security Administration.

THE FROZEN MISSOURI AT THE MANDANS, FEBRUARY, 1834.

Charles Bodmer, 1834. From Maximilian, Tab. 15.

Courtesy, Bureau of American Ethnology.

SHOSHONI:

Washakie's Lodge in the Wind River Mountains. Photo by W. H. Jackson, 1870.

pany was moving up the Grand, Henry directed two men to precede the rest as hunters. Glass was not detailed to the duty but went ahead anyway. He was a good man to have at hand in a pinch, but self-willed and insubordinate. Short of shooting him, it was difficult to get any obedience from him—and in this Glass was only too typical of the mountain men.

He was a short distance in advance of the party when he stumbled on one of the "white bears" the Ashley men were learning about this year—a she grizzly of tremendous size who sprang upon him with the incredible speed and ferocity of her kind. At Glass's screams Henry's men came thrashing through the brush to his assistance, and though the grizzly chased two of them into the river, a volley brought her down.

Glass lay on the earth in a welter of his own brightly flowing blood. Arms, legs and body, all had been torn open, and the wound in his neck was such that it could hardly be understood how he breathed. That a man could survive such wounds seemed impossible, and for minutes that stretched out to the rest of the day, Henry waited for him to die. At nightfall Glass's tortured breathing continued, and Henry faced the fact that the dying might take a long time. If he halted the entire party to await the event, the Rees might discover their presence, in which case the bones of a good many others would bleach here too. Beyond that, he had his duty to Ashley, the Company, and all his men in the mountains; he must get to Fort Henry as soon as possible. Henry asked for volunteers to remain with Glass until he died or could travel. The reward he offered was substantial—half a year's wage at the going rate—and two men spoke up. The elder was John S. Fitzgerald. The younger was a stripling named Jim Bridger.[2]

Next morning early, Henry took the trail. He ran into trouble on the way; one night his camp was fired on by a war party, two men and two horses being killed; he fired back, and in the morning found a dead Mandan in the brush—a find unpleasant in its implications, for no Indians on the Missouri had been so consistently friendly to the whites.[3] However, Henry reached his fort without further mishap. A few days later Fitzgerald and Bridger came in to report that Hugh Glass was dead. They had waited five days until the end came and then had buried him decently. Glass's rifle, knife and other fixins they brought with them as evidence of his death.

Glass was far from dead. In no man has the will to live ever burned more fiercely. He awakened one morning to find himself abandoned. How this could have happened has always passed understanding, for men in the West have not taken lightly their obligation to one another in extremity. Perhaps Glass fell into a coma hardly distinguishable from death. Perhaps the fears of Fitzgerald and Bridger worked on them with mounting intensity through the days and nights of their vigil, and at last they fled from themselves. Perhaps the decision was made in cold blood, an objective weighing of Glass's chances. All that can be said is that Bridger in after years had a blameless reputation among the mountain men, and if in his youth he made a mistake, it was not held against him.

Glass awoke to find himself helpless and alone. His life hung by a few small threads: a spring was close enough for him to inch his way to it; above the spring branches of wild cherry hung down, heavy with ripe fruit; and in the thicket round about tart buffalo berries grew in profusion. No less important, when Glass lifted his head from the ground he found his wallet under it. The contents were worthless with one exception: in the wallet was his razor, which could serve him as both knife and fire steel. Yet how desolating the realization! There was no help nearer than Kiowa, distant half the length and width of South Dakota, and he scarcely able to crawl.

For ten days Glass remained beside the spring. To stay longer was to accept the sentence of death Fitzgerald and Bridger had passed on him, and Glass began the long journey. He had scarcely strength to drag one leg after another, no weapon but his razor, but he had fortitude. And luck. Perhaps more than anything else, it is the luck of Hugh Glass that has made him immortal. He had not gone far when he came on a buffalo calf brought to bay by wolves. He stood by until the wolves had hamstrung their prey, then advanced to drive them from the carcass. The wolves showed him their teeth, and he retreated, baffled.

Then he remembered his razor, and with the aid of a flint and a few dry leaves set fire to the grass.

The flames leaped up, putting the wolves to flight, and nearly the whole of the calf fell into Glass's hands. Here was meat to put strength back on his bones, and he remained by the carcass for days, gorging on the buffalo flesh, until his wounds had healed a little. These wounds had been a fearful presence, for they bled at the slightest exertion; some of them filled with insects, and those on his back he could not dress at all. Not many of the details of Glass's journey back to civilization are recoverable; for the man himself the days must have had a nightmare quality. At first a mile a day exhausted him, then he could manage two miles, five, ten, living the while on berries, rose haws, roots, decaying buffalo carcasses, anything that came to hand. Perhaps in this way he covered the whole terrible distance to Kiowa, but two of the contemporary accounts of his adventures say that he fell in with a band of Sioux who had come up the Missouri to do some final gleaning in the Ree cornfields, and that they took him down the river with them. However it happened, he reached Kiowa, a man who had stretched his luck to the limit.[4]

Experiences to last any other man a lifetime Glass had crammed into six weeks, but his epic was not even well begun. At the time he reached Fort Kiowa, Joseph Brazeau was outfitting a party to ascend the river, the first to risk the passage of the Missouri since the dispersion of the Rees. "Cayewa" was an old trader among the Arikaras, and if in the present dangerous state of affairs any man could establish the trade of the French Company above the Sioux, it was he. Brazeau could not go himself, but he counted on the power of his name to get the boat through to the Mandans. He had five men to make up the party, which he placed in charge of Antoine Citoleux, *dit* Langevin; as a sixth he threw in Toussaint Charbonneau, whose services as interpreter were of small use this far down the Missouri but would be of considerable value above.[5] Glass made a seventh.

The pirogue set out from Fort Kiowa about October 10, 1823. Langevin did not share Brazeau's optimism over this venture, and on October 15, at Simoneau's Island thirty miles below the mouth of the Teton, made his will—a circumstance that gives us the one firm date in Glass's life through the whole of this extraordinary autumn. What moved Glass to join this hazardous upriver voyage we are left to conjecture. (It is possible that he did not get all the way down to Fort Kiowa, and meeting Langevin's party on the river was glad to accept their invitation to come along, no matter where they were going.) Perhaps, quite simply, Glass wanted to rejoin his companions and seized the first chance that offered. More dramatically, it may be that he was resolved to have an accounting with the men who had left him to die.

The voyage up the Missouri required about six weeks. Notwithstanding the misgivings of Langevin and the fears of Charbonneau, the ascent of the river was just the routine hard work of any voyage. The fire-blackened Ree towns were found deserted, no sign of an enemy about. Charbonneau was not reassured; the Rees had found refuge among the Mandans and would massacre them on sight. By a strange fatality, at some point on the river below the Mandans, Glass passed unknowing three men who had left Henry on the Yellowstone to make their way back to Fort Atkinson: one of the three was Fitzgerald, who had Glass's rifle with him in the boat.

On the day before Langevin's party expected to reach the Mandans, Charbonneau's medicine told him it was time to quit the little company. The others could, if they wished, finish the journey by water, but he would go by land and with proper circumspection.[6] His companions jeered but let him go.

When the pirogue was within ten miles of the Mandan towns, Glass was put ashore to hunt. The boat had to buck the current around a wide bend, and he expected to be waiting for it with fresh game when it reached the far end. Glass had gone only a few miles when he stumbled on the answer to what had become of the Rees: a party of warriors gave chase to him. Glass was by no means recovered from his wounds even yet, and the race would have ended early except that it amused fate to take a hand. A mounted Mandan who chanced on the unequal race swung the white man up on his horse and bore him off in safety to Tilton's Fort, the Columbia Fur Company post. Charbonneau was at the fort already or arrived soon after, but Langevin and the rest were never seen again. The Rees fell on the pirogue, killed all her crew and carried off as spoils the goods that were to have opened the trade with the Mandans. As an added touch, shortly after, the Rees killed one of Tilton's men, forcing him to abandon his post and move in with the Mandans for safety.

Undaunted by this narrow escape, Glass set out afoot for the Yellowstone, only taking the precaution to ascend the Missouri's left bank. It took him two weeks to reach the mouth of the Yellowstone, and he met with neither white man nor red. On a raft made of two logs tied together with bark, he crossed over to Fort Henry, to find the post abandoned.

Henry had evacuated the fort soon after his arrival from Kiowa. During his absence some ill-disposed Indians had made off with nearly two dozen horses, and they came back to pick off seven more shortly after he reached the fort. Realistically there was no reason for maintaining Fort Henry now that operations on the upper Missouri had been given up. If he was to confine his trapping to Yellowstone waters, it was better to move his base higher up the river, where he would have a degree of protection from the Crows and could back up his field parties more effectively. Caching some of his goods, Henry embarked the rest and set out up the Yellowstone. He was able to ascend as high as the Powder before rapids put an end to boat travel so late in the season, and fortunately near the Powder he fell in with a band of Crows. Obtaining forty-seven horses from them, he outfitted a party for the Big Horn—the same with which Jedediah wintered. The rest of his men the Major kept with him temporarily to build his new fort at the mouth of the Big Horn,[7] but some he later sent off to trap the tributaries of the Yellowstone. Presumably before abandoning Fort Henry the Major posted on the gate information as to where he was going, for Glass hardly paused in his journey. He continued up the Yellowstone, and near the end of December 1823 reached the new post.

The turn of the year was always a festive time in the fur trade, and Henry's men had just begun to get a good glow on when the gate of the fort was pushed open and Glass entered. Features sunken, arms and hands wasted, all skeleton and skin,

Glass's aspect was that of a man who had just left his grave. A feeling akin to terror ran through the onlookers till Glass spoke to them. They came forward and touched him, then threw their arms around him and tilted the keg again to give the moment true solemnity.

The walking of ghosts unnerved young Jim Bridger even more than his companions. It did not help matters when the apparition proved to be a living man; he could scarcely be induced to enter Glass's presence. One of the early chroniclers, who insists that a passion for revenge sustained Glass through all these adventures, gives the scene a fitting climax. With dignity and severity, he says, but with great feeling Glass addressed the stricken youth: "Young man, it is Glass that is before you; the same that, not content with leaving, you thought, to a cruel death upon the prairie, you robbed, helpless as he was, of his rifle, his knife, of all, with which he could hope to defend or save himself. . . . I swore an oath that I would be revenged on you, and the wretch who was with you, and I ever thought to have kept it. For this meeting I have braved the dangers of a long journey. . . . But I cannot take your life; . . . you have nothing to fear from me; go,—you are free;—for your youth I forgive you." [8]

Far down the Missouri, meanwhile, Colonel Leavenworth was keeping an anxious ear open for information on the state of things above. On December 13 he sent General Henry Atkinson in St. Louis a report from several of Pilcher's men, to the effect that six or seven of Henry's party had been attacked near the Mandans and three killed.[9] A week later Fitzgerald with his two companions reached Fort Atkinson, enabling Leavenworth to relay to Army headquarters the first reliable news from the upper river since August. The Colonel's letter is illuminating enough to be printed in full; it suggests faintly the violence of the controversies which by now had boiled up around the Arikara campaign.

Fort Atkinson Decr. 20th. 1823

Dear Sir,

On the 18th Inst. three men arrived here from Major Henry's party of Trappers and hunters.

I loose no time in sending you a statement of the Information which they bring.

About the 20th. of August [September?] last Maj^r Henry's party, while on their way to the mouth of the Yellow Stone river, were fired upon by a War party of Indians Two men were Killed, and Two Wounded—He also at the Same time lost two horses—This took place at considerable distance from the river.

When Majr. Henry arrived at his Establishment at the mouth of the Yellow Stone river, he found that 22 or 23 of his horses had been Stolen—and as was Supposed by the Blackfoot or Assinnaboin Indians —A short time after his arrival he lost 7 more horses. He embarked his goods on board his boat, abandoned his Establishment, and ascended the Yellow Stone river, to the mouth of Powder river. He was then prevented from going further with his Boat, by the rapids of the river. He there met the Crow Indians from whom he obtained 47 horses. With these he started a trapping party, in a south Western direction towards the Mountains. He intended to start one other party, in a short time afterwards.

My informant whose name is Harris and who appears to be a Correct & intelligent young man, and two other men, One also named Harris,[10] and the other Fitzgerald left Major Henry's party at Powder River and Came down in a canoe. Mr. Harris gives a Verry unfavourable account of the Situation & prospects of the Trapping and hunting parties at the mountains. He says that the Indians frequently visited the Establishment of Major Henry at the mouth of Yellow Stone, & behaved very well. They also frequently met with the men while out hunting, and did not molest them. But they would steal their horses whenever they could get an opportunity to do so. They received information from the Crow Indians, that the Blackfoot Indians were determined to hunt Continually for the trapping parties and destroy them, whenever it was possible to do so. This was also the expectation of the whole party. Mr. Harris says that Major Henrys party have not made over 25 packs of Furs since they have been in the Country, & that about two packs of those were purchased. Mr. Harris says that on their Way down they stopped at the Grosvont [Minnetaree] Village & were treated in a very friendly manner. He also stopped at the Mandan Village & went to the trading house of Mr Tilton—He there learned that it was a War party of the Mandans who had fired upon Major Henry's party. One of the party had told of it, but the Chiefs afterwards made him deny it. But Mr. Harris saw one of the Indians who was wounded at the time, and he also saw, and knew one of the horses which the Indians took from the party.

At Mr. Tilton's he saw four Aricara Chiefs—He understood from them, and from Mr. Tilton, that they professed to be anxious to preserve peace with the whites, and to have traders come amongst them.

But it was thought by him, that the Chiefs would not be able to controul their young men, in consequence of their Towns having been burned by McDonald & Gordon. They however behaved very well towards Mr. Tilton, and all the people about his Establishment.

The Aricaras had purchased a dirt Village of the Mandans and were living in it, about one mile below the Mandan Towns.

Mr. Harris was informed that the Aricaras had sent two War parties to the scite of their old Villages to fight the Sioux & to obtain some corn if possible. These he was advised to avoid. He accordingly started from Mr. Tilton's at about 10 O,clock at night—near day light supposing that they had passed those parties, they landed for the purpose of remaining through the day, but found that they were Very near one of those War parties—They accordingly Re-Embarked, and as they were in a narrow Channel of the river, and the Indians below them, they proceeded up the river to the head of that Channel—the Indians then discovered them, and fired at them but, did no injury.

They made for the opposite shore, and some of the Indians pursued them. They left their Canoe, & went into the bottom about a Mile, and hid themselves all that day. They saw no more of the Indians On their way down they saw a band of Siones (Sioux) opposite to the Scite of the old Aricara towns, & was verry Kindly treated by them. The Indians were well supplied with corn which they had obtained from the Aricaras Towns. They also saw the Tangtons (Sioux) who were also very friendly.

The Trader which Mr. Brazeaux had sent up to the Aricaras, had not arrived when they passed. It was from information said to have been derived from Mr. Harris & his Companions that four of the Missouri fur Company reported, that Mr. Brazeaux's trader had been robbed. Mr. Harris says that they never told any thing of the Kind.

The names of the men of Major Henry's party who were Killed, by the War party of the Mandans were James Anderson, an American, & August Néll a Frenchman. Mr. Harris says that this war party at the time they attacked Major Henry were ignorant of the result of our late expedition against the Aricaras, & that their Chiefs are much concerned about it. This letter I have carefully read over to Mr. Harris, and he says that it is correct. This has been done because I am aware that a different representation has been made upon the same information.

I have the honor to be
With great respect
Your Obt Servant
H. Leavenworth

N. B. Mr. Harris says that Major Henry's party planted some corn at the mouth of the yellow Stone, but the ground was so dry that it did not even swell or rot—There had not been sufficient rain the year past "to wet a man through his shirt sleeves."

Major Genl. A. McComb

The foregoing, (above my signature) is a copy of a letter written by me to Genl. Atkinson—You will therefore perceive that it may perhaps be improper to let it be published. I send it to you that the information may be at Washington sooner than it would go through the official channel—I am more anxious because I know that some individuals in this quarter are using every possible means to deceive the Government & the nation

H. L.[11]

It was the beginning of March before word came down the river that the rumor had been well founded after all, that the five men of the French Company and one of Tilton's were lost. Brazeau had vainly hoped all winter that his traders were safe at the Mandans, and even when word came along by the Indian news service that they were dead, he clung to the hope that they had been killed by the Yankton Sioux rather than by his old friends, the Arikaras. The suspicion flared that the Columbia Fur Company, two of whose partners until lately had owed allegiance to the British crown, was behind these troubles, and that company was soon making annoyed protestations of its loyalty and good conduct.[12] But no more news of what was going on in the high country, no word at all until late in the spring.

That lack was not the fault of Henry. Or of Hugh Glass. For late in February the Major undertook to send an express down to the Bluffs and, mindful that he had some unfinished business with Fitzgerald, Glass volunteered for the mission. He set out from Henry's Fort on the Big Horn February 28, 1824, with four companions—E. More, A. Chapman, one Dutton, and one Marsh.[13] At this season the great rivers were icebound, and to descend by land would have been foolhardy in the extreme. It was decided that the express should try a new route, going up the Powder to its sources, across to the Platte, then down it to the Bluffs, keeping well west and south of the Rees.

Why Henry should have found it necessary to send an express to Ashley at the cost of five men lost to his trapping force it would be interesting to know. Perhaps it was essential that Ashley be advised of Henry's prospects. Perhaps Henry had decided to quit the business and was giving Ashley notice. (A great deal about the affairs of the partnership at this stage is obscure: why, for instance, Ashley was sending no boat to the mountains this spring—not even as high as Fort Kiowa.) Some of the rest of what the letter contained can be guessed. Henry would have reported the news which had in some way reached him, by courier or by the return of Weber's party, that "Captain Smith, with some of the party, had crossed the Mountains." [14] He would have added that the Missouri Fur Company had got a party to Wind River to compete for the Crow trade. Finally he would have had something to say about the removal of his fort from the mouth of the Yellowstone to the Big Horn and about the steady wasting of his party. On the whole, a bleak letter.

Glass and his companions were well paid for the mission, and left the Big Horn in high spirits. This was a cold season for travel, as Jedediah Smith was learning on the Sweetwater, but the five trappers had no trouble on the first stage of their journey. The wide, shallow Platte was still icebound when they reached it, but soon after the ice broke up. Men in the mountains never wore out shoe leather if a river could be made to carry them, so Glass and the others set about making a bullboat. In most seasons even the shallow draft of these skin boats was too great for the Platte, but with the spring rise coming on, the five trappers pushed out hopefully on the swirling muddy waters.

The bullboat bore them down the swift upper course of the Platte as far as the junction with the Laramie.[15] On the river bank here stood thirty-eight Indian lodges, which the trappers supposed could only be Pawnee. They paddled to shore and were received with great cordiality, invited to a feast. All except Dutton left their rifles in the bullboat and proceeded to the lodge of the chief.

They had fallen into the hands of the Rees. When most of the tribe went up the river, a small band came west to visit their cousins, the Pawnee Loups. This was the band of Grey Eyes himself, led by Langue de Biche, Elk's Tongue, the first soldier of the tribe after Grey Eyes, whom Leavenworth mistakenly supposed to have been repudiated. Glass and his companions did not for some time dream of their peril, but while they were eating, a few words were dropped which led Glass to suspect the truth. Horrified, he said to one of his comrades, "These are Ricarees!" The chief, understanding him, replied, "No, Pawnees we." The whites had been foolhardy but they were not fools. They burst out of the lodge and ran for their boat.

Their rifles were gone, of course. They piled into the bullboat and made for the far shore. This was a sport the Rees enjoyed, and like so many hunting dogs plunged into the river in pursuit. As soon as Glass and his companions reached the opposite side, they scattered, hoping some would get away. Dutton was lucky; he still had his rifle and was not pursued. Marsh was even luckier; unarmed as he was, he outdistanced his pursuers and later managed to find Dutton, after which the two men made their long way down the Platte, arriving at Fort Atkinson sometime in May to report their three companions dead.[16] Luckless were Chapman and More. Language hardly suffices to describe the special case of Hugh Glass, who for the fourth time in ten months found his life thrown into the balance. Unperceived, he gained a point of rocks from which he saw Chapman and More overtaken and slain, one within a few yards of where he lay. When night came on and the Rees gave up their search for him, Glass began to hope again. He would have to follow down the Platte, how many hundreds of miles he had no way of knowing, to reach civilization. Yet how much better off was he now than he had been in September! "Although," as he said afterward, "I had lost my rifle and all my plunder, I felt quite rich when I found my knife, flint and steel, in my shot pouch. These little fixens make a man feel right *peart*, when he is three or four hundred miles from any body or any place—all alone among the painters and wild varments."[17]

A fortunate circumstance was that at this season the buffalo calves were only a few days old. As the country through which he must travel was an almost continuous buffalo pasture, it was at first no great task to overtake a calf as often as his belly nagged him. The journey grew harder as it lengthened, so that he turned to the bark of trees and roots, anything resembling food. But luck abided with him still; half starved and nearly exhausted, he fell in with a Sioux hunting party who took him to Fort Kiowa. He arrived there early in June 1824, and after resting a few days, went down the river to Council Bluffs. There he had a glad reunion with Dutton and Marsh. And settled accounts with Fitzgerald.

The faithless Fitzgerald, who had stayed on at the fort, in April had enlisted as a private in the Sixth Infantry. It was not the custom of the colonel of that regiment to permit his privates to be shot up by civilians, and Glass was taken aback to find his man in uniform. Leavenworth ordered his rifle restored and furnished him with such fixens as put him in shape to take the field again—but let George Yount give this story its final flourish. At Fort Atkinson, Yount says:

Glass found the recreant individual, who had so cruelly deserted him, when he lay helpless & torn so shockingly by the Grizzly Bear —He also there recovered his favorite Rifle—To the man he only addressed himself as he did to the boy—"Go false man & answer to your own conscience & to your God;—I have suffered enough in all reason by your perfidy—You was well paid to have remained with me until I should be able to walk—You promised to do so—or to wait my death & decently bury my remains—I heard the bargain—Your shameful perfidy & heartless cruelty——but enough—Again I say, settle the matter with your own conscience & your God."

Much there is in Hugh Glass's story of courage, perseverance and the indomitable will to live, but above all it is brimming over with luck. Perhaps for that reason especially the West took Hugh Glass to its heart and has never allowed him to die; the West has always valued luck. But a man can press his luck too far, and Glass may have considered that it was time to leave the Missouri. Soon after arriving at Fort Atkinson, he joined a company bound for Santa Fe, and it was four years before his trail again crossed that of Jedediah Smith.

This spring, and on through the summer, the Platte saw a veritable parade of men set adrift on the incalculable unknown. Dutton and Marsh reached Fort Atkinson first, the indestructible Glass soon after. The summer wore on, and here came Jim Clyman ragged and starving, as much dead as alive. Clyman had scarcely reached the fort when in walked Fitzpatrick, Branch and Stone in more wretched condition still. Clyman and Fitzpatrick had stories to set beside the epic of Hugh Glass, and their adventures cast a longer shadow in the history of the West.

Clyman's personal saga was eloquent of the way in which a man in the mountains could have the world fall away under his feet. When he separated from Fitzpatrick in June, he supposed that Fitzpatrick and the men would join him within a day or so. Making his way down the Sweetwater as far as the North Platte, he prepared to await his companions there. After cutting himself a lodging place in a clump of willows, he gathered some driftwood and was on the point of striking fire when he heard the sound of voices.

Along the bank of the stream, here some four rods wide, came a number of mounted Indians. They stopped nearly opposite and soon had four or five fires blazing. In all, Clyman counted twenty-two Indians and thirty horses. This was a party the lank mountain man did not feel like joining, and there were altogether too many Indians at hand. The country for half a mile back was bare and sandy, and the moon nearly full; it would be almost as easy to track him as if the land were covered with snow. Watching his chance, Clyman walked backward across the sandy stretch to a narrow, rocky ridge, then followed the ridge to where the river broke through it. After crossing over to the east bank of the Sweetwater, he climbed a high point of rocks and prepared to keep watch on his disagreeable neighbors from a distance of forty rods.

Some of the war party lay down and slept while the rest

kept up the fire. Toward midnight all arose and collected their horses. Two of the animals, however, crossed the Sweetwater, chased by two of the braves. A shout was raised and eight or ten more joined the chase. There was much riding to and fro while Clyman debated the probability that his trace would be discovered, but finally the war party made off to the north.

Next day Clyman went to have a look at the abbreviated canyon subsequently famous as Devils Gate, through which the Sweetwater plunges "fearfully swift without any perpendicular fall." While up on the high cliffs, he saw about twenty Indians approach the stream where he had been half an hour before, all on foot. They made a small raft of driftwood, piled their war equipment and clothes on it, swam the stream and moved off to the south. This was the day Jedediah Smith came down the river in search of him; Jedediah arrived while Clyman was off examining the Devils Gate, and he narrowly escaped falling in with the second of the two war parties. Clyman returned to his observatory and remained there eleven days, racking his brain for some explanation of Fitzpatrick's long delay, and getting distinctly lonesome.

At length Clyman examined his supply of ammunition. Although he had plenty of powder, there were only eleven balls in his shot pouch. Suppose he were to spend a week looking for his companions and not find them: he would not have balls enough left to take him to civilization. It seemed advisable to head down the river. But what a prospect! He was not sure whether he was on the Platte or the Arkansas, and there was only one way of finding out.

On the afternoon of the twelfth day Clyman left his lookout and headed down the Platte. The days were warm, and he had to keep near the water. At length, as he told the story, "I found a bull boat lying drifted up on a sand bar and the marks of a large Indian ranch on the main shore I knew by the boat some white men had [been] here for the Indians never made such boats this gave me a fient hope of meeting some white men in this Indian world." By the time he told this story at Fort Atkinson, he had another viewpoint on this "fient hope." The bullboat was that from which Hugh Glass and his companions had fled; the Indians were the Rees; near by the bones of Chapman and More were bleaching in the sun. Farther down the river, Clyman saw the Rees running buffalo on the far side of the Platte, but at too great a distance to make them out.

Great herds of buffalo were crossing the river. Clyman shot a buffalo and dried some meat, halting two days in the hope of meeting with some human being; the burden of his solitude had become such that even a friendly Indian would have been a relief. No one appeared, and he resumed the journey. Coming to a grove of large cottonwoods where a number of martins were nesting, he lay down in the shade and for some hours enjoyed the soft twittering of these birds—"it reminded me of home & civilisation." He saw wild horses at a distance, and when next he killed a buffalo, he made a halter of rawhide. A fine black stallion came down to the river to drink, and Clyman fired, hoping to stun the animal by shooting him through the neck just above the spinal column. The stallion plunged up to the main bank, and Clyman ran to capture him, but the horse never moved again; his neck was broken.

The loneliness of his journey had become unbearable, and when Clyman came to a large and recent lodge trail crossing the Platte, he waded across. The Indians were Pawnees. They robbed him of knife, blankets, balls, firesteel and flint, and might have made off with his life except that the whim to save him took one of the Indians.

Clyman now left the trail. The grass was so thick and tall as to be difficult to break through, and he resorted to the ridges. The last few days of the journey were the kind of nightmare Glass had known. Clyman had only a few grains of parched corn the Pawnees had given him, but he stumbled on two badgers fighting and killed them both with bones snatched up from the ground. The mosquitoes tormented him, and it rained incessantly. At last, as Clyman told the story:

I struck a trail that seamed to lead in the right direction which I determined to follow to its extreeam end on the second day in the afternoon I got so sleepy & nervous that it was with difficulity I kept the trail a number of times I tumbled down asleep but a quick nervous gerk would bring me to my feet again in one of these fits I started up on the trail traveled some 40 rods when I hapened to notise I was going back the way I had come turning right around I went on for some time with my head down when raising my eyes with great surprise I saw the stars & stripe waving over Fort [Atkinson] I swoned emmediatly how long I lay unconscious I do not know I was so overpowered with joy The stars & striped came so unexpected that I was completly overcome being on decending ground I set contemplating the scene I made several attempts to raise but as often fell back for the want of strength to stand after some minnites I began to breathe easier but certainly no man ever enjoyed the sight of our flag better than I did I walked on down to the fort there beeing no guard on duty I by axident came to the door of Cap Rileys quarters where a waiter brought out the Cap who conducted me to [Colonel] Leavenworth[18]

Clyman had been at the fort about ten days when to his surprise "Mr Fitspatrick Mr Stone & Mr Brench arived in a more pitible state if possible than myself." Now he learned how Jedediah Smith had searched vainly for him in June, and why his fellow trappers believed his flowing locks to hang in a lodge somewhere. Had Clyman remained at the Sweetwater even a day longer, he might have seen Fitzpatrick come boiling down the river in his bullboat—and become involved in fresh disaster. For when the unsuspecting Fitzpatrick shot down into the swift water at Devils Gate, his boat filled and sank with the whole of its valuable cargo. By great exertions, swimming and diving in the stream, the three men salvaged most of the furs. They dried them thoroughly and cached them at a likely point a few miles below, a great upthrust of red granite which later became one of the most famous of American landmarks, Independence Rock (named, it is thought, because Fitzpatrick cached his furs there on the Fourth of July).[19] Fitzpatrick, Stone and Branch lost two of their guns and all their balls. First and last, they had a rougher time getting in than Clyman.

Fitzpatrick now showed his mettle. Delaying only to write a letter to Ashley announcing his return from the mountains, the first direct word Ashley had had from Jedediah Smith's party, with full information about the discovery of South Pass, their success in trapping beyond the divide, and his own subsequent mishap, Fitzpatrick borrowed horses and set off for the mountains. Bound to bring in the furs which had cost so much trouble, he left Fort Atkinson about the beginning of September.[20]

During the spring and summer Ashley had made an unsuccessful campaign for the governorship of Missouri, running a few votes behind the plodding Frederick Bates. So he would be out of politics for a while. It had begun to seem likely that he would soon be out of the fur trade as well. The first bad news had been of minor note: late in the spring a party of Rees had come down to Fort Recovery and in broad daylight had run off several of the horses Ashley had lost to the Sioux the year before, which since had been rounded up by Pilcher. In June came word of Glass's misadventures. In July Bill Gordon of the Missouri Fur Company had reported in: He and Keemle had been robbed by the Crows after spending the winter with them, and had had to return to Fort Recovery by water. Gordon's party had had a look at the Columbia Fur Company's Mandan post on the way down, and a dismal sight it was, gates and doors cut down, floors torn up, everything topsy-turvy. In the wake of Gordon's arrival Major O'Fallon had written blackly from Fort Atkinson: "Mr. Vandeburg & C°. have returned [that is, Fort Recovery itself had been abandoned]—The surrounding trappers and hunters are descending from the mountains and are going out of the Indian country, leaving the upper Country stained with the inocent blood of the most daring and enterprising portion of our people." [21] Fort Kiowa was now the sole bastion of the fur trade above the Bluffs.

Still later had come word that the Minnetarees had discovered Henry's cache at the mouth of the Yellowstone and robbed it of powder, lead, blankets, clothing, kettles, everything.[22] And finally, riding the crest of this high tide of disaster, Henry himself, who got back to St. Louis the last week of August. The arrival made a brave show in the newspapers; the *St. Louis Enquirer* said on August 30: "After an absence of nearly three years, we are happy to announce the safe return of Maj. Henry, (of the firm of Ashley and Henry,) with a part of his company, from the Rocky Mountains. He descended the Missouri in boats to St. Louis, with a considerable quantity of valuable furs, &c." The *Enquirer* did not say that Henry had made a despairing final effort and launched Weber beyond the mountains; neither did it say that the Major had another six men dead, four killed on the Yellowstone by Minnetarees, two on the Missouri by Sioux; especially the *Enquirer* did not say that there were too few, by far, of the "valuable furs." [23]

Fitzpatrick's letter reporting that he had furs in quantity and was going back to the mountains for them was the one note of hope 1824 had brought. Jedediah Smith had found a rich beaver country beyond the mountains, and got down an earnest of its wealth. He and Weber might do still better this year. Henry would have to go back to the Rockies, following the trail Jedediah Smith and his men had blazed. Or if Henry had had enough, Ashley would go himself. Another year would decide whether William H. Ashley was to be a man of independent fortune or a bankrupt.

6. *THE STAKES OF THE COLUMBIA*

When Jedediah Smith separated from Thomas Fitzpatrick on the Sweetwater early in July 1824 to turn back across South Pass, his purpose was to press his hunt as far as the Columbia. In the Green River Valley he had reached the farthest limits of the British fur frontier. Now he would launch himself into the heart of the British domain.

It is more fruitful to think of Jedediah Smith's fall hunt of 1824 in these terms than as an exploration. He was the first American to have got west of the continental divide in ten years, but Jedediah's significance this year is that in his own person he is the American oncoming, the long-delayed frontal challenge to the maintenance of the British position in Oregon.

That such a challenge was developing, the Hudson's Bay Company had seen clearly for two years. On September 4, 1822, when Andrew Henry was still cutting pickets for his post on the Yellowstone, and Ashley and Jedediah Smith were laboriously engaged in the ascent of the Missouri, the Governor and Committee in London addressed a letter to their subalterns on the Columbia. With news from American papers that a party of 150 men had left St. Louis on a fur-trading expedition across the Rocky Mountains, they enclosed advices from Washington that the American government contemplated forming a settlement on the Columbia. Information was requested concerning these developments, and the gentlemen in Oregon were reminded, "we depend on your strenuous exertions to secure the Fur Trade to Great Britain by your liberality to and kind treatment of the Natives." [1]

The situation west of the mountains cannot be hewed into simplicity with a few sharp words, and explanation is required.

In 1822 the Hudson's Bay Company was still trying to heal the open wounds remaining from its long and nearly mortal struggle with the North West Company. Trading southward from its historic posts on Hudson Bay, the English company had clashed with a powerful group of Montreal traders who had made their way up the St. Lawrence and through the Great Lakes to Hudson Bay waters. The Nor'Westers were as formidable an opposition as any fur company ever faced anywhere, and a murderous trade war that lasted through more than a generation brought both companies virtually to their knees before a merger was agreed on in 1821.

Notwithstanding the violence of this struggle, the North West Company had the energy and found the resources to push entirely beyond the area of conflict, to the waters draining the western and southern slopes of "the height of land." The first man to complete the continental crossing north of Mexico was a Nor'-Wester; and it was Nor'Westers who built the first trading post west of the great divide. The same restless energy took the North West Company south to the headwaters of the Columbia, on which its men were trading as early as 1807, and though John Jacob Astor's bravely conceived Pacific Fur Company anticipated the Nor'Westers in establishing a post at the mouth of the great river, the tide of disaster which overwhelmed Astoria late in 1813 transformed the whole vast basin of the Columbia into a private preserve of the Canadians. The charter of the Hudson's Bay Company down to 1821 limited it to waters that drained into Hudson Bay, and only a single servant of the company penetrated to Columbia waters, a foray that reached no farther than Flathead Lake and was never followed up.

Against all expectations, the effective monopoly established by the North West Company on the Columbia profited the Company nothing. Fort George, as Astoria was renamed, had been envisioned as a main base for all the western operations of the Company. It would be supplied by sea, and the returns made there instead of being carried all the way back to the St. Lawrence; there were many ramifications to the idea, including the marketing of the furs in China in defiance of another great British monopoly, the East India Company. The whole concept was breath-taking in its boldness but it did not work out, and exploitation of the province was a more dismal failure still.[2]

In 1816 the Company sent the former Astorian, Donald Mackenzie, out to the Columbia in the hope that he would revitalize the interior trade. Mackenzie's first two years went largely into combating the inertia which reigned at Fort George, but in the summer of 1818 he founded Fort Nez Perces near the junction of the Columbia and the Snake, and from this base he took a column into the Snake Country, a region which had been grossly neglected.

Mackenzie's three Snake Country expeditions merit a great deal more space than we can give them.[3] His men roved as far south as the Bear River and as far east as the Green River Valley, trapping its productive streams a full three years before Jedediah Smith penetrated there across South Pass; and they trapped the Snake almost from source to mouth, giving various tributaries names which still endure. Mackenzie's Snake Country expeditions were a distinguished episode in exploration. They were also a momentous innovation in the conduct of the western fur trade. The basis of the fur business in North America had always been manipulation of the Indians. You got them to come to you, if possible, but if necessary (and under the stress of competition it always became necessary) you went to them, made them dependent on your goods, and waited for the skins to flood in. The system had worked everywhere else, but it did not work in the West. Even before Mackenzie's time and on the American side of the divide, the character of the fur trade had begun to alter under the pressure of necessity. White hunters by twos and threes could trap the streams more efficiently than the Indians, and the operations of the Missouri Fur Company on the Yellowstone and the Missouri in 1809-1810 had taken this turn.[4] To no purpose, for the Blackfeet scourged them out of the country. Auguste Chouteau and Jules De Mun experimented along the same lines on the upper Arkansas and the South Platte in 1815-1817, but that venture too came to naught when the Spanish authorities sent out a military force and installed the whole operation in the Santa Fe *calabozo*.[5] It was left to Donald Mackenzie to demonstrate the real potential of the trapping brigade.

With a motley group of Iroquois and Abenakis from the St. Lawrence, "Owyhees" from the Sandwich Islands, superannuated freemen (servants whose term of service had expired), and a few Canadian *engagés,* Mackenzie made history. His bold and imaginative use of his men for trapping rather than for manning trading posts; his system of supply and the transport of his furs, which involved the use of horses in place of the boats to which the fur trade had been wedded; his maintenance of his trapping force in the field almost uninterruptedly for three years—all this displayed genius and laid the groundwork for the revolution which Jedediah Smith and his associates were about to effect in the conduct of the American fur trade.

Mackenzie's returns during his three years in the Snake Country are difficult to estimate, perhaps a quarter of the whole returns of the Columbia Department. Alexander Ross has said that one year Mackenzie brought in enough skins to compensate for all deficiencies elsewhere and leave a handsome surplus; and again, that of a total year's hunt of some 14,000 skins Mackenzie produced nearly half. There remains some doubt that Mackenzie's Snake Country hunt ever exceeded 4,000 beaver, and in no year down to 1821 does the Columbia Department seem to have broken even.[6] The North West Company considered abandoning the Columbia, but it was a first principle with the Nor'Westers to give up nothing they ever got their hands on, and they hung on stubbornly down to the merger with the Hudson's Bay Company. That company in turn began to weigh the advantages and disadvantages of withdrawal, but the question was still open when Ashley and Henry launched their first expedition up the Missouri.

At stake was an empire in fur. Somewhere that empire had to be fought for. If the Columbia were abandoned, if the Company withdrew northward, Americans would be sucked into the vacuum. Astor had never been happy about the fate of his Pacific Fur Company; new competition might come by sea. Or, failing that, by land across the Rockies. In either case the struggle for furs would begin all over again, and on the borders of the richest fur country west of the Rockies, New Caledonia (British Columbia). The shock of the American oncoming logically should be met on the farthest frontier. To keep the Americans at a distance, even operations at a loss could be contemplated with equanimity—if the losses were not beyond all reason.

The question was not one of furs only. An important national interest was involved. In the negotiation of 1818 the United States and Great Britain had been unable to settle on a satisfactory partition of Oregon. The United States had stubbornly contended for a boundary along the forty-ninth degree all the way to the Pacific, while Britain just as stubbornly had contended for a boundary that would carry the line along the forty-ninth degree as far as the Columbia, then down the Columbia to the sea—a division of the Oregon country that would have left British the richest part of the modern state of Washington. The importance of the Columbia to the fur trade of the Pacific had been primarily responsible for the British obstinacy. Unable to agree on anything else, the negotiators had agreed on joint occupation of Oregon for ten years. When the question of the boundary was reopened, physical occupation of the country might weigh heavily; thus the imperial interest as well as its own urged the Hudson's Bay Company to stand fast on the Columbia. Through 1822-1824 while the American fur trade of the Far West was struggling to survive in the face of the disasters on the high Missouri, the Company anxiously debated a course of action, and a firm decision was not reached until the fall of 1824, when Americans, in the persons of Jedediah Smith and his six companions, had already burst on the scene.[7]

The Hudson's Bay Company's energetic North American governor, young George Simpson, had not required prodding from London to direct his attention to the Columbia. As early as July 1822, in writing the London office of an encouraging increase of returns from the remote department on the Pacific, he had observed that although large profits could scarcely be expected, "yet by oeconomy and perseverance" the trade might be made to support itself. Provided, however, and always provided, "that no formidable opposition from the Americans assail us, in that quarter." [8]

An inexorable logic was at work: Find some means of keeping the Americans at a distance. In practice, that meant to strip the country bare along the line of the American advance. As it happened, the large strategical objective exactly dovetailed with the local tactical situation. When the five years Donald Mackenzie had contracted for ended in the summer of 1821, no one on the Columbia felt it either his interest or his duty to take Mackenzie's place at the head of the Snake brigade. If the man's returns had been impressive, so were his casualties. Yet the trappers who had composed the Snake brigade went right on eating, and if they were not out hunting beaver, they ate horseflesh and still more expensive fare at the Company's posts on credit. Nine months of this was more than enough, and early in 1822 the Iroquois and freemen who had been loafing about Spokane House and Flathead Post were dispatched into the field under Michel Bourdon.[9]

That the Snake Expedition of 1822 was based on the more northern houses rather than on Nez Perces was in itself a novelty. The arrangement may have resulted from local convenience, but something was to be said for it on practical grounds. A Snake Expedition starting from Flathead Post (just above Thompson Falls on Clarks Fork of the Columbia) had a much greater distance to travel, but approaching from a different direction might open up fresh trapping grounds. Neither was it unimportant that the start was from Flathead country, for the amiable Salish had been convoying trappers to and through the Blackfoot lands for years.

Little more is known about Bourdon than that he was "a young man" employed as a "Conductor of Trappers." He had been with Mackenzie on the first Snake Expedition of 1818-1819; it was he who made the British discovery of Bear River (and gave it the name which still endures); his own name was briefly applied to Blacksmiths Fork in Cache Valley, and except for one of the whims of fate, he might have been the discoverer of Great Salt Lake.[10] Not much more is known about his Snake Expedition of 1822 than about the man himself, but it would appear that he got as far south and west as the Blackfoot River,[11] employing a dual crossing of the continental divide that was used in each of the next three years, the only practicable route to the Snake lands from the Flathead country. He got back to the inland headquarters, Spokane House, on September 13, 1822; the post journal that night says:

> About sun down M. Burdon arrived from the Snake Country he has left seven of his party of free men at the Ear Ring [Pend d'Oreille] Indians they having left their horses near the Flat Heads and come down with canoes to that place M. B.'s party have made out very well but were very much drove about by the common enemy in that country, that is the black feet. They had several skirmishes with them M. B. had two of his party killed & two wounded the enemy had seven killed, the wounded not known. M. Burdon represents that country as the best for beaver on this side of the mountains he lik[e]wise informs us that a party of free men have gone towards Fort Nez Percês but that the party in all had killed 2200 plues beaver but he could not get the Iroques to come on with their furs to the fort.[12]

Fourteen men deserted Bourdon, at least four of whom were not Iroquois but men who had come overland with Wilson Price Hunt's Astorians of 1811.[13] Instead of going to Fort Nez Perces, they had headed east across the continental divide to the American frontiers. When the fact of their desertion could no longer be doubted, the Company's officers had to conclude that the runaways had taken themselves to the new posts building on the Yellowstone, and nothing appeared more certain than that they would be back with Americans in tow. . . . In fact, these deserters had embarked on an odyssey. They may have made their way east by the Astorian track of 1811; it is even conceivable that they rode east through South Pass a year before Jedediah Smith came through it westbound—the details of their journey are not recoverable. But sometime in the winter of 1822-1823, having crossed the mountains, they fell among Crow and Cheyenne Indians who killed several, robbed the rest of all they possessed and made captives of their women and children. In this extremity they made the long journey down to Fort Atkinson, arriving at the end of July 1823 to beseech aid from the U. S. authorities in having their families restored to them.[14] . . .

If there had been reason to get a Snake Expedition into the

field in 1822, there was more compelling reason still in 1823. Owing to the defection of his freemen, Bourdon had had to cache seven hundred skins, nearly a third of his hunt, and these had to be recovered. Also, in the fall of 1822 a number of freemen from Fort des Prairies, the North Saskatchewan post, had drifted westward across the divide and on down to Spokane House; they should be put to work. And there was no getting away from it, the Snake Country was "the Source from which we draw the Major part of our Returns." In the spring of 1823 the chief factor in charge at Spokane fitted out Finan McDonald with five *engagés* and Bourdon to conduct the freemen a second time into the Snake Country. Although McDonald would have to return to direct the winter trade at Flathead Post, it was hoped the freemen could be maintained in the field throughout the winter.[15] Summer furs were poor in quality, and to have the men set out in the spring, return in the fall, and winter about the Company posts as they had done of late was the worst kind of management.

A six-foot-four-inch giant with a tremendous pair of shoulders and a wildly red-whiskered face, Finan McDonald had somewhat the aspect of a prophet who had missed his calling. He had been on the Columbia a long time, having crossed the mountains with the great geographer David Thompson in 1807.[16] McDonald had eruptive courage and the restless energy of a rumbling volcano, but he entered on his service in the Snake Country without enthusiasm, and returned in the fall disposed to thank God he had got home safe, frank to say that when the Snake lands should see him again, the beaver would have "Gould Skin." A letter about his experiences that he wrote in April of the year following has only recently become known and supplies some valuable information about one of the obscurest chapters in the history of the West:

We had Saviral Battils with the nasion on the other side of the Mountins Poore Meshel Bordoe was kild with 5 more of the Band there dath was revenge as well as we Could revenge it for no less than 68 of them that remane in the Planes as Pray for the wolves and those fue that askape our Shotes they had not Britch Clout to Cover them selves we Shoe them what war was they will not be so radey to atack People another time we got all there from them and made Pease with those that we kild they Promis they would not return agane to make ware. I got Last Summer as far as the Croe Indian Cuntre on the rail Spanish river from where we return Back separate saveral times in two Bands on acount of the Band being two strong and we ware onley 45 free men and six Engage men so you may se that the rivers is not altogether alive with Beaver but for all it is the richest Cuntre that I noe of on this side of the mountins and onley the Cuntre that free men is able to do sumthing—for the Flat Head Cuntre is rouint of Beaver For Free men to hunt I Sa the Musasourey Last fall down as far is the falls in that Part of the Cuntre is rouint of Beaver By the Amaricans for they hade fort there fue years agoe about ½ mile beloe Corta is old Fort[17] it is fine river all long and about the size of the N Parsey [Snake] River Varey Strong Currant.[18]

The embittered conflict with the Piegans which cost McDonald the lives of Bourdon and five others, the nearest thing to a pitched battle the British ever had to fight in the Snake Country, was fought in the service of the entire fur trade, for during the next few years Blackfoot war parties which roamed the Snake lands hunting horses and glory refrained from any but adventitious murders, and this relative immunity to attack did much to secure the fortunes of Jedediah Smith and his associates.

The Hudson's Bay Company's advance base, Flathead Post, was situated on the right bank of Clarks Fork at present Eddy, Montana. The trail to the Snake Country angled away from the river, east into the Horse Plains, on into Camas Prairie, and then south to cross the Flathead River at present Perma. After ascending the Flathead some miles, the trail turned south up the Jocko River and passed over a low divide to the site of Missoula. Here, at the confluence of Clarks Fork and the Bitterroot River, two alternative routes opened up. One trail continued south up the Bitterroot to its head and across Gibbon Pass to Missouri waters; this was the route that became familiar to Jedediah Smith. The other trail turned east into Hell Gate, the narrow canyon above Missoula, and followed Clarks Fork all the way up to Deer Lodge Prairie. Thence by Deer Lodge Pass it crossed over to Missouri waters, reaching the Big Hole River at its northernmost bend, some twenty miles below the point where the Bitterroot road arrived on that stream.

McDonald probably took the trail via Clarks Fork and Deer Lodge. Once on the Big Hole, he went up it to its sources and then crossed over to the Beaverhead, arriving on it immediately below Lemhi Pass. Scarcely had he recrossed the divide than he ran into a Blackfoot ambuscade. The balls that whistled about his startled party did no damage, but in the slashing counterattack McDonald immediately organized, several of his men were killed.

The Hudson's Bay men had had more than enough of the gentle ways of the Blackfeet; back on the Big Hole one of the party had been killed in a parley with the Piegans, and the man's scalp, flaunted on a coupstick, they had only now recovered. Ranging themselves in front of the dense thicket in which the Blackfeet had taken refuge, the trappers poured into it volley after volley of buckshot. The Piegans, short of ammunition, responded mainly with screams of defiance, but now and then a shot rang out, and three more of the besiegers were picked off. Utterly exasperated, McDonald's men took up a position to either side of the thicket, then contrived to fire it. With a strong wind blowing, the flames leaped up furiously. A dreadful moment, and then the shrieking Piegans burst out of their refuge to run the gantlet. The wonder was that as many as seven of the seventy-five who made up the war party got away; ten of them burned to death in the thicket. A more sanguinary battle was never fought in the Snake Country, and something of its horror attached to the spot for years after.[19]

McDonald went on south, up over the Salmon River Mountains to the Snake, then farther south still, as far as the Bear. When Bourdon reached this stream in 1819, he supposed that he had found the Spanish River, the Rio Colorado. Mackenzie in 1820-1821 had shown that was a mistake by getting his party over into the Green River Valley proper, but the Bear was still conjectured to be a branch of the Spanish River.[20] McDonald like Bourdon had his opportunity to become the discoverer of Great Salt Lake, but he turned up the Bear, and as his quoted letter now for the first time makes clear, got over into the valley of the Green, the "rail Spanish river."[21] This was late summer 1823, when Jedediah Smith had scarcely finished fighting with Rees and was yet a thousand weary miles' travel short of South Pass.

But now McDonald turned back to the Snake, very likely by the well-worn Indian trail north into Jackson Hole and over the Tetons to Henrys Fork. He may here have had another brush with Blackfeet, inconclusive but sufficient to force him to break off trapping.[22] Turning north again, he recrossed the Salmon River Mountains and went on down the Lemhi River to where the trail veered east across Lemhi Pass. Thence he trapped his way down the Missouri to Great Falls. This was the farthest east any Hudson's Bay Company party ever ventured on American soil, and rumors of McDonald's foray, carried by the Indian news service to Fort Atkinson far below, served to build up pressures for a military expedition up the Missouri to bind the Indians to the American interest.[23]

McDonald brought out of the Snake Country 4,339 beaver, perhaps the best hunt that had ever been made there, and when he reached Flathead Post, he received the welcome news that someone else would have the job of trying to improve on his returns. The North American Governor and Committee, meeting at York Factory in the summer of 1823, had decided to continue the Snake Expedition and had appointed Alexander Ross to its command. (Mr. Ross was cautioned against opening a road for the Americans.)[24]

Ross had been on the Columbia longer than anyone but McDonald, having come out on the *Tonquin* in 1811. Unlike most of Astor's clerks, he had stayed on with the North West Company. When Mackenzie returned to the Columbia in 1816, Ross became his principal supporter; he assisted in building Fort Nez Perces, and had it in charge till 1823. Beyond anyone who remained on the Columbia, Ross was the champion of the Snake Country, though not pleased by the change which based the expedition on Flathead Post. Of Scotch birth, Ross had the physical courage, the immutable prejudices, and the tart tongue that have distinguished his countrymen throughout history. Among the most unalterable of his prejudices was his conviction that the Iroquois were good for nothing. "Unruly, ill-tongued villains" is one of the more charitable expressions his journal employs; and his opinion of the freemen in general was little higher: "A more discordant, headstrong, ill-designing set of rascals . . . God never permitted together in the fur trade." [25]

Notwithstanding the desertion of Bourdon's men in 1822, nobody in the Columbia Department understood how grave was the disaffection among the trappers. So wide was the gulf between the commissioned gentlemen and the working hands that trouble was easier conceived as a reflection of human depravity than the result of a defect in the system. Governor Simpson expressed the general view in calling the freemen "the very scum of the country and generally outcasts from the Service for misconduct . . . the most unruly and troublesome gang to deal with in this or perhaps any other part of the World," requiring very superior management to make anything of them.[26]

It was only a question of management, and Simpson was going to find sourly that Ross simply did not have the capacity for command. But even Ross, who for £120 a year had taken on the least popular job on the Columbia, did not understand where the trouble lay. The North West Company had never worked out a policy for the freemen who had accumulated in increasing numbers on the Saskatchewan and the Columbia; it had taken beaver from them almost at Indian rates, and sold them goods at high prices. The men were reduced to virtual serfdom; however large their annual catch, it was swallowed up in their debt. As beaver had small value for them, they took little interest in pursuing it and at the slightest adversity were prepared to abandon their hunts; they much preferred to spend their time running buffalo or racing their horses with the Indians. Nor had any great change taken place after the merger of the North West Company with the Hudson's Bay Company. Soon now it was going to become abundantly clear why Bourdon's men had wandered off, but through 1824 the whole trouble was laid to the fickleness and lack of principle, the irresponsibility and worse, of the Iroquois and half-breed freemen.

Ross got off from Flathead Post early in February, about the time Jedediah Smith, far to the east in the Crow country, chafing over his long detention by snow and cold, set out for the Sweetwater. Through March and the first week of April, while Jedediah was finding his way across the wind-swept reaches of South Pass and down to the new trapping grounds in the Green River Valley, Ross was forcing his way up the snow-choked Bitterroot Valley and across Gibbon Pass to the Big Hole, whence by the familiar route to Lemhi Pass he got over into the Snake Country and could consider his spring hunt fairly begun. After some weeks on Salmon waters, Ross crossed the divide south. There, yielding to the importunities of a dozen of his Iroquois, he divided his party. Most of his brigade he took west toward the head of the Boise, and on that stream, the Payette and the Weiser he made a rich haul before turning east again. Meantime, however, his Iroquois ran into trouble.

Ross had been reluctant to detach the Iroquois in the first place, remembering the endless troubles Mackenzie himself had had in similar circumstances. But it was certainly true, as Finan McDonald had observed, that a brigade could be "two strong" for its own good. The British practice was to maintain the Snake brigade in sufficient strength to protect itself from the tribes. That this was sound practice is shown by the fact that after McDonald's set-to with the Piegans in 1823, British scalps were lost at rarest intervals. The Americans, in penetrating the West, would not and could not profit by this example but scattered everywhere in small parties, sometimes of four men and less, which made for efficient trapping but at the cost of high casualties. These the Americans blamed on British subversion of the Indians, refusing to face the fact that the price was one their system of trapping required them to pay. But Ross's Iroquois did have a valid point. The larger the party, the richer a river had to be to justify trapping it; relatively, a small party might do better on a stream already worked over than a large one on virgin waters. So after being badgered for weeks, Ross gave his consent for the Iroquois to trap by themselves.

The Iroquois were headed by a personality of note, "Old Pierre" Tivanitagon, whose name through all the great years of the fur trade was preserved in Pierres Hole under the Tetons. Old Pierre made first for Henrys Fork and the famous Hole, then trapped down the south bank of the Snake as far as the Blackfoot and Portneuf.[27] Ross said later that the conduct of the Iroquois was blamable from the time they left him, that they "passed the time with the Indians and neglected their hunts, quarrelled with the Indians at last, were then robbed and left naked on the plains." [28] But that was Ross's spleen. While Ross was in the western reaches of the Snake Country, a number of his traps were stolen by the Snakes. To force their return, he seized horses belonging to the thieves, and though this got his traps back, the Indians went off ready to vent their ill temper on the first object that offered, the Iroquois. A Snake chief was killed in the scuffle, and all things considered, the Iroquois were fortunate to get off with their lives.[29] When, unexpectedly, Jedediah Smith and his six men in the late summer of 1824 stumbled on the forlorn Iroquois in the vicinity of present Blackfoot, Idaho, the British trappers begged the Americans to convoy them to Ross's camp, and offered in payment such beaver as they still retained.[30]

It was probably about mid-September 1824 that Jedediah Smith entered on this scene. Where he had been since parting from Thomas Fitzpatrick is one of the minor conundrums of a life not yet wholly unriddled. The only thing resembling a statement of his route is a vague remark made by Ashley a year and a half later. Jedediah, Ashley said, "stated that he had in the fall of 1824 crossed from the head waters of the Rio Colorado to Lewis' fork of the Columbia and down the same about one hundred miles, thence northwardly to Clarks' fork of the Columbia." [31] This has been interpreted to mean that Jedediah traveled northwest out of the Green River Valley to the Hoback River, down it to Jackson Hole, across the Tetons by Teton Pass, down into Pierres Hole, across the Snake plain to the Three Buttes, and then north to Columbia waters proper.

Such a route does not in all respects conform to Ashley's description; and the interpretation rests in part on a confusion of the Three Tetons with the Three Buttes. It is entirely possible that when Jedediah recrossed South Pass, he headed southwest, returning to the country he had trapped in the spring. He would have moved over the Bear River Divide, followed down the Bear a hundred miles, and then struck north to the sources of the

CAMP OF THE GROS VENTRES OF THE PRAIRIES ON THE UPPER MISSOURI

Charles Bodmer, 1833. From Maximilian, Tab. 38.

Courtesy, Coe Collection, Yale University.

TRAPPERS MAKING THEIR ESCAPE FROM HOSTILE BLACKFEET

Alfred Jacob Miller, 1837.

Courtesy, National Park Service.

SCOTTS BLUFF NATIONAL MONUMENT

DEVILS GATE ON THE SWEETWATER RIVER

Frederick A. Piercy, 1853. From *Route from Liverpool.*

Blackfoot. From here he would have had a continuous northing all the way to Flathead Post.[32]

These details of the itinerary are important to local history and to the record of western exploration, but how Jedediah reached the Snake has only trivial significance compared with the fact that hereabouts he fell in with the Iroquois. En route to this rendezvous, Jedediah and his men trapped with conspicuous success; Ross heard later that they had in two different caches 900 beaver, which would be a famous three months' hunt for a party of seven. Ross suggested long afterward that the Americans had acquired the whole by intriguing with his Iroquois, and the remark has given rise to supercilious comment about Jedediah's ethics. The idea is implausible on its face, and is not supported by anything in the record. The story Ross had from Jedediah, that the Iroquois traded him 105 beaver for supplies and escort back to Ross, was probably correct—and let us observe that what was asked of Jedediah was not guide service in a country the Iroquois knew better than he, but armed protection through a bristling region.

That his Iroquois should come back "trapless and beaverless, naked and destitute of almost everything" was for Alexander Ross a hard blow. He had done well after a poor spring hunt, and had counted on the Iroquois for additional hundreds of skins. Worse still, here were Americans to remind him of the pointed instructions from York Factory. Ross gave Jedediah Smith his due in the words that everybody used about him, "a very intelligent person," but his quality made him all the more disturbing, for Ross took these seven Americans to be rather "spies than trappers," and in his journal set down something of his disquiet:

It is evident part of [our deserters of 1822] have reached the American posts on the Yellowstone and Big Horn with much fur. I suspect these Americans have been on the lookout to decoy more. . . . The quarter is swarming with trappers who next season are to penetrate the Snake country with a Major Henry at their head, the same gentleman who fifteen years ago wintered on Snake River. The report of these men on the price of beaver has a very great influence on our trappers. The seven trappers have in two different caches 900 beaver. I made them several propositions but they would not accept lower than $3 a pound. I did not consider myself authorized to arrange at such prices. . . . They intend following us to the fort.[33]

If Ross was correctly informed as to the number of beaver Jedediah had trapped, he had acquired enough to strain his resources in horses and men getting them out of the mountains. He could very well break off his hunt for the sake of some firsthand information about British operations. Ross might not like being accompanied back to his base, but there was no way he could prevent it.

So the combined party crossed Lemhi Pass October 28, and four days later recrossed the divide to the Bitterroot. The going was hard, with much ice and snow. Getting across Clarks Fork was especially disagreeable; one of the horses was drowned and two of the men came near sharing its fate.[34] But the worst was then past, and on November 26, 1824, Ross got back to Flathead Post. "All things considered," Ross says pridefully, "our returns were the most profitable ever brought from the Snake country in one year; amounting to 5000 beaver, exclusive of other peltries." [35] Viewpoint of Mr. Finan McDonald:

Mr. Ross had more luck then I had the [year] Before he had no Batil with the Black Feet fue [horses] stold by the Snakes. Brought out upwards of 4900 Beaver, Large and Small—561 over and above Last year he was better furnish in traps than I was the year before and he was noways trouble by our Anemis of the year before.[36]

Jedediah's arrival at Flathead has left remarkably little deposit in the Hudson's Bay Company records, yet the whole Columbia Department was already clangorous with what he symbolized. Less than a month before, Governor Simpson had arrived on the Columbia direct from York Factory, bringing with him a new chief factor, Dr. John McLoughlin, a man fully competent to run this long mismanaged Department. Simpson had passed down the river taking deadly aim at everything that smacked to him of waste or extravagance; shrewd, dynamic and ambitious, there was little that escaped the young governor, and he was full of ideas about everything. Simpson was confident that his measures of "oeconomy" would make the Columbia a paying proposition from this time forward, and he was determined that the Snake Expedition should be made an effective instrument to shield the Columbia from the advancing Americans. The man best qualified to lead the brigade, Simpson decided, was the tough, belligerent Peter Skene Ogden. During the year past Ogden had had a soft berth in charge of the Spokane District, and he would have been satisfied to stay put, but it was in large part to Simpson that Ogden owed his having been taken into the Company after being passed over in the merger of 1821; he would do as Simpson desired.

Ogden stands second only to Jedediah Smith among the field captains of the fur trade in this decade. Born of Loyalist American parents in Quebec about 1794, he was five years older than Jedediah Smith, and down to this time had lived a considerably more varied life. His father had designed him for the ministry or the law, but at the age of seventeen Ogden entered the service of the North West Company. For seven years he was in the thick of the fight with the Hudson's Bay Company, so much so that when indictments began to be found, his Company thought it expedient to send him out to the Columbia. His world fell apart with the merger of 1821, but two years later he was given a chief tradership by the H. B. Company and now Simpson had plans for him.[37]

The governor instructed Ogden to meet the incoming expedition at Flathead Post, refit it, and get it back into the field without delay. This would be the last time the brigade was based on Flathead Post. Simpson liked Fort Nez Perces as a base no better than Flathead, and he proposed a genuine innovation for the year's operations. Ogden and his men were ordered to proceed

direct for the heart of the Snake country towards the Banks of the Spanish River or Rio Colorado, pass the Winter & Spring there and hunt their way out by the Umpqua and Wilhamet Rivers to Fort George next summer sufficiently early to send the returns home by the Ship; and in future instead of incurring the heavy Expence of sending the Equipment round by the Spokane & Flat Head Posts . . . outfit it direct from the Depot on the Coast.

These were merely the mechanics of the operation; Simpson never for a moment lost sight of the large objective. The Snake Country was a rich preserve of beaver they must undertake to destroy. As long as it existed, there were compelling reasons for the Americans to cross the divide. If the region could be converted into a fur desert, it would be difficult for the Americans either to reach or to maintain themselves on the Columbia. In 1818 it had been pretty well settled that when partition finally came, all the country south of the Columbia would pass into American hands. Since the Company must sooner or later be ousted from that area, the intelligent thing was to get everything out of it they could. Elsewhere in the Columbia Department it might be to the interest of the Hudson's Bay Company to trap on a sustained yield basis, but the Snake Country must be ruined, the faster the better.[38]

It may have seemed to George Simpson that his crisp directions settled all the problems. What these directions involved, what actually he was requiring to be done, he had hardly the faintest conception. Simpson assumed: That there was nothing wrong with the organization and operation of the Snake Expedition that an iron hand could not straighten out in the field. That the Americans would not understand, resent and react violently to the purposeful destruction of a fur country for political ends. And that his geographical concepts were sound. These assumptions had now to be put to the test.

7. *ACTION ON THE FUR FRONTIER*

Peter Skene Ogden reached Flathead Post with the outfit for the Snake Expedition on November 26, 1824, just a few hours before Alexander Ross came in with Jedediah Smith.[1] If Ross was disappointed at the change in command and his new appointment in charge of Flathead, he mastered his feelings. He fell to work helping Ogden get the brigade in shape to take the field again, and during the three weeks this required, Jedediah Smith lazed around the fort, enjoying in wry fashion the spectacle of the winter trade.

Like most trading houses in the Indian country, Flathead Post was more imposing in its name than in the fact, "a row of huts 6 in number, low, linked together under one cover, having the appearance of deserted booths," the function of which was mainly to keep the rain off trade goods and furs. A brass three-pounder was the principal reminder to the Indians that correct conduct was expected of them. It was not needed, for the Flatheads had always been friendly and Blackfeet never got this far west in any numbers.

But the winter trade with the Flatheads, Pend d'Oreilles, Kutenais and a few Nez Perces and Spokanes was truly a spectacle, the like of which Jedediah had nowhere seen east of the divide. Some 861 men, women and children had assembled, with several thousand horses. Each tribe had its appointed day, beginning with the Flatheads on November 30. The manner of it was ceremonious in the extreme and instructive to watch. The Flatheads came up in a body, mounted and chanting the song of peace. At a little distance from the fort, they halted and discharged their guns in salute, a compliment returned by the brass three-pounder. When the echoes had died away, the head chief advanced to make a formal speech, welcoming the whites to these lands and apologizing for having so few beaver to trade. The entire cavalcade then moved up. The chiefs were invited to smoke, and the women of the camp came up on horseback, leading animals laden with provisions. The trade which followed lasted until dark. So each of the tribes in turn. By December 3 the trade was over and the Indians were leaving for their wintering grounds. In all, the Hudson's Bay Company had traded 1,183 beaver, 14 otter, 529 muskrat, 8 fishers, 3 minks, 1 martin, 2 foxes and 11,072 pounds of dried buffalo meat. Although the returns averaged hardly three skins to the Indian, it looked effortless, and Jedediah could not be unaware of the grip the British maintained on the tribes through this trade.

During the three weeks at Flathead Post there is only a single mention of Jedediah's presence, a notation by Alexander Ross in the post journal on December 12: "In course of this day, we traded from the American hunters I met in the Snake Country, 40 Beaver at Freemen's prices." [2] Ross thereby bought for sixty cents or so apiece skins worth in St. Louis from eight to twelve dollars. And payment made for them, probably tobacco or gunpowder, was in goods sold at an advance of seventy per cent on prime cost.[3]

The Snake Expedition got off from Flathead Post December 20, 1824—"the most formidable party," Ross remarked, "that has ever set out for the Snakes." Besides two gentlemen, Ogden and William Kittson, it was made up of eleven *engagés*, and forty-six freemen. They had 61 guns, 268 horses and 352 traps.[4] As there was no particular hazard the first few days of the journey, Jedediah and his men did not join up till December 29, when the British column was nearing Hell Gate. The men who composed Jedediah's party have gone unidentified all this time for lack of any real information about them, but there is good warrant for thinking that one was William L. Sublette as Jedediah's clerk, another Thomas Eddie, and a third possibly Arthur Black.[5] The Americans made a small show in comparison with the genuine spectacle of the British column, and Ogden did not notice them in his journal until he had been four months on the way. Kittson had a livelier interest, and from time to time his diary makes a useful note concerning the Americans—the more useful in that Jedediah's own journal for this period has never been found.

Short of stature, Ogden was powerfully built, capable of manhandling any three of his party. He had a gift for leadership, and before his years in the Snake Country ended would demonstrate his capacities, but in 1824 he still had much to learn. There was a wild streak of humor in him, an exuberance that found expression in spectacular practical jokes, but it was compensated in some degree by a disposition to look on this as the worst of possible worlds. His journals were intended for the eyes of his superiors, and his persistent pessimism may have been a shield held high against outrageous fortune, but also it reflected a genuine outlook on life.

William Kittson had not attained to Ogden's eminence in the Company, but he had had the toughening experience of a winter in the Snake Country, having been with Donald Mackenzie in 1819-1820. In Simpson's vinegary phrase, he was "a sharp, dapper, short tempered, self sufficient petulant little fellow of very limited Education, but exceedingly active and ambitious to signalize himself"; he was at this time about thirty-two years old. As a second lieutenant in the Canadian Voltigeurs, he had seen service in the War of 1812, and had afterward joined the North West Company as an apprentice clerk.[6] Both he and Ogden had taken Indian women to wife, the one a Kutenai, the other a Nez Perce. There were thirty women altogether in Ogden's party, and thirty-five children, with at least two more to be born along the way. This was the Indian mode of conducting a march or trapping operation; the Americans would come to it also, but for Jedediah Smith, as 1824 ran out, a party organized in this fashion was still as strange as the country itself.

The route adopted was that by which Jedediah had journeyed to Flathead Post in the fall. The weather was cold and snowy, with game scarce, and barely enough grass for the horses. On January 12 the party arrived at the foot of Gibbon Pass, and the next two days were occupied in crossing over to the Big Hole River. The snow on the heights was from two to three feet deep, but this was an easy traverse of a pass which had cost Ross a month's detention and the hardest kind of labor to get across at all. They came down into the Big Hole Prairie with sharpened eyes, for they were now fairly "in the Black feet Country of Wars & Murders."

This was the second time in three months Jedediah Smith had been on American soil with a British trapping party. National boundaries are most important to those who suffer by their infringement, and this trespass on American territory did not sit well with any of his company. It was bad enough that the British trapped the waters east of the continental divide with the same casualness they trapped those of the western slope, though in consequence of the Blackfoot interdiction this made no practical difference to the Americans. But British trapping in the Snake Country hurt. If the British could not enter the Snake lands except by a trespass on American soil, it was high time the integrity of the American boundary was asserted. Yet for the moment they were dependent on the British for safe conduct through a war country. Jedediah's men kept their mouths shut.

Ogden's education on the subject of freemen was already well advanced. Rules he made for the conduct of the march and the security of the camp were no sooner agreed to than violated. Friendly Indians were a bane, for the freemen would trade anything they owned, traps, guns and ammunition not excluded, for a good buffalo horse. Yet the men could not be induced to keep watch over their horses, and a Piegan raid to leave them all afoot was a daily possibility. When buffalo were plenty, the men were not content simply to hunt but must give themselves up to the pleasure of running them, so that the buffalo were harried out of sight and the camp went hungry. In more favored localities, command might have a military starkness, but in the Snake Country a brigade proceeded only by the continual exercise of jawbone diplomacy. On January 31, 1825, while the expedition was still on the Big Hole, two dozen of the freemen's horses were run off. Though chase was made after the thieves, only nine animals were recovered. At so unfavorable an omen, the freemen were minded to abandon the year's enterprise forthwith. Ogden argued them out of the notion, but his hope that they would profit by the lesson was not well founded.

By February 6 the brigade had reached the Beaverhead below Lemhi Pass. Here they suffered their first loss, one of the Iroquois in the party being accidentally killed by his wife. The misadventure cast a gloom over the camp, but as Ogden could note with surprise, "it is Contrary to the Canadian character that it Should last long," and by evening all was gay again. This understanding of the mercurial nature of the Canadians was vital to leadership in the Snake Country, and Jedediah Smith not less than Ogden could profit from it, for French-Canadians were the working hands of the fur trade everywhere.

On February 11 the combined party went up over Lemhi Pass[7] as Ross had done the year before to reach the waters of the Salmon; as Ogden says, "we Started & ascended a high mountain the ascent great & descent equally So & then proceeded along a narrow Defile an awful looking place, here a dozen Blackfeet Indians Could without exposing themselves destroy an army without a chance of any escaping." Down in the valley were buffalo by the hundreds, with plenty of coarse grass for the horses, an abundance which lifted the spirits of all.

The camp was now only eight days' march from the Snake, where the spring hunt would properly begin, but the number of buffalo in the Lemhi Valley was disquieting, for it indicated that heavy snow in the passes to the south kept the herds penned up, and the horses of the brigade were too enfeebled to stand up under hard going. These misgivings were fully borne out when at the end of February Ogden sent eight men for a look at the trail across the divide. The men came back to report that they had found the snow four feet deep and for three encampments no grass whatever: "This is really discouraging," Ogden wrote, "& from the present weak state of our horses it would be folly in me to attempt proceeding for two thirds would fall ere we reached the main river for without them we might as well retrace back our Steps to the Flat Heads."

For seven weeks Ogden was imprisoned in the Lemhi Valley, only shifting his camp when in need of grass or buffalo. On March 17, finally, Kittson made a casual entry in his diary, "Some talk of moving upwards to morrow." This talk may have proceeded out of Jedediah Smith's restlessness, for next day Kittson wrote, "The seven Americans are preparing to leave us tomorrow and try to make their way to snake river." Nothing more was needed to galvanize Ogden:

I feel So anxious to proceed that I shall again Send a party to examine another Defile to *examine* if it is possible for us to Cross over even at the sacrifice of Horses, if we Cannot we may give up all hopes of a Spring Hunt, how Cruelly mortifying after spending the winter in this dreary Country to loose the main object of our voyage when almost within reach of it.

Kittson's journal for the nineteenth is more illuminating:

The Americans traded some ammunition and Tobacco from us for Beaver at the same price as our freemen. About noon they left us well satisfied I hope with the care and Attention we paid them. For since we had them with us no one in our party ever took any advantage of or ill treated them. One Jedidiah S. Smith is at the head of them, a sly cunning Yankey. Mr. Ogden has just now ordered me to prepare against tomorrow to head a party of five men on discovery, for the purpose of ascertaining the present state of the snows and grass in this defile, leading to the same route Mr. Finan McDonald took to come out of the Snake river, and also to notice the way the Americans went.

Kittson got off early on the morning of March 20, instructed to examine the pass at the head of the Lemhi opening on Birch Creek.[8] Mounted on good horses, the six men made eighteen miles on dry ground and then went another twelve miles driving 600 buffalo ahead to trample out a road. On the rising ground the snow was from two to three feet deep, but it diminished to a few inches on the other side of the divide. There was little grass to subsist horses, but otherwise the way looked practical. Next morning, however, Kittson ran into a Blood war party numbering over thirty men. The reconnaissance was like to have had a sad issue, but the Indians were so cautious in their approach that Kittson was able to extricate himself, and late that night got safely back to camp.

If Blackfeet were infesting the Birch Creek divide, that was the very way Ogden did not wish to go, and when he got the brigade under way on the twenty-third, he chose the Little Lost

River route which had looked so dismaying in February. This, as it turned out, was the way Jedediah Smith had gone—a fortunate choice in Kittson's view, for "had they taken the one I visited they would have met with certain death, as they appeared when with us not to be over watchful."

Getting across the divide, even after Jedediah Smith had shown the way, was a severe trial, the road so steep that many of the horses fell with their loads. The summit was reached only with extraordinary labor, and on the far slope they wallowed down through snow shoulder-high, but on reaching the valley bottom were rewarded with grass, water, wood and others of the comforts of life. As soon as possible Ogden sent off a party of thirteen men under Francois Payette "to oppose the Americans and get a share of the beaver by trapping."

The expedition by then had nearly reached the sink of the Little Lost River, on the verge of the Snake Plain. Three buttes already famous as landmarks rose midway in the dark lava desert, and the road went straight south, just east of the middle butte. This was a bad trail, for there was little grass, in summer not much water, and the lava cut up the horses' hoofs. But Jedediah Smith and his own advance party were out ahead, and Ogden pressed after them, reaching the Snake opposite the mouth of the Blackfoot at sunset April 6. Next day he crossed the Snake, making contact at once with Jedediah Smith's party. The American camp, Kittson remarked, was "without any person in care, the beaver they had taken 80 in number were spread on the ground." This was better than Ogden's own men had done, but when they came in a little later he was happy to hear that they had sixty-three beaver and an otter.

Next day for the first time Ogden mentions in his own journal the Americans who had been so long in his company. As the Americans intended to separate on the morrow, he observed, they "requested to trade & tho' they found the prices high say the Freemens Tariff . . . being in Want they were obliged to Comply & traded 100 Lar. & Sm. Beaver this is Some recompence for the Beaver they traded with our party last Summer." Here is an interesting reference to the beaver Jedediah had obtained from Ross's Iroquois; on balance, the British were now ahead, for in three transactions they had gained rather more than they had lost.

Almost certainly it was ammunition of which Jedediah was in want. He had been out from his base eighteen months; from the time he left Fort Kiowa there had been no possibility of supplying himself, and he could not have been sure when and where he would again fall in with Fitzpatrick, the single strand of contact he had with St. Louis. Jedediah may also have known that Bloods were prowling in the vicinity. It was only the roll of the dice that Ogden's party, rather than his own, this very day paid fee to their presence.

Early that morning, when Ogden's detached party were visiting their traps, they were set upon by Bloods. There was a scramble into the bushes and into the water, and all but one got away. The unlucky Antoine Benoit was found after a two-day search. He had been shot through the body and head, three times stabbed, scalped and stripped naked. This happening cast a deep gloom over the camp, and the freemen showed the profoundest disinclination to go on. Be the country however rich, a dead man could have little enjoyment of it. Though Ogden finally got the camp moving, they were jittery.

On April 11 Americans and British set out up the Blackfoot River, and the next few days are a history of jockeying for advantage. On April 16 Ogden writes:

> Being informed by the Trappers who had gone a head with their Traps yesterday that they had Seen the Americans about ten miles ahead of us at their encampment from what they Could observe had taken 50 Beavers as these fellows by going a head will Secure the Beaver I assembled the Freemen & Selected 15 with orders to proceed to the Sources of this River & Secure all they Could this may be means of Sending . . . them off Sooner than they probably intend at all events we must endeavour to annoy them as much as we possibly Can.

The main camp was taken up beyond the American camp, but Jedediah moved up in turn and the two parties spent the night in close proximity. On the seventeenth Jedediah camped three miles ahead, but Ogden observed with satisfaction, "this will avail them naught as independent of our party we have traps 12 Miles a head."

Next day it developed that the route to the Bear by way of the sources of the Blackfoot was still snowbound. Reluctantly Ogden retraced his steps a distance, then swung west to the Portneuf. "The Americans," he noted, "have also been obliged to retrace back their Steps & will I presume follow us altho' they will nearly double their distance."

The seeming familiarity of Jedediah's party with the course of the Blackfoot, and their choice of it as a route to the Bear, may have an important bearing on how his party had reached the Snake the previous fall. If he knew nothing of the geography of the interior basin, the course he chose in working back toward Fitzpatrick is at least surprising. There is the question, too, of what he did to recover the furs left in cache the previous fall. Either the two deposits Ross heard about were along the present line of travel, or one of them was far to the east, perhaps as far as the Sweetwater.[9] It is certain that the caches were not along the trail via the forks of the Snake and Jackson Hole, for no effort was made this year to revisit that country.

By April 20 Ogden was on the upper Portneuf, his position vis-à-vis Jedediah irritatingly the same, "the Americans . . . not far a head Buffalo very Scarce & many in the Camp Complaining of Starvation." From the quantity of snow this quarter had had a severe winter, but frogs could be heard croaking—"this then may be Called Spring." Ogden was hopeful of an improvement in his returns when he should reach the Bear, but how vexing to have the Americans always out ahead: "some of the trappers keep in Company with them so as to annoy them & with the hopes they will Steer another Course."

On the twenty-third another in the long succession of calamities befell the party when twenty horses were run off by the Blackfeet. These belonged, Ogden observed, "to three men Old Pierre, Goddin & Geaudreau altho' the first lost everything he had last Summer nearly on the Same Spot[10] & the last two Suffered this Winter Still they allow their horses full liberty all night & the Consequence they are this day at the mercy of Canadians

& Iroquois & on that account & the loss they will Sustain in their hunts I feel for them." Six men, started in pursuit, came back with only one animal, the raiders having killed six and got off with the rest.

For a few hours the Snake Expedition came to another of its full stops, as the freemen came forward and announced their determination of abandoning the hunt—"to what end do we labour and toil, we are now only at the commencement of the season and already one Man has been killed, and one half of our horses have been stolen." But threats and promises had their effect, Ogden got the brigade moving again, and on the afternoon of April 26 they reached the banks of that large river "which the Deceased Michel Bourdon named Bear river from the great number of those animals on its borders." Thus Kittson; Ogden adds, "the upper part has been trapped twice but the lower part never has been it . . . was supposed to be the Rio Colorado & even now Said to be a Fork of the same as our route is to follow it we shall be enabled to ascertain this point."

From October through April the British brigade leaders have kept tally on Jedediah Smith for us, but now the parting of the ways has come. Kittson does us a last service in saying as he arrives at the Bear, "the Americans have gone upwards and we are to follow it downwards in order to find where it runs to." This information cannot be taken at full value; although Jedediah started up the river, he soon came back down it. For, through Indian information or direct observation, he discovered what Ogden himself was about to learn. Other Americans the previous fall had penetrated to the Bear; they had wintered on its banks, and even now were trapping the country below. Jedediah could hardly doubt that these were Ashley men, and it was his business to seek them out.

Among the obscurities that cloak the history of the fur trade in this decade, fewer have been more difficult to penetrate than the identity and experiences of the trappers who wintered on the Bear. No substantial narrative by any of the party has ever come to light, and only by bits and pieces has its history been put together. On the basis of no facts whatever, William L. Sublette has usually been identified as its leader. The Bear River company was the right wing of Ashley and Henry's two-pronged assault on the Rockies, and rather than William L. Sublette, its head was Captain John H. Weber. More or less independent groups of free trappers had attached themselves to the party along the way —most notably, one headed by Johnson Gardner—but this was the spearhead Major Henry had started up the Big Horn toward the mountains in the fall of 1823, and which cut loose from its base when Henry abandoned his fort on the Big Horn. The names of a very few of those who composed the company are known—Weber himself, Daniel Potts, Jim Bridger. Two others are accounted for by the laconic casualty lists of the fur trade, one of which tells us that in 1824 "Thomas, a half breed, was killed by Williams, on the waters of Bear river, west of the mountains." [11] Weber's party crossed over into the valley of the Bear probably by way of Blacks Fork, for Daniel Potts says that after passing from the Green River Valley in a southwesterly direction they "had very good travelling over an inconsiderable ridge" and "fell on a considerable river, called the Bear River," on which stream, its tributaries and the adjacent country they took beaver with great success from "the autumn of 1824." [12]

How many men composed Weber's party has been left for the British records to state, though on the authority of Indian information, which may explain why the number is given as both twenty-five and fifty men.[13] This party has been chiefly celebrated for Jim Bridger's discovery of Great Salt Lake, but its importance in the history of the fur trade comes from its head-on collision with Ogden.

That there were more Americans in the region who had reached his trapping grounds before him Ogden did not discover for days. On May 4 he fell in with a party of Snakes, who "appeared very doubtful of us & we so equally in regard to them." This mistrust was well founded, for these were Snakes of the band that had stripped Ross's Iroquois the previous year, and had been up to worse mischief since.[14] From them Ogden learned that a party of Americans had wintered near by and were gone in the direction he had intended taking—"if this be true which I have no reason to doubt it will be a fatal blow to our expectations." That was merely the two-way stretch of Ogden's pessimism, and he had no thought of turning back, but the remark was sound prophecy.

The Hudson's Bay party was now fairly in Cache Valley. Beaver sign was abundant, but it could be assumed that the Americans had cleared off all the streams, as high up the canyons as the snow had permitted. Since the Americans had gone down Bear River into the valley of the Great Salt Lake, the British continued up the south end of Cache Valley, trapping with encouraging success its several small creeks. On May 16 Ogden crossed the divide at the head of the long valley, now farther south than British traders had ever been, and descended into the beautiful mountain basin which now bears Ogden's name. Here, over the next six days, Ogden averaged better than eighty skins a day, which was the kind of trapping that had given the Snake Country its reputation; moreover, the beaver were still in prime condition.

On Sunday morning, May 22, as Ogden was breaking camp, one of his trappers rode up. With him were two of the freemen who had deserted Michel Bourdon in 1822. They had an amazing story. They were associated with a party of American trappers which had penetrated to this point by a long journey from New Mexico. Some thirty men made up the party, which was led by two French-Canadians, Provost and LeClerc. They had spent the winter in this quarter, but had met with little success. Ogden was informed that he was a mere fifteen days' march from Taos, the "Spanish Village," and he got an alarming picture of a rival operation supplied by wagons. (The wagons, of course, went only as far as the New Mexican settlements; from there supplies had to be packed into the mountains in the usual fashion.) The whole country was overrun with beaver hunters, for less than three weeks back Ogden had crossed the trail of one party on Bear River, and here was another which knew nothing of the first. Ogden also learned that he was now on the lands of the "Utas," a tribe represented as friendly to the whites; some of these Indians accompanied Provost's men, so decorated with crosses that the British were disposed to regard them as Christians.[15]

But it was the story of the deserters that interested Ogden most. As his party began the slow six-mile journey over the next divide south and on down to the new camp in the canyon of the Weber, he jogged along listening to the two men. Of their story he wrote little enough in his journal, merely that "of the 14 who deserted 6 are dead & the remainder with the Spaniards at St. Louis & Missouri," and that the party to which they now belonged "had a battle last fall with the Snakes & 7 of the [Americans] & one of our deserters Patrick O'Connor were killed & only one Snake fell." These shorthand notes we must elaborate, for deserters and their leader alike have become important to this narrative.

Etienne Provost is a figure in the history of the American fur trade badly in need of clarification. Few men who reached the mountains in this decade have been more misunderstood. Provost has been regarded as an Ashley man, even as leader of the party which was headed by Weber; there has been wide speculation that it was he rather than Jedediah Smith who led the vanguard of the American trappers through South Pass; and he and Ashley are often said to have broken in 1826—but an association between them never existed. Provost entered the mountains as an independent, from a different direction entirely; and already, in May 1825, he had made a notable contribution to mountain history.

Provost became a butterball of a man, and even in 1825 he may comfortably have filled his buckskins. His early life is obscure. Born in Canada about 1782, by 1815 he had removed to St. Louis, for he was one of the party Chouteau and De Mun took to the upper Arkansas that year. Two years on the Arkansas and South Platte made a mountain man of him, and two months in jail in Santa Fe put a high gloss on the finished product, for like the rest of the Chouteau-De Mun party he was rounded up by Spanish soldiery as a trespasser on the soil of His Most Christian Majesty. Chouteau and De Mun got back to St. Louis in

September 1817 to make loud complaint to their government, and Etienne Provost's "X" affixed to this bootless document is our first evidence that the fur trade had become his life.[16]

Having thrust his head into view in this single instance, Provost, turtlelike, drew it back into the horny shell of his anonymity, not to emerge for another five years. But after William Becknell got back from Santa Fe in February 1822, every American who had ever been in that country, in jail or out, made haste to return. Provost must have been one of the earliest, for he was back from Santa Fe by August 1, 1823, when we find Benjamin O'Fallon writing the governor of New Mexico that he had been informed "by Mess[rs]. Provot, Leclere, and several other Americans," of the governor's wish to make peace with the Pawnees. O'Fallon's letter is the more enlightening in that on the same day he wrote it he was interesting himself in the straits of the Hudson's Bay Company's forlorn "Iroquois." [17]

Not realizing how sad a fiasco the Arikara campaign was going to be, nothing to be done this year or the next to recover their captured women and children, the Iroquois waited patiently at the fort through August 1823 for some fortunate turn of events. Instead they became the victims of a prevailing epidemic. Several died, and most of the rest were glad to join Provost and LeClerc when the partners arrived back at the fort with a new outfit. The story of these deserters was remarkable enough already; with their return to the mountains in Provost's company it becomes truly extraordinary. Consider their three-year odyssey: Into the Snake Country with Bourdon, east across the continental divide on their own, down to the American military frontier, back to the mountains on the Santa Fe Trail (a course nearly at right angles to that on which they had left the mountains), and from Santa Fe all the way back to the Snake Country—a three-year wandering during which they fought with Blackfeet, Crows, Cheyennes and Snakes, lost furs, horses and women, and now had encountered their own people again. Had one of these men kept a journal of his experiences, it would be one of the immortal narratives of Western history.

As much can be said for Etienne Provost. A journal kept during these years would be a document beyond price. For lack of such a record, not even the first name of his partner can be stated with any confidence. So many LeClairs, LeCleres and LeClercs floated around in the fur trade that identification of any one of them at a given time or place is usually an act of faith.[18] Provost seems to have been the dominant personality in the partnership, but it could be that LeClerc was the stabilizing force in it, for with LeClerc's disappearance from the record in 1825 Etienne Provost becomes just another mountain man.

The partners were back in New Mexico by the fall of 1823, and that winter they launched their own trapping operation northwest from Taos into the Colorado Rockies.[19] That the northern villages of New Mexico were excellent bases from which to trap the southern Rockies occurred to many others, and some famous reputations were about to be made, but none got off to so brilliant a start as Provost and LeClerc. How far north and west the partners penetrated in 1823-1824 is not known, but next year they ranged over into the Green River country below the Uinta Mountains. During the early summer of 1824 while Jedediah Smith was trapping the upper valley of the Green, the two French-Canadians were just across the mountains south of him. That fall, while Jedediah was seeking out the British in the Snake Country, Etienne Provost was pushing west up the Strawberry River and on over the rim of the Great Basin to the beautiful river that now bears his name.[20] By late fall he had got as far as the valley of the Great Salt Lake itself—and here he was called on to pay the blood debt to the Snakes which had accrued from the misadventures of Alexander Ross and his Iroquois.

The set-to was less battle than massacre. As the tale went, Provost fell in with a Snake chief, Bad Gocha, bad left-handed one, while on "a stream flowing into the Big Lake" (apparently the Jordan). The chief invited the whites to smoke with him, but insisted that it was contrary to his medicine to have any metallic object near while smoking. Provost set aside his arms, and allowed his men to follow his example, when the Indians fell on the whites with knives concealed under their robes. Provost managed to extricate himself, and with three or four others succeeded in escaping, but the rest were slaughtered.[21] Provost must have fled back across the Wasatch Mountains to join

LeClerc in the Uinta Basin. Resupplied and reinforced, perhaps convoyed by friendly Utes, in the spring of 1825 he returned to the Great Basin. Instead of going down the Provo, this time he turned down the Weber. He had not yet reached the mouth of that canyon nor discovered that other Americans were in the country when he fell in with Ogden.[22]

So then, on the morning of the twenty-third Provost rode into Ogden's camp. His was a curious party, for Kittson says that it included "3 Canadians, a Russian, and an old Spaniard"—the mention of the Russian especially provocative. The meeting of the two parties cannot have been cordial, for rivalry over furs quite aside, the Americans blamed the British for provoking the Snakes to the massacre of the previous fall; in fact, Ogden observed, the Americans "would most willingly shoot us if they dared." [23]

The arrival of Provost at Ogden's camp subsided into the character of a minor event when, late in the afternoon, something very like a parade, complete with flying colors, emerged from the canyon below. The marchers consisted of 14 of Ogden's absent trappers and some 25 Americans. The column halted a hundred yards from Ogden's camp for its leader to bawl out to the British trappers the news that they were now in that land of liberty, the United States territory. Indebted or engaged, they were all of them free. Showing the uses of liberty, the American announced that the British trappers could sell him their beaver for $3.50 a pound, and buy goods from him cheap in proportion.

These were Americans from the party that had wintered in Cache Valley; they are described as being under "different heads," which means that the majority were free trappers, but the leading spirit among them was Johnson Gardner. Since Weber is not mentioned, probably he remained in his camp on the river below. It appears that Jedediah by now had reached Weber's camp, along with William L. Sublette and the other five of the winter adventurers; they had not cared to join in baiting John Bull, but their tales of a British column moving through this country flaunting a scarlet banner had helped to arouse Weber's party.[24] Bound to avenge this insult to national honor, their patriotism the more inflamed by news of the mounting British beaver catch, the American trappers had come up the river to deal with the intruders.

The sun had sunk below the line of the mountains, and nothing more happened this night. Ogden suspected that his freemen "in lieu of Seeking Beaver have been with the Americans no doubt plotting," and Kittson says that "Strick watch" was set, but it was not until morning that Gardner made his play. He came then to Ogden's lodge to demand whether the Britisher knew in whose country he was. Ogden replied that he did not; it had not been determined between Great Britain and the United States to whom this region belonged. (Ogden and Gardner alike supposed themselves still in Oregon; both were now south of 42° and therefore on Mexican soil.) Unblushingly Gardner declared that the country had been ceded to the Americans; as Ogden had no license to trade or trap on American soil, he must get out. Ogden had not been born the day before, and he answered that when he received orders from his own government to withdraw, he would obey. "Remain at your peril!" Gardner said ominously, and left the tent.

Ogden followed the man outside and saw him enter the lodge of John Grey, a half-Iroquois, half-American whom Alexander Ross had described the year before as "a turbulent blackguard, a damned rascal," but who from this time would be reputed among the bravest and most spirited of mountain men. In no mood to permit Gardner to intrigue among his trappers, Ogden strode into Grey's lodge only to have the Iroquois turn on him: "I must tell you, sir, that all the Iroquois as well as myself have long wished for an opportunity to join the Americans. If we did not sooner it was owing to our bad luck in not meeting with them, but now we go and all you can say cannot prevent us!"

Gardner interposed virtuously, "You have had these men already too long in your service and have most shamefully imposed on them, treating them as *slaves*, selling them goods at high prices and giving them nothing for their skins," and Grey picked the words up passionately: "That is true! The gentlemen in the Columbia are the greatest villains in the world, and if they were here this day I would shoot them. As for you, sir, you have dealt fair with me and with us all, but go we will. We are now in a free country and have friends here to support us, and if every man in the camp does not leave you, they do not seek their own interest!" He shouted orders to his partners to raise camp, and all the Iroquois were instantly in commotion.

As the lodges began to fall around him, Ogden ran to lay hands on the property of men still absent from the camp while Kittson raced up to seize the horses previously lent to the Iroquois. The moment was critical, for the Americans, headed by Gardner and accompanied by two of the deserters of 1822, advanced with guns cocked to support all who might be inclined to desert. Ogden paid them no attention, determined not to be pillaged of his horses and calling for the assistance of two *engagés*. Before so bold a front Americans and Iroquois contented themselves with heaping insult and obscenity on the British. The Iroquois, however, could not be prevented from conveying their furs to the American camp: "we were overpowered by numbers & these Villains 11 in number with Duford, Perrault and Kanota escaped with their Furs in fact some of them had conveyed theirs in the night to the American Camp." Nor was this the end of the matter, for two of the Company's freemen, Alex Carson and Joseph Annance, paid their debts and left in the wake of the Iroquois.

The Americans moved off about half a mile and encamped. After a while Carson came back to warn Ogden that the Americans and Iroquois were talking of coming on the morrow to pillage him. Ogden set double watch through the night and at daybreak on the twenty-fifth gave orders to raise camp. Scarcely had his men begun to load their horses than the Americans and Iroquois rode up. Finding the British prepared, as Ogden thought, they kept their peace, but three more of Ogden's freemen came forward to announce their intention of joining the Americans.

I endeavoured to reason with Mr. Montour [Ogden says] but all in vain, the reasons he gave for his villany were the Company turned me out of doors they have £ 260 of my money in their hands which they intend to defraud me of as they have refused to give me interest for [it] but they may keep it now for my debt & Prudhoms. which we have Contracted in the Columbia as for Clement he had a Balce. in the Compys. Book; go we will where we shall be paid for our Furs & not be imposed & cheated as we are in the Columbia.

[The three men] were immediately Surrounded by the Americans who assisted them in loading & like all Villains appeared to exult in their Villany we then Started but on my mounting my Horse Gardner Came forward & Said you will See us shortly not only in the Columbia but at the Flat Heads & Cootanies as we are determined you Shall no longer remain in our Territory, to this I made answer when we Should receive orders from our Government to leave the Columbia we would but Not before to this he replied our Troops will make you this Fall we then parted.[25]

Back the British column went, back over the route they had taken outbound with such high hopes. "I kept behind all day through Mr. Ogdens orders," Kittson remarks, "fearing that more would leave us on the road." And Ogden after encamping glooms to his journal:

Here I am . . . Surrounded on all Sides by enemies & our expectations & hopes blasted for returns this year, to remain in this quarter any longer it would merely be to trap Beaver for the Americans for I Seriously apprehend there are Still more of the Trappers who would Willingly join them indeed the tempting offers made them independant the low price they Sell their goods are too great for them to resist & altho' I represented to them all these offers were held out to them as so many baits Still it is without effect.

Ogden himself was impressed with the arithmetic. The Americans would give for beaver eight times the Company price.

The headlong flight north continued. On May 29 three more men deserted, leaving behind "Women, Children, Horses, Traps & Furs so greatly are they prepossessed in favor of the Americans." Including those who directly deserted his party and those out trapping who did not rejoin him, Ogden had lost twenty-three men, half of all the freemen with whom he had set out in December. With them had gone no less than seven hundred skins, to say nothing of his prospects.[26] Simpson would not like this.

The governor might like it still less that Ogden had not followed the return route prescribed for him. He was to have turned west toward the Pacific at about the point of his farthest south; all Simpson's plans had been predicated on his completing his fall hunt at Fort George. This plan Ogden thought practicable; his men had informed him of a great lake just west of the chain of valleys through which he had traveled, a lake as large as Lake Winnipeg which might extend a hundred miles west: no doubt this was the rumored lake at the head of the Umpqua. But to have gone the route Simpson directed would have opened a road to Fort George, and Ogden was prepared to believe that the mere appearance of the Americans on the Columbia might bring the whole structure of the Company crashing down. Simpson had better like it that Ogden was making straight for the post from which he had started. For, like it or not, this was all that was possible: "nearly one half of the Trappers are determined to return to Fort des Prairies . . . I must bend & Submit to the will of the party."

Ogden reached the Snake June 5, crossed, and was about to make for the Salmon when he learned that the Flathead camp was in the vicinity of the forks of the Snake. At the news his men brightened, and announced their willingness to change their course for Henrys Fork. Ogden reached the Flathead camp June 15, and "many wonderful accounts do they give of the Americans which they have received from the Peagans." At least the Flatheads were not yet in contact with the Americans. But within the week reports were heard of five lodges of Americans, from thirty to forty men, coming down the Snake.[27] Even as rumor this was enough to put Ogden into a state: "knowing too well from dear bought experience the loss I should sustain if the Freemen were once more to meet with them and the tempting offers they would make the Flatheads I resolved on leaving."

Ogden's adventures through the rest of the summer cannot be described in detail. Kittson got his spring hunt to Flathead Post under convoy by the Flatheads, and Ogden took a few more beaver on the Missouri and Clarks Fork; finally he got a skeleton party to Fort Nez Perces in November. His year's returns amounted to 3,188 "made beaver" (large skins or their equivalent),[28] but this had been a disastrous expedition. Ogden would not venture beyond the limits of the Snake Country for four years; there was the gravest doubt whether a British expedition could even be held together in the same country with the Americans. If the Snake Country was converted into the fur desert Simpson had contemplated, it now seemed likely that the Americans would do the job.

8. *RENDEZVOUS: 1825*

At what time Fitzpatrick's letter announcing his arrival from the mountains reached Ashley in St. Louis is not known exactly, but it was by the third week of September 1824. On the twenty-fourth of that month Ashley obtained a new license to trade with the Indians, and the information in the license could have been based only on advices from Jedediah's clerk.

This document authorized Ashley to trade with "a band of the Snake Indians, West of the Rocky Mountains, at the junction of two large rivers, supposed to be branches of the Buonaventura and the Colerado of the West, within the territory of the United States."[1] The reference obviously—even frivolously—is to the Snakes who had made free with Fitzpatrick's horses; the geography is confused but may have had reference to the junction of the Green and the Big Sandy. That Indians were mentioned in the license illustrates how far the laws of the United States lagged behind reality; the delusion persisted that fur trade and Indian trade were still one and the same, and as late as May of this year Congress had passed a law the intent of which was to force white traders to locate at designated points for trade with specific tribes and bands. (That was one of the remoter consequences of the public row which had followed the Arikara campaign.) It was another half dozen years before the United States government began to wake up to the fact that it was "altogether by hunting" that so much beaver was brought down out of the Rockies.[2] There were other interesting features to this license. It was issued to "William H. Ashley," nothing said about Henry. It was for three years. And the capital employed was a respectable $8,000.

Something of Fitzpatrick's letter also seeped out to begin a slow change in the nation's concepts of the West. The St. Louis press credited Andrew Henry with the news, but there is no doubt where Henry's information came from: "we learn that his party have discovered a passage by which loaded wagons can at this time reach the navigable waters of the Columbia River. This route lies South of the one explored by Lewis and Clarke, and is inhabited by Indians friendly to us." These remarks were picked up by papers all over the country, including the universally read *Niles' Register*. Here is the dawn of South Pass on the American consciousness, and two years would not pass before the fact was blazing in the West with noonday brilliance.[3]

That Henry should leave the stage of history honored only as a prophet is sad. He retired to a frustrated end in Washington County, dying in 1833 to have it said of him that he was his own worst enemy.[4] This end to his bid for wealth and public esteem is the more melancholy in that up to the time of Ashley's departure for the mountains in November, the General clung to the hope that Henry would come along.

Once his outfit was completed, Ashley wasted no time getting off to the frontier. On October 21 the sutler at Fort Atkinson noted in his diary that Ashley had arrived with a party of "Trappers and hunters, destined for Spanish Country," and five days later he had news in counterpoint, "Fitspatrick & party have come in & brot Beaver."[5] So Fitzpatrick's trip back to Independence Rock to retrieve his cache had ended well; the furs were safe. Nevertheless a letter Ashley wrote from Fort Atkinson on October 29 to his friend Dr. William Carr Lane had a gloomy tone. Since his arrival at the fort, he said, he had remained

> . . . with hopes of Maj. Henry's Joining me, and that a difference between the Agents of the U S at this post, and the Pawney Indians (out of which serious consequences may result) would be amicably settled. These are matters of much importance to me, but there is little, or no probability of my wishes in either case being realized I shall therefore have to accompany my party of Mountaineers to their place of destination, and be the first to encounter the hostile disposition of those savages.[6]

The difficulty to which Ashley alluded had arisen out of an offense committed by the Pawnees; Major O'Fallon always took a very high tone in such matters, and it was not until November that the affair was smoothed over.[7] By then the General had set out for the mountains.

The break with the traditional mode of conducting a fur-trading operation in the mountains was now all but complete. Ashley had not even used boats to get his outfit to Fort Atkinson. Pack mules and horses served from the time he left the settlements. There was plenty of precedent for this in the operations of traders on the Santa Fe Trail, who had had to use wagons and pack animals or carry their goods on their own backs. The efficiency of water-borne operations was a memory that died hard, and the example set by Jedediah Smith the year before, and by Fitzpatrick going and coming in the valley of the Platte this year, was too new for Ashley to have perfect faith in it.

The General got off to the mountains on November 3, 1824, and two days later overtook his party, some twenty-five in number, which had started off in advance with fifty pack horses, "a wagon & team, &c." [8] The mention of the wagon is tantalizing, for so far as known no wheeled vehicles had ever set out for the Rockies in these latitudes, but Ashley has nothing more to say of it. Neither did he have much to say about the men who composed his company, for Ashley like most other men of affairs before and since his time tended to view the world from the elevation of the first person perpendicular. All the same, this party was impressive. Fitzpatrick was going back to the mountains again, and Jim Clyman. Zacharias Ham, Ashley seems to have regarded as of equal caliber with Fitzpatrick and Clyman.[9] Possibly though not certainly the company included an Irishman going to the mountains as one of the earliest "lungers"—a young man named Robert Campbell of whom much was to be heard in the West. Most joyfully a member of the party was James P. Beckwourth, "the gaudy liar." To be a gifted liar was as much a part of mountain honor as hard drinking or straight shooting. Embroider your adventures, convert to your uses any handy odyssey, and spin it all out in the firelight, the only sin the sin of being dull. Jim Beckwourth's *Life and Adventures* has this immortality: it is an approximation of what was heard around the campfires in the West when the stars burned bright and fat cow sizzled over the coals. The book had to be lived before it could be written, and its writing was still thirty years in the future when Jim Beckwourth set out for the mountains. Son of a Missouri planter and a slave woman, as a boy Jim had been apprenticed as a blacksmith, and it was evidently in this capacity that he engaged with Ashley.[10]

Most of the way to the mountains Ashley and his men had a hard time of it. The General left Fort Atkinson under the impression that he could get sufficient provisions at the Pawnee villages to subsist his party until he reached the buffalo country, but the Pawnees had departed for their wintering grounds. Snowstorms howled down on the party, high winds and intense cold, and a few miles' travel a day became a major achievement. A dismal passage, this, as Jim Beckwourth remembered—"No jokes, no fire-side stories, no fun; each man rose in the morning with the gloom of the preceding night filling his mind; we built our fires and partook of our scanty repast without saying a word." Their allowance was half a pint of flour a day per man, made into a kind of gruel. With the ground covered two feet deep with snow, the horses had to be subsisted on the bark of the round-leaf cottonwood, and presently the men were reduced to living on the flesh of the horses that died.

In this fashion they traveled west to the Loup Fork of the Platte and some distance up that stream, essentially the same trail Stephen Long's expedition had traveled to the Rockies four summers before, and one the Mormons would beat into a road a few decades later. Finally the beleaguered company turned south to the Platte, and with the change in course their luck changed; they arrived on the banks of the river November 22 to find game in abundance and rushes on which their starved horses fed with relish.

On December 3, a hundred miles above, Ashley fell in with the Grand Pawnees, en route to winter on the Arkansas. The going would be harder from here on, the Pawnees said. Ashley would find little fuel or food for his horses except at the forks of the Platte; they urged him to take up winter quarters at the forks, saying that he would endanger the lives of his whole company if he attempted to advance farther before spring. The weather was, in fact, extremely cold, accompanied by frequent light snows. Ashley went up the river another eight miles, and, falling in with the Pawnee Loups, traveled with them the rest of the way to the forks, their usual wintering place. His men, Ashley says,

> . . . had undergone an intense suffering from the inclemency of the weather, which also bore so severely on the horses as to cause the death of many of them. This, together with a desire to purchase a few horses from the Loups and to prepare my party for the privations which we had reason to anticipate in travelling the next two hundred miles, (described as being almost wholly destitute of wood) induced me to remain at the Forks until the 23d December, the greater part of which time, we were favoured with fine weather, and notwithstanding the uplands were still covered with from 18 to 24 inches of snow, the Valleys were generally bare and afforded a good range for my horses, furnishing plenty of dry grass and some small rushes, from the use of which they daily increased in strength and spirits.

The Loups were more than generous; notwithstanding their own severe losses they traded to Ashley twenty-three horses, some buffalo robes and dried meat, putting him in shape to go on. He would have preferred the direct route up the North Platte, but since the South Platte was said to afford more wood, he set out up that stream. The weather was fine, the valleys covered with buffalo, and everything 'seemed to promise a safe and speedy movement to the first grove of timber on my route, supposed to be about ten days march."

The Loup Pawnees, anxious to establish friendly relations with the Arapahoes and Kiowas, sent five men with Ashley to seek them out. There was now danger from war parties, and Ashley moved carefully, looking to the security of his camp. The day after Christmas a blizzard blew up which cost him four horses and left the ground so deeply blanketed with snow that it was only by courtesy of the buffalo moving down the river that Ashley could proceed; "the paths of these animals were beat on either side of the river and afforded an easy passage to our horses." On January 1, 1825, about the time Jedediah Smith's party far to the north and west was starting up the Bitterroot, Ashley and his men reached a grove of cottonwood "of the sweet bark kind, suitable for horse food, situated on an Island, offering among other conveniences, a good situation for defence." Here Ashley thought it expedient to recruit his horses, so the Loup delegation left; they dried a few pounds of meat, and with bundles of wood tied to their backs set out for the Arkansas.

Ashley remarks:

Being informed by the Pawneys that one hundred of my old enemies (the Arikara warriors) were encamped with the Arkansas Indians, and my situation independent of that circumstance, being rendered more vulnerable by the departure of the Indians who had just left us, I was obliged to increase my guard from eight to sixteen men; this was much the most severe duty my men had to perform, but they did it with alacrity and cheerfulness, as well as all other services required at their hands; indeed such was their pride and ambition in the discharge of their duties, that their privations in the end became sources of amusement to them.

Ten days on the island recruited the horses considerably, and the party began moving again. The going was hard, for the weather continued extremely cold, but each day a small supply of driftwood and willow brush was found, sufficient for fuel.

Now a faint blue mass rose above the horizon. They were in sight of the Rocky Mountains, and by February 4 Ashley reached their base. He encamped on a small branch of the South Platte, perhaps the Cache la Poudre, in a thick grove of cottonwood and willows, and there he remained for three weeks, the world to the limits of vision "one mass of snow and ice." The prospect of getting across the mountains was not encouraging, but as Ashley's business "required a violent effort . . . things were made ready, and on the 26th we commenced the doubtful undertaking."

It has been said that Ashley was the first white man to undertake the crossing of the Front Range in this latitude. Very likely Chouteau and De Mun preceded him in 1816-1817, since their men penetrated to the Park at the head of the North Platte and gave it a name which long endured, "The Bull Pen." [11] The earlier travelers, however, undoubtedly crossed the mountains at a more clement season. Ashley's own passage across the first range, "exceedingly difficult and dangerous," required three days, but the country relented as he advanced, the valleys and south sides of the hills but partially covered with snow; "the latter already presented in a slight degree the verdure of spring, while the former were filled with numerous herds of buffaloe, deer, and antelope." He had reached the Laramie plains. All the cottonwood he saw was the narrow-leaf or bitter variety horses could not eat, and his animals had to subsist "upon a very small allowance of grass, and this, too, (with the exception of a very inconsiderable proportion) entirely dry and in appearance destitute of all nutriment." But Ashley was discovering a key fact about the western ranges: "my horses retained their strength and spirits in a remarkable degree."

After an unsuccessful effort to cross the Medicine Bow Mountains (the snow in places five feet deep), the party moved north along the eastern base of the range looking for a likely pass. This country was something of a paradise, even in mid-March:

> I was delighted with the variegated scenery presented by the valleys and mountains, which were enlivened by innumerable herds of Buffaloe, Antelope, and Mountain sheep grazing on them and what added no small degree of interest to the whole scene, were the many small streams issuing from the mountains, bordered with a thin growth of small willows, and richly stocked with Beaver.

Ashley slowed his pace to five or six miles a day, giving his men a chance to clean out the beaver.

Thus far on his journey we have followed Ashley through a narrative he wrote in December 1825 for General Atkinson, but from here on an important new Ashley diary amplifies the record.[12] By March 23 he had reached the pass between the Medicine Bow Range and Elk Mountain, promising enough to justify another attempt to turn west. Progress was slow, but on the afternoon of March 25 Ashley emerged into "a beautiful vallie of a sercular form"—the valley of the North Platte. As March ran out, he moved on to the continental divide itself. He was well south of South Pass, south even of the modern railroad and highway through the Great Divide Basin. The rather indeterminate depression by which he passed from Atlantic drainage is today known as Bridgers Pass, but might better bear Ashley's name, for he is the first white man of record to have used it.

On April 1 the Wind River Mountains were glimpsed far to the northwest, but Clyman and Fitzpatrick had never seen the range from this angle and were not sure of their whereabouts. The horses were much reduced by fatigue and hunger, and Ashley was anxious to find the river of which he was in search. Hoping to orient himself, on April 5 with a few of the men he climbed North Pilot Butte but gained no information that did him any good, and he attracted the attention of Crow horse thieves, who followed him back to camp and made off with seventeen of his best horses. This mishap reduced him to a dreadful condition, for he was obliged to burden his men with the packs of the stolen horses while with more courage than discretion he and one other pursued the fugitives. Two of the stolen animals were recovered but that was not saying much: they had given out and the Crows had abandoned them.

Artfully the Crows left behind a Snake arrowhead, which with "other appearances," as Ashley says, persuaded him that the miscreants were Snakes. On the eighth he dispatched nine men in further pursuit of the thieves, and took the rest of the company on. It was April 14, and he had reached the Dry Sandy when his posse rejoined him. "The men who went after the horses," Ashley remarks, "followed them to Sweetwater & found that they had been taken by a party of Crows, so finally made their escape with Them." At least he now knew where he was. Wind River Mountains, Sweetwater, valley of the Green, the whole geography fell into place, and on April 19 he reached "the Shetskedee."

Far to the south, forty to fifty miles, the jagged crest of a mountain range lifted along the sky, the snowy heights glinting through the blue distances. Small wonder Jedediah Smith had ridden off in that direction the year before; Ashley himself responded to the lure. Moreover, he was anxious to learn how the Shetskedee fitted into the geography of the West. Small though his party was, he divided it into four detachments, three to trap the country while he took the fourth on a voyage of discovery.

The arrangements he made before starting initiated the first great rendezvous of the fur trade.

The following [Ashley writes in his diary] are the directions given to Mrs. Ham & Clyman who conduct Each a party, one of six; The other of five men—To wit That I will transport the goods and extra baggage down the river to some conspicuous point not less than 40 or 50 miles from this place should the river not pass will Make choice of the Entrance of some river that may Enter on the West side of the Shetskedee for a deposite should there be any such River, should the mountains through wich the river firt [?] passes be a less distance than was immagined, the deposite will be made on or near the river a short distance above the mountain at some suitable place —The place of deposite as aforesaid, will be The place of rendavoze for all our parties on or before the 10th July next & that the places may be known—Trees will be pealed standing the most conspicuous near the Junction of the rivers or above the mountains as the case may be—. Should such point be without timber I will raise a mound of Earth five feet high or set up rocks the top of which will be made red with vermillion thirty feet distant from the same—and one foot below the surface of the earth a northwest direction will be deposited a letter communicating to the party any thing that I may deem necessary—Mrs C. & H will Each at a proper time apoint Each a man of their party to take charge of their business should by axident any thing occur to make it necessary.—The men so appointed will be informed of my arrangements, will, with their party proceed accordingly in the most carefull & best manner for my intrst—copies of the foregoing directions were delivered to Messrs Ham Cly. & Fitzpatrick, our boat launched and at 3 ock P. M. The parties started. Clyman with six men to the sources of the Shetskadee Ham—Westerly to a mountanous country That lay in that direction Fitzpatrick with 6 men southwardly—& myself with 7 men Embarked on board the boat with all my goods and the extra baggage of the men. . . .

By the disposition Ashley made of his men, Clyman was to return to the tributaries of the Green he had trapped the previous year; Ham was to go directly west (and thus doubtless he fell upon Hams Fork, which still bears his name); and Fitzpatrick was to go south and ascertain whether there was a stream running immediately at the base of the Uinta Mountains. (There was: Henrys Fork. That Fitzpatrick knew nothing of its existence is good evidence that Jedediah Smith's spring hunt of 1824 had taken him only as far south as Blacks Fork.)

Before following Ashley down the Green, it is expedient to take a look at the fabled geography of this wilderness—a geography Ashley and his men would be hard put to reduce to reality.

John King Robinson's *Map of Mexico, Louisiana, & the Missouri Territory &c*, published in Philadelphia in 1819, sums up the state of knowledge down to Ashley's time. This map, which borrowed liberally from Pike and Humboldt, as also from William Clark's map of 1814, had as its most prominent feature west of the mountains a large lake, the Laguna de Timpanogos (misspelled by Robinson *Tinpanogos*), from the southwestern extremity of which a river of the same name flowed to the Bay of San Francisco. Northwest of the Laguna de Timpanogos was a high range of mountains, on the western slope of which rose a tributary of the Columbia, the Multnomah, which Lewis and Clark had conceived as paralleling the course of the Snake far to the south and east. South of the Timpanogos River, and almost exactly paralleling it was a Rio de Sta. Buenaventura which headed with the Snake, the Big Horn, the Arkansas and the Rio Grande; this mighty river flowed some distance southwest into a lake Robinson did not name but which other mapmakers called the Buenaventura or the Salado, and from that lake the Buenaventura continued southwest to reach the Pacific south of Monterey.

To a degree this information reflected actual exploration—the journey the Franciscan friars Escalante and Domínguez had made from Santa Fe to the Green River and the Great Basin in the summer and fall of 1776. The friars had got as far north and west as Utah Valley before turning south through the heart of Utah; the lake they called the Timpanogos was Utah Lake; but the cartographers had joined to this body of water the rumor of Great Salt Lake to the north, and for good measure had given the combined lake an outlet to the sea. Again, their Buenaventura was a combined concept of Green River and the Sevier, both of which the friars crossed in their travels. The lake—Buenaventura or Salado, whatever it might be called—had a factual basis in Sevier Lake though the further course of the Buenaventura to the sea was altogether fabulous.[13] To all the fables there was an admixture of fact, and Ashley this spring, and Jedediah Smith for three years to come, was going to have a rough time sorting out verifiable truth from fantasy. What Ashley was immediately anxious to establish was whether the Shetskedee was the Buenaventura or whether it was the Colorado of the West, which in Robinson's view rose a good deal farther south; Ashley had been uncertain on this point as far back as September, when his application for a license to trade had allowed for either possibility.

The voyage down the Shetskedee began bravely enough on the afternoon of April 22, 1825. Ashley wrote in his journal that the bullboat, a craft sixteen by seven feet, more than exceeded his expectation—it was easily navigated and carried as much again as he expected. On the twenty-third he dropped down the river to the mouth of the Big Sandy. Soon, however, he was finding the boat "inconvenient for hunting and from the bulk of the cargo The men much confined," so he stopped, killed four buffalo and from the hides constructed another boat. While he was so engaged Fitzpatrick arrived, supplied himself with meat and continued down the river toward his assigned territory. Early on the twenty-fifth Ashley set out again, and on the twenty-ninth overtook Fitzpatrick, who by then had descended the Green to a point two miles below the mouth of Blacks Fork; Ashley directed Fitzpatrick to "Encline towards the mountain b[earin]g Southwardly where in all probability he would find a small river running along the mountain," and himself continued down the river another six miles. There he cached part of his goods. On May 1, the cache completed, he resumed the voyage. Ten miles farther down, Ashley found a beautiful bottom where he made sign for the various parties to rendezvous, but four miles below, on May 3, he came on Henrys Fork, the existence of which he had gratifyingly foreseen. There was much beaver sign on this stream, beautiful bottoms with a considerable growth of small willow, and large timber higher up: "finding this a much more suitable place for a Randavouze I have made marks indicative of my intention to randavouze here & in consequence . . . have given the creek the name of Randavouze Creek." [14]

Below Henrys Fork, as Ashley observed, the Shetskedee plunged into the maw of the mountain; he had reached Flaming Gorge, and from now on this was a journey of such kind as to have given Major John Wesley Powell forty-four years later an enduring reputation as an explorer. The mountains had an oppressive aspect—"They are Entire rock generally of a redish appearance," rising to a height of from two to four thousand feet, "on the one side or other of the river perpendicular or projecting over—on the other side so steep & rugged as to prevent the passage of a man over them."

Ashley was plunging headlong into a kind of country nothing in the American experience had prepared him for. Almost at once he came to "a fall of 10 or 15 feet in the distance of 150 feet caused by the mountains given way and throughing rock from 20 to 40 feet in diameter Entirely across the river, it is not possable for boats of any description here we performed a portage of 100 yards." [15] In a canyon farther down: "The Channel of the river is more confined by this than by the mountain above the walls of the mountain are perpendicular on each side of the river and much obstructed by rocks which make it exceedingly dangerous to descend." Next day the river was "so verry bad that we were unable to proceed with our canoes loaded we discharged them and performed a portage of half mile which in consequence of the roughness of the side of the mountain along which we were obliged to pass made it extremely difficult and tedious." And on the day following: "we decended the river to day about 4 miles S W and have 5 portages to perform—at many of these places the river is not more than forty or 50 yards wide Roling over rocks with great violence some of my men are the most skilful of watermen or I could not have proceeded at all."

The voyage got worse as it lengthened, and on May 14 achieved a climax. Let Ashley tell the story. He was in Split Mountain Canyon, caught in a series of rapids:

although the fall continued and the waves were verry high I concluded to proceed with the boats believing that should the river become impassable or more dangerous, that we could discover it, and land the boats—but after proceeding about one and an half miles we discovered at the distance of about 4 or 500 yards by the motion of the water &c a verry great & dangerous fall and attempt was immediately made to land the large boat (the small one being in the rear a considerable distance and had fortunately capsized which had detained here [her] untill the information relative to this fall was communicated to the men) but we were already in the draft to land was impossible I discovered from the appearances of the rocks that our only way & that doubtfull to avoid immedeate destruction was to lay the boat straight with the current and pass in the middle of the river I directed the steersman accordingly my orders were obeyed & the men performed their duty handsomely, but soon after entering the heavy billows our boat filled with water but did not sink she was in that situation thrown against a rock at or near the foot of the falls, and near a large eddy, to which by the rock she was inclined and entered, two of the most active men then leaped in the water took the cables and towed her to land just as from all appearances she was about making her exit and me with her for I cannot swim & my only hopes was that the boat would not sink.

Jim Beckwourth later made a famous story out of how he saved the General from "the Suck," but at the time he was 150 miles or more away, on the other side of the Uinta Mountains in Jim Clyman's party.[16]

Ashley was happy on May 16 to see the mountains withdraw from the river; he had reached the Uinta Basin. That night he encamped at the mouth of the affluent since called Ashleys Fork. And that night the General made contact with another salient of the advancing fur frontier—two members of Provost and LeClerc's party. From these trappers Ashley learned that the country for a great distance below was entirely destitute of game:

these men with 20 or 30 others crossed the Country from Toues 4 of whom descended the river in a canoe but finding it so verry dangerous and destitute of game returnd they gave a lamentable account of their voyge. they had to live on the skins of beaver which they had caught in this neighbourhood. They also inform me that the

Indians generally in this country are hostile desposed and have killed & robed 15 or 20 men who were from the neighborhood of St Louis.[17]

The General cached most of the goods his boats still carried before continuing down the river. On May 21 he reached the mouth of the Duchesne, and two miles below, where the White River flows in from the east, came on "the wintering place of Mess. Provo &c." There he found a paper directing Provost's hunters who were in the mountains trapping to descend the river six miles "where they would find Mr. Laclare with articles for them." Ashley acted on the hint only to find that LeClerc had left his camp in pursuit of game—there was none in this neighborhood.

Having reason to believe that Provost's men would not return for six or eight days, Ashley cached the rest of his cargo and sent three of his men to procure game for their return. With the remaining three Ashley embarked in two dugouts, his object being to find Indians from whom he could buy horses, and at the same time "ascertain the true situation of the country described as so verry mountanous and barren." Unfavorable as was the account of the country below, he had to enter it without provisions. This day and the next Ashley paddled down the Green, a distance by his estimate of twenty-four miles, finding the country "a barren heap of rocky mountains." [18] Except for a goose, he and his men were able to kill nothing. But they did find a fresh Indian trail, with indications that the Indians had camped and hunted in this neighborhood for some days. On May 24 Ashley followed the Indian trail far enough to determine that the red men were ascending the river. So he directed the men to return by water, while he himself vainly attempted to follow the Indians. This was a hungry day for all, and they had another on May 25, Ashley meanwhile having rejoined his men.

On the twenty-sixth, a novelty, the first Indian Ashley had seen since January. The red man met him

with great familiarity and Ease as much so as if he had been accustomed to being with white men all his life calling aloud American, I answered in the affirmative he then advanced and extended his hand, and by signs asked many questions to wit how many men were with me. where they were and my object of our pursuit in this country all of which I gave him to understand by signs—after passing about an hour with me during which time I made Enquiries relative to the Country Westwardly, his knowledge of any white men in the country &c &c he departed with a view [to] notifying a band of his nation to which he belonged and who were not more than a days march from my camp of my situation, and to Endeavour to induce them to bring and seli me 7 horses of which I informed him I was in want.

It took longer than anticipated for the Indians to arrive, but during the two-day wait Ashley and his men had some success in fishing. Ashley had supposed these Indians to be Snakes, but now he correctly identified them as Utes.

I invited their chiefs & warriors to smoke informed them That I wanted to purchase 7 horses & showed them the goods that I would give for them. They expressed satisfaction at the liberal offer made them, but such is the use that they make of their horses and the value the[y] set on them that I with difficulty purchased two—they expressed great friendship for the Americans & their conduct verrify their professions I was much surprised at the appearance of these people I expected to find them a poor lifeless set of beings destitute of the means or disposition to defend themselves; alarmed at the sight of a white man but to the contrary they met me with great familiarity and ease of manner were clothed in mountain sheep skin & Buffalow robes superior to any band of Indians in my knowledge west of Council Bluffs—have a great number of good horses & about the one half, well armed with English fusees others with bows & arrows Tomahawks & a number of them were ornamented with perl & sea shels which they informed me they purchased from Indians who lived on the borders of a great lake, none of them have been to the Pacific nor have they an Idea of its extent farther than 40 or 50 miles.

Finding that he could obtain no more horses from the Utes, Ashley moved up to "a camp of 6 frenchmen about 6 miles distant." The three horses he acquired there were not enough, and when he turned west up the wide valley of the Duchesne on June 3 he had to leave his goods in cache. The trail he was following was the one used by Escalante in 1776, in that notable journey from Santa Fe which brought white men for the first time into the Great Basin. Pursuing this trail, on June 7 to his surprise and satisfaction Ashley met "Mr. Provo and party consisting of 12 men[19] who informed me that Mr. Weber had wintered on the south waters of the Columbia & & had heard of my being in the Country that he had gone over to green River in search of me."

It was just two weeks since Peter Skene Ogden had parted from Provost and Gardner in Weber Canyon; it is evident from what follows that Ashley learned from Provost of the defection of Ogden's freemen and he was suddenly anxious to talk business with them. Much more in this brief diary entry is notable: Ashley's belief that Weber had wintered on Columbia waters (the character of the interior basin was not yet clear to him or anyone else; he had the Multnomah in mind). And for the first time in his diary Ashley has used the name "green River" for a stream he had called the Shetskedee; the name was of Spanish origin, and Provost had brought it from Taos; Ashley could now feel assured that, whatever its name here, this stream was the Rio Colorado.[20] That Weber had learned of Ashley's presence in the country means that by the end of May, Ham's detachment had made contact with him, or that the information had reached him through the Indians.

The encounter with Provost was helpful to Ashley beyond the news he brought, for the French-Canadian agreed to transport to "the waters of the Columbia" the goods Ashley had left in cache on Green River. Turning back on the trail as far as the junction of the Strawberry and the Duchesne, Ashley set up a camp and waited a week while Provost went over to Green River and raised the cache. On June 15 the reunited party took the trail west again.

The route by which Provost guided Ashley to the Weber was presumably that by which Provost first reached the Great Basin in the fall of 1824. This trail struck west to the headwaters of the Strawberry, keeping north of that river's wild and canyoned course until it reached Strawberry Valley. Here in 1776 Escalante had turned southwest, eventually emerging into Utah Valley by Spanish Fork Canyon, but Provost followed the Strawberry up to its source, crossed the Rim of the Basin there, and descended Center Creek on the other side of the divide. The canyon of this creek led Ashley down to the open valley in which Heber City stands, whence he turned north along the foothills, crossed a low divide and arrived on the bank of the Provo River at the south end of Kamas Prairie. In the fall of 1824 Provost had probably gone down the river which bears his name, following it all the way to its mouth in Utah Lake; but on returning to the interior basin in the spring of 1825 he had found another way to the valley of the Great Salt Lake. For now he led Ashley across Kamas Prairie to the Weber River. Both these rivers, Ashley heard, ran into "the lake which is about 30 miles W of this route"—the Great Salt Lake.

He had descended the Weber—"Lake River," Ashley called it—only as far as Echo Canyon when he learned that "Johnson Guardner—& party of whom we are now in search" had gone east up a small stream passed earlier in the day. Turning about, Ashley followed Gardner's trail up Chalk Creek Canyon to reach the Bear River a little south of where the Mormon Trail later crossed it; he then moved on across the Bear River Divide substantially by the Mormon Trail of later years.[21] These details of Ashley's itinerary are the more interesting to us because it is a virtual certainty Jedediah Smith had taken the same trail east a couple of weeks before, traveling with Gardner and Weber.[22]

Unfortunately Ashley's diary ends June 27, 1825, when he had reached a point on the Big Muddy a little west of modern Carter, Wyoming. He was then, on an airline, about sixty miles northwest of his caches on Henrys Fork, which he probably reached the last day of June. All he has to say on this score is that by the first of July all the men in his employ or with whom he had any concern in the country, "together with twenty-nine who had recently withdrawn from the Hudson Bay Company, making in all 120 men," were assembled in two camps near each other, about twenty miles from the appointed place of rendezvous. Jim Beckwourth adds that while waiting for the General's arrival the men had occupied themselves with hunting, fishing, target shooting, foot racing, gymnastic "and sundry other exercises."[23]

In small parties the Ashley men had been scattered over the territory west of the mountains from perhaps the thirty-eighth to the forty-fourth degree of latitude, sustaining no injury by Indian depredations except the seventeen horses stolen by the Crows, and one man in Clyman's party killed on LaBarge Creek by Arapahoes or their cousins, the Gros Ventres of the Prairies.[24] One can picture the pleasure with which Jedediah wrung Jim Clyman's hand after a year of believing him dead. The reunion with Fitzpatrick must have been as warm; and the sight of others, to us mere names, evoked for Jedediah all the experiences of three eventful years.

In the next decade rendezvous became synonymous with saturnalia, but this first gathering of the mountain men was almost decorous. Exact memoranda exist of the goods Ashley deposited in his caches; he had in quantity sugar, coffee, tobacco, lead, powder, knives, bar iron and Indian trinkets.[25] But no rum. The demand existed, and he would send up rum this very fall, but the institutions of mountain life were only now being worked out.

The logic of rendezvous was just dawning on Ashley and the mountain men: Summer furs had dubious value, and in summer beaver appeared to lose the lodging habit, scattering about the country to eat grass.[26] In July and August it was scarcely worth while to put a trap in the water, and it would suit the trappers to assemble at some predetermined point to supply themselves for the next year's hunt. Under the compulsion of circumstance, Ashley had come to the mountains in winter, and a very hard journey he had had. Travel for a supply caravan was easiest in the season during which it was most convenient for the mountain men to rendezvous. Over the course of the next few years, that would fix the pattern of mountain trade. This summer of 1825, however, all was improvisation. Ashley had not foreseen that his men and the free trappers might become so attached to this mountain-desert country as to be content to remain forever; if he was their only contact with civilization and its comforts, his supply job became that much more complex and remunerative. It had not been possible to foresee the desertion of the Hudson's Bay Company freemen, most of whom had Indian wives and families, with varied wants. Ashley talked to Old Pierre, and the notes he made in his journal about goods to be sent to the mountains are illuminating; they include sewing silk and very small needles, assorted ribbons, combs, earrings, soap and "slay bells"—this "fofarraw," as the mountain men called it, fully as important as kettles, ammunition, trap springs, gun locks, rum, flour, sugar and coffee.

Other notations are interesting among Ashley's accounts at rendezvous. At $3.00 a pound, he buys 202 pounds of beaver from Caleb Greenwood, 189 pounds from Isaac Galbraith, 107¼ pounds from William Bell, 156 pounds from Robert Nutt and so on. Robert Nutt, Stephen Terry and Thomas Eddie get only $2.00 a pound for their beaver: is it in bad condition or have they been with Jedediah Smith on a wage basis? The Hudson's Bay Company deserters are handing over their beaver too, 36 pounds from this man, 41 from that, 136 pounds from Thyery Goddin as the largest single transaction. And meanwhile Ashley is selling them goods—knives at $2.50 apiece, coffee and sugar at $1.50 a pound, blue cloth at $6.00 a yard, moccasin awls at $2.00 a dozen. Jedediah Smith hands in beaver by the bale; one can distinguish at least 12 packs with which Ashley credits him. Ashley's accounts indicate that altogether he picked up 8,829 pounds of beaver, worth in St. Louis from $45,000 to $50,000.[27]

But the furs had to be got down to St. Louis. Ashley set out for home July 2. He would try to take his furs down by water, via the Big Horn, the Yellowstone and the Missouri. This year that was likely to be the safest route, for a military expedition was to have ascended the Missouri this summer to negotiate treaties with the Indians. If Ashley were fortunate in his timing, he could look for an impressive escort home. There was this additional consideration: He was short of both men and horses. If he went down by way of the Big Horn, fifty men would be enough to see his furs to a point of embarkation, and he could send half of that force back to the fur country with all the horses—some of which were borrowed.

All that had happened during the winter vitally concerned Jedediah Smith. Ashley had to have a partner. If not Andrew Henry, someone of equal energy, intelligence, business sense, integrity and guts. Necessity had brought Ashley to the mountains this year, but his whole life was oriented to the Missouri community. Someone else would have to take on the field captain's job. We do not know when the General put the proposition to his scarred young partisan, but it is almost certain that they came to an agreement at rendezvous. Somebody had to bring back to the mountains this fall the goods ordered by the free trappers, and this necessity brought Jedediah down to St. Louis with Ashley.[28]

That homeward journey we shall not follow in detail, though it was not lacking in excitement. Ashley sufficiently described, to General Atkinson, their passage to the Big Horn:

I had forty five packs of Beaver cached a few miles east of our direct route. I took with me 20 men, passed by the place, raised the cache, and proceeded in a direction to join the other party, but previous to joining them I was twice attacked by Indians, first by a party of Black-feet about 60 in number—they made their appearance at the break of day, yelling in the most hideous manner & using every means in their power to alarm our horses which they so effectually did that the horses although closely hobbled broke by the guard and ran off. A part of the Indians being mounted they succeeded in getting all the horses except two, and wounded one man.[29] An attempt was also made to take our camp, but in that they failed. The following night I sent an express to secure horses from the party of our men who had taken a direct route, in two days thereafter I received the desired aid, and again proceeded on my way, made about ten miles, and encamped upon an eligible situation that night, about 12 o'clock we were again attacked by a war party of Crow Indians which resulted in the loss of one of the Indians killed and another shot through the body, without any injury to us. The next day I joined my other party and proceeded direct to my place of embarkation just below the Big Horn mountain where I arrived on the 7th day of august.

Luck was running Ashley's way, for the U. S. forces had arrived at the mouth of the Yellowstone August 17, just two days before Ashley with his heavily laden bullboats reached that point. Ashley's hundred packs of beaver were stowed aboard the government boats, and the rest of the way there was just one anxious moment. One of the government boats was stove in by a snag a few miles above the James River. Ashley's beaver got a ducking, but after being thoroughly dried was as merchantable as ever.[30] The *Missouri Advocate* of October 5, 1825, expressed the feelings of the West in welcoming Ashley home:

> Our fellow-citizen, Gen. Ashley, has just returned from his adventurous enterprize to the Rocky Mountains, bringing with him one of the richest cargoes of fur that ever arrived at St. Louis. He spent the past winter in the bosom of the mountains, and made excursions in the spring down several of the rivers which go to the Pacific ocean. The furs obtained by him were brought on horses to the waters of the Big Horn, where they were embarked about the middle of Aug. and after a voyage of three thousand miles arrived at St. Louis on the 4th inst. It is thus, by the effort of heroic enterprize, Gen. Ashley has indemnified himself for all the losses occasioned by the murderous attack of the Arikara's in the summer of the year 1823.

9. *PARTNER IN THE FUR TRADE*

Jedediah Smith arrived in St. Louis with Ashley on October 4, 1825. Just twenty-six days later he was off for the Rockies at the head of a party of 70 men, with 160 horses and mules and an outfit valued at $20,000.[1] No four weeks of his life were ever so filled with concentrated activity, and he must have found in them the kind of intoxication lesser members of Ashley's company were content to have served up to them out of the cellar of LeBarras' Hotel. Gunsmiths, blacksmiths, saddlers and horse and mule dealers filled Jedediah's days while the senior partner in the new firm dickered for the thousand and one articles they had engaged to deliver in the mountains.

Beyond most men of his time, William H. Ashley had a flair for public relations. Grant him also administrative genius, extraordinary energy, willingness to break with tradition, moral stamina and physical courage. But wish that occasionally the limelight had been permitted to play on his associates. No notice of Ashley's activities this fall even intimates that he had taken a new partner. Jedediah's departure from St. Louis October 30 the *Missouri Republican* remarked only to say:

> We understand that a party of men in the employ of Gen. Ashley, started from this place for the Rocky Mountains on yesterday. The party consists of about 70 men. They go by land, and are furnished with mules and horses to transport the goods and articles necessary for the expedition.

Modest and reserved, Jedediah himself had little more to say about this notable development in his life. A new-found letter, written a year later, says merely that "having left S^{t}. Louis, in the state of Missouri, on the first of N°. 1825 as a partner of *Gen Wm* H Ashley's in the Fur Trade and Trapping Business—with 60 men & an equipment for prosecuting our business W^{t} of the Rocky *Mount* we arrived at the place of destination in June."[2] All the same, the memory of those weeks in St. Louis must have stayed with him to the end of his life, the furious round of activity with Ashley, the letters written home in moments stolen from sleep, the rare privilege of worshiping on Sundays in the old courthouse with his fellow Methodists, the brilliant social display attendant on the General's marriage October 26 to Miss Eliza Christy. Perhaps above all, the circumstance of his call on General Clark to procure his license. Although Ashley's license to trade west of the mountains still had two years to run and the partners did not bother to take out a new one, Jedediah had to obtain an authorization to enter the Indian country. He had left St. Louis in the spring of 1822 as one of the greenest of Ashley's raw recruits, but he had come back possessed of a fund of information and a far-ranging experience to which even William Clark could listen with profit. Jedediah's composed manner belied his torn face; he had made himself master of a strange, cruel, exalting world, and men respected him.

Almost nothing is known about Jedediah's return trip to the Rockies. It is probable that he was the first to travel purposefully the Oregon Trail west from the mouth of the Kaw. Ashley the previous year had gone up the left bank of the Missouri, crossed the Missouri at Fort Atkinson and moved on west by what became the Mormon Trail, but the southern route was shorter and Jedediah, like all mountain men, never went the long way round if he could help it. The cutoff would have led him up the Kaw River some miles on the Santa Fe road, then off northwest to strike the Platte near the head of Grand Island. That Jedediah traveled by this route is mainly inference: There is no mention of his party's having visited Fort Atkinson; and the trail was used a year later by an express which came down from the mountains.

Once Jedediah reached the Platte, his travels can be described with more confidence, though all we have to go on are some sketchy indications of an itinerary on David Burr's map of 1839, which was based on Jedediah's, and some even more sketchy remarks in Jim Beckwourth's book. Our gaudy liar is busy spinning an extravaganza, in which he figures as a hero who for $1,000 had agreed to carry an express from Ashley to his parties in the mountains—(this through a country "considered dangerous even for an army")—and it is only reluctantly that Jim takes his humble place as one among Jedediah's seventy men. In fact, all Beckwourth is willing to grant us is that he traveled up the north branch of the Platte and crossed over to Green River, striking it higher up than previously. He adds that after crossing the Green he held his course to "the head of Salt River," and there falling in with an Ashley party, made his way to Cache Valley, the place of rendezvous for the trappers who had remained in the mountains.[3]

The Burr map is somewhat contradictory, but it can be interpreted to say that after reaching the upper Green River Valley, Jedediah turned northwest to the Hoback River, followed this stream down into lower Jackson Hole, crossed the Tetons to Henrys Fork, went down that stream and the Snake to the mouth of Salt River, ascended the Salt to its head, descended Smiths Fork to the Bear, and followed that river to Cache Valley. If this itinerary properly interprets the Burr map, it was a tremendous, even incredible journey to make in late fall.

Jedediah had now mastered the technique of moving large parties to and from the mountains. A clear description Ashley wrote in 1829 of how it was done would represent some of the fruits of Jedediah's experience. No officer in the United States Army then possessed this kind of practical knowledge.

In the organization of a party of, say from 60 to 80 men, four of the most confidential and experienced of the number are selected to aid in the command; the rest are divided in messes of eight or ten. A suitable man is also appointed at the head of each mess, whose duty it is to make known the wants of his mess, receive supplies for them, make distributions, watch over their conduct, enforce order, &c. &c.

The party thus organised, each man receives the horse and mules alloted to him, their equipage, and the packs which his mules are to carry; every article so disposed of is entered in a book kept for that purpose. When the party reaches the Indian country, great order and vigilance in the discharge of their duty are required of every man. A variety of circumstances confines our march very often to the borders of large water courses; when that is the case, it is found convenient and safe, when the ground will admit, to locate our camps (which are generally laid off in a square) so as to make the river form one line, and include as much ground in it as may be sufficient for the whole number of horses, allowing for each a range of thirty feet in diameter. On the arrival of the party at their camping ground, the position of each mess is pointed out, where their packs, saddles, &c. are taken off, and with them a breastwork immediately put up, to cover them from a night attack by Indians: the horses are then watered and delivered to the horse guard, who keep them on the best grass outside and near the encampment, where they graze until sunset; then each man brings his horses within the limits of the camp, exchanges the light halter for the other more substantial, sets his stakes, which are placed at the distance of thirty feet from each other, and secures his horses to them. This range of 30 feet, in addition to the grass the horse has collected outside the camp, will be all sufficient for him during the night. After these regulations, the proceedings of the night are pretty much the same as are practised in military camps [except that sentries ordinarily did not move about: a moving figure at night presented too good a target]. At day light (when in dangerous parts of the country) two or more men are mounted on horseback, and sent to examine ravines, woods, hills, and other places within striking distance of the camp, where Indians might secrete themselves, before the men are allowed to leave their breastworks to make the necessary morning arrangements before marching. When these spies report favorably, the horses are then taken outside the camp, delivered to the horse guard, and allowed to graze until the party has breakfasted, and are ready for saddling. In the line of march, each mess march together, and take their choice of positions in the line according to their activity in making themselves ready to move, viz: the mess first ready to march moves up in the rear of an officer who marches in the front of the party, and takes choice of a position in the line, and so they all proceed until the line is formed; and in that way they march the whole of that day. Spies are sent several miles ahead, to examine the country in the vicinity of the route; and others are kept at the distance of a half mile or more from the party, as the situation of the ground seems to require, in front, rear, and on the flanks. In making discoveries of Indians, they communicate the same by a signal or otherwise to the commanding officer with the party, who makes his arrangements accordingly.[4]

Instances are almost unknown of men in such parties being cut down by Indians. The hazard came after the companies reached the mountains and split into small parties for trapping. Horses might be run off; Ashley himself had lost horses to the Crows and the Blackfeet in the spring and summer of 1825, but the mountain men had learned from that experience, and from this time one hears little about the loss of horses on the march.

Few among Jedediah's company can be named. The probability is that Robert Campbell made one of the party, perhaps as Jedediah's clerk. Campbell may have gone to the mountains with Ashley the previous year, and it is just possible that he and Jedediah became good friends while traveling down from rendezvous. But it is more likely their acquaintance dates from this fall; no other opportunity ever offered for them to become such fast friends that in drawing up his will Jedediah named Campbell his executor; the closeness of the bond between them is touchingly reflected in one of Jedediah's letters of 1830. The young Irishman was soon to become leader of a brigade in his own right; in the '30s, he was associated with William L. Sublette in one of the fur trade's best-known partnerships; still later he became one of the most respected and wealthy of St. Louis merchants. In each period he left his impress on the West. Gay, intelligent, forthright, Robert Campbell had the power to warm men's hearts; everybody liked him, including the men who called him "booshway." [5]

Whatever is doubtful about Jedediah's return west, there is no question that he ended up in Cache Valley. Jim Beckwourth and a mountain man no less celebrated, Louis Vasquez, agree on this. Vasquez goes on to say that the winter became so severe, the snow falling to a depth of eight feet, that the trappers had to move down into the valley of the Great Salt Lake, which they found free from snow and well filled with buffalo; they divided into two camps, "one party, under Weber, wintering on the river which now bears his name; the other party wintering on Bear river, near its mouth."[6] This latter encampment probably was Jedediah's.

One dark and stormy night a considerable number of horses, eighty by Jim Beckwourth's accounting, were run off by the Indians; Jim says that the thieves were Bannocks, and that a party of forty men, including himself, Fitzpatrick and Jim Bridger, followed on foot, not only recovering their own animals but making prize of a number belonging to the Indians. On the other hand, Peter Skene Ogden intimated in the spring of 1826 that the thieves, Snakes by his understanding, made good their escape.[7]

Beckwourth says that on his return from the chase after the stolen horses he found "an encampment of Snake Indians, to the number of six hundred lodges, comprising about two thousand five hundred warriors," which entirely surrounded the American camp. Reduce these figures by two thirds, a standard discount for Jim's numbers, and they would be about right. These Snakes were perfectly friendly, Jim adds, and the whites apprehended no danger from their proximity. Peter Skene Ogden met up with these Snakes March 24, a month after the winter encampment broke up; he then estimated their number at two hundred lodges and observed, "it appears these fellows have spent their winter with the Americans and from their own accounts have made peace with them this I am inclin'd to belive is the case as they have received an American Flag and appear pleased and contented with the reception they have received from them." The Snakes told him that the American camp consisted of twenty-five tents—perhaps a hundred trappers.[8]

With the opening of the spring hunt, the Americans split into at least three and probably four or more detachments. Ogden met one of these parties on the Snake April 9; it consisted of twenty-eight men, including several of his deserters of the previous year. This company went north to the Flathead country, and in August John Work, conducting the Hudson's Bay Company's summer trade with the Flatheads, listened to tales of Ashley's intention to establish a post in the Big Hole Prairie and of the imminent ousting of the Hudson's Bay Company from the

Columbia by men coming on American ships. A principal figure in this party, which seems not to have made it back to rendezvous in 1826, was John Grey.[9]

Another company was that with which Jim Beckwourth trapped; Jim says that it was led by Fitzpatrick.[10] Beckwourth and his fellows trapped the Bear and the adjacent tributaries of the Snake, but what is chiefly remembered of their adventures is the circumstance that gave name to Cache Valley—up to this time it had been called Willow Valley. Jim says that at the opening of spring, whites and Indians moved back to Cache Valley, and soon after their arrival the whites commenced digging caches to deposit seventy-five packs of beaver, the fruits of their fall hunt. While the cache was being dug, the earth caved in, killing a trapper whom Jedediah later remembered as one Marshall. His companions, Warren Ferris relates, "*believed* him to have been instantly killed, *knew* him to be well buried, and the cache destroyed, and therefore left him 'Unknelled, uncoffined, ne'er to rise, Till Gabriel's trumpet shakes the skies,' and accompanied their object elsewhere." Trust Jim Beckwourth to figure large in the sequel. His was the privilege of taking for servant the widow of the man killed in the bank. "She was of light complexion, smart, trim and active, and never tired in her efforts to please me, she seeming to think that she belonged to me for the remainder of her life." Jim, whose mother was a slave, had never had a servant before, and he found her of great service "in keeping my clothes in repair, making my bed, and taking care of my weapons." [11]

When Jedediah broke up his winter camp at the mouth of the Bear, he plunged straight into the unknown, the country north and west of Great Salt Lake.

At rendezvous the previous summer Jedediah and Ashley had threshed out with the Hudson's Bay Company deserters what was known about this region. Ashley had been disposed to think that the Bear, the Weber, the Provo and the "Grand Lake" itself were sources of the Multnomah. The British trappers had corrected him; there was a great deal they did not know about "the Spanish waters," as they called the country lying south of the Snake, but they did know from firsthand observation the high degree of fantasy that had got into William Clark's conception of the Willamette, the river he called Multnomah. Far from rising in the Rockies, it had its sources in the Cascades, only a few hundred miles from its mouth.[12]

Ashley then guessed that the lake was the Timpanogos, but that idea he discarded; Great Salt Lake became for him the Buenaventura. All the maps showed a river draining from that lake into the Pacific, and Ashley understood the Indians to confirm this information, "at the extreme west end of this lake, a large river flows out, and runs in a westwardly direction." [13] (He was hearing about the Humboldt, which rises in the Independence and Ruby Mountains 150 miles west of Great Salt Lake and manages to flow most of the way across Nevada before expiring in the Humboldt Sink.) The Hudson's Bay Company's George Simpson, who had no belief in the Buenaventura but did have information about the Umpqua and had heard rumors of a lake in which it rose, had contemplated that Ogden should trap this enticing river, but Ogden had been prevented even from trying. It was left to Jedediah Smith to find out what the mass of rumor boiled down to.

This narrative has evaded coming to grips with the complicated question of when and by whom Great Salt Lake was discovered, but the principal factors are now all in and it is time to meet the question head on. On August 28, 1834, William Marshall Anderson asked some questions around a mountain camp fire, and wrote in his diary that "the great salt lake at the termination of Bear river, which has been claimed to be discovered by Genl. Ashley & which in the U. S. bears his name, I am informed by good authority has never been seen by him. . . . Tis believed the credit, if there is any in the accidental discovery of a place is due to Weaver or Provost." [14]

Later Anderson became an impassioned advocate of Provost and declared extravagantly that Provost had reached, trapped on, and "circumambulated" the inland sea as early as 1820, so that to him alone belonged the credit of having discovered and made known its existence.[15] There is little doubt that Provost laid eyes on the Great Salt Lake as early as the fall of 1824, but the priority of discovery has been fantastically complicated through the nearly simultaneous approach to the lake of many different parties. For Weber's party the discoverer was Jim Bridger; the fact is well attested though there is some doubt whether the event occurred in the late fall of 1824 or the early spring of 1825. Bridger's own statement, as elicited by Robert Campbell in the spring of 1857, was that

a party of beaver trappers who had ascended the Missouri with Henry and Ashley, found themselves in pursuit of their occupation on Bear river, in *Cache* (or Willow) valley, where they wintered in the winter of 1824 and 1825; and in descending the course which Bear river ran, a bet was made between two of the party, and James Bridger was selected to follow the course of the river and determine the bet. This took him to where the river passes through the mountains, and there he discovered the Great Salt lake. He went to its margin and tasted the water, and on his return reported his discovery. The fact of the water being salt induced the belief that it was an arm of the Pacific ocean. . . .[16]

Weber's party had gone on down into the valley of the Great Salt Lake before Peter Skene Ogden's brigade reached Cache Valley in May 1825. The first intimation of the existence of the great lake in the British journals is a notation by Ogden May 5; on seeing thousands of small gulls flying about Cache Valley, he reasoned that near at hand was a large body of water "at present unknown to us all." A week later the interpreter Charles McKay climbed the mountains overlooking the camp and came back to report a "large lake into which Bear River falls," twelve miles to the southwest. Ogden was more interested in beaver than in geographical discovery, and he continued his march south through the chain of valleys which lie east of the valley of the lake. Kittson several times refers to the existence beyond the range to the west of "the Large Bear Lake," but it was not until May 22, when the brigade had reached its farthest south in the canyon of the Weber, that the new-found lake made an impression on Ogden's journal:

From two of our trappers who Came in [I learned] they had Seen a large lake equal in Size Winipeg & that Bear River & New River [a name Ogden applied indiscriminately to the Weber and the Ogden] discharge their Waters in the Lake so the point is now ascertained that Bear River has nothing to do with the Spanish River from what they could observe the Lake runs due west, if so & as the Natives inform there is a large river at the west end this must be the Umqua.

Ogden was soon in flight back to the Snake, and it was three and a half years before he himself laid eyes on this singular mountain sea.[17]

No claim of prime discovery can be made for Jedediah Smith, though in following Weber's party down into the great valley he had the experience of seeing the vast lake open out before him, burnished by sun and space. From that time Jedediah began to have a proprietary feeling about the Great Salt Lake, and by the summer of 1827 he was speaking of it as his home of the wilderness.

The search Jedediah launched for the river which flowed from Great Salt Lake to the sea apparently led directly to the first exploration of the lake by water. It has long been known that a party of four trappers paddled around the lake in the spring of 1826, but it is now possible to see that exploit in new perspective.

On breaking up his winter camp, probably in late February 1826, Jedediah took his party around the head of Bear River Bay and on across the Promontory Mountains, a route later adopted for the Pacific Railroad. West of the summit where the Golden Spike was eventually driven, the lake opened to view again, the wide reaches of Spring Bay veiled at this season with gray wraiths of fog. The country here had a savage monotony, for a wintry dryness rested on the land, the sagebrush gray and contorted, the scattered dark junipers unrelated to anything, not even one another. Clouds of waterfowl wheeled overhead, and as the party came down to the shore they found numerous springs pouring a desperate abundance into the lake. Many of these were brackish, some as salt as the lake itself. Coming finally to the northwest corner of the lake, where beyond all doubt the shore line turned south, Jedediah was confronted with the necessity of continuing his reconnaissance by water.

There is no way of determining how far Jedediah and his men attempted to investigate the west shore of the lake on horses. Probably not very far, for though an outsize salt lake might be impressive as a spectacle, it was hard to live with. The water was eight times as salty as the ocean, totally undrinkable, and the scattered, salt-resistant greenery that fought for life along the storm line was fare the horses and mules would not touch. It was the part of wisdom to detail four men to build a bullboat, the reliable skin canoe which had proved its worth all over the West; and Jedediah would have been more attracted by this alternative if (as one of the accounts suggests) he was short of horses.

Four men, it may be assumed, were detached for the reconnaissance. It took them twenty-four days, and a very thirsty time they had of it before they reached the fresh-water springs at the south shore of the lake. When they turned up at the rendezvous in Cache Valley, it was an odd report they made; they had not exactly ascertained the outlet of the lake, but they had passed a place where they supposed it to be. The explorers had evidently observed the opening along the western shore line through which the lake during late Pleistocene times had retreated from the Salt Desert. On various occasions Jim Clyman, Louis Vasquez and Black Harris claimed to have floated around the lake, and the same claim was made for Henry G. Fraeb, so it may be that these were the four men who "coasted the lake." [18]

When he parted from his seafarers, Jedediah may have expected to meet them at some point on the Buenaventura farther west, though it must have troubled him to reflect that a river flowing from so salty a body of water must be salt also—and that would mean no beaver. Jedediah's narrative of his exploration northwest of Great Salt Lake is another of the lost documents of American history, and indeed it is barely established that he made such a journey. The slim record is composed of a few notations in the journal of Peter Skene Ogden and an itinerary depicted on the Burr map.

It would appear that Jedediah got into the dry, hungry country which rims the smoking-white Salt Desert, south of the later trails by which immigrants traveled to California. As he continued west into the arid reaches of eastern Nevada, he found no beaver, very little game and not much water. In desperation he turned north toward the Snake, coming on Salmon Falls Creek and going down it to the great South Branch. So Ogden understood, for on May 21, at Salmon Falls Creek, he heard from the Snakes "that about a month since a party of Americans about 30 in number had descended this Stream on their return from Salt Lake without Beaver." And again, on June 2, when Ogden had descended the Snake to the Bruneau, he noted the probability that a fur country existed to the south, discharging its streams into the Gulf of California:

it appears from the accounts we have again received from the Indians here, the Americans have made an attempt to reach it but starvation had Driven them back and they had crossed over from the entrance of Bruneau's River to the North side of the South Branch . . . when last seen they were destitute of both [beaver and game] and were Killing their Horses.[19]

So much for the tales of a majestic river flowing to the sea. Jedediah must have been glad to reach the Snake, a country sufficiently desolate, but offering at least the prospect of something to eat. In fact, after so unpromising a beginning, his spring hunt must suddenly have come alive. The Burr map enables us to follow its further course in at least rough approximation: Jedediah crossed the Snake below Lower Salmon Falls, struck north to the Boise, then again north to the Payette, and trapped that river clear to its source in Payette Lake ("Ward's Lake," the map names it, perhaps for a member of Jedediah's party). After retracing their steps as far as the Boise, the Americans made their way east to the Malade (present Big Wood), and after trapping some distance up that river, crossed over to the sources of the Big Lost, which brought them back down to the lava plain Jedediah had crossed and recrossed in 1824-1825. All of these streams had been trapped by Alexander Ross in the summer of 1824, but the country should have recovered somewhat, and it seems likely that Jedediah had a fruitful hunt. By what course he found his way back to Cache Valley is obscure, but the Burr map might indicate that he moved east to Henrys Fork, on around the Tetons to Jackson Hole, down the Snake and back to the Bear by way of Salt River, the Blackfoot or the Portneuf.

Cache Valley was the place appointed for the second great summer rendezvous. Accounts of the American fur trade have usually placed this rendezvous in the valley of the Great Salt Lake, but it is apparent that Cache Valley was the locale, the vicinity of present Hyrum.[20] From hundreds of miles in all directions the mountain men converged on this valley, and Ashley himself was present, having come up from St. Louis with a new consignment of goods.

The General had set out from St. Louis March 8 with twenty-five men, his departure evoking the usual huzzas from the press: "Such enterprise richly merits, and we hope will meet with, ample success." [21] Before his departure Ashley had given out to the newspapers some interesting ideas about the significance of what he and his men were learning of the West, and they are worth quoting; they have the ring of the future about them:

> Heretofore, those great barriers of nature, the Rocky Mountains, have been called up in judgment against the practicability of establishing a communication between this point and the Pacific Ocean. But the Great Author of nature, in His wisdom has prepared, and individual enterprize discovered, that so "broad and easy is the way" that thousands may travel it in safety, without meeting with any obstruction deserving the name of a MOUNTAIN.
>
> *The route* proposed, after leaving St. Louis and passing generally on the north side of the Missouri river, strikes the river Platte a short distance above its junction with the Missouri; then pursues the waters of the Platte to their sources, and in continuation, crosses the head waters of what Gen. Ashley believes to be, the Rio Colorado of the West, and strikes for the first time, a ridge, or single connecting chain of mountains running from north to south [the Bear River Divide]. This, however, presents no difficulty, as a wide gap is found, apparently prepared for the purpose of a passage. After passing this gap, the route proposed, falls directly on a river, called by Gen.

Ashley, the Buenaventura, and runs with that river to the Pacific Ocean.

The face of the country, in the general, is a continuation of high, rugged, and barren mountains; the summits of which, are either timbered with pine, quaking-asp, or cedar; or, in fact, almost entirely destitute of vegetation. Other parts are hilly and undulating; and the valleys and table lands, (except on the borders of water courses, which are more or less timbered with cotton-wood and willows,) are destitute of wood; but this indispensable article is substituted by an herb, called by the hunters, wild sage: which grows from one to five feet high, and is found in great abundance, in most parts of the country.

Soil.—The sterility of the country, generally, is almost incredible. That part of it, however, bounded by the three principle ranges of mountains, and watered by the sources of the supposed Buenaventura is less sterile; yet the proportion of arable land even within those limits, is comparatively small; and no district of the country visited by Gen. Ashley, or of which he obtained satisfactory information, offers inducements to civilized people, sufficient to justify an expectation of permanent settlements. . . .[22]

There is no detailed narrative of Ashley's journey this spring, only the briefest of summaries printed in the *Missouri Herald and St. Louis Advertiser* after his return home: "He went to the station of the party which he had left beyond the mountains when he came in a year ago, and thence descended a river, believed to be the Buenaventura, about one hundred and fifty miles to the Great Lake." This would indicate that from Henrys Fork, Ashley crossed over to the Bear and then followed the path his men had beaten out the past two years, down the circuitous course of the Bear to Cache Valley.

As many as a hundred men may have been present at rendezvous, though less than half were in Ashley's immediate service. Free trappers were on hand in numbers, including, it would seem, Etienne Provost. In a life of boundless obscurity, nothing is more obscure than how and why Provost's partnership with LeClerc ended in ruin. It may be that LeClerc the previous fall had gone down to the States via Taos and the Santa Fe Trail, and that he was killed by Indians en route.[23] If this happened, and if Provost had depended on him to bring a new outfit to the mountains, the game was up. All that is certainly known is that Provost went back to the States this fall and made proposals to the Chouteaus to be taken into their service, proposals that were finally accepted.

Captain Weber, too, may have left the mountains this fall, though the tradition preserved in his family was that he came back from the Rockies in 1827. The way the family remembered his story was that Weber made about $20,000 by hunting, trapping and trading in the Rockies, "but was beaten out of what was then a fortune by dishonest partners. He never made or saved much wealth afterwards and died poor." After his return to St. Louis the Captain moved to Galena, Illinois, in the spring of 1832, and twelve years later across the Mississippi to Bellevue, Iowa. It is said that he became a victim of neuralgia. "Life became a burden to him and he . . . deliberately committed suicide in 1859 by cutting his throat, bleeding to death in a few minutes."[24] Weber's name was all but lost from the record of the West, preserved solely in the name of the Weber River, and only now is his role in the mountains coming to be understood.

The great event of the summer was Ashley's selling out to a new firm, Smith, Jackson & Sublette. Ashley's association of Jedediah with himself in the firm Ashley & Smith led logically to this development, and Jedediah's partnership with Ashley furnished both the funds and the practical experience which made possible the organization of the new firm. Smith, Jackson & Sublette became so famous a concern as to obscure the nine-months partnership of Ashley & Smith which paved the way to it, but Jedediah became senior partner in the new firm for sufficient reasons.

William L. Sublette's entrance into the new partnership is understandable enough; he had been with Jedediah constantly from 1823 to 1825, and this past winter had emerged as a booshway in his own right.[25] But it is difficult to make much of David E. Jackson. Down to the moment he signed the instrument of partnership with Smith and Sublette, scarcely his existence can be demonstrated. He is said to have been with Jedediah on the beach before the Ree towns in 1823, and he has been misidentified as the George C. Jackson who was one of Ashley's officers in Leavenworth's campaign against the Rees.[26] As far as the American trappers were concerned, he was the discoverer of Jackson Hole, but no one knows when he first got into that locality. Possibly he was one of the twenty-five men who in the summer of 1825 escorted Ashley to the Big Horn, and afterward turned back across the divide to make the discovery for which he will be longest remembered.

The actual instrument by which Ashley was bought out has not been preserved, but a letter the General wrote the Chouteaus later in the fall sets forth the essentials. On leaving the mountains, Ashley explained, he

> placed under the direction of three young men, Messrs. Smith, Jackson and Sublett, my remaining stock of merchandise, amounting altogether, to about sixteen thousand dollars, which (after deducting therefrom five thousand dollars which I paid Mr. Smith on a dissolution of Partnership with him) they promise to pay me in Beaver fur delivered in that country at three dollars pr. pound or I am to receive the fur, transport the same to St Louis and have it disposed of on their account, deducting from the amount of sale one dollar twelve & half cents per pound for transportation, and place the net proceeds to their credit in discharge of the debt aforesaid. I have also transfered to the sd Smith, Jackson and Sublett, the services of a number of men employed by me as hunters, whose time of service will expire in July next [there were forty-two of these in all, engaged to Ashley & Smith]. . . . They bound themselves to deliver me all the beaver furs they may collect from the time I left them, until the first of July next . . . any amount which may appear from the proceeds of the fur after paying for the goods already delivered and any ballance which may be due the men transferred as aforesaid, is to be appropriated towards the payment of the goods to be delivered in July next, and any ballance of that debt which may remain after that appropriation, is to be paid on or before the first of July 1828.[27]

Ashley had made money enough the year before to clear his debts, and he had on hand another 123 packs of beaver, sufficient to provide him with a comfortable fortune if he got them down to the States. The arrangement he described, and another we shall describe, involved only a limited liability and would permit him to remain in Missouri and cultivate his temporarily arrested career in politics.

One document that has survived from these negotiations, the earliest known instrument bearing Jedediah Smith's signature, is an agreement between Ashley and the new partners concerning goods to be brought to the mountains next year. Entered into "this 18th day of July 1826," its most interesting feature follows on an itemizing of the merchandise:

> . . . which merchandise is to be by said Ashley or his agent delivered to said Smith Jackson & Sublett or to their agent at or near the west end of the little lake of Bear river a watter of the pacific ocean on or before the first day of July 1827 without some unavoidable occurrence should prevent, but as it is uncertain whether the situation of said Smith Jackson & Subletts business will Justify the proposed purchase of Merchandise as aforesaid it is understood and agreed [that the new partners] shall send an Express to said Ashley to reach him in St Louis on or before the first day of March next, with orders to fo[r]ward the merchandise as aforesaid, and on its arrival at its place of destination, that they the said Smith Jackson & Sublett will pay him the said Ashley the amount for Merchandise sold them on this day for which the said Ashley holds their notes payable the first day of July 1827 for, and it is further understood that the amount of merchandise to be delivered as aforesaid on or before the first of July 1827 shall not be less than Seven Thousand dollars nor more than fifteen thousand. . . .
>
> and it is understood and agreed between the two said parties that so long as the said Ashley continues to furnish said Smith Jackson & Sublett with Merchandise as aforesaid That he will furnish no other company or Individual with Merchandise other than those who may be in his immediate service[28]

Ashley returned to St. Louis the last week of September to the usual spate of compliments from the papers: "We sincerely rejoice that the efforts of this worthy and enterprising individual have been again crowned with success."[29] A more reflective piece was published November 8 in the *Missouri Herald and St. Louis Advertiser*. The editor of that paper was Charles Keemle, who had given up the fur trade to return to his first love, newspapering, but who now and ever after lent a sympathetic ear to the tales of men down from the mountains. Keemle wrote:

> The recent expedition of General Ashley to the country west of the Rocky Mountains has been productive of information on subjects of no small interest to the people of the Union. It has proved, that overland expeditions in large bodies may be made to that remote region without the necessity of transporting provisions for man or beast. Gen. Ashley left St. Louis in March last, and returned in September. His return caravan consisted of upwards of one hundred horses and mules, and more than one half that number of men. . . . His return march to St. Louis occupied about seventy days, each mule and horse carrying nearly two hundred pounds of beaver fur—the animals keeping their strength and flesh on the grass which they found, and without losing any time on this long journey. The men also found an abundance of food; they say there was no day in which they could not have subsisted a thousand men, and often ten thousand. Buffaloe furnished the principal food—water of the best quality was met with every day. The whole route lay through a level and open country, better for carriages than any turnpike road in the United States. Wagons and carriages could go with ease as far as General Ashley went, crossing the Rocky Mountains at the sources of the north fork of the Platte, and descending the valley of the Buenaventura towards the Pacific Ocean. . . .
>
> In the whole expedition, Gen. Ashley did not lose a man, nor had any one of those died whom he left behind last year, many of whom have been out four or five years, and are too happy in the freedom of those wild regions to think of returning to the comparative thraldom of civilized life. It would seem that no attempt has been made to ascertain the precise latitude and longitude of the point at which Gen. Ashley crossed the mountains.—It is to be hoped that this will not be neglected on the next expedition. From all that we can learn, the elevation is exceedingly small where the passage of the mountains was effected—so small as hardly to affect the rate of going of the caravan, and forming at the most, an angle of three degrees, being two degrees less than the steepest ascent on the Cumberland road.

So much for Ashley, beginning to reap the fruits of all that he had done for himself, all that had been done for him, beyond the continental divide. But Jedediah and his new partners had futures of their own to seek out.

10. THE SOUTH WEST EXPEDITION

The journey that brought Jedediah Smith to California as the first explorer overland from the American frontier is touched with paradox, for he avowed after reaching the Pacific that necessity alone had driven him to an exploit for which he may be longer remembered than for his discovery of South Pass. Moreover, the daybook of his clerk, begun at rendezvous some weeks before the journey began, speaks merely of a "South West Expedition," with no intimation that California figured in the plans for the year's hunt.[1]

Daniel Potts wrote his brother from rendezvous on July 16, 1826, two days before the firm Smith, Jackson & Sublette came into being, that he expected to start in a short time "to explore the country lying S. W. of the Great Lake where we shall probably winter. This country has never been visited by any white person—from thence to what place I cannot say, but expect the next letter will be dated mouth of Columbia River."[2] Potts's hope of sharing in this exploration was not fulfilled, but that he anticipated reaching the mouth of the Columbia by traveling southwest from the Great Salt Lake is worth meditation. And after Jedediah did emerge upon the California coast, a journey north to the Columbia seems never to have been far from his thoughts.

Jedediah himself says simply that he started southwest in the hope of finding beaver, and that in consequence of not coming on beaver in sufficient numbers to justify his stopping to trap, he kept on till his party was reduced to such straits as forced him to cross the desert to the California missions. Logically the object of the South West Expedition was to determine once and for all whether the Buenaventura River existed. In the spring

Jedediah had vainly sought this river in the country west and northwest of Great Salt Lake. If it existed at all, he had to assume that it rose southwest of that lake. Jedediah might have contemplated seeking out the sources of the Buenaventura, wintering on it and following it to the sea. Depending on which map he was using, that would bring him to the Pacific at a point south of Monterey or at the Bay of San Francisco. Thence, perhaps, he could go up the coast to the Columbia, trapping that great river and the Snake en route back to rendezvous.

The fall hunt of 1826 for Smith, Jackson & Sublette was important, for what it developed of their prospects would determine whether a midwinter express was sent down to Ashley confirming the contract for a new outfit. Jackson and Sublette took parties north at the same time Jedediah rode off to the southwest;[3] the Snake Country had a known potential, and Jackson and Sublette had a fair chance of clearing the commitment to Ashley. It is doubtful that anything was expected of Jedediah's party; the junior partners would carry the burden this fall, and the payoff on the South West Expedition would come later.

As his clerk Jedediah chose Harrison G. Rogers, who in 1819 had been a resident of the Boonslick country of Missouri,[4] but otherwise managed to live his life in perfect privacy; he is first connected with the fur trade by the journal and daybook he began to keep for the South West Expedition in August, 1826.[4] From the evidence of his fragmentary journals, Rogers was a man of angular Calvinist upbringing who walked unbending in the path of duty. Educated, intelligent, sharply observing, he had pride of spirit which could assume the form of an unexpected diffidence, but to any warmth he responded with grace and charm. To read Rogers' journals is to be impressed with the variousness of the men in the mountains, how different they were from the stereotype of the mountain man that has become fixed in the American legend.

The rank and file are worthy of remembrance. The members of the party were Arthur Black, Robert Evans, Daniel Ferguson, John Gaiter, Silas Gobel, John Hanna, Abraham Laplant, Manuel Lazarus, Martin McCoy, Peter Ranne, James Reed, John Reubascan and John Wilson. This adds up to fifteen men who made the whole journey, as shown by Rogers' journal and accounts. Two others, Manuel Eustavan and one Neppasang (doubtless a Nipissing Indian from Canada; there were many in the trade), accompanied the expedition at least part way. Louis Pombert was in California next year, associated at that time with Jedediah's party, but if he got there as a member of the expedition of 1826 he was totally self-sufficient, for Rogers issued him no supplies and never referred to him in his diary. Black had the longest history in the mountains; Laplant proved most useful, in consequence of having a smattering of Spanish; but Ranne is perhaps most interesting, for he was "a man of color"—the first of his race to enter California, as far as known.[5]

Jedediah said a year later that the South West Expedition got off about August 22, 1826, but by then he had reached Utah Valley. The actual date of starting can be fixed on the best possible authority, for on August 15 Rogers issued to the men a quantity of rum. The amount varied with the capacity or affluence of each man, from a pint to a gill, but the occasion is recognizable: this was the big blowout on the day before the party launched on its journey.

From rendezvous in Cache Valley Jedediah rode southwest into the valley of the Great Salt Lake, then south to Utah Valley. The Utes had lived in this valley from time immemorial, and had been visited here in September 1776 by the Spanish friars Escalante and Domínguez. The padres had envisioned a mission, but the half-century had brought only occasional illicit trading parties, slipping in from the deserts to the south and east. Etienne Provost had come in from the east by the same trails two years since, but none of the American trappers had been south or west of "the Little Uta Lake."[6]

To the Utes, on August 22, Jedediah handed out the usual munificent gifts—three yards of red ribbon, ten awls, a razor, a "durk knife," a "Brass handle Knife," a pound of powder, forty balls, some arrow points, half a pound of tobacco—but if they could tell him anything of the country below Utah Lake, he could make nothing of it. He had seen enough of the West not to venture improvidently into an unknown land; Jedediah carried seven hundredweight of dried buffalo meat. He was soon glad of his forethought, for after leaving Utah Valley he saw no more buffalo, nothing but an occasional antelope, a mountain sheep or what was most plentiful, "black-tailed hares."

Perhaps three days after parting from the Utes, Jedediah reached the Sevier River some thirty miles above its great bend. So far as it had any foundation in reality, he had found his Buenaventura River, but from its course where he struck it and its relative nearness to Utah Lake, Jedediah supposed it to empty into that lake. Turning up "Ashley's River," as Jedediah named it, on August 27 he encountered another Ute band, "a nation of Indians who call themselves Sampatch." These Indians received Jedediah cordially and in turn received of his largess. The Ute trade had never amounted to much and never would, but presents like these were the price of Jedediah's admission into the country.

The Sevier was a handsome stream, at this season from three to four feet deep and about twelve yards wide. The long valley through which the river wound was spacious, but arid and destitute of timber. So dry and unstable was the soil that the horses kicked up dust in choking clouds, but where side streams had flooded the bottoms, grass grew belly-high to the horses. Seventy miles of this and the mountains closed up, bringing the party to a full stop. The tangle of rock, brush and taller timber out of which the river burst was clearly impenetrable, and Jedediah turned west up Clear Creek, soon gaining the summit and descending the far slope to the rolling, sage-covered valley where Cove Fort now stands.[7]

Again south along the base of the mountains, through the searing September heat. Off to the west the country was so inhospitable that the mouth dried contemplating it. Sterile hills, faintly touched with color, floated on the horizon, but Jedediah's eye came back to the solid green of the junipers that marched along with him; they were rooted in reality. This stretch of his trail Jedediah described as "a Country of Starvation—Sandy plains and Rocky hills once in 20 30 or 40 m[iles] a little pond or Spring of water with a little grass." The infrequent Indians were shy and wild, disappearing among the rocks like mountain sheep.

About September 8 the party came on a small stream tumbling down out of the mountains; Jedediah named it Lost River—the Beaver. Farther south, the color of the earth began to change. There was a red tinge to the mountains, and the soil became a reddish sand. Scattered clumps of sagebrush took on heightened color; junipers struck the eye like a blow. This was not beaver country; it never had been and it never would be. The men had been unruly and quarrelsome from the time they started, and there was nothing about travel like this to improve their disposition.

The country grew more strange as they climbed over the Rim of the Basin and descended Ash Creek toward the Virgin River. To the east the mountains had begun to break up into spires and battlements, flaming red, and the vegetation was changing, thorned and armored against the furnace dryness. September was well advanced when in a red-walled valley Jedediah came on a swift little river running to the southwest—the first stream meriting the name of river he had seen since leaving the Sevier. The Virgin River, as it was named later, was muddy and brackish, but Jedediah named it the Adams in compliment to his President and turned down it.[8]

His supply of dried buffalo meat was gone. Jedediah was happy, a day's journey down his new-found river, to come on the Santa Clara flowing in from the north; he named the stream Corn Creek, for on its banks he found rude patches of corn and pumpkins, the first Indian agriculture he had seen west of the Mandans. The Indians called themselves Pa-utches or Paiutes, and were evidently related to the Utes. Nearly naked, dirty, willing to eat anything that crawled or hopped or ran on the ground, they were a poor people—their poverty reflected in their lodges, which were insubstantial shelters made of long branches of willow and cottonwood, with cornstalks interspersed. But Jedediah obtained from them a little corn and some pumpkins. These Indians had interesting pipes carved from green marble, which they obtained somewhere to the south. Jedediah acquired one to give to General Clark for his museum of Indian curiosities, but he was more interested in specimens of rock salt. The American people had found salt difficult to come by as they moved across the continent, and throughout his wanderings in the West salt was a great marvel to Jedediah. This rock salt the Indians obtained farther down the Virgin; they found it in a cave.[9]

Parting from the friendly Pa-utches, Jedediah followed the Virgin into the rough canyon it has cut through the mountains below St. George. He had a difficult time, having to travel in the river bed much of the way, but below the canyon the going improved. No game was to be seen, however, nothing but an infrequent hare, and so changed was the vegetation as to baffle his powers of description. Horses as well as men were showing wear and tear, and Jedediah watched them with an anxious eye, for in the West men without horses were scarcely men.

During September two of Jedediah's party disappear from Harrison Rogers' accounts. On September 8 Manuel Eustavan received his last supplies, two knives and a moccasin awl; and on September 22 Neppasang was issued "1 Beaver Chissel & Spear." Neither is heard of again in connection with the South West Expedition, and it may be that they deserted in the valley of the Virgin. It is also possible, though unlikely, that he sent them back to advise his partners of his exploration thus far.

Jedediah says that he traveled down the Virgin about ten days, when its course changed from southwest to southeast; he might better have said south, for the Virgin was now hastening to give itself to the Colorado. About October 1, only two days' journey above the mouth of the Virgin, Jedediah found the salt cave of which the Indians had told him; he explored it curiously, naming it like the river in compliment to John Quincy Adams.

It was about October 3 that Jedediah came back to an old friend, the Seedskeeder. Like his own party, the river showed the effects of its passage through the red rock country above. The color of its waters, a warm reddish brown, made understandable the name Colorado; the Seedskeeder was also vastly swollen, a surging, powerful stream which was clearly one of the great rivers of the continent.

Jedediah could have found a way down the Seedskeeder's right bank,[10] but he chose to cross and go down its left bank. An old "Pautch farmer" could be seen on the east side of the river, and perhaps the hope of profiting from his corn patch justified the considerable trouble involved in crossing.

It is likely Jedediah crossed the Colorado on October 4, 1826, and started down it next day. A copy of a letter he wrote the following summer says that he was four days descending the Colorado to the Mojave Villages, but it is impossible that he could have covered so much rough country in so short a time; more probably 21 days was misread by the copyist as 4.

This was a country "remarkably barren, rocky, and mountainous," with many rapids in the river. To travel along the margin of the river was all but impossible, but Jedediah's party had no water other than what the river provided. By the time Jedediah reached the Mojave Villages he "had lost so many Horses that we were all on foot—my men & the remainder of my Horses were worn out with fatigue & hardships & emaciated with hunger." The men got through alive, but more than half the horses died.[11]

This journey down the Virgin and the Colorado was a genuine labor of exploration. Escalante and Domínguez, coming south through Utah in 1776, had reached the Virgin where Jedediah did, but they crossed the river and went on south, hunting a way through the Colorado River badlands to take them back to Santa Fe. Another of the great Franciscan explorers, Garcés, had got no higher up the Colorado than the Mojave Villages, and Spain had sent no more explorers into this arid, brilliantly colored land.[12]

The valley in which the Mojaves lived was broad and beautiful, though the sun had plundered it of the fresh color which in late winter and early spring would make it a garden place. Even so there was a refreshing glint of green along the riverbanks —willows and mesquite. Far down the valley, the slender pinnacles later called the Needles stabbed at the sky; on all sides were the hazy blue mountains which had so surprisingly withdrawn to make space for this oasis.

The Indians Jedediah found here were tall men, well proportioned and powerfully built, wearing—those who wore anything —nothing but a loincloth. The women were short and stout, with plump, amiable faces, though some of the young girls were so pretty and gracefully proportioned as to draw even Jedediah Smith's eye; the women went unclothed above the waist, but wore a short petticoat fashioned from strips of bark which with somewhat comic effect stuck out eight inches or so behind.[13]

The Indians who called themselves "Ammuchábas" (as Jedediah Smith's ear rendered this word of many spellings) cultivated the soil, raising corn, beans, pumpkins, watermelons, musk melons and a little cotton and wheat. For fifteen days Jedediah remained among the Mojaves, to give men and animals a chance to recruit. Meanwhile he questioned his hosts about the country: one of the Mojaves, who answered to the name Francisco, spoke a little Spanish, and Abraham Laplant had a sketchy command of that tongue. Jedediah learned that "it was not far to some of the Missions of California & I detirmined (as this was the only resort) to go to that place as soon as my men & horses should be able to travel." But first he exchanged some of his horses for better ones, and purchased a few animals stolen from the mission herds.

Guided by two runaways from the missions, on November 10, 1826, Jedediah set out on the last stage of his long journey overland to the Pacific. The trail he took across the Mojave Desert and up the river of the same name was an age-old road—the trade route by which the Mojaves brought from the seacoast iridescent sea shells. (The further course of Indian trade spread those shells far and wide—Ashley had found specimens among the Utes in May 1825.) By the same trail Garcés had traveled from the Mojave Villages to Mission San Gabriel in the spring of 1776.

To cross the desert to the San Bernardino Mountains took Jedediah fifteen days,[14] the country one of "complete barrens," over which he generally traveled from morning till night without water. He crossed a broad plain topped by a thin crust of beautiful white salt which blazingly reflected the November sun, and beyond this plain he fell upon a river appropriate to such a land. Inconstant River, Jedediah called it, for often it ran beneath the surface. When the caprice took it to flow above ground, desert willows and delicately gold cottonwoods lifted to the sky in revolt against the universal sterility, but the plant life more characteristically was spiny cactus and yucca. Jedediah followed the Mojave all the way to its sources in the San Bernardino Mountains, and crossed that range south of Cajon Pass by the Mojave Trail.[15]

On November 26, 1826, sixteen days from the Colorado, Jedediah came down out of the rocky hills into the broad San Bernardino Valley. Columns of trees wandered through the plain in humble attendance on the numerous watercourses; dark live oaks grew everywhere; but what captivated the eye was the young green of the first winter grass: they had journeyed into spring.

Here in the valley was abundance after the starving times, cattle by thousands, horses, sheep. They met Indian herdsmen, and presently "there came and old Ind. to us that speaks good spanish, and took us with him to his mansion, which consisted of 2 Rows of large and lengthy Buildings, after the Spanish mode, they remind of the British Barracks—so soon as we enc. there was plenty prepared to eat, a fine young cow killed, and a plenty of corn meal given us." Afterward two friars appeared, having in their gray habits "the appearance of Gentlemen." Jedediah went with the friars to the mission four or five miles off, while Rogers stayed with the company.[16] There was, Rogers says simply, "great feasting among the men as they were pretty hungry not having had any good meat for some time."

On Jedediah's arrival at the mission, he gave up his arms to the corporal in charge, then sat down to write the Governor.[17] Describing his distressed situation, he requested some horses and permission to pass through the country to the Bay of San Francisco. The dream of the Buenaventura died hard, for having failed to find the sources of that river, Jedediah now proposed to ascend it from its mouth: "I wished to follow up one of the largest Riv[ers] that emptied into the Bay cross the Mou[ntains] at its head and from thence to our Deposit on the waters of the Salt Lake."

An express rode off to San Diego with the news of this singular arrival out of the deserts, the first of its kind in the history of California. Jedediah wrote Rogers that he had been received as a gentleman, and instructed him to bring the company on to the mission. Rogers arrived late on the twenty-eighth, being received very politely, though his arms were taken from him. About 10:00 P.M. supper was served and Rogers "was introduced to the 2 Priests over a glass of good old whiskey—and found them to be very Joval friendly Gentlemen."

The head of Mission San Gabriel was Father José Bernardo Sánchez. Kind and generous in his disposition, lively of manner, he charmed all who met him, including these two ragged Americans. Within a few days Rogers was writing in his journal, "I must say he is a very fine man and a very much of a gentleman," and two months later, feelingly:

> old Father Sanchus has been the greatest friend that I ever met with in all my Travels, he is worthy of being called a christian, as he possesses charity in the highest degree—and a friend to the poor and distressed, I ever shall hold him a man of God, taking us when in distress feeding and clothing us—and may god prosper him and all Such men.

Jedediah expressed his own feeling by naming the Sierra Nevada itself for the good father, "Mount Joseph." [18]

Jedediah reached Mission San Gabriel very nearly at the height of its prosperity. Secularization of the missions was to come within a very few years, bringing inevitable destruction to a way of life which had its harsh aspects but was an effective instrument of colonization. A handful of friars presided benevolently if autocratically over the daily lives of several thousand Indian neophytes who dwelt at the mission or in small rancherías scattered over the mission's far-flung grazing lands. As nominal protection from the wild Indians of the interior, a corporal's guard of soldiers was domiciled at the mission.

Rogers thought the situation of the mission very handsome, with pretty streams of water flowing from all quarters, "thousands of acres of Rich and fertile land, as level as a die in view, and a part under cultivation, surrounded on the N. with high and lofty mou[ntains], handsomely timbered with pine, and Cedar, and on the S. with low mou[ntains], Covered with grass and Cattle." The mission owned upwards of 30,000 head of cattle, with "Horses, sheep, Hogs &c in proportion"; the chief source of income was the sale of cattle hides and tallow to shipmasters trading on the coast. The mission was laid out in the form of a square, the chapel facing east and the guardhouse west, with the workshops on north and south. Rogers observed further:

> they have large vine yards, Apple and peach orchards, & some orrange Trees and some fig trees they manufacture Blankets, and sundry other articles, they distill whiskey and grind their own grain, having a water mill, of a tolerable quality, they have upwards of 1000 persons employed men women and children Inds. of different nations.

More attention was paid to the wants of Jedediah and his clerk than to those of the men, but when Jedediah spoke to the *comandante,* his men were removed to good quarters and furnished with cooking utensils and plenty of provisions. A more somber note: "Our 2 Ind. guides were imprisoned in the guard house the 2nd. day after we arrived . . . and remain Confined." One of these Indians died in prison; the other, sentenced to death, was at last pardoned through the intercession of the priest.[19] The lot of runaways, even those who voluntarily returned, was not a happy one.

Jedediah set his blacksmiths to work on a bear trap for the mission orchards, and courtesy met with courtesy: "The Priest presented Mr. S. with two pieces of shirting containing 64 yards, for to make the men shirts, all being nearly naked. Mr. Smith gives each man 3½ yards and kept the same number for himself, Each man getting Enough to make a shirt." The spirits of the men revived, and next day Rogers began issuing a new species of merchandise, "Finger Rings" by the dozen and half dozen. The men distributed these purely out of the goodness of their hearts, for the women about the mission, as Rogers observed, thought it "an honnour to ask a white man to sleep with them." One came to his own lodgings and asked him to "make her a *blanco Pickanina,*" get her a white child, but Rogers did not oblige—"seeing her so forward, I had no propensity to tech her."

Jedediah wrote letters for his men and drew maps for the priest; he drank chocolate, sampled the mission wines and strolled about the sunny gardens. But he grew restive waiting on word from below. On December 1 he went with Laplant to visit Pueblo de Los Angeles,[20] nine miles west; he came back the next evening, having been promised as many horses and mules as he wanted when the Governor should approve his leaving. Rogers' journal from December 5 to 7 is a litany:

> we are still remain[in]g at the mansion of St. Gabriel, waiting the result of the Governor's answer to a letter that Mr. S. addressed to him on the 27th of November. . . . no answer from the Governor as yet; we are waiting with patience to hear from the Governor. . . . No answer as yet from the Governor of the Province. Mr. S. and all hands getting impatient. There was a Spanish Gentleman arrived yesterday Evening . . . [who] advises Mr. S. to go an see the governor in case he does not receive an answer in a few days—he is a man of Business and is well aware that men on Expenses and Business of importance, should be preservering—he appears anxious as respects our well fare—Mr. S. has some Idea of going in company with him to Sandeigo, the residence of the Governor.

At last, on December 8, word from San Diego, brought by Captain William H. Cunningham of the ship *Courier,* a Bostonian who had been on the coast since the previous June.[21] The Governor required Jedediah's presence in San Diego. The following morning Jedediah set out on horseback with the Captain, taking the black boy, Peter Ranne, as a servant, and having, as Jedediah says, "a Soldier for a guide or guard (furnished by the Gov.)."

They reached San Diego at 2:00 P.M. on December 12.[22] It had suited the Governor-General, José María Echeandia, to administer the affairs of the province from this sun-baked place rather than from the old capital, Monterey; some said the climate was the attraction, others looked knowingly at a lady of the town. The presidio stood on the slopes of a barren hill, enclosed by high walls of dark, unburned brick. On one side of the square thus formed stood the accommodations built for the officers and their families; opposite were the chapel and storehouses. Directly in front of the gateway was the residence of the *Comandante,* which not only overlooked the square but afforded a magnificent view of the seacoast.[23]

Echeandia turned out to be a thin, juiceless man who towered three or four inches above Jedediah's six feet. His gaunt, almost emaciated face gave little hint of his thoughts, but these were sufficiently revealed by his questions. "Much of a Gentleman but very Suspicious" was Jedediah's impression of him; three times in four days he called in the young American to question him about the circumstances of his entrance into California. Beaver hunters were a species of humanity the Spanish language scarcely sufficed to name, and the aptest description Echeandia could find for Jedediah appeared to be *pescador,* fisherman. To the Governor it made better sense that the American should have come in out of the deserts on a military mission than that he should have arrived in pursuit of animals. When Jedediah produced his license from General Clark, Echeandia was made the more suspicious: here were five passports for fifty-seven men, but Jedediah had come in to San Gabriel with but fourteen men[24]—where was the rest of his party? Jedediah expounded, expostulated and explained, endeavoring to convince the Governor "of the truth that I was only a hunter & that Dire necessity had driven me here." He gave the Governor his journal and wrote out his ideas of the country, all to no purpose. On December 16 Jedediah wrote Rogers to pick out eight of the best beaver skins he had and send them down to San Diego; he would show the officers how to face their cloaks and thereby give them some dim understanding of the uses of beaver.[25] Also he wrote the American minister in Mexico, for it seemed only too likely that he would be detained two or three months and still be under the necessity of going to Mexico. If the Governor detained him until perfectly satisfied that he was no spy, Jedediah might lose the spring hunt. The Governor had been so kind as to say that if detained Jedediah should want for nothing, but what Jedediah wanted was not to be detained.

Jedediah's reactions were those of a businessman impatient of the subtleties of politicians, but Echeandia saw more realistically than Jedediah the significance of the young American's arrival in his province. Just as Jedediah's appearance in the Snake Country two years before had announced to the British the American oncoming, so now his bursting on the California scene announced to Mexican authority the disintegration of a historic barrier. Within the decade, the Spanish empire had broken apart; the fragmentation was still going on, and with this arrival out of the deserts a new stress began to operate. Whether or not it rose to the level of conscious thought, this appreciation of the situation would have affected Echeandia's whole attitude. At the same time, the American confronted Echeandia with the disagreeable necessity of having to exercise authority without being able to calculate all the consequences. If he allowed Jedediah to go about his business, he might get himself into trouble in Mexico. If he detained him, he might let himself in for still more trouble; the young man bore licenses signed by a general and had lately been the business partner of yet another general; generals tend to be people with influence, and influence has a long arm.

It would have suited Echeandia best to ship Jedediah off to Mexico and let higher authority wrestle with the problem. But Jedediah found a solution. From the shipmasters in the harbor at San Diego he obtained a certificate vouching for the authenticity of his papers and the purity of his motives. This document, drawn up December 20, eased Echeandia's mind, and he gave the necessary permissions, balking on one point only. Jedediah would have to go back the way he had come; the Governor could not permit him to go up the coast toward the Russian establishment at Bodega.[26]

The obliging Captain Cunningham sailed Jedediah up to San Pedro, and on January 10 Rogers was overjoyed to see his captain again. It took a week to buy horses and supplies, but on January 18 Jedediah got his party moving. Ferguson had tired of the mountain man's life and hid himself until his countrymen had left, and some weeks later Wilson was kicked out of the party,[27] but the rest seemed happy to take up the quest for beaver, hoping for a better showing than the miserable forty skins of the fall hunt.[28]

Echeandia had ordered Jedediah to take his South West Expedition out of California by the same route he had entered. But California for Jedediah and all mountain men after him was a territory narrowly delimited—at this time the settled belt along the coastal plain, and later so much of the country as lay west of the Sierra Nevada. When Jedediah had gone as far back on his trail as the San Bernardino Valley, he considered that he had complied with the Governor's orders. He recrossed the San Bernardino Mountains, but then turned north along the edge of the Mojave Desert, crossing Antelope Valley and the Tehachapi Mountains and coming down into the south end of the great San Joaquin Valley.[29]

Spanish explorers had preceded him, the soldier Fages in 1772, the missionary priest Garcés in 1776, Moraga and Zalvidea in 1806. From the north the valley had been extensively reconnoitered in 1810 by the priest José Viader; the entire valley was known, as far north as the Sacramento.[30] But known in a cloudy, half-forgotten fashion. Jedediah had been able to learn at San Gabriel little more than that in a great valley to the north there were lakes and beaver—"plenty beaver at a lake. . . . Plenty of beaver."[31] The words in Rogers' journal have a little the sound of prayer, for Jedediah had to show for his exertions thus far only sixty-odd horses and a few Indian curiosities. Advances in geographical knowledge counted for little in the fur trade unless they brought a payoff in beaver.

The country into which Jedediah led his men was not at first encouraging; he rode down out of bare, rolling hills into desolate alkali plains, and when he came on the promised lakes, he found them surrounded with endless tule marshes, almost impossible of access. But on the east a high range of mountains lifted, and as Jedediah moved north, swift streams began to tumble down out of these mountains, joining as a great river which flowed north toward San Francisco Bay. Beyond Kings River, called by Jedediah the Wim-mul-che,[32] the country took on a more fertile aspect, with oaks and sycamores growing along the streams; he found beaver again, and elk, deer and antelope in abundance. The Indians he met, a people who cut their hair oddly short, seemed remarkably poor in view of the richness of the country. Naked and destitute of arms save for a few bows and arrows, they lived mainly on fish, roots, acorns and grass. But they were friendly.

By the end of April Jedediah had worked two hundred miles farther north, as far as the American River, and his horses were packing over fifteen hundred pounds of beaver.[33] Getting these furs to rendezvous was beginning to worry him. No river yet seen looked like a reasonable facsimile of the Buenaventura, nor in 350 miles had he found a break in the high wall of the Sierra. The first week in May 1827 he undertook the passage of this barrier range; he turned east up the rugged canyon of the American River.[34]

The snow was too deep. His horses floundered in it and starved; five died before he gave up. Jedediah's journal a year later has a memory of this vain endeavor, the smothering weight of the snow, more snow flaking off the sky, his horses dying, his men discouraged, all in danger of freezing to death.[35] It was sufficient achievement to get down out of the snow and the dark pines, down to the receiving warmth of the flowering valley. Jedediah turned back on his trail seventy-five miles to what he called the Appelaminy—the Stanislaus—where he would find game and the opportunity to recruit.[36]

Meanwhile, disturbing rumors had reached the coastal settlements of Jedediah's passage up through the interior. Relations were never very good between the white settlers and the wild Indians of the San Joaquin who periodically raided the mission herds and offered a haven to runaway neophytes. Both the mission heads and the military authorities were alarmed by the reports of Jedediah's presence among the *gentiles.* On May 16 Father Narciso Durán at San Jose, president of all the missions, wrote Ignacio Martínez, the *comandante* at San Francisco:

This is to inform you that last night and this morning about four hundred souls ran away from this mission to their villages at the Tulare. The reason for this is that the Anglo-Americans sent several communications to people in that part of the country, offering them protection to abandon the mission and Christian obligations and return to their villages to live and die gentiles.

These men have been in the rancherías of the Muguelemnes and Cossmines several days and their stay brought about this inconvenience to this mission, which may be the beginning of such troubles and happenings in other missions. I believe them to be the same people who were in San Gabriel, and who have come all along the chain of missions causing trouble. [37]

Some rumor of Father Durán's disquiet reached Jedediah in his camp on the Stanislaus, and on May 19 he wrote the father explaining his presence in the country: Unsuccessful in crossing the mountains, he had returned to wait until the snow should melt; he was a long way from home and anxious to get there as soon as possible.[38]

Something of a saint, something of a bigot, Father Durán declined to receive Jedediah's letter. It was handed over to the *comandante,* who sent it down to Monterey, where Echeandia now was. Meanwhile Martínez had investigated the situation at San Jose, and on May 21 he wrote the Governor that one of the Christian Indians was at the bottom of the unrest, "that the running away of the Indians was advised by him, using the specious pretext of the Americans." Nevertheless, as a good military man, Martínez took steps against the Americans' coming in to San Jose; he ordered Sergeant Francisco Soto "not to let them advance a single yard, because, though they do not seem to come with any bad intentions, it is not right that they should see what we have here and to permit them to map this territory."

Echeandia himself thought it time to be stern. On May 23 he ordered Martínez to inform Captain Smith that his passport did not authorize him to inspect the settlements, he had aroused the suspicions of the entire province and must be on his way. The Captain might, if he chose, come in to San Jose and after being disarmed, remain there while awaiting orders from Mexico or a ship that would convey him to Oregon. At all events, the Captain was to be taken into custody.

When the Mexican soldiery reached the camp on the Stanislaus, they found that the American captain had already disappeared into the Sierra. Rogers behaved judiciously, for the soldiers left the Americans who had remained behind in peaceful occupation of their camp.[39]

The failure of his first effort to cross the Sierra had taught

Jedediah circumspection. Mount Joseph could be crossed with his whole force this early in the year only at the hazard of losing all his horses. If he was to reach rendezvous by July 1, he would have to get off at once. Jedediah left Rogers and the rest of the men to look after his furs and the horses while with Silas Gobel and Robert Evans he attempted to cross the mountains to rendezvous. He would be back, he promised, within four months.

Jedediah's crossing of the Sierra Nevada, the first by any white man, he described in the most frugal detail. He started May 20, 1827, with seven horses and two mules, loaded with hay for the horses and provisions for the men, and in eight days succeeded in crossing the mountains, having lost only two horses and one mule. The snow on the summit was from four to eight feet deep, but so well packed by the heat of the sun that his animals had relatively little trouble. Apparently Jedediah made his way up the north fork of the Stanislaus to Ebbetts Pass, and on down the eastern slope by a route which took him south of Walker Lake; two maps based on his own, the Gallatin map of 1836 and the Burr map of 1839, depict his route as crossing two northward-flowing streams which must have been the east fork of the Carson and the west fork of the Walker, while the Burr map shows the trail running south of three lakes, close enough to one of them to justify the inference that Jedediah saw Walker Lake.[40]

The course of Jedediah's further journey across the Great Basin, until he reached the present Utah line, must be conjectured on the basis of what was possible. He himself says only that he traveled over a country completely barren and destitute of game, sometimes without water for two days at a time; he adds, "when we found water in some of the rocky hills, we most generally found some Indians who appeared the most miserable of the human race having nothing to subsist on, (nor any clothing) except grass seed, grasshoppers, &c." The route is most nearly approximated today by US 6, though for a good half of the distance across Nevada, Jedediah traveled from thirty to forty miles north of the modern highway.[41] This area, as far south as the Mojave, he called the "Great Sandy Plain," and the Burr map preserves his memory of it: "Some Isolated Mountains rise from this Plain of Sand, to the regions of Perpetual snow, the small streams that flow from these, are soon absorbed in the Sand. It contains a few miserable Indians, and but little Game."

Jedediah was unlucky in not having succeeded in getting across the Sierra at the head of the American River, for that would have brought him down into the basin of the Humboldt River; he would have stumbled on the natural route across the Great Basin. But the Humboldt was a discovery left for Peter Skene Ogden to make, a year and a half later; the route Jedediah took eastward condemned him to eating the leathery flesh of his horses as they gave out. Three had gone into the kettles by the time Jedediah had crossed Nevada, and the three which still staggered along were so feeble as scarce to be able to carry the little camp equipage he had.

When Jedediah's journal takes up his story, on June 22, 1827, he had just crossed the present Utah line near Gandy and was moving north along the base of the Snake and Deep Creek ranges. The journal opens abruptly:

North 25 Miles. My course was nearly parallel with a chain of hills on the west [Deep Creek Mountains], on the tops of which was some snow and from which ran a creek to the North East. On this creek [Thomas Creek] I encamped. The Country in the vicinity so much resembled that on the south side of the Salt Lake that for a while I was induced to believe that I was near that place. During the day I saw a good many Antelope but could not kill any. I however, killed 2 hares which when cooked at night we found much better than horse meat. June 23d N E 35 Miles. Moving on in the morning I kept down the creek on which we had encamped until it was lost in a small Lake. We then filled our horns and continued on our course, passing some brackish as well as some verry salt springs [Salt Wells], and leaving on the north of the latter part of the days travel a considerable Salt Plain [the Salt Desert, the northern reaches of which he had seen the year before]. Just before night I found water that was drinkable but continued on in hopes of finding better and was obliged to encamp without any. June 24th N E 40 Miles I started verry early in hopes of soon finding water. But ascending a high point of a hill I could discover nothing but sandy plains or dry Rocky hills with the Exception of a snowy mountain off to the N E at the distan[c]e of 50 or 60 Miles [the Stansbury Range]. When I came down I durst not tell my men of the desolate prospect ahead but framed my story so as to discourage them as little as possible. I told them I saw something black at a distance, near which no doubt we would find water. While I had been up on the [hill] one of the horses gave out and had been left a short distance behind. I sent the men back to take the best of his flesh, for our supply was again nearly exhausted, whilst I would push forward in search of water. I went on a short distance and waited until they came up. They were much discouraged with the gloomy prospect but I said all I could to enliven their hopes and told them in all probability we would soon find water. But the view ahead was almost hopeless. With our best exertion we pushed forward, walking as we had been for a long time over the soft sand. That kind of traveling is verry tiresome to men in good health who can eat when and what they choose and drink as often as they desire, and to us worn down with hunger and fatigue and burning with thirst increased by the blazing sands it was almost insurportable. At about 4 O Clock we were obliged to stop on the side of a sand hill under the shade of a small Cedar. We dug holes in the sand and laid down in them for the purpose of cooling our heated bodies. After resting about an hour we resumed our wearysome journey, and traveled until 10 O Clock at night, when we laid down to take a little repose. previous to this and a short time after sun down I saw several turtle doves, and as I did not recollect of ever having seen them more than 2 or 3 miles from water I spent more than an hour in looking for water, but it was in vain.[42] Our sleep was not repose, for tormented nature made us dream of things we had not and for the want of which it then seemed possible and even probable we might perish in the desert unheard of and unpitied. In those moments how trifling were all those things that hold such an absolute sway over the busy and prosperous world. My dreams were not of Gold or ambitious honors but of my distant quiet home, of murmuring brooks of Cooling Cascades. After a short rest we continued our march and traveled all night. The murmur of falling waters still sounding in our ears and the apprehension that we might never live to hear that sound in reality weighed heavily uppon us. June 25th. When morning came it saw us in the same unhappy situation pursuing our journey over the desolate waste now gleming in the sun and more insuportably tormenting than it had been during the night. At 10 O Clock Robert Evans laid down in the plain under the shade of a small cedar being able to proceed no further. We could do no good by remaining to die with him and we were not able to help him along but we left him with feelings only known to those who have been in the same situation and with the hope that we might get relief and return in time to save his life. The Mountains . . . was apparently not far off and we left him and proceeded onward in the hope of finding water. . . . After traveling about three Miles we came to the foot of the Mt and there to our inexpressible joy we found water.[48] Goble plunged into it at once, and I could hardly wait to bath my burning forehead before I was pouring it down regardless of consequences. Just before we arrived at the spring I saw two indians traveling in the direction in which Evans was left, and soon after the report of two guns was heard in quick succession. This considerably increased our apprehension for his safety but shortly after a smoke was seen back on the trail and I took a small kettle of water and some meat and going back found him safe. He had not seen the indians and had discharged his gun to direct me where he lay, and for the same purpose had raised a smoke. He was indeed far gone being scarcely able to speak. When I came the first question he asked me was, have you any water? I told him I had plenty and handed him the kettle, which would hold 6 or 7 quarts in which there was some meat mixed with the water. O says he, why did you bring the meat and putting the kettle to his mouth he did not take it away until he had drank all the water, of which there was at least 4 or 5 quarts and then asked me why I had not brought more. This however revived him so much that he was able to go on to the spring.

The three men remained the rest of that day, June 25, 1827, at the springs in Skull Valley to rest their "wearied and emaciated bodies." Meanwhile Jedediah cut up the starved flesh of the dead horse and spread it out to dry. Next day he moved north along the base of the Stansbury Mountains, camping at some brackish water after having passed during the day a lodge occupied by two Indians, a squaw and two children. The Indians were somewhat alarmed but friendly, and cheerfully shared with the whites a little antelope meat they had; they gave Jedediah to understand that buffalo country was not far off. He could learn nothing from them of the Great Salt Lake, but next day another ten miles along the base of the mountains brought them to

an expanse of water Extending far to the North and East. The Salt Lake a joyful sight was spread before us.

Is it possible said the companions of my sufferings that we are so near the end of our troubles. For myself I durst scarcely believe that it was really the Big Salt Lake that I saw. It was indeed a most cheering view for although we were some distance from the depo, yet we knew we would soon be in a country where we would find game and water which were to us objects of the greatest importance and those which would contribute more than any others to our comfort and happiness.

Those who may chance to read this at a distance from the scene may perhaps be surprised that the sight of this lake surrounded by a wilderness of More than 2000 Miles diameter excited in me those feelings known to the traveler who, after long and perilous journying, comes again in view of his home. But so it was with me for I had traveled so much in the vicinity of the Salt Lake that it had become my home of the wilderness.

Jedediah swung around the south shore of the lake, finding fresh water at intervals and seeing antelope, but unable to get a shot. On June 28 he reached "the outlet of the Uta Lake," the Jordan River, swollen with the spring runoff. For some distance on either side, the river had overflowed its banks to the depth of two or three feet, and it was difficult to force a way through the thick cane grass and bulrushes. The channel itself was deep and about sixty yards wide; at the present stage of the river, the current was rapid. Jedediah cut a quantity of cane grass which he tied into bundles. These, attached together, made a raft sufficiently strong to carry his possessions. Now, Jedediah relates:

I swam and lead my horse over the mule following to the opposite bank which was also overflowed. I then returned and attaching a cord to the raft and holding the end in my mouth I swam before the raft while the two men swam behind. Unfortunately neither of my men were good swimmers and the current being strong, we were swept down a considerable distance, and it was with great difficulty that I was enabled to reach the shore, as I was verry much strangled. When I got to the shore I put my things on the mule and horse and endeavored to go out to dry land but the animals mired and I was obliged to leave my things in the water for the night and wade out to the dry land. We made a fire of sedge and after eating a little horse flesh we laid down to rest.

Next morning Jedediah brought his things up from the water and spread them out to dry. All three men were worn down with suffering and fatigue, but they could believe themselves near the end of their troubles, for it was not more than four days' travel to where Jedediah expected to fall in with Jackson and Sublette. By midmorning they were moving again, and they made fifteen miles by nightfall. Jedediah had a shot at a bear and wounded him badly, but the bear got away. At supper they ate the last of their horse meat and talked a little of the probability of their suffering being soon at an end. "I say we talked a little for men suffering from hunger never talk much but rather bear their sorrows in moody silence which is much preferable to fruitless complaints."

The following day, June 30, Jedediah brought down a fat buck, after which he and his two men employed themselves very pleasantly, for two hours forgetting that they were not the happiest people in the world. That afternoon they moved fifteen miles north along the lake shore and another twenty-five miles on July 1. By now they had reached the locality of present Brigham City, and on July 2 they left the lake, turning northeast through the mountains to Cache Valley. Here Jedediah fell in with two hundred lodges of Snakes and learned that the whites were assembled at "the little lake," twenty-five miles distant. The Snakes were themselves en route to rendezvous, and Jedediah encamped with them.

Next morning he hired a horse and a guide and at 3:00 P.M. arrived at Bear Lake.[44] "My arrival," Jedediah says briefly, closing the record of an extraordinary journey, "caused a considerable bustle in camp, for myself and party had been given up as lost. A small Cannon brought up from St Louis was loaded and fired for a salute."

11. RENDEZVOUS: 1827

During Jedediah Smith's absence in California, much history had been made, and Smith, Jackson & Sublette had been brought a long way on the road to solvency. Some of this was David Jackson's doing; in his quiet way, he had brought in the beaver on which everything depended. But this was a year of achievement for William L. Sublette in particular.

To begin with, Sublette made a memorable fall hunt. Daniel Potts, who had not succeeded in getting off to the southwest with Jedediah Smith, ended by accompanying the junior partner, and thereby Sublette's company acquired a historian. A reluctant historian, it is true, for Potts took his departure toward the Blackfoot country only because he could make a party for no other route. Sublette, whom the Indians called "Cut Face" for a scar on his chin, or "Fate" for reasons unexplained,[1] led his company north to the forks of the Snake, and then up Henrys Fork some thirty miles, after which he circled the Tetons into upper Jackson Hole. Most of the way he was harassed by Blackfeet.

In Jackson Hole, Sublette's party again fell upon the principal branch of the Snake. They followed it up to its source, then went on north across a divide to the source of the Yellowstone, which proved to be "a large fresh water lake . . . about one hundred by forty miles in diameter, and as clear as crystal." They were the first white men since John Colter to lay eyes on Yellowstone Lake,[2] and Potts's description is the earliest of record. But Daniel Potts had a much more significant discovery to report, no hint of which had got into the legend of Colter's wanderings:

On the South border of this Lake is a number of hot and boiling springs, some of water and others of most beautiful fine clay, resembling a mush pot, and throwing particles to the immense height of from twenty to thirty feet. The clay is of a white, and of a pink color, and the water appears fathomless, as it appears to be entirely hollow underneath. There is also a number of places where pure sulphur is sent forth in abundance.

An experience many later visitors to Yellowstone will understand:

One of our men visited one of these whilst taking his recreation—there at an instant the earth began a tremendous trembling, and he with difficulty made his escape when an explosion took place resembling that of thunder. During our stay in that quarter I heard it every day.

Evidently Sublette had reached the West Thumb of Yellowstone Lake, its paint pots and geysers more active than now. From this time, tales about the Yellowstone would get around in the mountains, laughed at by those not simple enough to be taken in by mountain yarning; formal "discovery" of this magnificent country would not come for over forty years.

Of Sublette's return to Cache Valley, Potts says merely:

From this place by a circuitous route to the North West we returned. Two others and myself pushed on in advance for the purpose of accumulating a few more Beaver, and in the act of passing through a narrow confine in the mountain, we were met plumb in the face by a large party of Blackfeet Indians, who not knowing our number fled into the mountain in confusion: we retired to a small grove of willows; here we made every preparation for battle—after which finding our enemy as much alarmed as ourselves we mounted our horses, which were heavily loaded, and took the back retreat. The Indians raised a tremendous yell, showered down from the mountain top, and almost cut off our retreat. We here put whip to our horses and they pursued us in close quarters until we reached the plains, when we left them behind. On this trip one man was closely fired on by a party of Black-feet; several others were closely pursued.[3]

Thus Sublette, late in the fall, got back to "the depot" in Cache Valley. What Jackson had been doing meanwhile remains something of a mystery: he is always a hard man to follow. It seems likely that Jackson headed for the lower reaches of the

Snake Country. Who made up his party is not known, but two years later Thomas Fitzpatrick was Jackson's clerk, and he may have acted in that capacity during all the years Smith, Jackson & Sublette operated in the mountains.[4]

Wherever Jackson went, whoever made up his party, he had a successful hunt. Either he returned in person to Cache Valley or he sent back an express with word of his prospects, for immediately after his own return from the Yellowstone country, Sublette took on himself the responsibility of getting the word down to Ashley. Such an express at this season involved a journey on foot, and Sublette had to go in person. He set out for St. Louis with a single companion, "Black" Harris.

Harris, the mountain men agreed, was the darnedest liar; lies tumbled out of his mouth like boudins out of a buffler's stomach. But he was also a "man of great leg," exactly suited to such a journey as this. His given name was Moses, and he was born, it is said, in Union County, South Carolina. He may first have gone to the mountains in 1822, and it is reasonably certain that he was one of the two men named Harris who in the fall of 1823 floated down the Missouri with John S. Fitzgerald. Beckwourth says he went to the Rockies a year later in Ashley's party. Harris looked and was tough; the painter Alfred Jacob Miller described him as "of wiry form, made up of bone and muscle, with a face apparently composed of tan leather and whip cord, finished off with a peculiar blue-black tint, as if gunpowder had been burnt into his face." He was a man of violent passions, but for all that, as Clyman once remarked, "a free and easy kind of soul Especially with a Belly full."[5]

Wearing snowshoes, the two men set out from the valley of the Great Salt Lake on January 1, 1827.[6] Horses would have been able neither to travel through the snow nor to find feed, so Sublette and Harris took with them an Indian-trained packdog, on the back of which they strapped fifty pounds of sugar, coffee and other provisions. On their own backs they carried a supply of dried buffalo meat.

As far as the valley of the Green they saw no buffalo sign; they came instead on evidences that Blackfeet were in the country. It seemed expedient to leave the traveled road for "the open plains," the approaches to South Pass south of the Sandy, where they were able to obtain water only by melting snow or ice. Of water in this form, however, there was no lack, for the whole countryside seemed drifted over with it. Two weeks' travel brought them to the Sweetwater, and on the fifteenth day they reached Independence Rock.

From here on the journey was a rugged one, for the plains were a formidable proposition in winter. As Sublette and Harris moved down the Platte, they encountered snowdrifts which compelled them to wear their snowshoes for half a mile at a time, and there was ever less wood: often they were forced to walk half the night to keep from freezing. Near Ash Hollow they came on Pawnee sign. A large party like Ashley's might be safe among the Pawnees, but what had befallen Jim Clyman in the summer of 1824 was a memory still fresh. Although they were beginning to stumble with weakness, Sublette and Harris veered away from the river for three days.

Afterward they fell on a large and recent trail made by Omahas. Sublette and Harris followed this trace four days before overtaking the camp. The chief, Big Elk, received them kindly, and other Indians they met subsequently were no less friendly. But the red men could afford the whites little in the shape of food. On one occasion Sublette traded his butcher knife, a mountain man's most prized possession, for a dried buffalo tongue—a dainty he and Harris devoured on the spot.

The dog was lame and starving. Each day it fell behind, limping into camp long after dark. The two men had got as far down the Platte as Grand Island, but the two hundred miles that separated them from the settlements seemed an infinity; both were in bad shape. One night they halted at a point where three elm trees grew. Sublette had barely strength to scrape the snow from the earth, gather his blanket about him and fall exhausted to the ground, but Harris broke dead branches from the trees and kindled a fire. When the dog crawled into camp, Harris proposed that it be killed. After a long wrangle Sublette gave in. Harris snatched up his ax and struck the dog. The animal fell, but staggered to its feet. Reeling with weakness, Harris struck again and missed. At the third blow the ax flew off the handle, and the dog, howling piteously, fled into the night. The frantic Harris called for Sublette's assistance, and the two men groped about in the darkness until they found the mourning dog. While Sublette held the animal, Harris stabbed it, then flung the carcass on the fire to singe it. But the dog still clung to life; convulsively it kicked off the fire. It was more than their nerves could stand. Sublette seized his ax and dashed in the animal's skull.

Sublette returned to his blanket. Harris roasted the dog and set aside some of the flesh for his booshway. By morning Sublette was able to choke down a little of it. This food carried them for another two days. They staggered along, now and then seeing a bird, without being able to bring it down. They had turned away from the Platte, taking the road southeast toward the Kaw,[7] but the going was desperately hard, for the snow was not crusted over sufficiently to bear their weight. They shot a rabbit, however, and soon afterward fell on a Kaw trail. The trail was a month old, but the Kaws had beaten down the snow, and they were able to make better progress. In a timbered bottom they killed four wild turkeys. That carried them to the Big Vermilion, and a few more days brought them to the Old Kaw village. Here they were fed and given something to drink, but the terrible pressure of time rode them, the necessity to be in St. Louis by March 1. Harris had sprained his ankle, but by giving up his pistol, Sublette got a horse for him to ride, and on they went, reaching the Missouri two days later. On March 4, just three days late, the two men rode into St. Louis.

This arrival was important to William L. Sublette and his partners to a degree they could scarcely have anticipated when, the previous July, they signed the contract with Ashley. For Ashley, Sublette found on reaching St. Louis, was by no means done with mountain adventures; he was full of plans to send an expedition to the Rockies which in effect would compete with Smith, Jackson & Sublette.

The idea may have been in Ashley's mind all along, for there is a curious stipulation in the contract the General drew up with the three partners in July 1826: "it is understood and agreed . . . that so long as the said Ashley continues to furnish said Smith

Jackson & Sublette with Merchandise . . . he will furnish no other company or Individual with Merchandise *other than those who may be in his immediate service.*" This was enough to put the squeeze on the free trappers, who would have to deal with Smith, Jackson & Sublette or develop a supply service of their own. But for Ashley himself the arrangement left a loophole large enough to drive a wagon through. He no sooner reached St. Louis than he began loading the wagon.

On October 14, 1826, Ashley addressed a letter to the partners of the French Fur Company, Bartholomew Berthold, Bernard Pratte and Pierre Chouteau. That letter has been quoted in part on page 190, but it is significant for other reasons than its account of Ashley's dealings the previous summer with Smith, Jackson & Sublette. The General went straight to the point:

> I contemplate sending an expidition across the R Mountains the ensuing Spring for the purpose of trading for and trapping Beavers, and from a conversation had with Genl. B. Pratte a few days since I am induced to propose to you an equal participation in the adventure.
>
> [He describes the arrangements he has made with Smith, Jackson & Sublette, including the prices at which some of the merchandise is to be delivered in the mountains, then continues:]
>
> The expedition which I propose sending in the spring will consist of about forty Men one hundred and twenty mules & horses, the merchandise &c necessary to supply them for twelve months, and that to be furnished Messrs Smith Jackson & Sublett, all of which must be purchased for cash on the best terms.
>
> If you are disposed to join me in the adventure you will please signify the same by letter previous to my departure for the East——[8]

Here are two separate though related business undertakings. Ashley is to act as supplier for Smith, Jackson & Sublette. But his expedition is to trap as well as trade for beaver; and it is to be equipped for twelve months. The logic is apparent. If men were to be sent out to the Rockies anyway, it would be a good idea to keep them there a full year, trapping beaver the while.

The partners in the French Company took Ashley's proposal under advisement. His rivals had been profoundly impressed with Ashley's successes of the past two years, but the mountains had ruined everybody else who ventured into them. A further complication was that Etienne Provost was back from the mountains asking to be taken into the company.[9] The partners in St. Louis wrote to Berthold, then upriver at Fort Lookout, requesting his advice. On December 9 he replied:

I dare not advise anything about the project with Ashley. However, it seems to me that it would be well for us to assure ourselves of Provost, who is the soul of the trappers of the Mountains [*l'âme des chasseurs des Montagnes*]. . . . Even if it was only to hinder the meeting between him and the Robidoux I would say it seems that he should be made sure of, unless you have other plans.[10]

Provost was put on the payroll, to remain the rest of his life. But the negotiation with Ashley dragged. On February 2, 1827, Ashley wrote Pierre Chouteau from Lancaster, Pennsylvania, trying to bring the business to a head.

Dr Sir

In addition to the terms of my proposition made to Messrs. B. Pratte & Co to equally participate with me in an expedition intended for the Rocky mountains—I propose to furnish what mules & horses I have (say about one hundred) with each a saddle & rope, the former at fifty five dollars & the latter at twenty five dollars pr head —all the merchandize which I now have intended for that Expedition, on terms equal to such as you may furnish similar articles for the same purpose, I will accompany the expedition as far as I may deem absolutely necessary, and receive for my personal services at the rate of two hundred & fifty dollars pr. month which sum is to be paid by Messrs. B Pratt &c—all the beaver which I may receive for debts now due me by the hunters west of the mountains shall be delivered to said concern as proposed, they accounting to me for the same at whatever price I receive it in that country which is in no case to exceed three dollars pr pound—after the conclusion of the hunt say about the first of July 1828 any remna[n]ts of merchandize or other articles (furs mules & horses for the transportation of the same excepted) is to be taken by said B Pratt & Co on their acct at a discount of thirty three & one third pr ct less than the retail price in that country & for one half of the whole amt. thereof the said B. Pratt will account to me for and pay the same at St Louis—Two confidential persons will be necessary to conduct the business to whome we must expect to pay saleries of considerable amt I should prefer Mr. August Chouteau [eldest son of Pierre Chouteau] being at the head of the business I would be willing to pay him one hundred dollars pr month for his services—The other person I will Select myself—If Mr. Chouteau or some other Gentleman equally qualified cannot be had on the terms before mentioned I would be willing to allow him or the person in charge of the business an equal participation in the profits we finding the whole capital, viz, this person to receive one third of the neat proceeds and he at the same time accountable for one third of any loss which may appear in the business—Messrs. B. Pratte & Co will not suffer any person trading for them at Taus or other place or places, directly or indirectly to interfere with the business of the proposed concern in any way whatever—or allow them to persue a similar business in the same section of country—my [word lost by seal] will not permit me at preasant to enter more minutely into the articles of the proposed assoseation, the outlines being understood, articles of a minor nature can be specifyed at St Louis—I must require of Mr. Chouteau an answer to this proposition in *positive terms*, befor I leave Pittsburg say by the 15th next—my health is much better than when I left Phi[a]—I shall go directly to Pittsburg——[11]

Replying from Philadelphia on February 10, Chouteau observed that in all their conversations the difficulty had been to decide who should conduct the enterprise. "I am convinced that with you in charge of the Expedition, you would prove of great service, not only in deciding upon the route to be followed, but to instill order and obedience, which are indispensable in a voyage of this sort. But you are aware General that your presence would be still more necessary in crossing the Mountains & for transactions with the Hunters, than it would be elsewhere." He proposed that they wait on the return of both to St. Louis, when an hour's conversation would be more effective than volumes of correspondence in deciding on a head for the expedition.[12]

Ashley went on back to St. Louis. There, on February 28, in the presence of Bernard Pratte, he drew up a memorandum covering the main points of the discussions previously had. Down to this moment, four days before Sublette reached St. Louis, the project still hung fire, for the memorandum ended, "should Genl.

Pratte exceede to these propositions, it will be necessary immediately to enter into articles of agreement."[13]

Unless it had been clearly understood the year before that Ashley reserved the right to trap on his own account, Sublette must have objected strenuously to any such project as he found shaping up in St. Louis. What it amounted to was that Smith, Jackson & Sublette, by purchasing goods through Ashley, underwrote the expenses of a rival operation. Sublette may have threatened to look for backing elsewhere, with good prospects of finding it despite the circumstance that the firm's returns for the present year were committed to Ashley. Another possibility is that Chouteau's reluctance to enter on an arrangement for a trapping venture which did not require Ashley's return to the mountains proved to be an insuperable obstacle. A final possibility is that Sublette made so good a proposition to Ashley that the General gave over his own plans.

This third idea has to be taken seriously, for there are facts to support it. The proposition might have shaped up like this: Merchandise to the amount of $15,000 would be taken up to the mountains this spring and the furs brought down in late summer. When the caravan reached Missouri, probably about the end of September, Ashley would meet it with an outfit for 1828. Smith, Jackson & Sublette would buy from Ashley all his mules and horses and use them to transport the new outfit back to the Rockies immediately. This would save the expense of wintering the pack animals in Missouri; it would return them to the mountains where an unfailing demand existed; and it would save the trouble of sending outfit 1828 to the mountains next spring. Above all, it would remove Ashley from the operating end of the business. Smith, Jackson & Sublette would find a new function for him; hereafter Ashley would serve as agent in marketing their furs.

The arrangement just described actually materialized, but we may never be sure to what extent the details were worked out beforehand. At any rate, nothing more is heard of Ashley's proposal to trap in the Rockies for a year, and the agreement he reached with the Chouteau interests was limited to the delivery in the Rockies of the goods ordered by Smith, Jackson & Sublette.

Courtesy, Bureau of American Ethnology.

CROW INDIAN, ET-TISH-EASTER-KO-KISH OR SPOTTED RABBIT

Photo by De Lancey Gill, 1910.

Courtesy, Coe Collection, Yale University.

GIVING DRINK TO THIRSTY TRAPPERS

Alfred Jacob Miller, 1837.

Courtesy, U.S. Forest Service.

THE FALLS OF THE POPO AGIE

Photo by A. H. Carhart, 1922.

Courtesy, U.S. Forest Service.

STRAWBERRY POINT, UPPER VIRGIN RIVER

Photo by Paul S. Bieler, 1941.

For this limited undertaking the French partners named as their agent James B. Bruffee, and Ashley picked as field commander Hiram Scott, one of the two captains (with Jedediah Smith) who had commanded his men in the campaign against the Rees.[14] The party got off from St. Louis late in March 1827 and, a distinct novelty, took along a piece of artillery, a four-pounder, mounted on a carriage drawn by two mules—the first wheeled vehicle that ever crossed South Pass.[15] (It was this cannon which saluted Jedediah Smith on his return from California.) Ashley accompanied the party only to the frontier in consequence of his "verry bad health," but he got the expedition off confident it was in good hands. "Messrs Bruffee & Scott appears alive to our intrest," he wrote the Chouteaus from Lexington on April 11, "the latter is entirely efficient & if properly supported by the former will keep all things in their proper channel." [16]

One detail William L. Sublette had to attend to personally was a license to trade with the Indians. Issued March 26, 1827, the license authorized Smith, Jackson & Sublette to trade for two years at "Camp Defence [Defiance], on the waters of a river supposed to be the Bonaventure.—Horse Prairie, on Clark's river of the Columbia, and mouth of Lewis' fork of the Columbia." The first location undoubtedly was the place of rendezvous in Cache Valley (Bear River as yet was shown on no maps, and the Buenaventura served to approximate the location for official purposes). Jedediah had some firsthand acquaintance with Horse Prairie, which was located a few miles east of Flathead Post. But none of the American trappers, to the time Sublette left the Rockies, had yet worked the country about the mouth of the Snake, the near vicinity of the Hudson's Bay Company's Fort Nez Perces. This may have been Jackson's objective at the time he and Sublette parted from Jedediah Smith at the rendezvous of 1826. The amount of capital employed was stated in the license as $4,335, which would seem to have been a gross understatement.[17]

Scant enough is the information as to what was happening in the mountains while Jedediah Smith was working his way north through California and William L. Sublette was wrestling with the destinies of the partnership in the lower country. Jackson presumably spent the time clearing off any beaver which remained on the Weiser, the Payette and the Boise after Alexander Ross's summer hunt of 1824 and Jedediah's spring hunt of 1826.[18] He lost no men and got back to rendezvous with good returns. The only definite information regarding the movements of any of the trappers is furnished by Daniel Potts. His narrative is worth quoting; he participated in an exploration which corrected a misconception Jedediah Smith had entertained about the course of the Sevier River, and he describes one of the first trapping forays into central Utah:

Shortly after our arrival last fall in winter quarters, we made preparations to explore the country lying south west of the Great Salt Lake. Having but little or no winter weather, six of us took our departure about the middle of February, and proceeded by forced marches into the country by way of the Utaw Lake—which lies about 80 miles south of the Sweet Water [Bear] Lake, is thirty miles long and ten broad. It is plentifully supplied with fish, which form the principal subsistence of the Utaw tribe of Indians. We passed through a large swamp of bullrushes, when suddenly the lake presented itself to our view. On its banks were a number of buildings constructed of bullrushes, and resembling muskrat houses. These we soon discovered to be wigwams, in which the Indians remained during the stay of the ice. As there is not a tree within three miles, their principal fuel is bullrushes.

This is a most beautiful country. It is intersected by a number of transparent streams. The grass is at this time from six to twelve inches in height, and in full bloom. The snow that falls, seldom remains more than a week. It assists the grass in its growth, and appears adapted to the climate.

The Utaw lake lies on the west side of a large snowy mountain [the Wasatch Mountains], which divides it from the Leichadu [Green River]. From thence we proceeded due south about thirty miles to a small river [the Sevier] heading in said mountain, and running from S. E. to S. W. To this I have given the name of Rabbit river, on account of the great number of large black tail rabbits or hares found in its vicinity. We descended this river about fifty miles to where it discharges into a salt lake, the size of which I was not able to ascertain, owing to the marshes which surround it, and which are impassable for man and beast. This lake is bounded on the south [north] and west by low Cedar Mountains, which separate it from the plains of the Great Salt Lake. On the south and east also, it is bounded by great plains. The Indians informed us that the country lying southwest, was impassible for the horses owing to the earth being full of holes. As well as we could understand from their description, it is an ancient volcanic region. This river is inhabited by a numerous tribe of miserable Indians. Their clothing consists of a breech-cloth of goat or deer skin, and a robe of rabbit skins, cut in strips, sewed together after the manner of rag carpets, with the bark of milk weed twisted into twine for the chain. These wretched creatures go out barefoot in the coldest days of winter. Their diet consists of roots, grass seeds, and grass, so you may judge they are not gross in their habit. They call themselves Pie-Utaws, and I suppose are derived from the same stock.

From this place we took an east course, struck the river near its head, and ascended it to its source. From thence we went east across the snowy mountain above mentioned, to a small river [the Frémont River] which discharges into the Leichadu. Here the natives paid us a visit and stole one of our horses. Two nights afterwards they stole another, and shot their arrows into four horses, two of which belonged to myself. We then started on our return. The Indians followed us, and were in the act of approaching our horses in open daylight, whilst feeding, when the horses took fright and ran to the camp. It was this that first alarmed us. We sallied forth and fired on the Indians, but they made their escape across the river.

We then paid a visit to the Utaws, who are almost as numerous as the Buffaloe on the prarie, and an exception to all human kind, for their honesty.[19]

Bear Lake, site of rendezvous this year, lies within the great bend of the Bear River, nearly bisected by the Utah-Idaho boundary along the forty-second parallel. The lake was probably discovered by the Nor'Westers, for Alexander Ross prints a letter written by Donald Mackenzie on September 10, 1819, from "Black Bears Lake," and in his account of his own adventures in the summer of 1824 Ross writes that his party considered proceeding "by the Blackfeet river to . . . Bear's lake, where the country was already known." Still, it is curious that William Kittson, who was a member of Mackenzie's party in 1819-1820, should later have drawn a map of the Bear River country which has no intimation that such a lake existed. For the Americans, Bear Lake undoubtedly was discovered by Captain Weber in the fall of 1824, because Jim Beckwourth calls it "Weaver's Lake." The lake had many other names—Little Lake, Sweet Lake and Sweet Water Lake (all serving to distinguish it from Great Salt Lake), Little Snake Lake and Trout Lake; it is one of the most beautiful bodies of water in the West, its waters profoundly blue under the sienna hills. Rendezvous was at the south end of the lake, near present Laketown. A trail south from Bear River ran along the west shore of the lake, and it was by this trail, undoubtedly, that the lake was first discovered, but it could also be approached from the east over a ridge, and from the west by the canyon of Blacksmiths Fork—the way Jedediah was led by his Snake guide on his return from California.[20]

The ingathering of the trappers at Bear Lake began in June, and was attended with a degree of excitement. Potts relates that a few days before his own return from the trapping expedition into central Utah

> a party of about 120 Blackfeet approached the camp & killed a Snake Indian and his Squaw. The alarm was immediately given and the Snakes, Utaws and whites sallied forth for battle—the enemy fled to the mountains to a small concavity thickly grown with small timber surrounded by open ground. In this engagement the squaws were busily engaged in throwing up batteries and dragging off the dead. There were only six whites engaged in this battle, who immediately advanced within pistol shot and you may be assured that almost every shot counted one. The loss of the Snakes was three killed and the same number wounded; that of the whites, one wounded and two narrowly made their escape; that of the Utaws was none, though they gained great applause for their bravery. The loss of the enemy is not known—six were found dead on the ground. a great number besides were carried off on horses.[21]

Jim Beckwourth participated in this battle, and the account he gives of it illustrates the facility with which he embroidered the facts; the fruits of victory, Jim says, "were one hundred and seventy-three scalps, with numerous quivers of arrows, war-clubs, battle-axes, and lances. . . . The trappers had seven or eight men wounded, but none killed. Our allies lost eleven killed in battle." But Beckwourth does furnish two details to amplify Daniel Potts's factual report: the scene of the fight was the shore of Bear Lake, perhaps five miles from camp, and William L. Sublette took a valiant part in the battle.[22]

Participation of Utes in the fight is the more interesting because a rumor of treaty making with that tribe penetrated all the way to Mexico and gave rise to diplomatic representations. The degree of exaggeration in those representations was something in which Beckwourth himself could have taken a just pride. The Mexican Secretary of State wrote the American minister on April 12, 1828, of intelligence lately received that

at four days' journey beyond the lake of Timpanagos, there is a fort situated in another lake, with a hundred men under the command of a general of the United States of North America, having with them five wagons and three pieces of artillery; that they arrived at the said fort in May, and left it on the 1st of August of the year last past, with a hundred horses loaded with otter skins; that the said general caused a peace to be made between the barbarous nations of the Yutas Timpanagos and the Comanches Sozones, and made presents of guns, balls, knives, &c., to both nations; that, of the above-mentioned hundred, five-and-twenty separated themselves to go into the Californias; that the Yuta Timpanago Indian, called *Quimanuapa*, was appointed general by the North Americans, and that he states the Americans will have returned to the fort by the month of December.[23]

Such happenings as these, and especially "the iruption of the twenty-five men into the Californias," were calculated to disturb the tranquillity of the republic, and the American minister was informed that "necessary measures" would be taken. He, however, replied suavely that on examining Melish's map of North America, he found the dividing line between Mexico and the United States to pass through the lake of Timpanagos.

Any point, therefore, four days' journey beyond that lake must be situated within the territory of the United States; and the only act set forth in your excellency's note of which this Government has any right to complain, is that of the entrance of the twenty-five men into California without passports.

Infractions of the laws of Mexico were to be deplored, but hunters passed the boundary of the United States ignorant that they were doing wrong, and pursued their hunting excursions within the territories of Mexico unaware that they were committing a trespass.[24]

Thus the far, faint international repercussions of the activities of Smith, Jackson & Sublette in the West. The gathering at Bear Lake was in fact a trespass on the soil of Mexico, for the site of rendezvous was some fifteen miles south of 42°, but no one knew where that vague abstraction, the boundary line, really ran. No one much cared. Effective sovereignty was exercised here by no nation; law was what could be agreed on with friendly Indians or enforced on hostile Indians.

More important to mountain history was the developing economics of the fur trade. The varied years since Ashley set out for the mountains had brought complications which by the time of rendezvous in 1827 were exerting a powerful pressure on the trade.

Ashley had introduced free trappers into the mountains in 1822-1823. The price for beaver then fixed, $3.00 a pound, held down to the flush times of 1833-1834, when under the pressure of competition it rose to $5.00 a pound in merchandise, $3.50 a pound in cash.[25] Since the price was fixed without regard to the fluctuating market value of the fur, the variable became the price of the goods which were exchanged for beaver. A good market for beaver just possibly might bring lower prices for goods; a poor market most certainly would result in higher prices.

When he sold out to Smith, Jackson & Sublette in the summer of 1826, Ashley stipulated that payment was to be made in beaver delivered at the mountain price, that is, at $3.00 a pound. (He was alternatively willing to transport it to the States and sell it for them, charging them $1.125 a pound for transport, which shows that Ashley was serious when he said, as he once did, that he would gladly pay $1.00 a pound to have beaver delivered in St. Louis from the mountains.)[26] Obviously, if the new partners paid the free trappers $3.00 a pound for their beaver, then turned around and sold it to Ashley at the same price, there was nothing in the deal for them. Their whole margin had to come from the goods they sold. Ashley had therefore stipulated also that he would supply goods to no other company or individual. Unless and until competition showed its face in the mountains, the free trappers would have to deal with Smith, Jackson & Sublette.

There was one other factor in this situation—men who were hired by the year and whose beaver catch, if any, was the property of the company. *Engagés* had always been necessary around the fixed posts, and they may not have been dispensed with when Ashley's men cut loose from their bases on the Missouri and the Yellowstone; camp tenders and horse wranglers as well as trappers were important to a hunt. And a certain number of engaged men was essential. Otherwise a brigade could go nowhere except by common consent. When Jedediah Smith returned to the mountains as Ashley's partner in the fall of 1825, a considerable proportion of his men, perhaps as many as forty-two, were *engagés*.[27]

Some of the men may have been hired at a fixed annual wage, say $200 a year.[28] Others may have been paid a minimum annual wage, plus a percentage of the value of the beaver they caught. When the engagements of his men ran out on the Oregon coast in July 1828, Jedediah agreed to pay ten of them $1.00 a day until they should get back to rendezvous,[29] but whether this was typical of contractual engagements it would be hard to say.

Throughout this period, however, the backbone of the trade remained the free trapper, who might attach himself to a brigade yet retain the right to deal independently with company partners or clerks in the sale of his beaver. And the free trappers, at rendezvous 1827, began getting an education in the manipulation of prices. That Smith, Jackson & Sublette were under heavy pressure themselves did not make the free trappers feel more kindly about it.

A table will illustrate what happened to prices in the mountains between 1825 and 1827. The first column lists the retail prices noted by Daniel Potts at rendezvous in 1827; the second column shows the prices at which Ashley agreed to deliver goods under the contract of July 18, 1826; the third column lists prices for the same goods found in Ashley's accounts of 1825.

Merchandise	Retail 1827	Wholesale 1827	Retail 1825
Powder	$2.50 per lb.	$1.50 per lb.	$2.00 per lb.
Lead	1.50	1.00	1.00
Coffee	2.00	1.25	1.50
Tobacco	2.00	1.25	3.00 [?]
Vermillion	6.00	3.00	....
Beads	5.00	2.50	5.00
Pepper	6.00	....	1.75 [?]
Blankets (three point)	15.00	9.00	9.00
Cotton Stripe, per yd.	2.50	1.25	....
Calico	2.50	1.00	....
Scarlet Cloth (coarse) do.	10.00	6.00	6.00
Blue Cloth (coarse) do.	8.00	5.00	5.00
Ribband, per yd.	0.75	[3.00 per bolt]	0.50
Brass nails, per dozen	0.50	....	....

No wonder Daniel Potts exclaimed that there was a poor prospect of making much money in the mountains; he cited the price of goods and horses, saying that horses cost from $150 to $300 apiece, and some sold as high as $500. (Potts lost one horse on the Yellowstone hunt and two on the central Utah hunt; his loss, he said, could not be computed at less than $450.)[30]

Potts was not the only one to resent the sudden upward surge of prices. We shall see in Chapter 13 that rising American prices and lowered British prices did much to alter the balance of economic force in the mountains. Meanwhile, observe Peter Skene Ogden entering in his journal on January 5, 1828, reports which had reached him of developments at the American rendezvous the previous summer:

. . . altho our Trappers have their goods on moderate terms, the price of their Beaver is certainly low, compared to Americans, with them Beaver large & small are averaged at five Dollars each, with us two Dollars for a Large and one Dollar for a small Beaver here then there is certainly a wide difference . . . it is optional with them to take their furs to St. Louis where they obtain five & half Dollars pr. lb., one third of the American Trappers follow this plan, it is to be observed goods are sold to them at least 150 p.Cent dearer than we do, but again they have the advantage of receiving them on the waters of the Snake Country and an American Trapper, from the short distance he has to travel, not obliged to transport provisions, requires only half the number of Horses we do, and are also very moderate in their advances, for Three years prior to the last one, General Ashly Transported supplies to this Country and in that period has cleared Eighty Thousand Dollars and retired, selling the remainder of his goods on hand at an advance of 150 Pr.Ct. payable in five years in Beaver at five Dollars per lb. or in cash optional with the purchasers, Three young men Smith, Jackson and Soblitz purchased them, and who have the first year made a gain of twenty Thousand Dollars, it is to be observed, finding themselves alone, they sold their goods one third dearer than Ashley did, but have held out a promise of a reduction in their prices this year, What a contrast between These young men and myself, They have been only six years in the Country, and without a doubt in as many more will be independent men. . . .[31]

Ogden's envious view of his young American rivals was a little astigmatic, but 1827 brought them over the hump. At Bear Lake, Jackson and Sublette delivered to Bruffee, as agent for "W. H. Ashley & Co.," 7,400⅝ pounds of beaver at $3.00 a pound, together with 95 pounds of castor at the same price, and 102 otter skins at $2.00 each, the proceeds of the year's hunt totaling $22,690. At the same time they accepted delivery on merchandise invoiced at $22,447.14, plus 5 horses valued at $30 each. There were some sundries among both the credits and the debits, but these balanced out at $22,929.[32] Apparently the invoice of merchandise delivered included the note given to Ashley the previous year, for the Sublette papers contain a quit claim by Ashley dated October 1, 1827, which says that if in July 1826 Smith, Jackson & Sublette gave a note in Ashley's favor for $7,821, "a ballance then due by them to me now therefore if any such note was given it is to be considered entir[e]ly void as they the said Smith Jackson & Sublette have since paid said amount." [33]

All this had been the doing of Jackson and Sublette, for the proceeds of Jedediah Smith's spring hunt of 1827 were still in California. On the whole, the partners had had an encouraging first year, and they were prepared to undertake something more ambitious. This year it had suited their convenience to hand over their beaver in the mountains at $3.00 a pound, letting Ashley run the risk and assume the expense of transport. Next year one of the partners would take down the year's hunt, and they might have a try at marketing their beaver themselves.

One detail remained, getting outfit 1828 up to the mountains this fall. It seems likely that an arrangement was entered into with Hiram Scott to handle this business for the partnership, for Scott came to a tragic end on the Platte next year, and this was the only opportunity that offered for him to get back to the mountains. He may, however, have returned in the capacity of clerk. If so, Jackson himself must have gone down with Bruffee and come back in charge of the outfit. Ashley says that he met the incoming party with everything necessary for another outfit, and that, turning back with the same horses and mules, they reached the mountains by the last of November. However, Peter Skene Ogden was informed in February 1828 that the American "Traders from St. Louis . . . did not return last fall . . . [owing to] the severe Winter." En route back to the mountains, this party seems to have lost a few horses to Pawnees; otherwise, nothing is known of their experiences.[34]

Rendezvous broke up July 13, 1827, ten days after Jedediah's arrival from California. The partners had made their plans.

Sublette was to take another party north, all the way to the Blackfoot lands; the opportunity might have arisen to open trade with these Ishmaelites. Jackson went down to Missouri and back, or more probably he spent the fall in the Utah country, wintering at "the depot" on Bear River. Robert Campbell seems to have remained with Jackson until the spring hunt of 1828, when the young Irishman took a party north to the Flathead lands.

Re-outfitted with eighteen men and supplies for two years, Jedediah proposed to rejoin his men in California, then trap his way up the California-Oregon coast to the Columbia. If he got back to rendezvous, which again next year would be held at Bear Lake, well and good. If not, his partners would see him in two years

12. THE CALIFORNIA QUAGMIRE

Eighteen men set out with Jedediah Smith on his second expedition to California. One of the eighteen was the durable Silas Gobel, but Robert Evans had had enough of the West for the time being; he left the mountains this summer and apparently did not return until 1834, when he was chosen by Nathaniel Wyeth to be the first bourgeois of Fort Hall.[1]

Aside from Gobel, these composed the company: Henry ("Boatswain") Brown, William Campbell, David Cunningham, Thomas Daws, Francois Deromme, Isaac Galbraith, Polette Labross (a mulatto), Joseph Lapoint, Toussaint Maréchal (or Marrishall), Gregory Ortago (a "Spaniard"), Joseph Palmer, John B. Ratelle, John Relle ("a Canadian"), Robiseau ("a Canadian half-breed"), Charles Swift, John Turner and Thomas Virgin. Maréchal, Ortago and Deromme had come to the Rockies only this summer, but the rest were old hands; Galbraith and Virgin had been in the mountains since 1824, at least. Two Indian women were probably squaws of the Canadians.[2]

Jedediah took this party south from rendezvous on July 13, 1827. He had learned enough of "the Sand Plain" on his eastward journey

> to know that it would be impossible for a party with loaded horses and encumbered with baggage to ever cross it. Of the [nine] animals with which I left the Appelamminy but two got through to the Depo, and they were, like ourselves, mere skeletons. I therefore was obliged to take the More circuitous route down the Colorado which although much better than that across the Plain was yet a journey presenting many serious obstacles.

His object, Jedediah adds, was to relieve his party in California and then proceed farther, examining the country beyond Mount

Joseph and along the sea coast. "I of course expected to find Beaver which with us hunters is a primary object but I was also led on by the love of novelty common to all which is much increased by the pursuit of its gratification." [3]

Perhaps it was this love of novelty which started him off for the south by a different route. Instead of heading for the valley of the Great Salt Lake, he took his party southeast, up over the ridge which divides Bear Lake from Bear River, then south up the Bear itself. When the Uinta Mountains loomed ahead, he veered off to the southwest, and probably by way of Chalk Creek came down to the Weber. He then followed in reverse Ashley's route of 1825 as far as the Provo River, and followed that stream down to Utah Valley.[4]

Here he found a large band of Utes encamped, the same with which he had made a treaty the year before. The Utes told him that in the spring some white men had come up from the south and turned east in the direction of Taos; these men were nearly starved to death. What had been an unknown land only a year before was already being transformed into a crossroads. The fur frontier was advancing all over the West, and Jedediah had barely preceded to California trappers who were operating out of New Mexico. The Utes had told a straight story, for along the Sevier, Jedediah found tracks of horses which had been made in the spring when the ground was soft.

His further journey to the Colorado, Jedediah dismisses in a few words. At Lost River the Indians who had been so wild the year before came to him by dozens; Jedediah's journal has an interesting allusion to his previous passage: "Every little party told me by Signs and words so that I could understand them, of the party of White Men that had passed there the year before, having left a knife and other articles at the encampment when the indians had ran away." Jedediah made these Indians further small presents and moved on to the Virgin and the Santa Clara. Not an Indian was to be seen, nor appearance of any having been in the locality during the summer; their flimsy little lodges were burned down.

Anxious to avoid a repetition of his experience in the canyon of the Virgin, Jedediah turned up the Santa Clara River some miles, "and then turning S W I crossed the Mountain without any difficulty and crossing some low Ridges struck a Ravine which I followed down to the bed of the dry River [Beaverdam Wash] which I call Pautch Creek which I followed down to Adam's River about 10 miles below the Mou[tn]." Thus Jedediah pioneered the road taken by present-day US 91 west from St. George. From the time he struck the Virgin, Jedediah had seen but one Indian, who kept as close to rock as a mountain sheep. The Indians continued wild all the way to the Colorado.

On reaching the mouth of the Virgin, Jedediah found "the old Pautch farmer still on the east side of the Colorado." He continues, giving us the barest glimpse of the difficulties of the first journey:

> From this place to the first Amuchaba village my route was the same as when I passed before with the exception that instead of taking the ravine [canyon] in which I had so much difficulty I took another further south and passed in to the river without difficulty.
>
> As there had been no indians to carry news of our approach on our arrival at the village the indians all ran off but finding an opportunity to talk with one of them the[y] soon returned and seemed as friendly as when I was there before.
>
> I remained a day to rest my fatigued animals and then moved down to the next settlement. The indians had heard of my approach and met me some distance above their village.
>
> I went to the place where I intended to cross the Colorado and encamped in a situation where I found good grass, with the intention of giving my horses some rest. I exchanged some horses, Bought some Corn and Beans and made a present to the Chiefs.

Francisco, Jedediah's interpreter of the year before, was still at the Mojave Villages, and he told the young American captain that after Jedediah set out for San Gabriel the previous November "a party of Spaniards & Americans from the Province of Sonora, by the way of the Gila," had appeared there. According to Francisco's story, the members of this party had quarreled and separated, one division continuing up the Colorado, the other taking another direction. This, Jedediah thought, "accounted for the tracks of horses and Mules I had seen on Ashley river and for the starved party which the Utas said had passed through their country."

It sufficed Jedediah that the small mystery of the starving whites had been solved, but this narrative must reckon with the appearance of a party of trappers at such a place and time. It is only surprising that Jedediah had not crossed trails with one of the New Mexico-based parties before now. Etienne Provost had been followed out of Taos by the brothers Robidoux, William Becknell, Ewing Young, Sylvestre Pratte—and a little later by Ceran St. Vrain and the brothers Bent. By the winter of 1824-1825 American trappers out of New Mexico were on the Green, the Grand and the San Juan, and farther south they were reaching the sources of the Gila and the Little Colorado; they may have crossed the continental divide at several points before Jedediah Smith made the momentous crossing farther north.

In September 1826 Sylvestre Pratte led one such party to the Gila; it consisted of fifteen men, including Milton Sublette, the rambunctious younger brother of William. They had a run-in with Coyotero Apaches, who drove them back to the Rio Grande, but after being reinforced by a party of sixteen men under Ewing Young, one of the outstanding figures of the southwestern fur trade, they moved back into Coyotero country. Seven Apaches were killed, after which the season for beaver opened again. Young trapped the Gila to its mouth, and then turned up the Colorado to the Mojave Villages. The Mojaves were not friendly, and in an attack on the party, a number were killed. When Jedediah reappeared in the Mojave Valley, the Indians were still aching from their wounds.[5]

The Mojaves dissembled well, and Jedediah had no intimation that their hearts were bad. He remained three days among them, recruiting his horses and trading a few articles of merchandise for beans, wheat, corn, dried pumpkins and melons. Jedediah's ability to learn from experience was evidenced by the superior condition of his party this year: three days' rest put his animals in shape to travel. It was probably about August 18 that he set about crossing the Colorado.[6]

Leaving the horses and half of the company on the left bank, Jedediah loaded a part of his goods on rafts of cane grass, and moved out on the broad river. The Mojaves had waited patiently for this moment. Raising the war cry, they fell on the ten men and two women who remained behind. Within seconds Brown, Campbell, Cunningham, Deromme, Gobel, Labross, Ortago, Ratelle, Relle and Robiseau were dead and the women made prisoners. Apparently Jedediah and the others were attacked also, for Thomas Virgin was badly wounded in the head by a Mojave war club.[7]

It seemed to the nine who still lived that they would join their companions soon enough, for hundreds of Mojaves were scattered along the banks of the river, and to defend themselves the whites had only their butcher knives and five guns. They had lost their horses and all their provisions but fifteen pounds of dried meat.

"After weighing all the circumstances of my situation as ca[l]mly as possible," Jedediah writes in his journal, "I concluded to again try the hospitality of the Californians. I had left with my party on the Appelaminy a quantity of Beaver furr and if the Governor would permit me to trade, and I could find any person acquainted with the value of furr, I might procure such supplies as would enable me to continue my journey to the north." But how big was the if: "I was yet on the sand bar in sight of My dead companions and not far off were some hundreds of indians who might in all probability close in uppon us and with an Arrow or Club terminate all my measures for futurity."

Such articles of his outfit as would sink Jedediah threw into the river; the rest he spread out on the sand bar. Telling his men the kind of journey they faced, he gave them permission to take with them whatever they chose. The remainder Jedediah scattered over the ground, hoping the Indians would quarrel over the spoils and give him more time to escape. His thoughts must have gone back to the defeat by the Rees four summers before; the ten men lost made this a disaster second only to Ashley's, and his situation now was incomparably worse than Ashley's had been.

Shouldering their small packs, Jedediah and his eight men turned their backs on the Colorado. They had not gone half a mile before the Mojaves closed around them. Jedediah thought it his best chance to move back to the river, and if the Indians allowed him time, select a spot where he and his men might sell their lives as dearly as possible. He succeeded in reaching the riverbank, and took up a position in a thicket of small cottonwood trees. Jedediah's journal continues:

> With our knives we lopped down the small trees in such a manner as to clear a place in which to stand while the fallen poles formed a slight breast work, we then fastened our Butcher knives with cords to the end of light poles so as to form a tolerable lance, and thus poorly prepared we waited the approach of our unmerciful enemies. On one side the river prevented them from approaching us, but in every other direction the indians were closing in uppon us, and the time seemed fast approaching in which we were to come to that contest which must, in spite of courage conduct and all that man could do terminate in our destruction. It was a fearful time Eight [nine] men with but 5 guns were awaiting behind a defence made of brush the charge of four or five hundred indians whose hands were yet stained with the blood of their companions. Some of the men asked me if I thought we would be able to defend ourselves. I told them I thought we would. But that was not my opinion. I directed that not more than three guns should be fired at a time and those only when the Shot would be certain of killing. Gradually the enemy was drawing near but kept themselves covered from our fire. Seeing a few indians who ventured out from their covering within long shot I directed two good marksmen to fire they did so and two indians fell and another was wounded. Uppon this the indians ran off like frightened sheep and we were released from the apprehension of immediate death.

Courage and conduct could sometimes be enough. The Mojaves did not press them again, and just before dark the nine men struck out into the desert. They traveled all night, and next morning reached the first spring. They had no way of carrying water and the desert was blisteringly hot, so Jedediah remained at the spring until evening. Lacking guides, they must depend on Jedediah's memory of a route he had traveled just once. "In a low plain," he says, "and in the night when I co[u]ld not see the distant and detached hills I had no guide by which to travel and therefore lost my way." At daybreak he ascended a hill, but could not ascertain on which side the trail ran. Observing a high hill nearly in the direction he wished to travel, Jedediah told the men which way to go in case he did not come back and, taking one man with him, pushed on in search of water. The ability to find water when life depended on it was one of the highest skills the mountain men possessed, and Jedediah had become a master mountain man. He found the water they had to have. Worn out by incessant anxiety and fatigue, he lay down to sleep while his man went back to bring on the party.

Awakened by their arrival, he climbed the highest hill in sight and established that they were about five miles to the right of the trail, nearly opposite a place where he had found water the year before.

We remained at the spring [Jedediah's journal continues] until nearly night and then bearing the spring on the trail to the left I struck directly for the next spring on the old route, traveling and resting by intervals during the night and the following morning until ten O Clock, when we got to the spring. We then remained during the remainder of the day and the following night, and in the morning early we started but instead of following the old trail I turned to the left and struck directly for the Salt Plain. My guides had told me of that route when I was there before, but it was considered too stoney for horses. The day was extremely warm and consequently we suffered much from thirst my men more than myself for they had not been accustomed to doing without water as much as I had. We found some relief from chewing slips of the Cabbage Pear, a singular plant . . . verry juicy although frequently found growing on the most parched and Barren ground. My men were much discouraged, but I cheered and urged them forward as much as possible and it seemed a happy providence that lead us to the little spring in the edge of the Salt Plain, for there was nothing to denote its place and the old trail was filled up with the drifting sand. Two of the men had been obliged to stop two or three miles before we got to the spring and although it was just night two of the men took a small kettle of water and went back, found and brought them up. After dark we proceed[ed] on across the Salt Plain and stopt at the holes I had dug when I passed before and there remained for the rest of the night.

On the following day Jedediah moved on to Inconstant River, the Mojave, finding it even drier than the year before. About eight miles up this fickle stream Jedediah came on two horses, and soon after two Indian lodges. As the Indians did not discover him until he had got close to them, they had no chance to run off. They were Paiutes. With some cloth, knives and beads he had carried from the Colorado, Jedediah purchased the horses, some sorghum candy, and a few demijohns for carrying water. Near the head of the river he fell in with a few lodges of another Shoshonean people whom the Californians called Serranos; from them he purchased two more horses. In continuing his journey, Jedediah says, "instead of traveling south East around the bend of the stream I struck directly across the Plain Nearly SSW to the Gape of the Mountain"—and thus he made for Cajon Pass.[8]

On emerging into the San Bernardino Valley, probably on August 28, Jedediah determined to kill a few cattle and dry meat enough to support his little party "through the Barren country Between Bernardino and the Appelaminy." He had several cows shot and began cutting and drying the meat. As the distance to San Gabriel was considerable, he did not go in but sent word to San Bernardino Rancho of what he had done. The overseer came out, Jedediah says, "bringing with him such little Luxuries as he had, and as he appeared anxious that I should go in and stay with him a night at the farm house I did so and was verry well treated." With the things he and his men had brought on their backs from the Colorado, Jedediah traded for horses enough to enable all his party to ride.

Jedediah had been nine and a half days coming from the Colorado, and he remained at the camp in the San Bernardino Valley five days. During his stay he obtained some paper and wrote Father Sánchez. He had not, he said, intended to return to the California settlements, but an attack by Indians had left him and his men destitute. He had killed four beeves, and for these and past benefits he thanked the good father. Two of his men Jedediah left at San Bernardino. Thomas Virgin was not yet recovered from his wounds, and the giant Isaac Galbraith, a free trapper, preferred to stay in this strange, sunny land.[9]

Directing Thomas Virgin to come on to San Francisco as soon as his health would permit, and leaving him a good horse,

Jedediah set out for the north.[10] With small exception he traveled the route he had taken the year before, and reached the camp on the Stanislaus September 18.

His men had become somewhat anxious about him, for he had told them to look for his return by September 20 at the latest, and their supplies were all but exhausted. "I was there by the time appointed but instead of Bringing them the expected supplies I brought them intelligence of my misfortunes." At any rate, Rogers and the rest of the men were well.

They had passed wh t hunters call a pleasant Summer not in the least interrupted by indians. The game consisted of some deer and Elk and Antelopes in abundance. They spoke in high terms of the climate. . . . A party of Spaniards had visited them in the summer having received intelligence of their being in the country from some indians who had gone in to the Missions. They appeared satisfied with the reasons Mr Rodgers gave for his being in the country.

Jedediah stayed two days with his party arranging them for trapping, then taking three men with him, set out for Mission San Jose, seventy miles to the southwest. This was a disagreeable necessity, but as Jedediah says, his "last and only resource [was] to try once more the hospitality of the Californias." Not unaware that this hospitality might be in some things lacking, he instructed Rogers if worst came to worst to take the party in to the Russian fort at Bodega, up the coast from San Francisco.[11]

Indians guided Jedediah in to Mission San Jose, where he arrived on the third day, about September 23, 1827.

I rode up in front of the Mission dismounted and walked in. I was met by two reverend fathers. One father [Narciso Durán] belonging to the Mission of St Joseph and the other father [José Viader] of the Mission of Santa Clara. The reverend fathers appeared somewhat confused by my sudden appearance and could not or would not understand me when I endeavored to explain the cause of my being in the country. They did not appear disposed to hear me, and told me I could go no further and soon showed me the way to the guard house. My horses were [taken] away and for two days I could get no satisfaction whatever. They would neither put me in close confinement nor set me at liberty. No provision whatever was made for my subsistence and I should have suffered much had it not been for the kindness of the old overseer, who invited me at each meal to partake with him. My men likewise ate at the same place.

Thus Jedediah's journal. His third-person letter to General Clark has an angrier bite, saying that on arrival at San Jose he

made known his situation and wants, [and] requested permission to pass through the province to the Governor's residence . . . but instead of complying with his request, he was immediately conveyed to a dirty hovel which they called a guard house, his horses seized and taken away, and only allowed the privilege of writing to the Captain of the Upper Province.

After two days, hearing of an American at Pueblo San Jose by the name of William Welch, Jedediah sent for him, and on his arrival sought an interview with Father Durán. This year Father Durán was not good company—a French visitor observed that "whether he chose the most melancholy works or had eyes only for the most lugubrious passages, he seemed no longer to perceive things except through a funereal veil: never has a soul held less cheerfulness than Fray Narciso's."[12] Unfortunately there was no easy quitting this sad abode; the only satisfaction the Reverend Father offered was to tell Jedediah that an officer would be up from San Francisco to inquire into his case.

When finally the *comandante*, Ignacio Martínez, arrived, Jedediah learned that he was to be tried as an intruder, and for claiming the country on the San Joaquin. On inquiry he found that an Indian had been over to the San Joaquin and returned with his own ideas of the intentions of Jedediah's party.

In the presence of the father [Jedediah says], the indian and my self were confronted, Lieut. Martinos sitting as judge. I put a few questions to him by which I ascertained that he had seen me just before my departure for the Depo and had once been with my party during my absence. But no circumstances could be proved against me and Lieut. Martinos instead of punishing me as the father desired Sentenced the indian to a severe flogging, which perhaps he did not deserve.

Father Durán, Jedediah observed shrewdly, "seemed much interested against me for what reason I know not unless perhaps It might be that he was apprehensive of danger to the *true faith*, for which reason he was anxious to stop my fishing around the country (for so he termed my traveling in their country)." Jedediah adds:

I gave the Lieu[t] to understand my situation and my wants and hinted at my desire to go directly to Monterrey, the present residence of the Governor for I considered this the most expeditious way to get through with my business. He told me I would be obliged to remain at the Mission until an express could go to and return from Monterey. Endeavoring to impress him with an Idea of the importance of despatch I urged him to expedite the business as much as possible. He prevailed on the father to furnish me with a room. After this my meals were sometimes brought to me in my room and sometimes I ate with the overseer as before.

Capt. [John Rogers] Cooper, a Bostonian who had married and resided in Monterrey & Mr [Thomas B. Park] supercargo of the Brig Harbinger from Boston, came up in company from Monterrey and remaining at St Joseph 2 days much relieved the anxiety of mind attendent on the uncertainty of my situation. Capt Cooper in particular seemed willing to afford me any assistance in his power. I was detained at St Joseph 12 or 14 days before I received a letter from the Gov and at the same time a guard to accompany me to Monterey.

The journey to Monterey was much like that to San Diego ten months before, but this time there could be no doubt that the four soldiers who made up the escort were a guard rather than a guide. When, near midnight on the third day, they arrived at Monterey, Jedediah was delivered to the *calabozo* and locked up for the night, unwashed and unfed. Morning brought Captain Cooper with some breakfast and a cheerful countenance, but Jedediah's frame of mind was not particularly happy when, late in the morning, he was taken to see the Governor.

The tall, gaunt Echeandia met Jedediah at the door, shook hands with him, and passed a few compliments in Spanish, after which they walked through a hall into a portico and sat down. Echeandia began talking in Spanish, but Jedediah interrupted to say that an interpreter would be necessary. The Governor agreed, suggesting that they solicit the services of William Hartnell, an Englishman trading on the coast whose command of French, German and Spanish had made him nearly indispensable to Monterey's official business.[13]

Hartnell was not available until evening, and the discussions at that time were not very rewarding. Jedediah found Echeandia "distinguished by the same traits as those that Marked his character when I saw him at San Diego." He could get nothing out of the Governor except the freedom of the town, the presidio and the harbor; Echeandia agreed, however, to another interview at Hartnell's house at a later date.

At another time Jedediah might better have appreciated Monterey's peculiar charm. The low, rounded hills back of the town were overgrown with beautiful dark pines; the blue Pacific creamed along the bay, and between presidio and castillo the forty-odd whitewashed adobe houses which made up the town had a piquant appeal. The townsfolk were warm-hearted and pleasure-loving, foreigners and Californians alike. Jedediah must have responded to the grace and warmth of this life and disapproved of it as well, for the men seemed not at all businesslike, and the women much too free in their language, manners and dress; the touch of the alien lay on everything.

Strolling about the town, Jedediah encountered Daniel Ferguson, who had deserted him at San Gabriel the year before, and John Wilson, the man he had discharged in the Tulares country. Apparently they stood a chance of being accepted into the community. But time hung heavy on his hands. Jedediah was happy, at a second session with the Governor, to come to grips with his problem.

Echeandia began this interview by observing that what the American stated with regard to his business might be true, but he could not believe it. "When you came to San Diego," he said sharply, "you represented the route by which you had come in to California as being a dry barren desert almost impassable and now you have come by the same route again. It is a very circuitous route, and if, as you say, your only object was to strengthen and supply your Appelaminy party, why did you not come directly across to them? And further, when you were defeated and came in so near San Gabriel, why did you not notify me of your arrival?"

Patiently Jedediah explained that it was very true that at San Diego he had represented the route by which he had come in as very bad, but on trial he had found the direct route much worse; in fact, he considered it entirely impassable for a party with loaded horses at that season and perhaps at any. Of two evils, it was natural and politic to choose the least. With regard to the notification the Governor spoke of, he had written a letter to Father Sánchez under the impression it would be forwarded to the Governor immediately.

Not in the least satisfied, Echeandia observed that this was altogether a mysterious business, and he must have time to consider. . . . The Governor seemed prepared to consider the subject forever, but Jedediah would not leave him in peace, and finally the Governor decided that the young American captain would have to go to Mexico. Jedediah replied that he was ready to leave, the sooner the better; the Governor said that he should go by the first opportunity.

A few days later, hearing that an English whaler was about to sail for Acapulco, Jedediah informed the Governor of the fact. And now Jedediah's journal rises to a pitch of indignation:

he merely said I might go. I soon found that he was not disposed to put himself to any trouble about it. I asked him if he intended that I should go to Mexico as a prisoner and at my own expense. He said most certainly, if I had the privilege of going in a foreign vessel, but if I would wait two or three months a Mexican Vessel would be going to Acapulco when he might perhaps as a favor from the Capt get a passage for me.

I[t] seemed that this man was placed in power to perplex me and those over whom he was called to govern. That a man in possession of common sense should seriously talk of making a man take himself at his own expense to prison. That he should talk to me of waiting 2 or 3 months for a passage to Acapulco. I plainly told him that on such conditions I would not go. Capt Cooper, knowing that I had no money, supposed that to be the reason why I refused to go and told me the want of money should not hinder me from going. I thanked him, but I told him I would not see Mexico on the terms proposed by his honor the Governor.

During both his visits to California, Jedediah was fortunate in finding friends when he needed them, and now the Englishman, Hartnell, did him a neighborly turn. Hartnell's opinion had almost the force of law for Echeandia, and he suggested a way Jedediah might be freed without the Governor's incurring any responsibility. The British law, Hartnell said, allowed four masters of vessels in a foreign port in times of emergency to appoint an agent who could act as consular agent until the home government could be advised of their action. Perhaps the Americans also had such a law. Jedediah says:

[This] seemed to please the governor and he said he would see what could be done. No sooner was the conference ended than I told Cap[t] Cooper of what had passed and also the Masters of the several vessels in port. They were not perfectly satisfied of the legality of the proposition, but thought the urgency of the case would justify the proceeding.

Captain Cooper was appointed agent. Echeandia thereupon proposed that the Captain not only become responsible for Jedediah's good conduct until he left California but also insure that he should not return again to the country on any pretense whatever. Jedediah would not agree to such a restriction and the Governor let the matter drop.

Meanwhile Jedediah's party on the Stanislaus had become a source of contention. Echeandia had requested Jedediah to order his party in to Monterey.

I told him they were nearer St Francisco than that place and he remarked that they might go in there. I therefore wrote to Mr Rodgers that it was the Governor['s] request that they should come in, and at the same time hinted at the treatment I had received. This I knew was sufficient for Mr Rodgers, who from what had passed between us would go in to Bodega. I carried the letter to the Gen[l] unsealed. He had it translated and took a day or two to consider its contents, then sent for me and said he was afraid to send such a letter for I had not ordered Mr. Rodgers positively to come in and that I had discouraged him from coming in from the manner in which I had spoken of the usage I had received at the same time he observed he would be verry sorry that his soldiers should have any difficulty with my party. I told him I thought what I had written verry reasonable but that if he would give me a copy I would write again. He said he could not do that. After getting the promise of the Govenor that they should not be imprisoned and should be furnished with provision I wrote to Mr Rodgers directing him to come in to San Francisco. The soldiers who carried the letters went by way of St. Joseph and one of my men accompanied them. Notwithstanding what the Genl had said about his soldiers and the smallness of my party I think he did not wish to have my party try their rifles on his soldiers, for there was some terrible stories in circulation about the shooting of my men. It was said they were sure of their mark at any distance.[14]

As an added complication, news came in from the south that another party of Americans were in the Tulares country. Jedediah assured the Governor that no Americans were there, but in this case rumor had a foundation in reality, for this must have been the party of Richard Campbell from New Mexico, the first to penetrate to California after Jedediah Smith. Campbell had brought in a company of thirty-five men in a journey which ended at San Diego; he reached the Colorado by way of the Little Colorado, but not much more is known about this venture, which presumably was provided with Mexican papers and met with no such trouble as Jedediah experienced.[15]

A letter arrived from Rogers announcing that the party had come in safely to San Francisco, and with Echeandia's permission, Jedediah wrote Thomas Virgin to come up from below and join him. On November 7 Jedediah called on Echeandia in company with Captain Cooper, who gave the Governor a written certificate setting forth the reasons which had brought Jedediah to California, outlining his needs and offering to become responsible for his conduct.

On these conditions, Echeandia said, he would give Jedediah three choices. He could wait until orders could be had from Mexico; he could go to Mexico himself; or he could go away with such men as he had in the same direction by which he had come in. Jedediah believed that by insisting on his traveling the same route and by preventing him from hiring more men Echeandia thought to retain him in the country until he could receive orders from Mexico. "But I told his excellency I would go if I had but 2 men." Echeandia bowed and said he would make a memorandum of what Captain Cooper must become responsible for.

While waiting on the Governor's convenience, Jedediah agreed with the master of the ship *Franklin* to sell his beaver at $2.50 per pound. If that was less than its value even in the mountains, it spared Jedediah the trouble and expense of transport, and more to the point, he needed money to outfit his party.

The bond was made and signed on November 12. In this document Captain Cooper guaranteed the good conduct and behavior of his countryman. It was agreed that in returning to "the settlement called the Salt Lake deposit," Jedediah would take the road from Mission San Jose by way of Carquinez Straits and Bodega, and that "under no condition will he delay on the way a longer time than is necessary, and that having reached his destination, he will make no hostile excursion, and will make no trip toward the coast or in the region of his establishment south of the 42nd parallel not authorized by his Government in accord with the latest treaties, unless he has a legal passport expressly [permitting it] from one or the other of the aforesaid Governments." [16]

Once the four copies of the bond had been signed, Echeandia requested a list of such things as Jedediah wished to purchase. He objected to none of the articles save horses and mules; about these there was some difficulty, but finally he gave permission. Gladly, on November 15, 1827, Jedediah received his passport and went on board the *Franklin*. The passport had been a laborious attainment, and Jedediah's eye would have run gratefully over its meager provision for his further journey:

> I hereby grant free and safe passport to Captain Smith, in order that, accompanied by the seventeen men he brought under his command, he may return to his settlement, each man carrying his own

fusil or gun; a total of seventy-five pounds of powder and one hundred and twenty-five pounds of lead, five loads of clothing, and other goods, six loads of provisions, two loads of merchandise for the Indians, one load of tobacco, and other loads comprising the equipment he brought; a total of one hundred mules and one hundred and fifty horses.

José Mª de Echeandia.[17]

At 2:00 P.M. on November 15 the *Franklin* sailed for San Francisco. Jedediah was soon seasick, and a gale that came on three hours after sailing made him still more unhappy. By nightfall next day the ship was off the Bay of San Francisco, but the wind being contrary, she stood off until noon of the seventeenth. There were, Jedediah says, seven sail in the harbor at the time. He called on Don Luis Argüello, formerly governor of California and now *comandante* at San Francisco, who seemed satisfied with his passport. Rogers and the men were well, though they had not been properly provisioned. They had received many courtesies from Henry Virmond, a German trading under the Mexican flag.

Next day, November 18, Jedediah had his furs taken on board the *Franklin;* they totaled 1,568 pounds of beaver and 10 otter skins. He received for the beaver $3,920, and for the otter pelts perhaps another $20; this was all he had to show for the hunt of three full seasons, and he was not yet clear of California.

From November 18 to 22 Jedediah was busy preparing his goods and trotting back and forth from ship to party to presidio. With the captain of the *Franklin,* he was invited to dine on board H. M. S. *Blossom,* the sloop of war in which Captain F. W. Beechey this year had made a distinguished exploration of the Northwest Coast; he was so long detained in business with Argüello as to be unable to attend, but some account of him got into the British journals nonetheless. The British officers had first met Jedediah while at Monterey, when James Wolfe wrote:

There was in the Praesidio a Mr. Smith, chief of a party, attached to a company of fur merchants at Kentucky, who had crossed the continent and being obliged to put into the missions, for supplies, had been taken up on suspicion of being a spy from the United States

Government. On leaving the deposit of St. Louis, on the Mississipi they made a westerly route across the Missouri territory, and after traversing the Chain called the Rocky mountains arrived at the Colorado River where they were treacherously attacked by a tribe of Indians whose friendship they had apparently gained by presents. The attack was made while in the act of crossing the River on rafts assisted by the Indians who observing that all the fire arms were on the headmost raft took the advantage of the opportunity to murder eight men & two women, and to plunder.

Mr. Smith describes the country to the Eastward of the Rocky Mountains as very fertile and abounding in Game in short affording all the desiderata for habitation from the great plenty not only of animal, but also of vegetable life. To the westward of this Chain which is itself a most formidable barrier, lie vast sand deserts, in traversing which they became so straitened for provisions as to be obliged to eat their dogs & horses. They travelled in rather a large cavalcade, each individual is necessarily a good shot with his rifle performing as we were told the feat of William Tell frequently for pastime.

When first brought in to the Praesidio Mr. Smith was treated as an already convicted criminal, and put into close confinement, Mr. Cooper however who was a merchant settled here and a fellow countryman became bond in his own person for the safety of Mr. Smith, and took him to live at his house. Several applications were made to the Governor to release him that he might return with his party (who also were confined in the Praesidio of San Francisco), but the Governor would not allow it until he had heard from Mexico, at the same time that he gave him liberty to quit the country by sea whenever he pleased. Mr. Cooper however at length bound himself in all that he possessed that, if Mr. S. should be permitted to return with his party, they should make the best of their way out of the Mexican dominions, without staying to hunt within the territory, and on these terms Mr. S. left for San Francisco, whither the reduced state of our stock of water obliged us to follow him.

. . . .

Mr. Smith who had been some time here [San Francisco] making the necessary preparations took his departure during our stay. Mr. Smyth was present when the party left the praesidio, the cavalcade consisted of 16 men well armed and mounted, with about 60 horses to carry baggage, and as relays presenting rather a formidable appearance. Mr. Smith seemed to think very lightly of his trip across the continent, and spoke with great acrimony of his long and unjust detention.[18]

This departure observed with so much interest by the British artist William Smyth took place November 26. As he could not get his work done at San Francisco, Jedediah had obtained Argüello's permission to move on to Mission San Jose, as that was on his line of march out of the settlements. The horses had nearly starved while at San Francisco, but Jedediah "got them up and moved off in the direction of St Jose." He reached there on the twenty-eighth and made arrangements with Father Durán to use the mission smithy for a week, also engaging a room for himself and two small rooms for his men.

A busy period of preparation followed. On December 6 Isaac Galbraith showed up. Jedediah must have bought some beaver from him, for before leaving San Jose he executed a promissory note in Galbraith's favor for $202.50.[19] Galbraith brought no news of Thomas Virgin, about whom Jedediah was beginning to be anxious. On the thirteenth, however—

Mr. Virgin arrived. He had been imprisoned for some time and frequently without anything to eat and strictly forbidden to speak to any one. and abused in almost every way.[20] On the 5th the Gen[l] on his way to St. Barbara saw him, released him and instructed the fathers to forward him on to St. Joseph. He was much rejoiced to see us and I am sure I was quite glad to see the old man again.

Happy to have an old friend delivered out of the hands of "Spanish cruelty," Jedediah by now was prepared to believe anything of this strange people who dwelt along the California coast, even that they had instigated or ordered the Mojaves to fall upon his party; everywhere he turned, he saw the iron hand of oppression, and all in the name of republican government and the true faith. He asked nothing of California now but to be quit of it.

By Christmas Day he was in shape to take the trail. He rode to San Francisco to make the necessary final arrangements with Argüello, for it had been stipulated that he should cross to the north shore of the Bay of San Francisco at the Straits of Carquinez, and Argüello had been ordered to detail ten soldiers to see Jedediah out of the territory.

> The time which the Genl had given me to remain was nearly expired [Jedediah explains] but I found it entirely impossible to procure a Launch to take me across the river [strait] without which it was impassible. . . . In this situation I made no doubt that Don Lewis [Luis Argüello] would consent that I should go up the River until I could find a place where I could swim my horses and carry my goods over on a raft which could not be done at the mouth. But he would hear nothing of this proposition but insisted that I should cross at the particular place directed by the Gen[l]. I then told him to furnish the boat and I was ready to cross. This he could not do but said I must wait untill the Gen[l] could be advised of the situation of things and give further instructions. I apparently acquiesced but left him with a determination fixed to take my own course without waiting for their tardy movements which the situation of my finances would not permit.

Back he rode to his party at Mission San Jose. There Jedediah sat down and wrote Echeandia and Argüello what he intended doing; and he also wrote the American minister at Mexico City complaining of the harsh treatment he had received. (This was not the end of the letter writing; the annoyed Echeandia on January 29 wrote his government complaining of the criminal conduct of "Smith, the fisherman's company." In Mexico City the Secretary of State, availing himself of the occasion to transmit the assurance of his distinguished consideration and respect, expressed confidence that the American minister would undertake such corrective measures as might be applicable.) [21]

With all this behind him, on December 30, 1827, Jedediah set out with his party in the rain. Having been so long absent from the business of trapping and so much harassed by the folly of men in power, Jedediah "returned again to the woods, the river, the prairae, the Camp & the Game with a feeling somewhat like that of a prisoner escaped from his dungeon and his chains."

13. *THE UMPQUA MASSACRE*

During the fall of 1827 a familiar word returned to Jedediah Smith's vocabulary. It is doubtful, after what he had seen of the Sierra Nevada, that he was able to conceive of a Buenaventura River rising far to the east, slicing through the mountains, and giving up its waters to San Francisco Bay. But when his northward movement through California brought him to the Sacramento, he applied the name Buenaventura to it, and the name came very close to sticking.

Information about the upper course of the Sacramento which Jedediah had sought in Monterey and San Francisco had been vague and unsatisfactory. In 1821 Don Luis Argüello had taken a party up the Sacramento—an exploration which everybody said had gone a great distance. A man in Argüello's company acquainted with the Columbia declared that they had gone nearly to that river, so the Sacramento must be a branch, or rather, a bayou of the Columbia; this had satisfied the Spaniards, but it did not satisfy Jedediah, who had acquired a realistic understanding of the nature of rivers and of western geography. He was the more contemptuous of "Spanish enterprise" that they should talk seriously of a "chalk mountain" which bounded the San Joaquin Valley, never having got close enough to the Sierra to establish that the chalk was snow.[1] But Spanish exploration and his own observation of the Sierra coincided on one conclusion: The Buenaventura headed in the north.

Once clear of the California settlements, it was Jedediah's purpose to head for the scene of his spring hunt of 1827, trap the Buenaventura as high up as practicable, then cut over to the coast and push on to the Columbia. Previously there had been talk about going into the Russian fort on Bodega Bay; he had sought Indian guides who could take him there, and when he left San Francisco, Jedediah carried a letter from Paul Shelikof, the

MOJAVE INDIANS

Balduin Möllhausen, 1853. From his *Tagebuch einer Reise vom Mississippi nach den Küsten der Südsee.*

VIEW OF THE MISSION OF ST. GABRIEL

From Alfred Robinson, *Life in California,* 1846.

Courtesy, U.S. Forest Service.

OCEAN SCENE AT SEAVIEW RANCH, OREGON COAST
Photo by E. Lindsay, 1936.

LOOKING ACROSS SMITH RIVER, OREGON, TO THE SITE OF THE UMPQUA MASSACRE
Photo by Harvey E. Tobie, 1952.

Russian agent, promising whatever facilities he might require to repair his things.[2] But no more is heard of Bodega after the arrangements to leave the settlements by way of Carquinez Straits fell through.

A large spring hunt could hardly be hoped for. Jedediah had only forty-seven traps left, and a steady wasting of these would come through loss, breakage and theft by the Indians. The young American would not have risen so far and so fast, however, had he not been of a resourceful turn of mind. A large part of the money realized on the sale of his furs he had invested in horses and mules, 250 of them at ten dollars apiece, which, added to the sixty-five horses he already possessed, gave him an imposing *caballada*. Jedediah proposed to drive these horses back to rendezvous and dispose of them to the free trappers; they would be worth a minimum of fifty dollars apiece, delivered in the mountains.[3] Thus Jedediah was pioneering in another field of enterprise; he was opening the continental trade in California horses.

There were twenty men in the party, Jedediah included, on its departure from Mission San Jose. Besides Rogers, nine men remained from the South West Expedition of 1826—Black, Gaiter, Hanna, Laplant, Lazarus, McCoy, Ranne, Reed and Reubascan; and these had been joined by Daws, Lapoint, Maréchal, Palmer, Swift, Turner and Virgin of the expedition of 1827. Jedediah would have liked to strengthen his party, but this had been forbidden by Echeandia. Notwithstanding, on December 20 Jedediah had taken into his service a little Englishman named Richard Leland who had been in the country about two years and was an excellent horseman; perhaps in the same way he added Louis Pombert. "Pompare" may have come to California with the expedition of 1826, but the probabilities are against it. On the other hand, no explanation has offered as to how Pombert could have reached California this early if he did not come with Jedediah Smith.

On leaving San Jose, Jedediah rode northeast and east through steady rain, and on January 1 "encamped on Buenaventura River which sometimes is called by the Spaniards the Piscadore." This was not the Sacramento but the Old River branch of the San Joaquin. Next day Jedediah moved on east to the San Joaquin itself. He carried his property across on rafts made of poles and flags, then made a pen on the bank of the river, and by driving his horses in small bands into the pen and from the pen into the river, he got the herd over without the loss of an animal.

All this with hardly a letup in the rain. It was apparent that not much could be done in the way of trapping without bullboats, and Jedediah sent out men to hunt elk for their hides. Despite his poverty in traps and the generally adverse weather, in two days he took forty-five beaver, which was more than his combined fall hunts of 1826 and 1827.

After the boats were built, Reed and Pombert were assigned to the detail which would trap by canoe, and on January 17 they came into camp with twenty-two beaver. Next day they started out again under orders to join the camp in one week on the Cosumnes River, but they deserted instead, and what was a worse injury, they took eleven traps with them.

Through January Jedediah trapped the lower tributaries of the San Joaquin—Lone Tree Creek, the Calaveras, the Mokelumne, the Cosumnes. The country at this season was a morass. Large sloughs thickly grown with tules extended for miles back from the river, and although these yielded a steady return in beaver, he moved his horses through the mud with the greatest difficulty, having to travel every point of the compass to make any forward progress. Still, the Indians were almost universally friendly, even those who had been hostile the year before; they were also the nakedest Indians he had ever seen, which was saying a great deal.

As Jedediah continued north, the Indians showed more alarm at his passage. Sometimes the men would remain in their little lodges of flag mats and straw, only taking the precaution to send off their wives, children and possessions, but sometimes the men fled too. The rain continued incessantly, rarely interrupted by a pleasant day, and the rising water made it impossible to set traps effectively.

On February 22 Jedediah crossed the American River, ferrying his goods over in a skin canoe while the horses swam. By now he had only thirty-two traps, and the difficulties of travel were serious. His journal entry for the following day is typical:

> I took all the trappers and went down to the forks and up the Main River but soon found slous so deep as to be swimming. I then turned back and endeavored to head them but found it so Muddy that the horses could not travel. . . . All appearances for progress were unfavorable for as far as I could see up the Main River The flag Ponds & Lakes extended. I hardly knew what course to pursue for it was impossible to travel North and useless to travel up Wild [American] River on which I was encamped for there was no Beaver in that direction. At 1 O Clock the weather became clear with a north wind I crossed over the slou by the means of my skin Canoes and a raft made of logs.

He turned up the American River, rafting the sloughs as he came to them (sometimes two in forty yards), but the mud was implacable, and there was regrettable trouble with the Indians:

> Two of my trappers Mareshall and Turner were up 3 or 4 miles from camp and seeing some indians around their traps who would not come to them but attempted to run off they fired at them and Turner killed one and Mareshall wounded another. I was extremely sorry for the occurrence and reprimanded them severely for their impolitic conduct. To prevent the recurrence of such an act the only remedy in my power was to forbid them the privilege of setting traps, for I could not always have the trappers under my eye.

It was the fate of all mountain men to learn about bears, and Rogers' turn came on March 8 when he was badly mauled while out hunting with John Hanna. Rogers' wounds were most painful, and for some days Jedediah dressed them with cold water "and salve of Sugar and Soap."

By the time Rogers was able to travel, the country had dried out enough to have a different aspect. Jedediah began moving north again, making a few miles a day and stopping to trap when he came on appearance of beaver. The Indians he encountered were honest and peaceably disposed, but they seemed "the lowest intermediate link between man and the Brute creation"; as home builders, "either from indolence or from a deficiency of genius inferior to the Beaver." This appeared to Jedediah the more strange in that these Indians dwelled in a country "rather calculated to expand than restrain the energies of man a country where the creator has scattered a more than ordinary Share of his bounties."

On March 28 Jedediah turned sufficiently west to come back to the Sacramento, which here was about 200 yards wide, deep and with a forcible current. Its banks were fringed with timber, principally cottonwood and sycamore. Far to the north, "verry high Peaks of the Mountain were seen covered with snow," and thus, from the vicinity of Chico, Jedediah was getting a look at Mt. Shasta. The valley here looked to be fifty miles wide. The mountains to the west were not high, but they were rugged and snow-capped. On the east the mountains were high, timbered and covered with snow. Two elk were killed and found to be in good order. But there was not much beaver sign.

In the vicinity of Deer Creek the Indians began to present a more respectable appearance. Although naked, they had not the miserable appearance of those below. A novelty, they labored under the impression that the horses could understand them, and when passing talked to them and made signs as to the men.

Some miles above, on April 7, Jedediah had two narrow escapes while hunting bears; he got clear the first time by plunging head foremost into a creek, and the second time he was mounted when the bear charged. "He was so close," Jedediah says, "that the horse could not be got underway before he caught him by the tail. The Horse being strong and much frightened exetered himself so powerfully that he gave the Bear no oppertunity to close uppon him and actually drew him 40 or 50 yards before he relinquished his hold." The bear did not continue the pursuit and Jedediah "was quite glad to get rid of his company on any terms."

The company was now approaching the head of the Sacramento Valley. Although the Sierra appeared lower, with less snow on it, the mighty range maintained its hostile aspect, and rocky hills blocked the way.

On April 11 Jedediah crossed the Sacramento just above the site of Red Bluff. Off to the northwest there was an inviting gap in the mountains, and on April 13 Jedediah turned in that direction. He had very rough going, and on the fifteenth was attacked by Indians, who showered arrows into his horse herd. These Indians followed all next day, whooping from the high points, and as the traveling was extremely bad, their attentions were not appreciated. After encamping, Jedediah went out with several men and endeavored by signs to persuade the Indians that his disposition was friendly. The red men had their bows strung and their arrows in their hands, and the violence of their gestures, their constant yelling and their refusal to approach were not reassuring. Mild man and Christian he might be, but Jedediah had lived through two defeats: "in order to intimidate them and prevent them from doing me further injury [I] fired on them. One fell at once and another shortly after and the Indians ran off leaving some of their property on the ground."

The following day, April 17, Jedediah got his horses across the divide to the Hay Fork of Trinity River, probably reaching it at present Wildwood.[4] He then turned down that stream. The trail was very difficult, at times winding among high, steep hills, at times running immediately along the riverbank, and the Indians continued hostile. He had to make another demonstration, and killed two.

There were occasional brushes with the red men afterward as Jedediah and his men forced their way down the Hay Fork and then down the South Fork of the Trinity, but the extraordinary roughness of the terrain impressed them most. The journey would have been hard enough had Jedediah possessed only pack animals; and he was driving ahead of him 300 head of half-wild horses and mules. The animals would go through narrow passes in a squirming mass, frantically trying to keep from being precipitated down the vertical cliffs, and inevitably knocking off one or two of their number to be crumpled on the rocks or drowned in the river below; they would get tangled in brush or timber, tied up in cul-de-sacs, their feet, legs and bodies cruelly mangled by sharp rocks or broken branches; and rarely would they find an open space in which to feed. To advance one mile might require a day's labor on the part of the whole company, and the horses would be unfit for travel for days after. When possible, Jedediah moved along the bank of the river, but often he had to twist and turn up over rocky, steep ridges, then down again through thickets and deep ravines; and though it was now late April, the horses occasionally floundered through snow three or four feet deep.

No longer were the Indians the short-haired type so strikingly characteristic of the Central Valley; they wore their hair long and were clad in deerskins. Their lodges were novel also; ten or twelve feet square, three feet high, and with peaked roofs, they were made with split pine planks. These Indians were Hupas, a people whose language served as a *lingua franca* for nearly all the northern California tribes. Occasional natives he encountered made signs to Jedediah of their desire to trade deerskins for axes and knives, and he saw trees on which axes had been used. These tools had been carried down the Oregon and California coast through the usual channels of Indian trade, but clearly Jedediah was approaching Hudson's Bay Company territory.

Back-breaking labor had brought them down the Trinity to the Klamath without delivering them from the natural prison to which their route had sentenced them. Some Indians came to camp, light-colored, small, talkative and somewhat afraid of the horses. Jedediah purchased their fish, gave them presents and endeavored through signs to ascertain something of the character of the country, but they could not understand him.

Two men sent out to reconnoiter came back to report that the ocean lay not more than twenty miles to the west. "I determined therefore," Jedediah says, "as traveling along the river was so bad to move towards the coast." But his party was in bad shape; it was a day before they could move at all, and three miles made on May 18 taxed their strength to the utmost. The men were almost as weak as the horses, for the poor venison of this country contained little nourishment. The weather was rainy and cloudy, and "so thick with fogg" that it was difficult to keep track of the horses.

On May 19 they moved west six miles along a ridge covered with spruce, fir and redwood—the latter the noblest trees Jedediah had ever seen—and that night they encamped in view of the ocean.[5] Rogers and Virgin next morning went out to examine the country and came back to report the route impracticable. The hills along the coast were heavily timbered and brushy, and rose abruptly from a rocky shore: they would have to go back the way they had come. Jedediah rode out in the rain and fog to see for himself, but the report was true. Rogers prayed: "Oh! God, may it please the[e] . . . to still guide, & protect us, through this wilderness of doubt & fear. . . . Oh! do not forsake us Lord, but be with us, and direct us through."

For two days they could not stir from camp. When the weather cleared, Jedediah started his party on the back trail, reaching the Klamath May 24 at the same place he had left it on the eighteenth. Somehow he had to find a way out of this labyrinth. After crossing the river, on the twenty-sixth Jedediah moved down it two miles, then struck east to a high range of hills. He was able to wind along the summit some distance, but again had to descend to the river. On May 28:

In consequence of the hills which came in close and precipitous to the river I was obliged to ascend on to a range of hills and follow along their summits which was verry difficult particularly as a dense fog rendered it almost impossible to select the best route. I encamped where there was verry little grass and near where the Mountain made a rapid descent to the north rough & ragged with rocks. I went to the brink of the hill and when the fog cleared away for a moment I could see the country to the north extremely Mountainous along the shore of the Ocean those Mountains somewhat lower. From all appearances I came to the conclusion that I must move in again towards the coast

He was within a few miles of the ocean, but it took ten days to get there. The fog closed around so thick that at times Jedediah dared not move; it poured rain, making the mountainsides slippery and the bottoms miry; it was almost impossible to drive the horses. An entry from Rogers' journal:

We made and early start this morning directing our course N. W. up a steep point of Brushy Mou, and Travelled about 2 m. and enc. in the River Bottom, where there was but little for our horses to eat, all hands working hard, to get the horses on, as they have become so much worn out, that it is almost impossible to drive through Brush—

we have two men, every day that goes a head with axes, to cut a road, and then it is with difficulty we can get along.

That was June 3. Next day Jedediah writes:

North 1 Mile. Whilst the party were preparing I went ahead looking [for] a route . . . and found one passible by the assistance of axe men to clear the way along a side hill. In passing along my horses were so much fatigued that they would not drive well and many of them turned down into the swamp from which we extricated the most of [them] with considerable difficulty. Where I encamped there was no grass for my horses I was therefore obliged to build a pen for them to keep them from strolling off.

June 5 got them only another mile and a half northwest. Two horses and a mule gave out and had to be left. The camp had been without meat since the morning of the fourth, and the ration these two days was half a pint of flour per man, plus the only dog they had in camp.

With no game to be had, Jedediah killed a young horse. Two of his hunters came in with reports of a pass to the northwest, and on the eighth Jedediah took his horse herd in that direction. Rogers says that the traveling was "ruff," but five miles brought them to the Pacific at the mouth of Wilson Creek, near present Requa, and next day Jedediah killed three elk.

The party remained in camp a day, making salt and drying meat. When they resumed the journey on June 11 the trail seemed as bad as before, up and down steep ridges, through timber and brush, but on June 14, in the vicinity of present Crescent City, travel became easier. They still had to take to the sea for three or four hundred yards at a time, the swells as high as the horses' backs, but there were clover and grass for the horses, and Lapoint killed a monstrous elk, weighing about seven hundred pounds.

On June 20 Jedediah crossed at its mouth the California river which today bears his name, and three days later, unknowingly, he entered Oregon, encamping on Windchuck Creek. In his journey up the coast, he moved along the shore when possible, though rocky bluffs often forced him inland. To cross the various small rivers he had to wait for low tide. Although less laborious than his passage through the mountains, this was not rapid travel; the twelve miles made on June 25 Jedediah called the best march for a long time. Deer continued plentiful, and occasionally the hunters brought in an elk.

They reached the Rogue River June 27. The Indians here were not friendly; horses came into camp with arrows in their sides, and the red men fled at the approach of the whites. Next morning, however, at low tide, Jedediah undertook the crossing of the river. A dozen or more horses drowned during the passage, and Jedediah observed that in three days he had lost by various accidents twenty-three animals.

Five days later, at the Coquille River, there was a last addition to the party. Jedediah, who was out ahead of the company —he had been, most of the way from the Sacramento—"discovered some indians moving as fast as possible up the river in a canoe. I ran my horse to get above them in order to stop them When I got opposite to them & they discovered they could not make their escape they put ashore and drawing their canoe up the bank they fell to work with all their might to split it in pieces." This, the last notation in Jedediah's journal, breaks off in mid-entry. Rogers says:

> [Jedediah] screamed at them and they fled, and left [the canoe], which saved us of a great deal of hard labour making rafts, after crossing our goods we drove in our horses and they all swam over, but one, he drowned pretty near the shore, we packed up & started again, after crossing along the Beach N and Travelled 5 miles more & encamped, saw some Inds. on a point close by the Ocean; Marishall caught a boy about 10 years old & Brought him to Camp I gave him some Beads & dryed meat, he appears well satisfyed, and makes signs that they Inds. have all fled in their canoes & left him.

This Indian boy they named Marion;[6] it appeared that he belonged to one of the Willamette tribes and had been held as a slave; he was glad to be taken along.

On July 5 two Indians who spoke Chinook came into camp; "they tell us," Rogers noted, "we are ten days Travell from Calapoo on the wel Hamett which is pleasing news to us." Pleasing because the Calapooyan tribes on the Willamette regularly traded with the Hudson's Bay Company. Even here on the coast there were abundant evidences of trade—knives, tomahawks and pieces of cloth.

These coastal Indians however had an uncertain temper. On the evening of July 8 a trading session ended badly: "we found they had been shooting arrows into 8 of our horses & mules, 3 mules and one horse died Shortly after they were shot the Inds. all left camp, but the 2 that acts as interpreters—they tell us that one Ind. got mad on account of a Trade he made and Killed the mules & horses." Next day, reaching the Coos River and meeting with a great many more Indians:

We talked with the Chiefs about those Inds shooting our horses, but could get but little satisfaction as they say they were not accessary to it, and we finding them so numerous and the Travelling being so bad, we thought it advisable to let it pass at present without notice. We Bought a number of Beaver Land & sea otter skins from them in the course of the day.

Harrison Rogers' diary continues four more days:

Thursday July 10th 1828. We commenced crossing the River early, as we had engaged canoes last night, we drove in our Horses, and they swam across, they had to swim about 600 Yards—our goods was all crossed, about 9 O.C. A M. and 2 Horses that was wounded, and one mule, remained, that Capt Smith and 5 men stay to cross, the 2 Horses dyed of there wounds, and Capt. Smith swam the mule along side of the canoe. He was some what of opinion the Inds. had a mind to attact him from their behaviour, and he crossed over when the swells was running pretty high, and, there being good grass, we enc. for the day; the Inds. pretty shy. . . .

Friday July 11th 1828. All hands up early, and under way had an Ind. who speaks Chinook, a long as a guide Our course was N along the Beach of the Ocean, 15 miles and struck a River that is about 300 yards wide at the mouth and enc, as it was not fordable, we Crossed a small creek, 30 yards wide, 10 miles from camp—to-day—we enc. where there was some Inds. liveing—a number of them speak Chinook—70 or 80 in Camp, they bring us fish & Berries and appear friendly, we buy those articles from them at a pretty dear rate—those

Inds call themselves the Omp quch. The day windy and cold—Several of the men unwell. Peter Ranne has been Sick for 6 weeks, with a swelling in his legs—the country about 1/2 mile back from the Ocean Sand Hills covered with small pine and Brush, the sand Beach quite continuous.

Saturday July 12th. we commenced crossing the River early and had our goods & horses over by 8 o.C. then packed up & started a N. E. course up the river and Travelled 3 M. & enc.—had several Inds. along, one of the Ind. stole an ax, and we were oblig to seize him for the purpose of tying him before we could scare him to make him give it up. Capt. Smith and one of them caught him & put a cord round his neck, and the rest of us stood with our guns ready in case they made any resistance, there was about 50 Inds present, but did not pretend to resist tying the other, the River at this place is about 300 yards wide & make a large Bay that extends 4 or 5 miles up in the pine Hills—the Country similar to yesterday—we Traded some land & sea otter & beaver fur in the Course of the day. Those Inds bring Pacific rasberrys and other berries

Sunday July 13th 1828. We made a pretty good start this morning, directing our course along the Bay, East and Travelled 4 miles & enc. 50 or 60 Inds in camp again to-day (we traded 15 or 20 Beaver skins from them—some Elk meat & tallow, also some lamprey eels)—a considerable Thunder shower this morning—and rain at intervals through the day Those Inds. tell us after we get up this River 15 or 20 miles we will have good travelling to the Wel Hammett or Multenomah—where the Callipoo Inds live—

The company had reached the confluence of the Umpqua and its north branch—which from this time on would be called Smith River. The route the Indians had pointed out would take them up the Umpqua to what was already known as the Labiche or Elk River, then across the Calapooya Mountains to the Coast Fork of the Willamette. On the morning of July 14 Jedediah set out as was his custom to find a road. The country being swampy in the bottoms and woody in the mountains, he departed in a canoe, taking with him Leland and Turner, with one of the natives as a guide.

Before leaving camp, Jedediah warned Rogers not to let these Indians—Kelawatsets, they called themselves—enter the camp.

Had Jedediah known it, these instructions were the more in point from the fact that the stealing of the ax on July 12, and its enforced restoration, had given mortal offense to one of the chiefs. He had urged an immediate attack on the whites, only to be overruled by another chief. As the Kelawatsets told the story later, however, the conciliatory chief himself was then affronted; he mounted a horse to ride around the camp, only to be compelled by Arthur Black to dismount.[7]

Rogers evidently trusted to the influence of the Hudson's Bay Company on these Indians, for he admitted about a hundred of them to the camp. While the Americans were busy arranging their arms, which had got wet the day before, the Indians suddenly rushed on them. Two got hold of Arthur Black's gun and in contending with them he was wounded on the hands by their knives. Another Kelawatset ran up with an ax to strike him on the head, but Black sprang to one side and received the blow on his back. He then let go of his gun and rushed into the woods. The last he saw of the camp, two Indians were on Virgin, Daws was in the water with Indians pursuing him in a canoe, and a third man was on the ground with a horde of Indians butchering him with axes.[8]

Black wandered in the woods for four days, finally making his way to the ocean a few miles above the Umpqua's mouth. Knowing that the British post, Fort Vancouver, was only about a hundred miles away, he headed north along the coast. He was stripped of his clothing and knife by Indians he met along the way, but friendly "Killimaux" guided him across the coast range to the Willamette, and he reached the British fort after nightfall on August 8. As Dr. McLoughlin described the event:

I was surprised by the Indians making a great noise at the gate of the Fort, saying they had brought an American. The gate was opened, the man came in, but was so affected, he could not speak. After setting down some minutes to recover himself; he told us he was, he thought, the only survivor of 18 men, conducted by the late Jedediah Smith, all the rest, he thought, were murdered. . . . At break of day the next morning, I sent Indian runners with tobacco to the Willamette chiefs, to tell them to send their people in search of Smith and his two men, and if found to bring them to the Fort and I would pay them, and telling them, if any Indians hurt these men, we would punish them, and immediately equipped a strong party of 40 well-armed men. But as the men were embarking, to our great joy, Smith and his two men arrived.[9]

It was about noon August 10 that Jedediah, Turner and Leland reached the fort, having come by almost the same route as Black. On the fatal morning, after proceeding a few miles, Jedediah had paddled back down the river. It struck him as strange that none of his men could be seen. While he was looking about for some sign of them, an Indian on the shore spoke to his guide. The man turned around in the canoe, seized Jedediah's rifle and dived into the river. Kelawatsets hidden in the bushes immediately fired on the boat. Jedediah paddled frantically to the opposite bank, then ascended a hill from which he could get a clear view of his camp. None of his party was to be seen, and from the fact that the sound of gunfire had brought no one to investigate, he concluded that they had all been cut off. Thereupon, as Dr. McLoughlin reported, he "shaped his course for the ocean & fell on it at Alique [Alsea] River & followed the Coast to the Killamau [Tillamook] Village," whence Indians guided him to Fort Vancouver.[10]

When Jedediah first appeared at a Hudson's Bay Company post in the fall of 1824, he was important only as a symbol. Not quite four years later he had become a personage. The Hudson's Bay Company might have a touch of contempt for Smith, Jackson & Sublette; in Governor Simpson's view they were merely "men who had formerly been practical trappers" and who on buying out Ashley "promoted themselves to the Travelling title of Captains." All the same, the Company felt a certain respect for Jedediah and his partners. Ashley's venture in the fur trade, with the emphasis he placed on free trappers, had seemed no regular company at all,[11] but Smith, Jackson & Sublette had impressed the British concern as a firm with which it might be worth while to come to an agreement concerning deserters.

The generosity with which Jedediah was received at Fort Vancouver is better appreciated if something is said about what followed on Peter Skene Ogden's debacle of 1825, and about Dr. McLoughlin and his post.

When George Simpson traveled to the Columbia from York Factory in the fall of 1824, John McLoughlin came with him. In his journal of the voyage Simpson described the doctor as

. . . such a figure as I should not like to meet in a dark Night in one of the bye lanes in the neighbourhood of London, dressed in Clothes that had once been fashionable, but now covered with a thousand patches of different Colors, his hands evidently Shewing that he had not lost much time at his Toilette, loaded with Arms and his own herculean dimensions forming a tout ensemble that would convey a good idea of the high way men of former Days.[12]

A veteran of the war between the Hudson's Bay Company and the North West Company, the doctor was a huge fellow, six feet four, with deep-set gray eyes and a shock of long white hair parted in the middle. Strong-willed, and possessed of a towering temper, McLoughlin was also the soul of honor and a man of deeply compassionate nature.[13]

On arrival at Fort George, he and Simpson set about demolishing that imposing bastion; Simpson thought the fort possessed "an air or appearance of Grandeur & consequence" not at all appropriate to an Indian trading post, and a more serious objection was that an establishment on the south side of the Columbia would pass into American hands whenever the Oregon boundary question was settled. It was his hope that a main base could be built much farther north, in British Columbia, but meanwhile he wanted the principal establishment on the Columbia removed to the north bank of the river, at some point where farming operations could be undertaken in its support. The site best adapted to this purpose was "Belle vue Point," seventy miles up the river, above the mouth of the Willamette. Here, in the spring of 1825, McLoughlin began to build Fort Vancouver,[14] and here, in August following, the first reports reached him of Ogden's disaster in the Snake Country.

McLoughlin's reaction to those reports was angry and defiant:

we are justified in resenting to the utmost of our power any attack on our persons and property or any assumption of authority over us by the Americans. . . . had we a party sufficiently strong to defend itself from the Natives and that could be depended upon—I would have no hesitation in making another attempt in that quarter if it was merely for one year to defy them to put their threats in execution.

He was also unwilling to admit that anything could be wrong with the system: "no Man was ever induced to buy a single article . . . they were in debt much against our will and inclinations." [15]

But the doctor was capable of facing up to the facts when he had had time to look them over. He got Ogden back into the field for a second year's hunt by the expedient of making two thirds of his trappers engaged men,[16] and thereafter he took a long look at the freemen's rates. In the summer of 1826 he wrote his superiors in the Company:

it is certain if Americans fall in with our party Unless we give more for Beaver than we have hitherto our people will desert us. We therefore have agreed to give them 10/– for every full Grown Beaver—half this amount for a cub and to allow them [to] purchase personal necessaries according to their abilities and means of from ten to fifteen pounds at European servants prices and hunting implements at Inventory prices. . . . I am convinced the measure adopted will be beneficial to the Concern, as the High prices charged the Freemen and trappers for their supplies prevented our getting several Thousand Beaver Skins from the Snakes more than we have, drove our people to desert from us and to work for others whom they are now Guiding to Countries Rich in Beaver and in opposition to us. I send you the Tariffe the Freemen hitherto paid for their Supplies and the price allowed them for their furs; several have killed a hundred and fifty made Beaver and this was not sufficient to pay their Hunting supplies and their Losses in Horses and traps stolen by the Natives.[17]

This action was approved in London. The Governor and Committee wrote Simpson in March 1827:

We can afford to pay as good a price as the Americans and where there is risk of meeting their parties it is necessary to pay as much or something more to avoid the risk of a result similar to that of M^r^

Ogden. By attempting to make such expeditions too profitable the whole may be lost and it is extremely desirable to hunt as bare as possible all the Country South of the Columbia and West of the Mountains.[18]

McLoughlin not only advanced to a more respectable figure the price paid for beaver but reduced the price of goods, especially trapping equipment, which was sold at inventory prices. Although the price for beaver remained less than the American figure, the prices placed on goods were much lower than those of Smith, Jackson & Sublette, and the quality of the merchandise was better.[19] The competitive position of the British concern from and after the summer of 1827 was such that many of the deserters of 1825 returned to the fold, and Simpson felt that had the Company been disposed to encourage desertion, it could have broken up the opposition.[20]

Meanwhile the Company's ideas about the Snake Country had not changed in the least. The new rate structure secured to the Company the loyalty of Ogden's men while he himself won their respect and confidence by his conduct in the field. In the spring of 1826 he trapped the Snake as high as the Blackfoot River; next year he trapped southern Oregon and northern California as far south as Pit River; and in the year just past, 1827-1828, he had again trapped the southern tributaries of the Snake, each of his expeditions bringing in better than 3,000 beaver.[21] The Americans certainly co-operated in the project of transforming the Snake Country into a fur desert, but Ogden's Snake Expedition was an effective instrument of the imperial purpose.

How steadfast was that purpose the Company's correspondence strikingly reveals. In September 1826 McLoughlin pointed out that the Columbia "affords the Easiest communication to carry on the Fur Trade in the Countries on the Head Waters of the Missouris, Rio del Norte and Bears River, and if the Americans Establish themselves here they will be able to compete with us for a Great part of the Saskatchewan trade"; he thought that the Company "could yet Employ during three years a hundred more Trappers than we have, Say Eighty about Henrys Forks and Trois Tettons . . . the present party under Mr. Ogden would find Employment in that part of the Country which Lies between Mr. Ogden's intended track of this year [southern Oregon] and the sea. At the End of that time we think the Country would be so Exhausted as no longer to afford Employment to such a number of men." [22] Simpson meantime was proposing that a trapping expedition be fitted out, partly from the Saskatchewan but chiefly from the Red River Settlement (Winnipeg), which in the fall of 1827 would make its way west to the Kutenai country, "renew their Hunts in Spring 1828 and scour the country to the Southward & Westward throughout the Summer Autumn, Winter and following Spring and get to Fort Vancouver with their returns Summer 1829." [23] This party was never organized, but the plans show how the wind was blowing.

The Governor and Committee in London were perfectly willing to see the country south of the Columbia trapped bare; they would have liked to divert as much of their man power to Oregon as possible, stripping what wealth they could from that country while giving the Far North a chance to recruit.[24] But Simpson was warned to keep his trappers west of the mountains; there must be no more trapping of Missouri waters. Confused by the way Ogden had wound back and forth across the continental divide in 1825, they were under the impression that the 700 skins his deserters had carried off had been lost on American soil, so that as trespassers they could make no demand on the American government for the restoration of their property.[25]

Still later, after the failure of renewed Oregon boundary negotiations in 1826-1827, the Governor and Committee wrote Simpson:

> . . . The Country on the West of the Mountains remaining common to the Americans and us for an indefinite period, terminable by a years notice from either Government, it becomes an important object to acquire as ample an occupation of the Country and Trade as possible, on the South as well as on the North side of the Columbia River, looking always to the Northern Side falling to our Share on a division, and to secure this, it may be as well to have something to give up on the South, when the final arrangement comes to be made.
>
> If the American Traders settle near our Establishments, they must be opposed, not by violence, which will only be the means of enabling

the Traders to obtain the interference of their Government, but by underselling them, which will damp their sanguine expectations of profit, and diminish the value which they at present put upon that Trade. It will be useful to give the Americans full occupation by active and well regulated opposition on the South of the river to prevent them advancing towards the North, and the general regulation of the Trapping parties call for your best attention and we think merit your devoting a year of your time to it. . . .[26]

This was the situation when Jedediah Smith arrived at Fort Vancouver in the wake of the Umpqua Massacre.

When the refugees from the south appeared at the gates of his fort, McLoughlin was in the midst of preparations for a trading and trapping expedition to the very region where the Americans had been slaughtered.[27] At the head of that expedition he had placed Alexander Roderic McLeod, who was now given the responsibility of recovering whatever he could of Jedediah Smith's property and restoring law and order to the British domain.

It took time to complete the preparations for McLeod's departure, and McLoughlin was anxious to do anything possible to rescue others who might have survived the massacre. He sent off Michel Laframboise to do whatever could be done.

Laframboise was a sufficiently remarkable person; he became the most celebrated French-Canadian of the Pacific Slope. At one time an Astorian, later a Nor'Wester, now a Hudson's Bay man, he could go alone and carefree through regions where heavily armed parties ventured with trepidation; one reason was that he had a wife in practically every tribe along the Oregon coast.[28] Laframboise had not yet returned from his mission when, on September 6, Jedediah left Fort Vancouver in McLeod's company, but two days later, near Champoeg, they met him en route back to Fort Vancouver. He had no word of more survivors, and it appeared that Jedediah's property was dispersed all over the country.[29]

The French-Canadian went on to Fort Vancouver to make his report but rejoined the party on September 13, bearing two letters from McLoughlin.[30] The first was addressed to Jedediah:

Fort Vancouver,
12th Sep[r]. 1828

J: S: Smith Esqr.,
Dear Sir,

I am extremely sorry to learn from Michel that your property is so scattered that their is little probability of recovering it, you write "In the meantime should you think it necessary for the benefit of your Company to punish these Indians you would confer a favour on your humble Servant to allow him and his Men to assist" I beg to assure you that in this case I am actuated by no selfish motives of Interest—but solely by feelings of humanity as I conceive in our intercourse with such barbarians we ought always to keep in view the future consequences likely to result from our conduct as unless those Murderers of your people & Robbers of your property are made to return their plunder, as we unfortunately too well know they have no horror or compunction of Conscience at depriving their fellow Man of Life—If strangers came in their way they would not hesitate to murder them for the sake of possessing themselves of their property, but as it would be worse than useless to attempt more than our forces would enable us to accomplish and as Mr. McLeod knows those Indians & knows best whether we can effect any good, he will decide on what is to be done most sincerely Wishing you success, Believe me to be

Yours truly
Jno. McLoughlin
Chief Factor
Hudsons Bay Co[y].

The second letter was for McLeod:

Dear Sir,

I received yours of the 8th per Michel Laframboise & I am extremely sorry to find by his Statement that Mr. Smith's affair has a more gloomy appearance than I expected & it seems to be in that state, either that we must make War on the Murders of his people to make them restore his property or drop the business entirely.

I know many people will argue that we have no right to make war on the Natives, on the other hand if the business is drop[p]ed, will not our personal security be endangered wherever this report reaches —Again suppose that by accident a Vessel was wrecked on the Coast, to possess themselves of the property would not the Natives—seeing these Murderers escape with impunity—kill all the Crew that fell in their power & say as these now do—We did not take them to be the same people as you—have not the Natives of Cape Look-out not many years since killed the Crew of a Vessel wrecked opposite their Village, and is it not our duty as Christians to endeavour as much as possible to prevent the perpetration of such atrocious crimes—& is their any measure so likely to accomplish so effectually this object as to make these Murderers restore at least their illgotten booty now in their possession—But it is unnecessary after the various conversations we have had for me to say any thing further on this subject—You know those Indians you know our means, and as a failure in undertaking too much, would make this unfortunate affair worse—& as you are on the spot—you therefore will decide on what is best to be done and depend that whatever that decision may be at least as far as I am concerned every allowance will be made for the situation you are placed in.

I am Sir
Yours truly
Jno. McLoughlin.

N. B. Laframboise and [Joseph] Cournoyer will go to the Umqua or return immediately as you think proper—Mr. Smith offers himself and party to accompany you to War on the Murderers—I refer him to you for an answer.

McLeod set out up the Willamette with twenty-two *engagés,* fourteen Indians and Jedediah and his three men. The journey was not a pleasant one. It rained constantly; the horses could not be broken to service, and Indian report was that the Kelawatsets and other tribes of the Umpqua, elated by their easy conquest of Jedediah's party, intended to ambush and pillage McLeod.

The party made its way up the Willamette past the site of Eugene to the vicinity of the present Cottage Grove, then over the Calapooya Mountains to the Umpqua. There was some apprehension that they might be ambushed in crossing the mountains, but the Indian story proved groundless. As they moved down the Umpqua, the Indians living along the river fled, but, McLeod says, they "were soon made to return, as their Countrymen accompanying us appeased their fear."

On October 10 McLeod sent a message to the chief of the Umpquas asking him to come in for a talk, meanwhile writing in his journal a curious rumor to the effect that four of Jedediah's men survived in the custody of the "Cahoose Indians," a rumor he hoped the old chief would be able to confirm.

The Umpqua chief arrived in camp October 11 bringing in eight of Jedediah's horses, but he had no definite information about survivors.

Before the Umpquas departed next day the chief inquired whether the whites intended to make war, to which, McLeod says,

> we answered in the Negative . . . being told our wish was to Establish Peace and Quietness and recover what could be got of Mr Smiths Property, and restore the Same, seemed to give Satisfaction, but privately with some of his intimate Acquaintances the Old fellow . . . expressed his surprise at our interference in aiding and assisting People that evinced evil intentions towards us, as he had been informed by the people who defeated the Party, they having communicated something about territorial Claim, and that they would soon possess themselves of the Country, makes the Natives about us very inquisitive not having ever heard such a thing before, and we avoid giving them any information, and treat the subject with derision. Mr. Smith when told of this, observed that he did not doubt of it, but it was without his knowledge and must have been intimated to the Indians through the Medium of a Slave boy attached to his Party, a Native of the Wullamette—he could converse freely with those Indians—as to the Origin of the Quarrel as Stated yesterday by the Old Chief Mr Smith affirms to have tied an Indian and set him free when the ax was restored, but denies having used blows or any manner of violence except Seizing him—Black acknowledges to have seen a Chief mount a horse without leave and ordered him to desist but not in an angry tone neither did he present his Gun, but had it in his hand, and he adds the Indian immediately dismounted, shortly after the party was attacked and defeated——

The Umpquas had managed to gather up twenty-six horses and mules. They were rewarded with small presents, and the party continued down the river toward the site of the massacre. They reached the Kelawatsets Village in a downpour October 21, and the same evening McLeod made demand on the village for the restitution of Jedediah's property.

The Kelawatsets obliged; they handed over 560 large and 28 small beaver, 23 large and 20 small land otter, 4 sea otter and such odds and ends as rifles, pistols, traps, cooking kettles, lead pencils, cotton shirts and beads. On October 28 McLeod continued down toward the sea, stopping, his journal says, "at the entrance of the North Branch, where Mr Smiths Party were destroyed, and a Sad Spectacle of Indian barbarity presented itself to our View, the Skeletons of eleven of those Miserabl Sufferers lying bleaching in the Sun."

McLeod says nothing of Jedediah's feelings, but they can be imagined, with devoted Harrison Rogers, old Thomas Virgin, Laplant, Hanna, Ranne, all reduced to gaping skull and naked bone. How many men had accompanied him to California, and how few still lived! And how strange that he himself should have survived so many disasters—the Ree affair of 1823, the Mojave Massacre of 1827, and now the Umpqua Massacre.

Only eleven skeletons were found. It might be that four men had drowned or been killed in the water trying to escape, but in view of the Indian report it was possible to hope. For a while.

After burying the remains, McLeod moved on to the sea, then north up the coast. The party went as high as the Siuslaw River, all the while recovering articles of Jedediah's incredibly scattered property—three horses, a musket barrel, a few beads, a woolen shirt, a rifle; on one occasion fifteen beaver. But nothing tangible was forthcoming about the four survivors.

On November 3 McLeod turned back toward the Umpqua, the principal reward of the return journey coming November 10, when "the following Articles were recovered—viz—3 horses—2 Mules, 7 Steel Traps, 1 Copper Covered Kettle—1 Rifle—1 Rifle Barrel—some Beads, Books, journals & other Papers." Thus the journals of Jedediah Smith and Harrison Rogers were preserved.

Two days later they "Encamped on the Island at the Entrance of the North branch, now called *Defeat River*." That name persisted quite a while, but Smith River won out finally. It occasioned Jedediah some trouble to move up the Umpqua the horses and mules collected from the Indians, but he and McLeod reached the latter's base camp November 22, arriving in the sluicing rain that was so characteristic of this country.

Next day Jedediah came to McLeod's lodge to say that he had resolved to proceed to Fort Vancouver and to discharge such of his men as pleased to accept their dismissal. He wanted to dispose of his horses to the Company, but McLeod could only say that Jedediah would have to settle that and other matters with his senior officer.

So miserable was the weather that it was November 28 before Jedediah got off for Fort Vancouver in company with Laframboise, and he might as well have stayed in camp, for McLeod, who set out for the fort on December 1, overtook him by 2:00 P.M. the same day. "Owing to the rise of the water in the Numerous Streams and the inundated State of the low land . . . travelling [is] extremely bad and very injurious to horses," McLeod observed; "it is therefore expedient to built temporary Canoes to descend the Wullamette River to Save the furs from further injury."

Rain-soaked, defeated and dispirited, Jedediah and his men returned to Fort Vancouver.

14. "GOOD, MERCHANTABLE BEAVER FURR"

While Jedediah Smith was south with Alex McLeod, Governor George Simpson turned up at Fort Vancouver from York Factory, his first visit to the Columbia in four years.

Simpson's westward passage had wrought some notable changes in his thinking about the Columbia. At the time of his visit in 1824-1825 he had anticipated the early removal of the Hudson's Bay Company's main base on the Pacific from the Columbia to Fraser River, which emptied into Puget Sound just north of 49°. Such a base, he felt, would be more centrally located, and less exposed when the partition of Oregon came. But the idea was practicable only if the Fraser was navigable into the back country. All this time Simpson had clung to the belief that the Fraser was adapted to river communication, and in voyaging west this summer he had undertaken to establish the fact by exploration.

In vain; Simpson had a terrifying passage down the Fraser, and reached its mouth stripped of all his illusions. He had come on to Fort Vancouver with a fresh appreciation of the importance of the Columbia, and in a mood to infuse the whole Department with a new energy. He meant to reinvigorate the Hudson's Bay Company's coastal trade, driving American ships from the northwest coast; he proposed to build up a timber trade and thereby tap new sources of wealth; and more than ever he was determined to keep Americans at arm's length in the interior.

Since the Governor's first visit to the Columbia in 1824, significant progress had been made toward self-sufficiency in the Department. There was no more importing of expensive European provisions; last summer Fort Vancouver alone had produced 400 bushels of corn, 1,300 bushels of wheat, 1,000 bushels of barley, 300 bushels of peas, 100 bushels of oats and about 4,000 bushels of potatoes, to say nothing of garden produce; and the number of cattle, hogs and goats had increased astonishingly. All this had followed from the abandonment of Fort George in favor of a new depot at Fort Vancouver. Similar if less spectacular results had attended the abandonment of Spokane House and the building of Fort Colvile on the Columbia near the Kettle Falls; Colvile now supplied all the grain required for the interior posts.

Such economies had considerably improved the competitive position of the Company, for to the extent that the overhead was reduced, prices could be slashed to undercut American competition without incurring ruinous losses. The Company might be muscle-bound to a degree, but it was big and powerful, having enormous staying powers, and with the general improvement of its position, Simpson could have some confidence in the Columbia Department's ability to cope with the Americans.

Notwithstanding the full stop put to Ogden's Snake Expedition of 1824-1825 by the desertion of his freemen, Ogden's returns that year had shown a profit of £3,700. The three expeditions which followed produced profits of £3,000, £2,000 and £2,500; thus the Snake Country was being turned into a fur desert not only without loss but at an actual profit. In the meantime the returns of the fixed posts had not been affected too adversely. Flathead Post was the one chiefly exposed to American pressure; the trade with the Flatheads had been lost to the Company in 1827-1828, and would be again this year. On the other hand, the new rates McLoughlin had put into effect in the summer of 1827 had already brought many of the deserters of 1825 back into the fold; their furs had nearly counterbalanced the loss of the Flathead trade.

Simpson could not rejoice over the presence of American trappers west of the continental divide; he estimated that they had cost the Company 1,700 beaver or £2,000 a year since 1824, and there had been further losses from the reduction in the profit margin in dealing with the Company's freemen. Still, the Governor conceived that

> the excellent footing on which the Trapping Expeditions were put, by Chief Factor McLoughlin after that disastrous affair [of 1825], has

proved highly advantageous in many points of view, as our own people are now perfectly satisfied with their situations, many of our late deserters find it advisable to return to their duty, and it has occasioned so much disaffection in the American camp, that several of their people have already joined us, and were we disposed to encourage desertions, very few would remain with them.

On the whole, Simpson was inclined to be optimistic. In March 1829 he wrote the Governor and Committee in London:

there is a probability of our being relieved from Opposition in the Snake Country for a time. That Country has never been rich for its extent, and is now much exhausted; but if undisturbed by the Americans, it will afford employment to a party of 30 to 40 men for several years to come, and while it even defrays the expences of such a party, we consider it good policy to keep them in that quarter. . . .

The American Trapping Expeditions are never sufficiently well organized to hold together for any length of time; the heads of the concern or Outfitters, are merely adventurers who have nothing to lose, and are ever on the watch to take some petty advantage of their followers, who being aware of this, have no respect for, and are always ready to cheat them in their turn. The conductors or Leaders of parties, are men who have been common Trappers, and therefore possess no influence: and the Trappers themselves are generally speaking, outcasts from Society, who take all their bad qualities along with them: this "motley crew" acknowledge no master, will conform to no rules or regulations, and are never on their guard, so that they are frequently cut off and their camps plundered. . . . We might repeatedly have broken up their parties, but the spirit of insubordination which characterises those fellows, is particularly infectious in the plains, we therefore allow as little intercourse as possible between them and our people, and in order to guard against the baneful influence of bad example, do not encourage desertion and have not at present above 10 or 12 of their people in our Service.

Simpson loved to sit in judgment; there was more than a touch of condescension in him; and he was most lacking in insight when thinking about the rank and file. It had taken him several years to disabuse himself of his prejudices about the Company's freemen, and he was not capable of seeing in the American free trappers a new breed of men.[1]

Jedediah Smith and Alex McLeod arrived from the south on December 14, 1828.[2] The reappearance of the latter at Fort Vancouver was a severe shock to Dr. McLoughlin, who had supposed that by now McLeod was trapping the "Bonaventura." McLeod's stated reason for returning to the fort was to obtain more horses, but as Simpson was about to argue to Jedediah that McLeod had more horses than he needed anyway, McLeod's return was not well received; he was accused of having come back for the sole purpose of seeing his family. Moreover, his handling of the Umpqua expedition was not approved; McLoughlin had not contemplated that he should waste the Company's time and money pursuing furs and horses all along the coast. McLeod set out for the south again in January 1829, and by April reached the valley of the Sacramento. He trapped as far south as present Stockton before turning back. Attempting to cross the mountains at the head of the McCloud River in December 1829, he was caught by heavy snows and lost all his horses; he put his furs in cache and got back safe to Fort Vancouver only to meet with severe criticism for his conduct of the expedition. It became expedient to transfer him out of the Columbia Department entirely, and the rest of his life he worked in the Far North. Nevertheless, trails had been beaten out, and until the middle '40s Hudson's Bay Company parties reaped a succession of rich harvests in the Valley of California.[3]

Ten days after Jedediah's return from the Umpqua, he had a formal conference with Simpson. He wanted to take his furs up the Columbia to Fort Nez Perces and leave them there while he traveled across country to the "Depot on Salt Lake." He also wanted the British Company to agree to exchange for the thirty-eight horses left on the Umpqua the same number of horses at Fort Nez Perces, his intention being to send during the summer of 1829 for both horses and furs. To these proposals Simpson replied formally by letter the day after Christmas.

First of all, he pointed out the inconvenience and expense Jedediah had occasioned the Company through the Umpqua Massacre and its aftermath.

When M^r^ McLeod and his party took their departure D^r^ McLoughlin did not conceive that any inconvenience or delay would have been occasioned by their visit to the Umpqua he did not therefore intend to have made any charge against you for the Services of Mr McLeod & his party in the recovering of your property but the time occupied in visiting the different Camps on the River & Coast with that object we now find has occasioned the loss to us of the Services of this Expedition for the whole Season thereby subjecting us to an expense of exceeding £1000 independent of the loss of Profits we had reason to calculate from the Services of this Expedition. [Had the American been in the condition of discussing terms, Simpson added] we should as a matter of course have insisted on your defraying the expenses, that the recovery of your property might have occasioned to us, but you was not in that condition consequently nothing was said on the subject, and altho' we are well aware that either in Law or Equity we should be fully entitled to Salvage, we make no claim thereto, on the contrary place the property which we have recovered at your disposal without any charge or demand whatsoever.

In order to suit your own convenience, you left 38 Horses at our Camp on the Umpqua which the Expedition had not the least occasion for as Mr McLeod having independent of them about 150 being more than sufficient we conceive to meet his demands; these and a few others expected to be received in order to accommodate you we are willing to take off your hands at 40/ St[erlin]g p. head, which is a higher price than we ever pay for Horses and the same we charge to our Servants & Trappers but if you are not satisfied with that price, they are still quite at your disposal.

. . . we should consider it the height of imprudence in you to attempt going up the Columbia with only your two followers either light or with property.—We a[l]tho' perfectly acquainted with every Indian on the communication rarely venture to send a party even with Letters and with property never less than from 30 to 40 Men; such a measure on your part would therefore in our opinion be sporting with Life or courting danger to madness; which I should not consider myself justified in permitting without pointing out to yourself and followers in presence of witness's the desperate hazards you would thereby run

I should consider it equally imprudent to attempt a Journey from Walla Walla to Salt Lake on many considerations, the most prominent of which are, the great danger to be apprehended from roving War parties, your total ignorance of the Country, the difficulty you would have in finding your way across the Blue Mountains, the inexperience of your people in Snow Shoe Travelling (one of whom I believe never saw a Snow Shoe) and the danger from Starvation as it is impossible you can carry provisions such a distance and the chase in some parts of the country through which you would have to pass is at this Season even to a hunting party a very precarious means of subsistance.—In reference to your demand upon us for Horses at Walla Walla it cannot be met by any possibility as by the last advices from thence we [have] none at that Establishment and our own business in the Upper parts of the Columbia requires at least five times the number we are likely to be able to collect in the course of next Season

You are well aware that we have already experienced much inconvenience incurred many sacrifices, and exposed the Concern to heavy loss, through our anxious desire to relieve, assist and accommodate you we are willing nevertheless to do whatever else we can without subjecting ourselves to further loss or expense in order to meet your wishes, I shall now suggest what I conceive to be the safest course you can pursue and the most eligible plan you can adopt.

Your Beaver which is of very bad quality the worst indeed I ever saw, having in the first instance been very badly dressed & since then exposed to every storm of Rain that has fallen between the Month of April & the 22nd. Inst. consequently in the very worst state of Damage, I am willing to take off your hands at 3 Dollars p Skin payable by Bill at 30d/ sight on Canada, which I conceive to be their full value at this place, and your Horses I will take at £2 St^{g} p Head payable in like manner But if these terms are not satisfactory to you the Furs may be left here until you have an opportunity of removing them & the Horses are at your disposal where you left them

In either case yourself and followers shall be made welcome to a continuance of our hospitality while you choose to remain at our Establishment—and if agreeable you shall be allowed a passage free of expense to Red River Settlement with me in the course of next Spring & Summer from whence you can proceed to St. Louis by Pra[i]rie du Chien or you may accompany our Snake Country Expedition next Autumn by which means you will in all probability have a safe escort until you fall in with your people at or in the neighborhood of Salt Lake

After you have fully considered these suggestions which are dictated by the best feelings towards you and an intense anxiety for the safety of yourself followers & property I have to request the favor of a reply thereon in Writing previous to M^{r} McLeod's departure[4]

Simpson had exhibited toward Jedediah on the part of the Hudson's Bay Company an undoubted generosity; the American was much better treated than he himself had treated the destitute Iroquois he had met in the Snake Country in the fall of 1824. But Simpson could not forbear rubbing Jedediah's nose in that generosity, and Jedediah must have resented it. His own reply, written the same day, has not survived, but Simpson's letter three days later preserves the substance of it.

Mr. J: S: Smith
Present

Fort Vancouver, Columbia River
29th. Dec[r] 1828

Dear Sir,

In reference to your valued communication of 26th Inst., and to our subsequent conferences I beg it to be distinctly understood that we do not lay claim to, nor can we receive any remuneration for the Services we have rendered you, any indemnification for the losses we have sustained in assisting you, nor any Salvage for the property we have recovered for you, as, whatsoever we have done for you was induced by feelings of benevolence and humanity alone, to which your distressed situation after your late providential escape & the lamentable & melancholy fate of your unfortunate companions gave you every title at our hands.—And I beg to assure you that the satisfaction we derive from these good offices, will repay the Hon[ble] Hudsons Bay Comp[y] amply for any loss or inconvenience in rendering them

I am exceedingly happy that you have consented to abandon the very hazardous Journey you contemplated and that you have allowed yourself to be influenced by my advice to pursue the safer yet more circuitous route by Red River, which notwithstanding the increased distance, will in point of time be the shortest, as thereby you will baring accidents be at St. Louis in the month of July next

With regard to your property, we are willing in order to relieve you from all further concern respecting it, to take it off your hands, at what we consider to be its utmost value here say Horses at 40/. each which you know to be a higher price than we ever pay for any, and Beaver at 3$ p[r] Skin Land Otters at 2$ p[r] Skin and Sea Otters at 10$ p[r] Skin which from their damaged state I conceive to be their utmost value here, fully as much as they will net to us in England, and after making a fair deduction for risk and expence of transport hence to St

Louis, more than they would yield you if taken to and sold in the States

But if these prices be not satisfactory to you, and that you prefer leaving your property here until a favourable opportunity should present itself for removing it, we shall with pleasure retain it for you, and deliver it when and to whom you may direct

With Esteem
I remain
Dear Sir
Yo: Mo: Ob^{t}: Ser^{t}:
Geo: Simpson[5]

Jedediah accepted Simpson's offer for his furs and horses, and on March 9, 1829, Simpson advised the Company's agent at Lachine that he had drawn a bill of exchange on him at sight in favor of Messrs. Smith, Jackson & Sublit for the sum of £541. 0s. 6d. Halifax Currency (£486. 18s. 5d. in Sterling, or $2,369.60), which amount was to be "charged in account with the Northern Department Outfit 1828 being the balance of Accounts of Furs and Horses sold to the Honble. Hudson's Bay Company" and delivered at Fort Vancouver.[6]

The winter at Fort Vancouver was profitable in information for both Jedediah and his hosts. California was still a semimythical land, and Jedediah's tales of the country and its people partook of the character of fable; it entertained Simpson vastly that "the Spaniards" could never bring themselves to believe that Jedediah's sole object was to hunt beaver, "an animal they scarcely knew by name, altho some of the Rivers within a few miles of their Settlements, abounded therewith." [7] But Simpson was pleased chiefly by Jedediah's account of his explorations, which enabled him to write London:

We learn from our American visitant Smith, that the flattering reports which reached St. Louis of the Wilhamot Country, as a field for Agricultural speculation, had induced many people in the States to direct their attention to that quarter; but he has on his present journey, discovered difficulties which never occurred to their minds, and which are likely to deter his Countrymen from attempting that enterprize. In the American Charts this River, (The Wilhamot or Moltnomah) is laid down, as taking its rise in the Rocky Mountains . . . and the opinion was, that it would merely be necessary for Settlers with their Horses, Cattle, Agricultural implements &c. &c. to get (by the main communication from St. Louis to Sta. Fee) to the height of Land in about Lat. 38, there to embark on large Rafts & Batteaux and glide down current about 800 or 1000 Miles at their ease to this "Land of Promise." But it now turns out, that the Sources of the Wilhamot are not 150 Miles distant from Fort Vancouver, in Mountains which even Hunters cannot attempt to pass, beyond which, is a Sandy desert of about 200 miles, likewise impassable, and from thence a rugged barren country of great extent, without Animals, where Smith and his party were nearly starved to Death. And the other route by Louis's River, Settlers could never think of attempting. So that I am of opinion, we have little to apprehend from Settlers in this quarter, and from Indian Traders nothing; as none, except large capitalists could attempt it, and the attempt would cost a heavy Sum of Money, of which they could never recover much. This they are well aware of, therefore as regards formidable opposition, I feel perfectly at ease unless the all grasping policy of the American Government, should induce it, to embark some of its National Wealth, in furtherance of the object.[8]

For Jedediah, meantime, everything he bent his sharp, observing eye on was information. If Simpson united his responsibilities to the Company with his duties under the crown, Jedediah was no less mindful how his obligation as an American citizen coincided with his personal interest. He was already composing in his mind the report he would make to his government when he got home again. This report is printed in full in the Appendix, but salient points merit notice. Fort Vancouver, he said, was situated on the north side of the Columbia, five miles above the mouth of the Willamette, on a second bank about three-quarters of a mile from the river; this was the original fort, but a large one, 300 feet square, about three-quarters of a mile lower down and within 200 yards of the river, was commenced in the spring of 1829. (The building of a new fort followed on Simpson's giving up the idea of a central base on the Fraser River; if Fort Vancouver was to be the principal depot, it had to be moved closer to the water's edge: this is the Fort Vancouver remembered in history.) The fort was defended, Jedediah noted, with a few twelve-pounders. What with mechanics of every sort, a good sawmill, and a small shipyard, Fort Vancouver had every requisite for becoming a British colony and a military and naval station: "As to the injury which must happen to the United States from the British getting the control of all the Indians beyond the mountains, building and repairing ships in the tide water region of the Columbia, and having a station there for their privateers and vessels of war, it is too obvious to need a recapitulation." There spoke the representative of the national interest. But in honor Jedediah was bound to add that he had met with kind and hospitable treatment, and that personally he owed thanks to Governor Simpson and the gentlemen of the Hudson's Bay Company for this hospitality and for the efficient and successful aid given him "in recovering from the Umpquah Indians a quantity of furs and many horses."

Apparently Jedediah at first intended to accept Simpson's invitation to accompany him east through Canada in the spring of 1829. It must have been the word that reached Fort Vancouver of the presence of American trappers in the vicinity of Flathead Post that changed his mind. Two different parties of trappers were wintering in the Flathead country. A surprise, one was headed by Joshua Pilcher. The other was led by Jedediah's own partner, David E. Jackson.[9] Jedediah improved the first opportunity to leave for the interior, and on March 12, thirteen days in advance of Simpson's departure, he set out up the Columbia.

Arthur Black went with him.[10] When Jedediah talked over his plans with Simpson in December, he had contemplated taking two men with him to the Depot on the Salt Lake, and the two must have been Black and Turner. Turner now chose to stay on in Oregon; he had a sufficiently eventful, often violent life, surviving yet other massacres on the California-Oregon trail to die in California in the spring of 1847.[11] The little Englishman, Richard Leland, dropped from sight so completely that it was long believed he must have left Oregon by sea. A cryptic letter from Dr. McLoughlin to John W. Dease, stationed at Fort Colvile, shows that he was taken overland to Canada in the summer of 1829; on July 11 McLoughlin advised, "Thomas Petit and Richard Layland are on their way to Canada there are heavy accusations against them, you will please keep them in confinement and if you apprehend any chance of their making their escape you will put them in Irons." What these heavy accusations were, what the disposition of the charges and even of Leland was, nothing in the Hudson's Bay Company archives discloses.[12]

Concerning his journey to seek out his partner in the Flathead lands, Jedediah is frugal with detail. His third-person letter to General Clark says merely that he remained at Fort Vancouver till March 12, when he ascended the Columbia to Fort Colvile; "from there he proceeded on, passing the Flathead trading post on the Flathead river, until he joined one of his partners (D. E. Jackson) in the Colanais country." The Burr map, somewhat more explicit, would indicate that Jedediah ascended the Columbia by boat to Fort Colvile, crossed over to Clarks Fork above Metaline Falls, and went up the north bank of Clarks Fork past Lake Pend d'Oreille to Flathead Post.[13] He then turned northeast, probably up the Thompson River, and crossed over to the Flathead River well above Flathead Lake. There, presumably, he found Jackson.

The reunion must have been a joyful one. Not, perhaps, of the back-pounding variety, for the emotional extravagances Jedediah permitted himself were chiefly religious, though there was a deep-running warmth in him for the men he called his friends. After his long absence, Jackson may have thought him dead, but more likely a journey lasting two years had been forecast when Jedediah left Bear Lake in July 1827. Having been so long separated from his partners, Jedediah would have inquired eagerly as to their adventures since parting from him, and this was a tale not told in an hour.

From Bear Lake, William L. Sublette had taken a party north to the Blackfoot country. Ashley said later that the Blackfeet "had always been considered enemies to our traders; but about that time some of them manifested a friendly disposition, invited a friendly intercourse and trade, and did actually dispose of a portion of their furs to Messrs. Smith, Jackson, and Sublette." This mood did not rest on the Blackfeet very long, and the life of the Iroquois leader, Old Pierre, became the price of the furs that were traded. According to Ashley, "P. Tontavantogan was killed by a party of Blackfoot Indians, who advanced near to where about

25 of our hunters were encamped, and proposed trading with them: Some difficulty arose—the Indians fired upon the whites, shot this man dead, and wounded another; took one horse and about one hundred and fifty pounds of beaver fur." This happened somewhere on the sources of the Missouri.[14]

Jim Beckwourth, a member of Sublette's party, says that the trading venture was preceded by news that the Flatheads and Blackfeet had achieved a fragile peace, following which one of the Blackfeet chiefs invited Sublette to come and trade. According to Jim, Sublette sent himself and two others on this mission. First and last, Jim makes quite a tale of it, including his acquisition of two Blackfoot wives. But he may descend to prosaic fact when he says that they left the Blackfoot country after a stay of twenty days, "having purchased thirty-nine packs of beaver and several splendid horses at a sum trifling in real value, but what they considered as far exceeding the worth of their exchanges." [15]

Apparently Sublette's party was accompanied north by a number of former Hudson's Bay Company freemen, who on hearing of the new rates established by McLoughlin chose to take their furs in to Flathead Post.[16] The rest of Sublette's party accompanied him on the back trail, which if Peter Skene Ogden's understanding was correct, took him all the way to Bear River before a paralyzing winter set in.

The only clue to Sublette's activities in the spring of 1828 comes through the loss of one of his men, Joseph Coté. Ashley, again serving as the historian of the mountain fur trade, relates that "Coty belonged to a party of fourteen men, under the immediate command of Mr. W. Sublette; he was shot while at his post on guard, on a very dark night, by (as since ascertained) a blackfoot Indian." This accident befell the party on "Godair's" or Little Goddin's River (the present Birch Creek), which in consequence for some years was known to the mountain men as "Coté's Defile." Therefore in the spring of 1828 William Sublette was north of the Snake Plain on the trails to and from Salmon waters, but whether he returned to this country at that season or after all wintered on the waters to the north remains a question.[17]

Still another party, numbering some forty men, during the

fall of 1827 ranged the lower Snake country. Peter Skene Ogden ran into some of this company as early as September 14, on the Weiser River, and at that time understood them to be working toward the sources of the Owyhee. These may have been free trappers rather than an organized brigade; some members of the party trapped in company with Ogden through much of the autumn, and when they separated from him at the end of November the British leader observed with satisfaction, "The beaver we have traded from them exceed 100. During the time they have been with us, they have trapped only 26, so they lost more by meeting with [us] than we have."

By the time Ogden made this journal entry he had reached the mouth of the Blackfoot River, where he set up a winter camp in the vicinity of a huge Snake camp. Late in December he was joined by a small party of Americans under Samuel Tullock, "a decent fellow," who had just crossed the Snake Plain from the Little Lost River. Tullock may have been a clerk for Smith, Jackson & Sublette, because he told Ogden that "his company would readily enter into an agreement regarding deserters. He informed me the conduct of Gardner's at our meeting 4 yrs. since has not been approved." (Ogden added in his journal, "I shd. certainly be shocked if any man of principle approved of such conduct as Gardner's.")

This was a fearful winter, one of the severest on record, and despite repeated efforts to cross the mountains to Bear River, Tullock could not get through. Ogden's diary, describing the repeated and almost laughable failures, speaks as if one at least of the American partners was at "the Depot" at this time, and it may be that both Jackson and Sublette were there.

Ogden's journal is eloquent about the weather and revealing as to the situation of his rivals:

[Wednesday January 16] . . . The Americans are now most anxious to procure snow shoes, and I am equally so they should not, as I am of opinion they are anxious to bring over a party of Trappers to this quarter . . . I have given orders to all not to make any for them. This day they offered 25 Dollars for one pair and 20 for another, but failed. . . .

[Tuesday January 22] . . . a Snake arrived and informed The American Trader, that one of their Cashes had been Stolen by the plain Snakes. . . . property . . . in it, about 600 Dollars, how long will the Snakes be allowed to Steal and Murder, I cannot say, The Americans appear and are most willing to declare war against Them, and a short time since requested to know, if they did in the spring, if I would assist, to This I replied if I found myself in Company with them at the time I would not stand idle, I am certainly most willing to commence but . . . not knowing the opinion of the Concern, it is rather a delicate point to decide on . . . acting for myself, I will not hesitate to say I would most willingly sacrifice a year and even two to exterminate the whole Snake Tribe, Women and Children Excepted, and in so doing I am of opinion I could fully justify myself before God and man. . . .

[Thursday, January 24] . . . The Americans are in three different places starving, no Buffalo in That quarter This year, and were reduced to eat their Horses and dogs . . . we could not ascertain [from Indians from Bear River] if the American Traders had returned from St. Louis. . . .

[Friday, January 25] Snow greater part of the day. The man who started on the 23rd Inst. in quest of his traps arrived . . . reports arriving from all directions relative to the distressed state of the Americans, Horses dead . . . Casches destroyed . . . The Americans here now appear determined to proceed and find their Traders, They now discover it is to no purpose these extravagant offers, and are making Snow Shoes themselves, this they ought to have done two Months since . . . I cannot ascertain the motive of their Journey but I principally dread their returning with liquor a small quantity they may succeed in bringing if so, it would be most advantageous to them but the reverse to me. . . . If they should succeed in reaching their Camp it will be to their advantage to bring twenty or thirty trappers to this quarter, This would also be most injurious to us . . . as all my hopes for a Spring Hunt, are in this quarter . . . as the party here have only ten Traps, no good can result to us, if they succeed in reaching their Depot, and returning here. . . .

[Wednesday, February 6] . . . The Americans again making preparations to Start for their Depot . . . from the precautions they now take will succeed in reaching it, This will be their third attempt, and They have no time to lose, if they wish to return here in time with a Party to assist us in trapping. . . .

[Tuesday, February 12] . . . a war Party of Black Feet has [been reported as] taking the direction of Salt Lake . . . the Americans here are alarmed at this News, not only on account of the two men who shortly started for Salt Lake, but also for their Party in that quarter.

[Wednesday, February 13] . . . the Americans . . . have now only 24 [horses] left from 50 they started from Nez Percy with. . . .

[Sunday, February 17] . . . the two Americans . . . arrived accompanied by one of their Traders and two men, they met these on Portneuf River, near its sources . . . he also informed me, they had a skirmish with the Black Feet, and old Piere the Iroquois Chief who deserted from me four years ago was killed and cut into pieces. . . . Their Traders from St. Louis . . . did not return last fall, their non arrival is attributed to the early and Severe Winter, which has been in the vicinity of Salt Lake most severe, with the exception of the Freemen from the Flat Heads all had reached the Depot in safety . . . their loss sustained in Horses by Black Feet, has been most severe amounting to 60; it was rather a novel sight in this part of the world to see the above party arrive with Dogs and sleds, for prior to this year, seldom has there ever been more than two inches of snow at any time. . . .

[Tuesday, February 19] . . . The Americans making preparations for their Journey to the Flat Heads . . . Their Trader Mr. Campble informed me that two of their Trappers Goodrich & Johnson, who Joined my Camp last fall with the intention of going to the Columbia, are heavily indebted to the Concern, to this I made reply that I had no knowledge of the Same, and as he was now here it was his duty to secure his debts and his men also . . . I [observed] that my conduct towards their party was far different from what I had received four years since, he said it was, and regretted that at that time there was no regular Company in the Country, otherwise I should have received far different treatment. . . .

[Wednesday, February 20] . . . The American Trader had a long conference with the two trappers who joined me last fall, and both have consented to return. . . .

[Thursday, February 21] Cold stormy weather . . . prevents the Americans from starting . . . 30 Tents of Snakes are now encamped within half a mile of our Camp, are Starving and very troublesome.

[Saturday, February 23] . . . American Party started for the Flat Heads, and probably another may go to the Kootenays . . . they have certainly a long Journey before them, but are well provided for it, while here they were very silent regarding the object of their Journey . . . I believe it is their intention to trap the Forks of the Missouri, for which they are sufficiently strong in numbers. . . .

[Wednesday, March 26] . . . the American party who have been with us since last December . . . took their departure for Salt Lake. We met and separated on good Terms. . . .[18]

This departure of Tullock's party for the Salt Lake had a regrettable sequel, for three or four days after leaving Ogden, while on the Portneuf, Tullock was attacked by thirty or forty Indians who killed three of his party, Pinckney W. Sublette, J. B. Jondron (or Gendreau) and P. Ragotte (or F. Rashotte), and as the tale was told afterwards, "plundered him of about four thousand dollars worth of furs, forty-four horses, and a considerable quantity of merchandise." Blackfeet were responsible for this outrage; they were in turn looted by the Snakes in May.[19]

Other men were lost this winter, four under mysterious circumstances: Ephraim Logan, Jacob O'Hara, William Bell and James Scott. According to Ashley:

Logan, O'Harrar, Bell, and Scott, the four men missing, were with 15 or 20 other men, on their way from the river Columbia to the Grand Salt Lake. The four in question diverged from a direct route to their place of destination, for the purpose of exploring some small rivers, intending to again join their companions in the course of two or three days; but since they left the party [about January 1828] . . . , nothing directly or indirectly has been heard of them.[20]

Evidently the four men were members of the party of forty which Ogden found operating in the western reaches of the Snake Valley in September 1827. Jedediah Smith, at rendezvous in 1827, must have been apprised of the intention of these men to trap in that direction, for after the Umpqua Massacre, when rumors were heard of four men held captive by the "Cahoose" or Coos Indians, Jedediah voiced to Alexander McLeod the interesting idea that these men were not survivors of the massacre at all; rather, "M^r^. Smith is of Opinion that Logan & three other Men have not visitted their Deposit last Season, and were proceeding toward his route, and possibly fell on his track and have come forward till their progress was arrested by the Natives." Their precise fate never was determined, but Indian report declared that they were killed by the Snakes.[21]

The year 1828 continued a bloody one. It was probably in

the spring that John Johnson and John Godan (or Goddin or Godair) were killed "near the Great Salt Lake, while attempting to pass from one American camp to another, but a few miles distant." These killings too were attributed to the Blackfeet, and Bear River is given as the place.[22] The most melodramatic happening of the spring belongs, however, to the history of Robert Campbell's party.

Ogden had noted Campbell's departure for the north on February 23, and accurately forecast his destination. According to Ashley, the party consisted of eighteen men and succeeded in making "a valuable collection of furs" in trade with the Flatheads. On the return march Campbell moved with all possible expedition, and had nearly reached rendezvous at Bear Lake when a war party of several hundred Blackfeet forced him to hole up in the rocks.

Jim Beckwourth has something to say about this exciting event, and the gaudy liar's account squares amazingly with the known facts. According to Jim, while he and two others at rendezvous were awaiting the ingathering of the trappers, they heard of the approach of Campbell's party and went out to meet them. "They had met with very good fortune in their *cruise*, and had lost none of their men. We encamped with them that night, and escorted them to the rendezvous the next day." When, the following morning, they were set on by the Blackfeet, the party had a running fight for six miles before they could hole up.

On the way we lost one man, who was quite old. He might have saved himself by riding to the front, and I repeatedly urged him to do so, telling him that he could not assist us [in the rear guard]; but he refused even to spur on his horse when the Indians made their charges. I tarried with him, urging him on, until I found it would be certain death to delay longer. My horse had scarcely made three leaps in advance when I heard him cry, "Oh God, I am wounded!" Wheeling my horse, I called on my companions to save him. I returned to him, and found an arrow trembling in his back. I jerked it out, and gave his horse several blows to quicken his pace; but the poor old man reeled and fell from his steed, and the Indians were upon him in a moment to tear off his scalp.

Veritable prodigies were performed by the defenders after

they holed up, Jim goes on to say, he himself receiving an arrow wound in the head. But ammunition was low, and it seemed inevitable that they must be destroyed unless help could be summoned. Jim volunteered for the mission.

Campbell then said that two had better go, for there might be a chance of one living to reach the camp. Calhoun volunteered to accompany me, if he had his choice of horses, to which no one raised any objection. Disrobing ourselves, then, to the Indian costume, and tying a handkerchief round our heads, we mounted horses as fleet as the wind, and bade the little band adieu. . . .

we dashed through the ranks of the foe before they had time to comprehend our movement. The balls and arrows flew around us like hail, but we escaped uninjured. Some of the Indians darted in pursuit of us, but, seeing they could not overtake us, returned to their ranks. . . . When about five miles from the camp we saw a party of our men approaching us at a slow gallop. We halted instantly, and, taking our saddle-blankets, signaled to them first for haste, and then that there was a fight. Perceiving this, one man wheeled and returned to the camp, while the others quickened their pace, and were with us in a moment, although they were a mile distant when we made the signal. There were only sixteen, but on they rushed, eager for the fray, and still more eager to save our friends from a horrible massacre. They all turned out from the camp, and soon the road was lined with men, all hurrying along at the utmost speed of the animals they bestrode. . . . The Indians were surprised at seeing a re-enforcement, and their astonishment was increased when they saw a whole line of men coming to our assistance. They instantly gave up the battle and commenced a retreat. We followed them about two miles, until we came to the body of Bollière—the old man that had been slain; we then returned, bringing his mangled remains with us.

At the last, Jim cannot refrain from improving on the facts, saying that Campbell lost four men killed and seven wounded, together with two packs of beaver, a few packs of meat and some valuable horses, while the whites took seventeen scalps and were satisfied they had killed at least a hundred more. But Jim's account ends on an authentic note when he says, "The battle lasted five hours, and never in my whole life had I run such danger of losing my life and scalp." The name of the man killed, given by Beckwourth as Bollière, is rendered Francois Bouldeau or Boileau in the casualty lists, and Lewis Boldue by Ashley. The latter's version of the affair, written in January 1829 on William L. Sublette's authority, is that when within about fifteen miles of rendezvous Campbell discovered two or three hundred Indians in pursuit of him:

he and party (Boldue excepted) succeeded in reaching some rocks near at hand, which seemed to offer a place of safety. The Indians, who proved to be Blackfoot warriors, advanced, but were repulsed with the loss of several of their men killed; they would, no doubt, have ultimately succeeded in cutting off the whites, had they not been so near the place of rendezvous, where, in addition to 60 or 70 white men, there were several hundred Indians friendly to them, and enemies to the Blackfoots. This fact was communicated to the assailants by a Flathead Indian, who happened to be with Mr. Campbell, and who spoke the Blackfoot language. At the same time, the Indians saw two men, mounted on fleet horses, pass through their lines, unhurt, to carry the information of Mr. C's situation to his friends. This alarmed the Indians, and produced an immediate retreat. Lewis Boldue, being an inactive man, was overtaken and killed before he had reached the rocks. Several others were wounded, while defending themselves among the rocks. The party lost about five thousand dollars worth of beaver furs, forty horses, and a small amount of merchandize.[23]

Since Ashley blamed all these murders and robberies on the British, he was not inclined to understate the losses, and his figures as a rule would do credit to Jim Beckwourth; in this instance he puts Beckwourth in the shade.

The fight made a lively overture for rendezvous 1828, fully comparable to that of the year before, and both staged along the shores of Bear Lake. None of the mountain rendezvous has been more obscure than the gathering of 1828, which down to this writing has never been correctly located, usually placed in the valley of the Great Salt Lake. There was no Smith, Jackson & Sublette supply caravan up from the States this year, the Company's goods having been brought up the previous fall. But as a novelty, competition of sorts reappeared at this rendezvous in the person of Joshua Pilcher.

Pilcher's Missouri Fur Company had failed in 1825. He ascribed the failure in part to the Immell-Jones disaster of 1823, and in part to "inveterate competition" by the French Fur Company for the trade along the Missouri River.[24] He had applied for, without getting, the job of secretary to the Atkinson-O'Fallon commission sent up the Missouri in 1825 to treat with the Indians;[25] always persistent, he had thereupon organized a new partnership in the fur trade, associating himself with Lucien B. Fontenelle, William Henry Vanderburgh, Charles Bent and Andrew Drips. With a capital which according to its license amounted to about $7,000, this partnership floundered along for two years.[26] Inspired by Ashley's successes, Pilcher and his partners got together an outfit and in the late summer of 1827 set out for the mountains in a last attempt to retrieve their fortunes.

Pilcher's party, 45 men with 104 horses, left Council Bluffs in September 1827. He followed the now well-beaten road up the Platte and the Sweetwater, but as he was approaching South Pass the Crows made off with practically all his horses. The luckless traders had to cache their goods and continue on across South Pass afoot, wintering on the Green. Next spring, with horses obtained from the Snakes, one of the partners returned to the cache only to find much of the merchandise destroyed by seeping water. Pilcher says:

> The remnant saved from this misfortune was carried across the mountains to the small lake called *Bear Lake*, a little to the west of the sources of the Colorado, then a rendezvous for hunters and traders. Here our traffic with these people was completed. My partners and most of the men set out on their return to the Council Bluffs; and myself, with nine men, commenced a tour to the northwest, with the view of exploring the region of the Columbia river, to ascertain the attractions and capabilities for trade. This was in July, 1828. . . .[27]

Fontenelle, Vanderburgh and Charles Bent went down to the States with a meager sixteen to eighteen packs of beaver, and it was reported on their arrival at the Bluffs in mid-September that Pilcher & Co. had broken up.[28] Drips remained in the mountains, trapping in the Crow country, he and Fontenelle seemingly having organized a new partnership out of the ruins of the old.[29]

Viewed as competition for Smith, Jackson & Sublette, Joshua Pilcher & Company had been a miserable failure, a grave disappointment to the free trappers, and Pilcher made out no better in following David E. Jackson to the Flathead lands. According to Pilcher, the journey required four months, and it was about December 1 when they took up winter quarters on the shores of Flathead Lake in northern Montana. John Work, in charge at Fort Colvile this winter, commented that the Americans considerably injured the British trade without materially benefiting themselves.[30] Simpson's viewpoint was that "Jackson, accompanied by a Clerk Fitzpatrick, and a Major Pilcher with a Clerk Gardner & 40 Trappers . . . had very few Skins, and of those few, about half fell into our hands in exchange for some necessary supplies." He observed that the same fate that overtook Pilcher's Missouri Fur Company probably awaited his present concern, "as it must have been in a desperate state indeed, when the head thereof, could not find better employment for himself and followers than watching the Flat Head Camp." [31]

Casting about for any alternative to ruin, on December 30, 1828, Pilcher sent some proposals down to Simpson at Fort Vancouver. It would appear that he contemplated a trapping venture in the Blackfoot country, the Hudson's Bay Company to furnish the outfit, he to conduct and front for the expedition so as to legalize its operations on American soil. To this letter Simpson wrote a stinging refusal, saying that as British subjects the officers of the Hudson's Bay Company could not openly infringe the territorial rights of the United States Government, "and although the protecting Laws of your Government might be successfully evaded by the plan you suggest still I do not think it would be reputable in the Honble Hudson Bay Co^y^ to make use of indirect means to acquire possession of a Trade to which it has no just claim." [32]

Pilcher was nearly finished, and the spring of 1829 completed the job. He resumed trapping in February, but he had more horses stolen, and he also lost a man, E. Marlow, killed by the Kutenais on the river that bears their name. Soon afterward he fell in with Jackson's party, and as his men were disheartened and had "no ultimate prospects sufficiently brilliant to bear them up under present hardships," Pilcher permitted all but one of them to join Jackson's brigade, sold Jackson his traps for $200, and frankly abandoned his mountain business for a tour of observation. (He made his way down to Fort Colvile, from which in the summer of 1830 the Hudson's Bay Company conveyed him east through Canada. The mountains would see Joshua Pilcher no more.)[33]

At the same time Jackson took a detachment north to the Flathead country, Robert Campbell led a brigade, including Jim Beckwourth and Jim Bridger, to the Crow lands. Sublette, however, set out for St. Louis with the year's returns. It seems probable that he journeyed down from the mountains with Pilcher's discouraged partners,[34] and it must have been in the course of this journey that Hiram Scott came to a celebrated end.

The record of Scott's life is sparse enough. In 1819 he was living in Dardenne Township, near St. Louis. That his fortunes were threadbare is evident from a notice in the St. Charles *Missourian* of February 21, 1822, to the effect that on the first day of the next circuit court for the county he would apply for final hearing and discharge under the act providing for the relief of insolvent debtors. That he was nevertheless much of a man is evidenced by Ashley's having appointed him to command a company in the Arikara campaign of 1823, and to conduct to the mountains the trading venture of 1827—a service for which Ashley paid him two dollars a day over a period of 140 days. But Scott was to be immortalized through his tragic death, which attached his name to a landmark in the valley of the Platte.[35]

Precisely what happened to Scott has been the province of folklore more than of history. But as Warren Ferris heard the story in 1830, Scott was

> a clerk in a company returning from the mountains, the leader of which found it necessary to leave him behind at a place some distance above [Scotts Bluff], in consequence of a severe illness which rendered him unable to ride. He was consequently placed in a bullhide boat, in charge of two men, who had orders to convey him by water down to these bluffs, where the leader of the party promised to await their coming. After a weary and hazardous voyage, they reached the appointed rendezvous, and found to their surprise and bitter disappointment, that the company had continued on down the river without stopping for them to overtake and join it. . . . They had, moreover, in descending the river, met with some accident, either the loss

of the means of procuring subsistence or defending their lives in case of discovery and attack. This unhappy circumstance, added to the fact that the river was filled with innumerable shoals and sand-bars, by which its navigation was rendered almost impracticable, determined them to forsake their charge and boat together, and push on night and day until they should overtake the company, which they did on the second or third day afterward. The reason given by the leader of the company for not fulfilling his promise, was that his men were starving, no game could be found, and he was compelled to proceed in quest of buffalo.[36]

Scott's bones were found the following summer. As the tale was embellished over the years, he had crawled hopelessly for sixty miles or so before finding his death at the magnificent bluffs which preserve his name. The tale is one that has captured the imagination of travelers from that day to the present and has given rise to a national monument. It has been supposed that Scott was one of Sublette's company, since Fontenelle, Vanderburgh and Bent would scarcely have had need of a clerk. However, Scott might have been traveling unattached, and there is presumptive evidence that Sublette had no part in abandoning him, for William Marshall Anderson, who traveled to the Rockies in 1834 with Sublette and who greatly liked and admired him, on briefly recounting the affair in his journal said that the "abandonment of this poor man by his leader and employer, was an act of the most cruel and heartless inhumanity, uncalled for and unnecessary. . . . I know the name of the soulless villain, and so does God and the devil."[37]

Whatever may have attended the downward passage, Sublette reached the States with his furs about the end of September 1828. An exact record of the returns is preserved in an account of Ashley with Smith, Jackson & Sublette; they consisted of 7,107½ pounds of beaver valued at $5.00 per pound; 49 otter skins at $3.00 apiece, 27 pounds of castoreum at $4.00 per pound, and 73 muskrats at 25 cents each, the total value being $35,810.75. This sufficed to pay various debts, including $9,010.40 owing Ashley for the second outfit of 1827, and leave a "Ballance due S. J & S this 26th day Octr 1828" of $16,000.[38] That represented the extent to which Smith, Jackson & Sublette by the fall of 1828 had emerged clear of debt—without benefit of any returns whatever from Jedediah Smith's two California expeditions.

Sublette remained in St. Louis through the winter of 1828-1829, preparing the outfit he would take to the mountains next spring, meanwhile furnishing Ashley with information about the state of things in the Rockies. During that winter, Sublette made a number of recruits who would be heard from in the mountains hereafter, including Samuel Parkman, Joe Meek, Robert Newell and George W. Ebberts.

Both Newell and Meek have left accounts of the journey to the Rockies in the spring of 1829, though Newell's account is laconic in the extreme, and Meek's was set down long afterward, with the usual lapses of memory. Both at this time were brash young men, the one from Butler County, Ohio, the other from Washington County, Virginia. Newell's memorandum says merely, "March 7 1829 I left St Louis with Mr W*m* Sublette who was the prop[r]ietor of our camp on a hunting expedit[i]on for beever 54 men in all arived at the foot of the mountains on Sweet water the 17th of July whare we met his hunters in part. . . ." [39] Meek relates that they traveled "across the country from near the mouth of the Kansas River to the River Arkansas; thence to the South Fork of the Platte; thence on to the North Fork of that River, to where Ft. Laramie now stands; thence up the North Fork to the Sweetwater, and thence across in a still northwesterly direction to the head of Wind River."

It is scarcely believable that Sublette took so wide a detour from the traveled trail as to have reached the Arkansas; Meek must have meant to say that they headed up the Kaw on the Santa Fe road for a few miles, then struck over to the Platte, went up that river and the South Platte a distance, crossed the latter to reach the North Platte at Ash Hollow, and went on up the North Platte and the Sweetwater to the mountains—one of the standard routes on the subsequent Oregon Trail. They had a scare by Indians along the way, but proceeded without other incident and, so Meek says, "arrived, about the first of July, at the rendezvous, which was appointed for this year on the Popo Agie." [40]

A good deal of confusion has marked accounts of the rendezvous of 1829 on the Popo Agie, which may not have been a general rendezvous at all, but a specifically appointed meeting with Robert Campbell, who had made his fall and spring hunt on the Big Horn, the Powder and other tributaries of the Yellowstone. Jackson did not get his party to the Popo Agie, and Sublette, after finishing his business with Campbell, continued on across the Wind River Mountains in search of him.[41]

Before following Sublette west, we must give some attention to Campbell's hunt of 1828-1829. Jim Beckwourth accompanied him on that hunt, so that a little more is known of Campbell's experiences than of Jackson's. Beckwourth says that the party consisted of thirty-one men, including Jim Bridger, most of them skilled trappers. Bridger's star had been rising for five years, and by 1829 his reputation was second to none. A description of him penned a few years later by David L. Brown applied now as then. He had, Brown wrote,

> a complete and absolute understanding of the Indian character in all its different phases, and a firm, though by no means over cautious, distrust with regard to these savages. . . . his bravery was unquestionable, his horsemanship equally so, and . . . he had been known to kill twenty buffaloes by the same number of consecutive shots. The physical conformation of this man was in admirable keeping with his character. Tall—six feet at least—muscular, without an ounce of superfluous flesh . . . he might have served as a model for a sculptor or painter, by which to express the perfection of graceful strength and easy activity. One remarkable feature of this man . . . was his neck, which rivalled his head in size and thickness, and which gave to the upper portion of his otherwise well-formed person a somewhat *outre* and unpleasant appearance. His cheek bones were high, his nose hooked or aqueline, the expression of his eye mild and thoughtful, and that of his face grave almost to solemnity. To complete the picture, he was perfectly ignorant of all knowledge contained in books, not even knowing the letters of the alphabet; put perfect faith in dreams and omens, and was unutterably scandalized if even the most childish of the superstitions of the Indians were treated with anything like contempt or disrespect; for in all these he was a firm and devout believer.[42]

From rendezvous in 1828, Beckwourth says, Campbell's party made its way to the Powder, and there commenced trapping.

To hear Jim Beckwourth tell it, the indestructible old mountain man, Caleb Greenwood, had persuaded the Crows that Beckwourth was born of that tribe, having been made captive by the Cheyennes when a boy, later bought by the whites, and now become a great chief. Consequently, Jim expected to fare well in the Crow country.

As Jim tells the tale, one day he and Bridger started out with their traps, intending to be gone three or four days. They followed up a small stream till it forked, then separated, setting traps up each fork. Beckwourth's fortune it was to fall in with the very band of Crows Greenwood had shown to be so gullible, who rejoiced that their lost son should be restored to them. They equipped him with a wife and other fixins, and he could not find it in his heart to tear himself away "from their untutored caresses." Thus commenced Beckwourth's life as a Crow chief. "I said to myself, 'I can trap in their streams unmolested, and derive more profit under their protection than if among my own men, exposed incessantly to assassination and alarm.' I therefore resolved to abide with them, to guard my secret, to do my best in their company, and in assisting them to subdue their enemies."

Jim adds that Bridger was a witness to his capture. Supposing the Indians to be Cheyennes, Bridger doubted not that he had been put to death, and went sorrowing back to camp. His fellow trappers pronounced their eulogies on his memory, and "having conceived a deep disgust at that vicinity, they moved their camp to the head waters of the Yellow Stone, leaving scores of beaver unmolested in the streams." [43]

All this makes a fine story, or it would not be authentic Beckwourth. But a document in the Sublette papers puts a different face on the matter. At Wind River on January 6, 1829, Beckwourth signed by mark a promissory note witnessed by Robert Campbell, "On a settlement of all accounts up to this date with Smith Jackson & Sublette there appears a Balance due by me to them of Two Hundred and Seventy five Dollars 17½¢ which I promise to pay in good merchantable Beaver Furr at Three Dollars per pound for value received." [44] Probably Beckwourth wanted to join the Crow camp, Campbell agreed to let him go, and Jim signed this note in acknowledgment of existing indebtedness or to secure an outfit. At any rate, on this day Jim Beckwourth passes beyond the ken of Smith, Jackson & Sublette.

Campbell must have made his spring hunt down the Big Horn, in the course of which he lost four men, Ezekiel Able, Peter Spoon, Philip Adam and Luke Lariour, killed by Blackfeet at "Bad pass of Big Horn"—the pass across the Big Horn Mountains. Drips likewise lost two men to the Blackfeet this spring on Yellowstone waters, their names remembered as Garreau and Mino (or Meno).[45] If all mountain men had a deep and abiding hatred of the Blackfeet, the reason is evident.

Following his rendezvous with Campbell, William Sublette started the young Irishman down to the States with the forty-five packs that were his returns. What remained of the party, reinforced perhaps by some men of the fifty-four just brought to the mountains, William placed in charge of his younger brother Milton and two free trappers, Henry Fraeb and Jean Baptiste Gervais, directing them to trap down the Big Horn.[46] Campbell left the mountains in company with Andrew Drips; the journey was uneventful, and Campbell got his furs to Lexington on August 20.[47] What value was placed on the furs no document discloses, but as the packs borne by mules and horses were relatively light, averaging fifty pounds each, Campbell's hunt might have been worth some $11,250 on delivery in St. Louis.

Having disposed of the first phase of the summer's business, Sublette set out in search of Jackson. Newell says that they "crossed the mountain from the waters of Missourie to the Columbia and on piers fork we fell in with Mr Smith & Jackson partners of Mr Sublette." This is in accord with Jedediah's own sparse record of the summer's events, which says that after joining Jackson "he proceeded and joined Mr W. L. Sublette, on the 5th August 1829, at the Tetons on Henry's Fork S. branch Columbia." Newell adds that they held "general rendezvous" in Pierres Hole on August 20 with about 175 men present; that would include a sizable number of free trappers.[48]

According to Governor Simpson, Jackson had done badly on his hunt in the Flathead and Kutenai country. He may not have done so badly as Simpson would have liked to think, and admittedly he had obtained nearly the whole of the Flathead trade this year.[49] Nevertheless, the partners must have had forebodings about the future. Where were they to turn for beaver?

Nothing Jedediah had seen in the country west and southwest of Great Salt Lake promised much. California was too far off, and they had had no luck there. The southern Rockies were overrun with trappers operating out of Taos.[50] The Utah country was trapped out. The Flathead lands were not a likely prospect for this year. The Snake Country, trapped by British and Americans alike, seemed all but exhausted. Since they had left the Snake Country undisturbed for a year, Jackson might try his luck there. Milton Sublette had already been detailed to the Big Horn. That left just one likely possibility, the Blackfoot country. Jedediah Smith and William Sublette would have to accept the risks and take to that country a party large enough to look after itself.

With his usual economy of phrase, Newell says concerning the fall hunt, "we went up henrys fork of Snake river on to Lewises fork crossed the mountain on to the waters of missouri took up winter garters [quarters] on the Bighorn and went to powder river and Remaned untill Spring." The mention of Lewis's fork, the Snake, must be mistaken. Joe Meek is more plausible in saying that Smith and Sublette's company "commenced moving back to the east side of the Rocky Mountains in October. Its course was up Henry's fork of the Snake River, through the North Pass to Missouri Lake, in which rises the Madison fork of the Missouri River." They arrived on the head of the Madison in November, having been harassed by Blackfeet most of the way; they moved on northeasterly over the rugged Madison Range to the Gallatin, and then again east across the Gallatin Range to the Yellowstone, which they probably reached twenty-five or thirty miles above present Livingston.

According to Meek, they crossed the mountains with difficulty and were resting the camp and horses on the Yellowstone River for a few days when Blackfeet attacked them, two men being killed. Meek must have been remembering some other deaths, some other year, for the casualty lists show no men lost this fall or in this country. However, he says that in consequence of the attack he was cut off from the camp and had to flee to the mountains, with mule, blanket and gun his only earthly possessions.

Young Meek decided that his only chance was to make for Wind River, which had been settled on as the place for the winter encampment. He had to abandon the mule, but killed mountain sheep enough to furnish food and chanced on a hot-spring area, the sulphurous warmth delightful after the freezing cold of the mountains. Though the place smelled of brimstone, Joe felt that "if it war hell, it war a more agreeable climate than I had been in for some time."[51]

Here Meek was found by two men sent in search of him and with them he proceeded to the camp, which he found attempting to cross the high mountains between the Yellowstone and the Big Horn. The snow was so deep that men had to go in advance to break a road for the animals. In these mountains, Meek says, they lost a hundred head of horses and mules, which sank in the snow and could not be extricated, but the party forced its way down into the Big Horn Basin, falling on the Sulphur Stinking Fork as then called, now more euphoniously the Shoshone River. Pronouncing this region the "back door to that country which divines preach about," the trappers pushed on to the Big Horn.

Here they found signs of the presence of another trapping party, which turned out to be Milton Sublette's, consisting, Meek says, of forty men. Jedediah and William Sublette cached the proceeds of their fall hunt, and the united companies headed south. The road up over the Littlehorns brought them to Wind River, and just before Christmas they reached winter quarters, having had, on the whole, a successful fall hunt.[52]

In view of their success, it was decided that a new outfit should be brought up in the spring. The job of getting down to the States was given to William Sublette. As he had done three years before, he elected to set out with a single companion, Black Harris, going on snowshoes with a train of pack dogs.[53] Jedediah would perhaps have liked to go down to the States himself, for how many years had he been from home! But the state of the partnership's affairs would not admit of his going; after his disasters of the last three years, Jedediah was badly in need of a good hunt. He had to be content with sending down letters which Sublette tucked into his capote on setting out Christmas Day.

15. THE THINGS OF TIME

The letters Jedediah Smith wrote home from Wind River the day before Christmas 1829 yield an insight into his mind and personality the more welcome for the consistent bareness of the record of his life. His years in the West are a sustained, almost unrelieved chronicle of physical endurance, unflagging courage and granitic purpose, with occasional climaxes in which his spirit burns clear and bright. Explorer, fur trader, fighting man—he was all of these; and as a symbol of the nation which launched him in the track of the sun, a great deal more. But Jedediah the man tends to be lost in Jedediah Smith the hero, the trail breaker, the public personality. His letters are almost the only window that opens on his heart.

Taking up his pen after an absence from home of nearly nine years, an "unworthy Son" once more undertaking to address "his Mutch Slighted Parents," homesickness came over him. Many times, he said, he had been ready to bring his business to a close and endeavor to come home; by the assistance of Divine Providence he would come as soon as possible. It comforted him, as it would comfort them, that he invoked the memory of a common worship. "God only knows, I feell the need of the wa[t]ch & care of a Christian Church . . . I hope you will remember me before a Throne of Grace."[1]

For all the tenderness with which he wrote his parents, a barrier stood between them, and it was rather to his elder brother that he opened his mind and heart. Since he left home, he wrote Ralph, he had passed through various vicissitudes; he had been fortunate in some respects, in others not:

I have passed through the Country from St. Louis, Missouri, to the North Paciffick Ocean, in different ways—through countrys of Barrenness & seldom one of the reverse, many Hostile Tribes of Indians inhabit this Space, and we are under the necessity of keeping a constant wa[t]ch; notwithstanding our vigilenc[e] we some times suffer; in Augt. 1827 ten Men, who were in company with me, lost their lives, by the Amuchabas Indians, on the Colorado River; & in July 1828 fifteen men, who were in Company with me lost their lives, by the Umpquah Indians. . . . My Brother believe me, we have Many dangers to face & many difficulties to encounter, but if I am Spared I am not anxious with regard to difficulties—for particular[s] you must await a meeting——

The religious feeling which ran through his life, a thread both shining and dark, finds clear expression in this letter. "As it respects my Spiritual welfare, I hardly durst Speak I find myself one of the most ungrateful; unthankful, Creatures imaginable Oh when Shall I be under the care of a Christian Church? I have need of your Prayers." And with a sudden rush of feeling:

Oh My Brother let us render to him to whoom all things belongs, a proper proportion of what is his due I must tell you, for my part, that I am much behind hand, oh! the perverseness of my wicked heart! I entangle myself altogether too much in the things of time—I must depend entirely upon the Mercy of that being, who is abundant in Goodness & will not cast off any, who call, Sincerely, upon him; again I say, pray for me My Brother—& may he, before whoom not a Sparrow falls, without notice, bring us, in his own good time, Together again.[2]

So also, a year later, he wrote his brother:

are we ungrateful to that God in whoom we live, and moove, and have our being, how often ought we on our bended knees to offer up our greatful acknowledgments for the gift of his Dear Son; is it possible that God "So loved the World that he gave his only begotten Son that whosoever believed on him Should not perish, but have everlasting life"

Then let us come forward with faith, nothing doubting and he will most unquestionably hear us—let us be often found in the means and take my word for it we Shall receive a blessing: some, who have made a profession of Christianity & have by their own negligence caused the Spirit to depart think their day of grace is over; but where did they find Such doctrine? I find our Saviour ever entreating & wooing us, useing the most endearing language and endeavoring by every means without compelling, for that would at once destroy our free agency), to bring us to him that we may have life, are we doeing our duty, do we regularly and without fail attend to *Prayers* & keep in mind that in due season we shall receive the Crown, if we faint not, oh! let us be engaged & to that end let us take a view of what the Poet says of the unhap[p]y close of life

> "How Shocking must thy summons be, oh death!
> To him who is at ease in his possessions!
> Who counting on long years of pleasure here,
> Is quite unfurnished for the world to come!
> In that dread moment, how the frantic Soul
> Runs round the walls of his clay tenement;
> Runs to each corner and Shrieks for help;
> But Shrieks in vain! How wishfully She looks
> On all She's leaving now no longer hers!

What a dreadful picture is this which we find in the English reader! But another Poet Sings the following lines

> Lord, I believe a rest remains
> To all thy People known;
> A rest, where pure enjoyment reigns,
> And thou art loved alone

Well, My Brother, will it be for us if we have faith in those last lines and make use of it in Such a way that it may produce good works[3]

It was said of Jedediah that he made the lone wilderness his place of meditation, the mountaintop his altar, and that he made religion an active, practical principle, from the duties of which nothing could seduce him.[4] His firm belief that faith must find expression in works emerges in a moving passage of the letter written from Wind River. Providence, he said, had made him steward of a small pittance, and his prayer was that while allowed the privilege of using it, he might use it without abuse. He was forwarding a little money which Ralph must assist him in expending:

in the first place my Brother, our Parents must receive of our beneficence, & if Dr Simons is in want I wish him to be helped. . . . The Sum for which you will expect to receive will be Two Thousand & Two hundred dollars . . . if any of our Friends are in a distrest Situation youl please let me know, recollect that we are Brothers! and I shall not forgive you, if you do not let me know your own Situation—be not too modest—

It is, that I may be able to help those who stand in need, that I face every danger—it is for this, that I traverse the Mountains covered with eternal Snow—it is for this that I pass over the Sandy Plains, in heat of Summer, thirsting for water, and am well pleased if I can find a shade, instead of water, where I may cool my overheated Body—it is for this that I go for days without eating, & am pretty well satisfied if I can gather a few roots, a few Snails, or, much better Satisfied if we can affo[r]d our selves a piece of Horse Flesh, or a fine Roasted Dog, and, most of all, it is for this, that I deprive myself of the privilege of Society & the satisfaction of the Converse of My Friends! . . . let no one know of this little money which is to be forwarded, except the one whoom you consult,—let it be the greatest pleasure that we can enjoy, the height of our ambition, now, when our Parents, are in the decline of Life, to smooth the Pillow of their age, & as much as in us lies, take from them all cause of Trouble

There was a sternness and austerity to his life. So far as the record shows, Jedediah had no interest in women, and there is no suggestion that he ever admitted a squaw, however eager or lovely, into his bed.[5] He had none of the comfortable vices of his men; he did not use tobacco or join in their sprees; and he drank sparingly of wine or brandy at formal occasions. With a fastidiousness not characteristic of the mountain men, he kept himself clean-shaven even on the trap trail.[6] There was in him nothing of uncouthness; "with his ears constantly filled with the language of the profane and dissolute, no evil communication proceeded out of his mouth." Gentle and affable, he was yet "exact in his requisitions of duty, determined and persevering, always confident of success." [7]

He may have been entirely humorless; in what has survived of his journals and letters there are only two remarks which have the ghost of a smile in them, and these contain as much of wryness as of humor. Yet there was an honesty, a directness, an openness about him that won him friends on brief acquaintance—and there were times during Jedediah Smith's years in the West when much depended on his ability to make friends. In the world in which he made his mark, courage was a commonplace, and skill, the intricate skills of survival. But intelligence has never been commonplace, in the West or anywhere, and everyone was struck with the quality of Jedediah Smith's intelligence. A close and accurate observer, he was able to profit by the variety of his experiences, and had life been kind to him, the world might have heard much of Jedediah Smith.

In most years Wind River was the best of wintering places, but in 1829 the cold was severe and game scarce. About the beginning of January 1830, Jedediah set out with the camp for the buffalo country on the Powder, 150 miles northeast. So says Joe Meek, in the book Mrs. Victor made of his adventures; Meek also intimates that Jackson had rendezvoused at Wind River with his partners, for he says that the furs collected by Jackson on the fall hunt were cached here, and that Jackson's party joined in the move to the Powder. They arrived about the middle of January, and remained until the first of April.[8]

Jackson then returned to the Snake Country, while the remainder, including Meek, started northwest with Jedediah as commander and Jim Bridger as pilot. Joe Meek's is the only account of that hunt, except that Newell remarks sparely, "that winter Mr Sublette went to St Louis and Mr Smith in the Spring went on serch of beever from Powder to Tongue River little horn clarks fork through priers gape to the yellow Stone River." According to Meek, after leaving the Powder

> the first halt was made on Tongue River. From thence the camp proceeded to the Bighorn River. . . . It was the design of Smith to take his command into the Blackfoot country, a region abounding in the riches which he sought, could they only be secured without coming into too frequent conflict with the natives: always a doubtful question concerning these savages. He had proceeded in this direction as far as Bovey's Fork of the Bighorn, when the camp was overtaken by a heavy fall of snow, which made traveling extremely difficult, and which, when melted, caused a sudden great rise in the mountain streams. In attempting to cross Bovey's Fork during the high water, he

had thirty horses swept away, with three hundred traps: a serious loss in the business of hunting beaver.

Trapping as they went, the company moved on across the Pryor Mountains through Pryors Gap, thence to Clarks Fork of the Yellowstone, the Rosebud and the Yellowstone proper, which they reached "where it makes a great bend to the east, enclosing a large plain covered with grass, and having also extensive cottonwood bottoms." This might have been at present Big Timber, Montana. It was necessary to resort to bullboats to get across the Yellowstone, after which Jedediah headed north to the sources of the Musselshell. Presumably he trapped this river down to its mouth, where he had wintered his first year in the mountains, then went as high up as the Judith before returning to the Big Horn.[9] But all that is known of this last phase of the spring hunt is what Mrs. Victor says of it. After crossing the Yellowstone outbound, she relates:

The camp was . . . in the excellent but inhospitable country of the Blackfeet, and the commander redoubled his precautions, moving on all the while to the Mussel Shell, and thence to the Judith River. Beaver were plenty and game abundant; but the vicinity of the large village of the Blackfeet made trapping impracticable. Their war upon the trappers was ceaseless; their thefts of traps and horses ever recurring: and Smith, finding that to remain was to be involved in incessant warfare, without hope of victory or gain, at length gave the command to turn back, which was cheerfully obeyed: for the trappers had been very successful on the spring hunt, and thinking discretion some part at least of valor, were glad to get safe out of the Blackfoot country with their rich harvest of beaver skins.

The return march was by the way of Pryor's Gap, and up the Bighorn, to Wind River, where the cache was made in the previous December. The furs were now taken out and pressed, ready for transportation across the plains. A party was also dispatched, under Mr. Tullock, to raise the cache on the Bighorn River. Among this party was Meek, and a Frenchman named Ponto. While digging to come at the fur, the bank above caved in, falling upon Meek and Ponto, killing the latter almost instantly. Meek, though severely hurt, was taken out alive: while poor Ponto was "rolled in a blanket, and pitched into the river." . . . Meek was packed back to camp, along with the furs, where he soon recovered.[10]

Jackson is said to have arrived at rendezvous from the Snake Country with plenty of beaver; characteristically, that is all that is known of his spring hunt. Peter Skene Ogden, who kept tabs of a sort on Jackson in previous years, in the fall of 1829 moved totally outside the limits of the Snake Country, down the eastern slope of the Sierra Nevada and back by way of the San Joaquin —an important exploration but one which yielded few beaver and no information about the parties of Smith, Jackson & Sublette.[11]

William Sublette, meanwhile, had been making a little history himself. No details of his journey down to the States with Black Harris are known; the presumption is that he had an easier time than in 1827. He appears to have reached St. Louis on February 11, 1830, the object of lively curiosity on the part of Pierre Chouteau, who wrote Astor, "*Je 'ai beaucoup questionné. Je N'ai rien obtenu de satisfaisant. Il me regard toujours comme un opponent.*" [12]

It was eminently sensible of Sublette to regard Chouteau in the light of a rival, and he wasted no time getting back to the mountains. He got his party off from St. Louis April 10 but was himself apparently detained a few days longer; a new license he took out for his firm is dated April 14. The license was for three years, and authorized trade with the Indians at "Camp Defiance, Horse Prairie, mouth of Lewis' fork of the Columbia, junction of the Little Horn with the Big Horn, and at the Quamash flats of Lewis' fork of the Columbia." The capital employed was stated to be a modest $8,205.[13]

On leaving St. Louis, Sublette's party consisted of eighty-one men, mounted on mules. What made the expedition significant was that Sublette took along ten wagons, drawn by five mules each, and two dearborns, drawn by one mule each. Ashley had set out from Fort Atkinson with a wagon in 1824, doubtless soon abandoning it in heavy snow, and a cannon had been taken on a carriage as far as Bear Lake in 1827, but this was the first serious effort to demonstrate that a natural wagon road existed all the way from the Missouri River to the Rocky Mountains.

The route followed "was nearly due west to the western limits of the State; and thence along the Santa Fe trail about forty miles; from which the course was some degrees north of west, across the waters of the Kanzas, and up the Great Platte river, to the Rocky mountains. . . ." Sublette thus took his wagons west by the same route he had used in coming down from the mountains in 1827; in after years he and his friends spoke of it as "Sublette's Trace." [14]

The experiment worked out very well; as the country was open and level, the chief obstructions were ravines and creeks, the banks of which required cutting down. To subsist his party until the buffalo country should be reached, Sublette drove along twelve head of cattle and a milk cow, but it had been necessary to kill only eight of the beef cattle when the company fell in with buffalo on the Platte, about 350 miles out. The remaining cattle and the cow went on to the Wind River rendezvous—the first cattle ever seen in the northern Rockies—and were eventually driven all the way back to Missouri.

Sublette and his wagons reached rendezvous July 16. He could have gone on across South Pass had there been any reason for it, but as rendezvous had been fixed for the Wind River Valley, it was left to Captain Bonneville, two years later, to take the first wagons across the continental divide. The sources are not quite explicit about the site of the 1830 rendezvous, saying merely that it was at "the head of Wind river, where it issues from the mountains," but the Burr map may be taken to indicate that it was just below the junction of Wind River with its southern fork, the Popo Agie. The same site served for rendezvous in 1838.

This was a significant rendezvous. As had Ashley four years before, Smith, Jackson & Sublette sold out to a newly organized firm, the Rocky Mountain Fur Company. Why this development should have come at just this time has never been explained. The possibility apparently had not been foreseen down to the time Sublette left for the States the previous Christmas, and the partners may not have decided to withdraw from the business until a week or more after Sublette arrived from the States. In December Jedediah had written his parents, "as our business is at present, it would be the height of impolicy to set a time to come Home," but now it was possible for him to write his brother, "Our business is so arranged that I am not under the necessity of visiting the mountains again." [15]

Jedediah's determination to return to the States may have had much to do with the dissolution of the partnership which had dominated the fur trade in the Rockies since 1826. The letters brought up to the mountains by Sublette carried word that his mother had died in the late winter of 1830, and his thoughts had also been turned homeward by a letter from his old friend, Dr. Simons. A conspicuously successful fall and spring hunt had changed his financial prospects for the better, and perhaps relieved a sense of obligation felt toward his partners. It would appear that Jedediah took the initiative in dissolving the partnership, for Jackson and Sublette promptly formed a new firm.

But larger considerations may have influenced Smith, Jackson & Sublette to withdraw from the trapping end of the fur trade at just this time. The progressive exhaustion of the fur country had impressed them all, and no one was better able to gauge its extent. Inexorably the center of gravity for the trade had moved toward the Blackfoot country—the sole rich beaver preserve that remained, and one to be trapped only at the hazard of immediate battle. Jedediah had shown this past year how the streams in the Blackfoot country could be trapped; the phrase "fur brigade" from this time begins to take on meaning. Still, this kind of trapping required an *élan* and a contentment with the country that Jedediah no longer felt. And there was yet another factor in the situation, new and incalculable: rival brigades were coming up from the Missouri and the Yellowstone to trap in earnest.

Earlier pages of this book have discussed the converging movement on the Mandan Villages which began in 1822 only to be brought to a standstill by the Ree troubles. The French Company waited two years after the slaughter of Langevin's party before venturing above the Sioux domain, and the Columbia Fur Company hung on at the Mandans through that time by the thinnest of margins. It was not until after the Atkinson-O'Fallon Expedition in the summer of 1825 that either company made good its hold on the Mandan trade.[16]

The two companies clashed at once; as the French Company began expanding up the Missouri, the Columbia Fur Company began an aggressive expansion downward. By 1827 the alternatives had become clear, some kind of merger or a full-scale trade war. The French Company meanwhile had been enormously strengthened through yielding to the insistence of John Jacob Astor that he be given a share in the fur trade of the Missouri; an agreement was signed in December 1826 by which the French Company (at this time going under the name of Bernard Pratte & Company) was transformed as the Western Department of the American Fur Company. The Columbia Fur Company had no resources to match those of the giant combine, but it did have a scintillating leader in Kenneth McKenzie, and when amalgamation of the Columbia Fur Company with the American Fur Company was agreed on in July 1827, McKenzie got nearly everything he asked.[17]

The Columbia Fur Company was renamed the Upper Missouri Outfit and assigned all the country above the Big Sioux River, the Western Department taking as its province the Missouri trade below that point. As early as September 28, 1827, Chouteau wrote McKenzie, "I have the satisfaction to inform you that our mountain expedition in connection with General Ashley has . . . reached the settlements in safety with the whole returns, which terminates our arrangements with the General. It therefore becomes necessary to learn from you with the least possible loss of time what is to be done to prosecute the business in the Rocky Mountains. . . ."[18]

McKenzie wanted to get an expedition off to the mountains as soon as possible, that is, during the summer of 1828. Down in St. Louis, however, Chouteau was a little appalled by the risks. He wrote McKenzie on April 25, 1828, "For three years these enterprises have succeeded well with General Ashley, but with him alone. . . . I believe that there is a great deal to gain if such an expedition succeeds, but there is also great risk to run. . . ."

In the end, the mountain expedition was postponed for a

year, while McKenzie put the firm's energies into fort building, Fort Floyd (later called Fort Union, and under that name one of the most famous of all fur-trading establishments) being founded at the mouth of the Yellowstone. But if the Upper Missouri Outfit was not yet prepared to launch a full-scale assault on the mountains, McKenzie wanted to bid immediately for the Crow trade, and that fall he sent Etienne Provost to their country.[19]

Unexpectedly, Hugh Glass came floating down the Yellowstone as an emissary from the free trappers. Rendezvous in 1828 apparently had brought no reduction in the price of goods, for the free trappers had sent Glass down with an invitation to McKenzie to send a party to the mountains to meet with them after the spring hunt of 1829.[20]

In retrospect the proposals of the free trappers to McKenzie resemble the invitation of the frogs to King Stork, but that the stubborn individualist Glass should have arrived at Fort Floyd in the fall of 1828 as the bearer of these proposals is wonderfully fitting. Glass had had a sufficiently wild career since 1824. He went out to New Mexico, trapped for a year with indifferent success, and got into fresh scrapes which necessitated his traveling 700 miles with an arrow festering in his back so that a fellow trapper could cut out the arrowhead with a razor.[21] Glass had turned up at Bear Lake in 1828, and was just the man to go in search of a better deal for the free trappers.

(The rest of his life Glass spent in the vicinity of Fort Union. He tempted fate by returning to the scene of his adventures of 1823-1824, and fate could not resist the temptation. In the winter of 1832-1833 Glass's old enemies, the Arikaras, caught him and Edward Rose on the frozen Yellowstone below the Big Horn; the Rees killed and scalped them. Johnson Gardner caught up with a couple of the murderers a few weeks later and burned them to death.)[22]

While McKenzie busied himself with preparations to invade the upper country, the Western Department bought out the last important opposition on the lower river; in October 1828 the Company came to terms with Joseph Robidoux, purchasing his goods for $3,500 and agreeing to pay him $1,000 a year for two years to stay out of the Indian country. Robidoux had been outfitting several parties, one of which, under William Henry Vanderburgh, was to have gone to the Pawnees. The Western Department took Vanderburgh into its service, too, and next spring sent him up the Missouri to head McKenzie's mountain expedition; Fontenelle & Drips were also bought out, so that three of Pilcher's former partners now owed fealty to the giant combine.[23]

Vanderburgh at the head of thirty men arrived at McKenzie's Fort Tecumseh (the precursor of Fort Pierre near the mouth of the Teton River) on June 4, 1829;[24] his force struck McKenzie as too weak, but some kind of a hunt was made, for in May 1830 McKenzie wrote down to Fort Tecumseh requesting as many horses as could be rounded up for the mountain expedition and "the Free hunters in the mountains," adding, "Mr. Vanderburgh and his party will be in I think about the last of June. Gordon with four or five men is trapping on powder River. Provost is with the Crows."[25]

It is obvious why, in February 1830, Pierre Chouteau should have been bursting with questions about the mountains, and why Sublette should have been unwilling to give out any information at all. Smith, Jackson & Sublette now had to reckon with opposition not only from the Upper Missouri Outfit but from a party the Western Department itself was sending to the mountains. Headed by Fontenelle, Drips and Joseph Robidoux, this second party got off from Council Bluffs in May 1830.[26] While Smith, Jackson & Sublette were rendezvousing with the free trappers on Wind River, Fontenelle was searching for them in the Green River Valley and the Great Salt Lake country. From now on, the mountain fur trade would have to be prosecuted in the face of a powerful opposition.

The partners who composed the Rocky Mountain Fur Company were, in the main, practical trappers. The brains of the firm was Thomas Fitzpatrick, and to a lesser extent, Milton Sublette. Jim Bridger was a tower of strength as a field captain, but he could not even write his name, and little more could be said of the other partners, Henry Fraeb and Jean Baptiste Gervais. The papers are not extant for the transaction by which they bought out Smith, Jackson & Sublette, but it would seem that the terms were similar to those by which the latter had got into business in 1826. That is, the merchandise on hand at the close of rendezvous was sold to the new concern, for which they gave their note payable in beaver at $3.00 a pound. Dated August 1, 1830, this note was for the sum of $15,532.23, due November 1, 1831.[27] Apparently the new partners made with Jackson & Sublette an agreement like that Jedediah and his partners had signed with Ashley in 1826, a provisional undertaking to buy at stated prices stated quantities of goods to be delivered in the mountains in the summer of 1831, this deal to stand only if the Rocky Mountain Fur Company got confirmation down to Jackson & Sublette by March 1 following.[28]

Free of the bonds which had tied him to the mountains, Jedediah left rendezvous for St. Louis August 4, 1830. "All the high points of the mountains then in view," he wrote subsequently, "were white with snow; but the passes and valleys, and all the level country, were green with grass. Our route back was over the same ground nearly as in going out, and we arrived in St. Louis on the 10th of October,[29] bringing back the ten wagons, the dearborns being left behind." During the summer they had no accident but the death of Ponto and the injury of Meek in the collapse of the cache on the Big Horn. Only one mule had given out; and two horses stolen by the Kaws was their only injury at the hands of Indians.

On reaching the line of the settlements, the last week of September, Jedediah must have been amazed to observe how civilization had marched up to the very borders of the Indian country. In the five years he had been gone a vigorous new town, Independence, had sprung up near the mouth of the Kaw as the latest of the many jumping-off places for the Santa Fe and mountain trade, and other new towns were strung along the Missouri like beads on a necklace. The capital of Missouri itself had been moved into the interior of the state, and though painfully unbuilt as yet, Jefferson City was full of the promise of the future. There were other changes. Fort Atkinson, up the Missouri from the mouth of the Platte, was crumbling into ruin; for more than three years now the principal military base on the Missouri had been Cantonment Leavenworth, forty miles north of Independence on the west bank of the river.

The incoming company reached Columbia October 5. This was the chief town of the Boonslick country now that old Franklin had been swept away by the Missouri, and Jedediah would have been entitled to reflect on that long-gone day when he had touched at Franklin in the *Enterprize,* for the *Missouri Intelligencer,* now removed to Columbia, gave the party its enthusiastic attention. Guessing wildly that their furs and mules might be worth $150,000, the *Intelligencer* observed on October 9:

> The cavalcade extended a considerable distance . . . a considerable number of large and substantial waggons, loaded with the fruits of their toils, accompanied them, exclusive of the pack horses and mules, of which there were a great number. We should judge there were about fifty individuals. These hardy and sun-burnt *Mountaineers* . . . exhibited great demonstrations of satisfaction, at their near approach to their families and homes.

More discerning comment was that by Charles Keemle in the *St. Louis Beacon* on their arrival in St. Louis. After noting that Jedediah had been out five years and had explored the country "from the Gulf of California to the mouth of the Columbia,"[30] Keemle trumpeted the significance of the year's work:

> They left St. Louis the 10th of April last with these . . . ten wagons, each drawn by five mules, arrived at the *Southern Pass,* which is the place of rendezvous for the traders, on the 16th of July; loaded with the furs previously collected; set out on the return on the 4th of August, and arrived at St. Louis on the 11th of October. The wagons did not cross the mountains; but there was nothing to prevent their crossing and going on to the mouth of the Columbia. The furs were at the place of rendezvous, and that was as far as the wagons needed to go. They could have crossed the mountains at the *Southern Pass,* which is at the head of Wind river, without difficulty. Messrs. Smith, Sublette & Jackson are the first that ever took wagons to the Rocky Mountains. The ease with which they did it, and could have gone on to the mouth of the Columbia, shows the folly and nonsense of those

"*scientific*" characters who talk of the Rocky Mountains as the barrier which is to stop the westward march of the American people.

The partners were fully aware of the significance of what they had accomplished, and on October 29 they wrote the Secretary of War. There were military implications in the ease with which a party like theirs had gone to the mountains; and beyond that, there was military significance to the British alienation of the tribes beyond the continental divide. The letter is a clear-sighted statement of the national interest, and the conclusions to be drawn from their experience in the West. Promptly published in a Senate document and reprinted in newspapers all over the land, the letter placed the West in startling new perspective before the American people.

One of Jedediah's first acts on reaching St. Louis was to go in search of Robert Campbell. He had not seen him in three years and he remembered Campbell with warmth and affection; had Jedediah died at the Mojave Villages or on the Umpqua, Campbell would now be executor of his will.[31] Campbell however had gone back to Ireland on a visit, and Jedediah had to be content to write his brother in Virginia. He seized the opportunity to ask for prices current in the East, for Jedediah and his partners were considering marketing their beaver themselves.

Before a reply could come from Virginia, the three partners decided, after all, to engage Ashley to sell their furs, giving him a commission of 2½ per cent. Ashley had excellent contacts, and "Ashley beaver" had become known on the market as an especially fine grade—a consequence of its having been taken in the mountains. Ashley's account subsequently rendered shows the precise value of the last hunt made by Smith, Jackson & Sublette; the furs sold for $84,499.14. Before leaving St. Louis for Philadelphia and New York, Ashley made the partners a cash advance of $23,889.53; he charged them 6 per cent interest on the money, and there were sundry expenses afterward, but when all these had been paid, an additional $53,920.92 remained to be divided among the partners.[32]

So Jedediah could look back to the days of his green youth,

when he had come to St. Louis owning the clothes on his back, a rifle, a Bible and very little else. He had started into the mountains knowing what he wanted to do, and determined to make the doing profitable. He had been fortunate in realizing his ambition in every particular. It remained to make a book of his travels and a map to illustrate them, but that would take time, and he was busy.

He gave his brother Ralph $1,500 to buy for him the neighboring farm of Major Tiller, for Green Township still had the power to compel his dreams.[33] But also he bought a house and lot on Federal Avenue in St. Louis, and two Negro servants to turn the place into a home.[34] He made it a home for his brothers as well, for Peter was already in St. Louis when Jedediah arrived there (he had come to Missouri more than a year before, seriously contemplating a journey to the mountains to find out whether Jedediah still lived); young Ira arrived late in December 1830, and Austin a month later. A city the size of St. Louis, its population now pushing past 6,500, struck Jedediah as no place for a young man of tender years and unformed character, and he hastily took Ira to Jacksonville and settled him in a seminary. Illinois College might not be quite sound in doctrine, being a Presbyterian institution, but Jacksonville was removed from the baneful influence of St. Louis and close enough for Jedediah to keep an eye on his brother. The possibility that the still younger Benjamin Paddock and Nelson might be sent to St. Louis to join him stirred him to anxious alarm: "my Brother! This is the last place to which youngsters should be sent." [35]

Meantime there was a letter from Hugh Campbell with disquieting information about the state of Robert's health. "With pain," Jedediah was moved to reply, "did I peruse that part of your Epistle, which Speaks of the ill health of My *much valued Friend*—Oh is it possible I Shall never again See him in the Land of the living? My Prayer to Almighty God, is, that I may again be allowed the Privilege of passing some time in company with my Friend——" Testimony of the universal esteem in which Robert Campbell was held, Jedediah added, "I have been under the necessity of going forward with a partnership amounting to part of My Capital, but Shall Still, unavoidable accidents excepted, have eight, or, perhaps, ten thousand Dollars, in March, or April next, which Could not be vested in any way to please me so well, as to have it aid both My FRIEND and me."[36]

Jedediah would have betrayed all the traditions of his forefathers if, possessed of capital, he did not put it to work. The partnership with Campbell he may have envisioned as a later possibility, when the remaining proceeds from the hunt of 1830 should have been received from Ashley. Meantime, it would appear, he had resolved on a trading venture to Santa Fe.

This project Jedediah must have conceived soon after returning to St. Louis, for Samuel Parkman, who had come down from the mountains with him and had been hired to copy his journals and aid in drafting his map, spent the winter studying Spanish.[37] Jedediah was scarcely prepared to begin keeping store, and there were interesting possibilities in the Santa Fe trade. That trade by now was well established, having come far since William Becknell's time. Moreover, the book and map Jedediah was going to publish would benefit if he could report at firsthand on the Southwest, the only part of the West of which he could not speak with authority.

Jedediah had committed himself to the Santa Fe project by the end of January 1831, for on February 11 Ashley, who was then in Philadelphia, wrote Senator Thomas Benton in Washington asking that he obtain for Jedediah a passport and certificate of good character, as this young man proposed "a trading Expedition to the Mexican Provinces." Benton and the State Department obliged, the passport being issued March 3.[38]

By the time this document was received in St. Louis, Jackson & Sublette were looking to Santa Fe also. March had come without bringing one of the partners of the Rocky Mountain Fur Company to validate the contract for goods, nor in the next three weeks was there any word whatever from the mountains. Confident that the contract would be confirmed, Jackson & Sublette may already have bought much of the merchandise. They decided to take their goods to Santa Fe. On March 23 Ashley wrote the State Department asking a passport for Sublette too. Mr. Sublette, he said, would accompany Mr. Smith "to a certain point, Thence they will take different directions." (This might mean that

Jedediah had it in mind to go down into Chihuahua.) Sublette was issued the requested passport on April 9. None was asked or issued for Jackson.[39]

Little enough of Jedediah's plans for the year appears to have got into his letters to his family; he was a man who could keep his own counsel, and as he wrote Ralph, "it is certainly verry far from my wish to have too much publicity given to our business." As a public man, Ashley had courted publicity; as a businessman, Jedediah had found that it invited competition. Nevertheless, he was energetic in his preparations for the Santa Fe expedition. He intended to take Peter and Austin with him, and Samuel Parkman was to go as clerk. Another recruit was young Jonathan Trumbull Warner of Lyme, Connecticut, who had come to Missouri in the fall of 1830 for reasons of health, and who called on Jedediah with a view to becoming a mountain man only to be dissuaded from embarking on what was scarcely a Christian life. Warner would now go out to Santa Fe, and on to Southern California, there to be transformed into that respected rancher and member of the community, Don Juan José Warner.[40] What Jedediah paid his two clerks, Parkman and Warner, the record does not disclose, but from a contract Jedediah signed with one Wilson Williams, it would seem that he engaged common hands for six months' service at thirteen dollars a month.[41]

Seventy-four men made up the combined party of Jedediah Smith and Jackson & Sublette. They had twenty-two mule-drawn wagons, of which eleven belonged to Jedediah, and ten to his former partners; the other, their joint property, carried a six-pounder. This cannon was mounted on the rear axle; the wagon was so constructed that it could readily be uncoupled and the hind wheels with the piece of artillery drawn out ready for action. Before leaving the frontier, two additional wagons joined the caravan, of which one was the property of Samuel Flournoy of Independence while the other, drawn by oxen, belonged to two men named Wells (or Mills) and Chadwick. These additions swelled the number of men to eighty-three.[42]

The party set out from St. Louis on April 10,[43] and by the end of the month had moved along the trail as far as Lexington, forty miles east of Independence. Jedediah may have thought it expedient, in view of Robert Campbell's continued absence and ill health, to draw up a new will, and this he did, as the instrument itself has it, on "April Thirty first." A simple document, it provided that Jedediah's father should receive an annuity of $200 the rest of his life, and that all his property beyond this legacy should be divided among his brothers and sisters. Jedediah's "particular and confidential friend," Ashley, was named executor.[44]

The wagons may have gone on ahead, perhaps in Jackson's care, for Warner says that they remained two or three days in camp near Independence, making final preparation. The party launched on its journey from the camp near the Big Blue, ten miles southwest of Independence, on the morning of May 4, 1831.[45] Beyond the narrow bottoms of this creek, the prairies began, extending all the way to the mountains which sheltered Santa Fe. This was a beautiful country, especially at this season; the road was plainly marked; and for hundreds of miles no danger need be apprehended from the Indians.

It was just before or just after the departure from Independence that Thomas Fitzpatrick made his unexpected appearance in camp. Two months late, here he was, down from the mountains anxious to come to some arrangement about merchandise. After the rendezvous of 1830 he, Bridger and Milton Sublette had taken sixty men into the dangerous Three Forks country. They had made a good hunt and returned to winter on the Yellowstone. Two other brigades under Fraeb and Gervais had gone to the Snake Country, and to the end of February had not been heard from, terrific blizzards which blew across the West perhaps making an express impossible. The partners on the Yellowstone had finally decided that the returns from their own foray into the Blackfoot country were good enough to justify the gamble on a new outfit, and early in March Fitzpatrick with one *engagé* set out for St. Louis. By Warner's reminiscent account, Fitzpatrick reached Lexington while the party was there; by the contemporary though hearsay account of Warren Ferris, Fitzpatrick arrived in Lexington two days after the party left, and overtook them after several days' hard riding. In either event, he wanted to know what could be done for him.[46]

Ordinarily, goods for the mountain and Santa Fe trades had marked differences, and this was a late hour for Fitzpatrick to be getting in his order. However, the trappers operating in the Southwest had been a potential market for the kind of merchandise Fitzpatrick wanted, and the wagons were not unprovided. It was agreed that he should accompany the party to Santa Fe, and that they would there fix him up, Jedediah to provide one-third of his outfit, Jackson & Sublette the rest.[47] Fitzpatrick could then buy pack animals and take the goods to Cache Valley where his partners awaited him.[48]

Fitzpatrick had news of his competitors, and these old friends and associates must have grinned at each other over the troubles of the greenhorns. In the summer of 1830 Vanderburgh had taken a party of perhaps seventy men from Fort Union to the Madison by way of the Yellowstone, but he had scarcely begun trapping when the Blackfeet fell on him. Vanderburgh had one man killed and two wounded; he also had ten horses killed and fifty wounded, which had been sufficient to drive him back to the Yellowstone.[49] The Rocky Mountain Fur Company would yet be humbled by the American Fur Company, but the cost to Chouteau and McKenzie was going to come high.

Although none of them had traveled the Santa Fe Trail before, Jedediah and his companions were old hands on the plains and took in their stride the protracted drizzles, punctuated by occasional violent winds out of the northwest, which soaked them to the skin and made the going miry; they were used to the erratic behavior of the mules, and they learned patience in getting the wagons across the occasional creeks which interrupted their progress. Council Grove, 109 miles out, was an important point of passage, for beyond here no wood fit for axle trees could be obtained, and it was the custom of the Santa Fe traders to lash a few spares under their wagons. Beyond Council Grove, too, there was more danger from war parties, especially Pawnees, Comanches, Kiowas—and of late Gros Ventres of the Prairies, who had come down from the north to visit the Arapahoes; a people who dwelt among the Blackfeet, their line of travel north and south on these visits generally was marked by a trail of blood.

East of Pawnee Fork the only trouble with the Indians occurred when several hundred mounted Indians—Comanches as the party supposed, but probably Gros Ventres—made a tentative charge on the wagons; the six-pounder barked angrily at them, and they fled. On reaching Pawnee Fork, however, nearly 300 miles out, Jackson & Sublette's clerk, Minter, "a very estimable young man" in Warner's view, was killed by Pawnees; while out hunting antelope, he dropped a little behind the party, whereupon a dozen mounted Indians fell on him. The future historian of the Santa Fe Trail, Josiah Gregg, who was making his first trip to Santa Fe this year a few weeks behind Jedediah's party, called Minter's death the only instance of loss of life by a trader while engaged in hunting; the tragedy occurred May 19.[50]

That incident should have taught Jedediah caution. But many times in the West he had, in the Indian phrase, thrown his life away when the safety or need of his men required, and now he threw it away forever.

South of the Arkansas lay a plain, forty or fifty miles wide, which had to be crossed to the Cimarron—a river as inconstant as the Mojave. This plain, "the water scrape," was the most dreaded stretch of the Santa Fe Trail. It was not only dry but flat, utterly featureless, and the more bewildering for the maze of buffalo trails which furrowed its surface. No discernible trace marked the course of the wagon road across this desert and Jedediah's party struck it at an especially bad time, when the country was parched by drought.

They had been three scorching days without water, and the teams were on the point of perishing when, on May 27, a last desperate effort was made to find water. Men were sent out in various directions, and Jedediah in company with Fitzpatrick headed south, the direction the teams were traveling. The two men came to a deep hollow which should have provided water, but the hole was dry. Instructing Fitzpatrick to wait till the party came up and meanwhile to dig for water, Jedediah pushed on south toward some broken ground, perhaps three miles off.[51]

None of his friends ever saw Jedediah again. What became of him was learned only after the search was given up and the party went on to Santa Fe. Mexicans who traded among the

Comanches rode into the city carrying his pistols and rifle, and from their understanding of what the Comanches said come the details of Jedediah Smith's death.

Apparently a Comanche hunting party, numbering fifteen or twenty men, lying in wait for buffalo at one of the water holes along the Cimarron, saw Jedediah approach and kept themselves concealed until he was too close to escape. Jedediah had seen too much of the West, and knew too well the reputation of this most savage of all the Shoshonean tribes not to be able to appraise his chances. A brave front was his only hope, and he rode directly up to the red men. A brief colloquy followed, but neither could understand the other, and they paid no attention to his signs of peace.

The Comanches began to spread out. Watchfully Jedediah tried to keep them from getting behind him. His horse danced nervously, and was suddenly startled into wheeling. Instantly the Comanches fired at Jedediah's exposed back, a musket ball entering his body near the left shoulder. Gasping at the impact, Jedediah turned his horse and leveled his rifle at the chief, killing him with the single shot he had time to fire. Before he could draw his pistols, the rest rushed on him with their lances, thrusting and stabbing.

"*. . . yet was he modest, never obtrusive, charitable, 'without guile' . . . a man whom none could approach without respect, or know without esteem. And though he fell under the spears of the savages, and his body has glutted the prairie wolf, and none can tell where his bones are bleaching, he must not be forgotten.*"

APPENDIX A

Letters by Jedediah S. Smith Relating to His Explorations

I.

[*To the United States Plenipotentiary at Mexico*]

Port of Sandieg[o] Province New California
16th [December] 1826

Dear Sir

being Detained by the Governor *Gen* of this place and thinking it verry probable that I Should be detained for 2 or three months & that perhaps I Should then be under the necessity of comeing to Mexico —I thought proper to inform you of my Situation—having left S^t^. Louis, in the state of Missouri, on the first of N°. 1825 as a partner of *Gen Wm* H Ashley's in the Fur trade and Trapping Business–with 60 men & an equipment for prosecuting our business W^t^ of the Rocky *Mount* we arrived at the place of destination in June–here we *recd* of men which had remained in the coutry for the purpose [of] Traping–a quantity of B*er* Fur with which the Gen Started for St Louis Messrs Jackson, Sublet & my self remained in the country having Bought the *Gen.* interest to prosecute the business Messrs Jackson and Sublet went to the N I with thirteen men went to the S W for the purpose of hunting B*er* but not finding them plenty enough to justify me in Stopping I pushed on through a Country of Starvation—Sandy plains and Rocky hills once in 20 30 or 40 *m* a little pond or Spring of water with a little grass after traveling 8 or 9 day in this way & turning my course from S W to S I fell on to a Riv 30 *yds* or more in width running S W by this time my [crossed out: dryed meat of which I had provided my self before our companies separated] provision were exhausted (dried meat, of which I had provided my self with 700 weight, before I left the C*ou* of B*uf*—I went down this river,—which after changing its course several times fell into the Colorado (or as it is called by the hunters in the *mou* Seetskeedee) in coming down this *riv* (which is a little Brackish) I found (by the Information of the *In* a cave which I examined–I entered by a mouth (at the foot of a hill) the entrance 6 or 7 feet wide 12 or 10 in heighth after descending 18 or 20 feet a room opens 25 or 30 feet in length and 14 or 15 in width the Roof Sides and floor of this room are solid Rock-Salt mostly pure some of it is a litle mixed with sand this river & cave I call Adams's river & Adams cave in honor of our President—I then followed down this Colorado untill I fell in with a Nation of *In* which call them selves Amuchabas from the time I first struck Adams *Riv* untill I fell in with the Amuchbas our living very hard some times 2 or 3 day without half a meal 2 [3?] times we fell in with *In* of whoom I got a litle corn & pompkins in coming through this *coun* of Starvation (for both men & Horses) I had lost so many Horses that we were all on foot—my men & the remainder of my Horses were worn out with fatigue & hardships & emaciated with hunger—there hapened to be at this place an *In* which could Speak Spanish & one of my men Spoke a little–by this means I found that it was not far to some of the Missions of California & I detirmined (as this was the only resort) to go to that place as soon as my men & horses should be able to travel in the mean time I exchanged some of my Horses for better ones & on the 10*th* of *Nov* Started for California (having engaged 2 guids) on the 27*th* I arrived at S*ta* Gabriel here the Commandant of the place required me to let him have my Arms which I did & an express was started immediately to San Diego to acquaint the *Gov Gen* of my arrival. I wrote liquise, stating to the *Gov Gen* my situation and requesting of him some Horses & permission to pass through this *coun* to the Bay of *St* Francisco–I wished to follow up one of the largest *Riv* that emptied into the Bay cross the *mou* at its head and from thence to our Deposit on the waters of the Salt Lake——After waiting for an answer 9 days (during which time my self & men were verry hospitably treated by the *Rev* Father and obliging little Commandant) I received an order to go to the *Gov* at Sandigo–on the 10*th* I Started in Company with Capt Cunningham of the Ship Courier from Boston which was lieing in the habor of San Diego–having Horses & a Soldier for a guide or guard (furnished by the *Gov*) 12th at 2 *oc* we arrived at Sandiego a distance of 50 Leagues here I have been questioned & crossquestioned three different times by the *Gov* (who appears to be very much of a Gentleman but very Suspicious) I have applied to him for Horses & endeavored to convince him of the truth that I was only a hunter & that Dire necessity had driven me here I am to call next tuesday [December 19] for to know whether I can pass, or be detained here 3 months, for an answer from Mexico—the

Gun is so kind as to say if he detains me I Shall want for nothing/I have found in Capt Cunningham of the Courier a friend which I stand much in need of as I am destitute of almost every thing, with the exception of my Traps (guns which I can not now call mine) Ammunition & [crossed out: 18 horses which I have left] the *Gov* requested my Journal my Licence & my Ideas of the *Cou* which I gave him–but instead of thanking me for the information which I have given him & assisting me to pass on about my business he seems to be for detain[in]g me untill he ascertains that I am no Spy–which will deprive me of making a valuable Spring hunt

To the United States Plenipotentiary at Mexico *Jedediah S. Smith*

P S Der Sir excuse my Scrawl, the Brig is now ready to Sail & I have no time to Coppy

J. S. Smith

II.

[*To Father Narciso Durán at Mission San Jose, May 19, 1827*]

Reverend Father:——I understand, through the medium of one of your Christian Indians, that you are anxious to know who we are, as some of the Indians have been at the Mission and informed you that there were certain white people in the country. We are Americans, on our journey to the River Columbia; we were in at the Mission San Gabriel in January last; I went to San Diego and saw the General, and got a passport from him to pass on to that place. I have made several efforts to cross the mountains, but the snow being so deep I could not succeed in getting over. I returned to this place (it being the only point to kill meat) to wait a few weeks until the snow melts so that I can go on; the Indians here also being friendly, I consider it the most safe point for me to remain, until such time as I can cross the mountains with my horses, having lost a great many in attempting to cross ten or fifteen days since. I am a long ways from home, and am anxious to get there as soon as the nature of the case will admit. Our situation is quite unpleasant, being destitute of clothing and most necessities of life, wild meat being our principal subsistence. I am, Reverend Father, your strange, but real friend and Christian brother,

J. S. Smith

May 19, 1827.

III.

[*To General William Clark*]

Little Lake of Bear River,
July 12th 1827

Gen[l] Wm. Clark,
Supt. of Indian Affairs
Sir,

My situation in this country has enabled me to collect information respecting a section of the country which has hitherto been measurably veiled in obscurity to the citizens of the United States—I allude to the country S. W. of the *Great Salt Lake* west of the Rocky mountains.

I started about the 22[d] of August 1826, from the Great Salt Lake, with a party of fifteen men, for the purpose of exploring the country S. W. which was entirely unknown to me, and of which I could collect no satisfactory information from the Indians who inhabit this country on its N. E. borders.

My general course on leaving the Salt Lake was S. W & W, Passing the Little Uta Lake and ascending Ashley's river, which Empties into the Little Uta Lake.—From the lake I found no more signs of buffalo; there are a few antelope and mountain sheep, and an abundance of *black tailed hares.* On Ashley's river, I found a nation of Indians who call themselves *Sampatch;* they were friendly disposed towards us. I passed over a range of mountains running S. E. & N. W. and struck a river running S. W. which I called *Adams River,* in compliment to our President.—The water is of a muddy cast, and is a little brackish. The country is mountainous to the East; towards the West there are sandy plains and detached rocky hills.

Passing down this river some distance, I fell in with a nation of Indians who call themselves *Pa Ulches** (those Indians, as well as those last mentioned, wear rabbit skin robes) who raise some little corn and pumkins.—the country is nearly destitute of game of any description, except a few hares. Here, (about 10 days march down it) the river turns to the South East. On the S. W. side of the river there is a *cave,* the Entrance of which is about 10 or 15 feet high, and 5 or 6 feet in width;—After descending about 15 feet, a room opens out from 25 to 30 feet in length and 15 to 20 feet in width;–the roof, sides

* In the original letter, which has disappeared, this was undoubtedly written *Pa Utches,* as pronounced and as published in the version of the letter which appeared in the *Missouri Republican,* October 11, 1827.

and floor are solid *Rock Salt,* a sample of which I send you, with some other articles, which will be hereafter described. I here found a Kind of plant of the prickly pear kind, which I called the cabbage pear, the largest of which grows about two feet and a half high and 1½ feet in diameter; upon examination I found it to be nearly of the substance of a turnip, altho' by no means palateable; its form was similar to that of an Egg, being smaller at the ground and top than in the middle; it is covered with pricks similar to the prickly pear with which you are acquainted.

There are here also a number of shrubs and small trees with which I was not acquainted previous to my route there, and which I cannot at present describe satisfactorily, as it would take more space than I can here allot.

The *Pa Ulches* have a number of marble pipes, one of which I obtained and send you, altho' it has been broken since I have had it in my possession; they told me there was a quantity of the same material in their country. I also obtained of them a Knife of *flint,* which I send you, but it has likewise been broken by accident.

I followed Adams river two days further to where it empties into the Seedskeeder a South East course. I crossed the Seedskeeder, and went down it four days* a South East course; I here found the country remarkably barren, rocky, and mountainous; there are a good many rapids in the river, but at this place a valley opens out about 5 to 15 miles in width, which on the river banks is timbered and fertile. I here found a nation of Indians who call themselves *Ammuchábas;* they cultivate the soil, and raise corn, beans, pumkins, water melons and musk melons in abundance, and also a little wheat and cotton. I was now nearly destitute of horses, and had learned what it was to do without food; I therefore remained there fifteen days and recruited my men, and I was enabled also to exchange my horses, and purchase a few more of a few runaway Indians who stole some horses of the Spaniards. I here got information of the Spanish country (the Californias) & obtained two guides, recrossed the Seedskeeder, which I afterwards found emptied into the Gulf of California about 80 miles from this place by the name of the Collarado—many render the river *Gild* from the East.†

* Four days being impossible, it is likely the original letter had a numeral 21 which in copying was misread as a numeral 4. This part of the letter was deleted in the *Missouri Republican* printing.

† The copy of this letter at Washington has a blank where the words "many render" here appear; this passage is omitted in the *Missouri Republican* version. Presumably the intent was to say that some maps show the river Gila entering the Colorado from the East above its mouth.

I travelled a west course fifteen days over a country of complete barrens, generally travelling from morning until night without water. I crossed a Salt plain about 20 miles long and 8 wide; on the surface was a crust of beautiful white salt, quite thin;—Under the surface there is a layer of salt from a half to one & a half inches in depth;—between this and the upper layer there is about four inches of yellowish sand.

On my arrival in the province of Upper California, I was looked upon with suspicion, and was compelled to appear in presence of the Governor of the Californias residing at St. Diego, where, by the assistance of some American gentlemen (especially Capt. W. H. Cunningham of the *ship Courier* from *Boston*) I was enabled to obtain permission to return with my men the route I came, and purchase such supplies as I stood in want of.—The Governor would not allow me to trade up the sea coast towards *Bodaga*. I returned to my party and purchased such articles as were necessary, and went Eastward of the Spanish settlement on the route I had come in. I then steered my course N. W. keeping from 150 to 200 miles from the sea coast—A very high range of mountains lay on the East. After travelling 300 miles in that direction through a country somewhat fertile, in which there was a great many Indians, mostly naked and destitute of arms with the exception of a few *Bows and arrows*, and what is very singular amongst Indians, they cut their hair to the length of three inches; they proved to be friendly; their manner of living is on fish, roots, acorns; and grass.*

On my arrival at a river which I called the *Wim-mul-che*, (named after a tribe of Indians which reside on it, of that name) I found a few beaver, and Elk deer, and antelope in abundance. I here made a small hunt, and attempted to take my party across—the [mountains] which I before mentioned, and which I called *Mount Joseph* to come on and join my partners at the Great Salt Lake. I found the snow so deep on Mount Joseph that I could not cross my horses, five of which starved to death; I was compelled therefore to return to the valley which I had left, and there leaving my party, I started with two men, seven horses and two mules, which I loaded with *hay* for horses and provisions for ourselves, and started on the 20th of May, and succeeded in crossing it in Eight days, having lost only two horses and one mule. I found the snow on the top of this mountain from 4 to 8 feet deep, but it was so consolidated by the heat of the sun that my horses only sunk from half a foot to one foot deep.

After travelling twenty days from the East side of *Mount Joseph*,

* The *Missouri Republican* version, evidently by misreading, has "grapes," rather than "grass."

I struck the S. W. corner of the Great Salt Lake, travelling over a country completely barren and destitute of game. We frequently travelled without water sometimes for two days over sandy deserts where there was no sign of vegetation and when we found water in some of the rocky hills, we most generally found some Indians who appeared the most miserable of the human race having nothing to subsist on, (nor any clothing) except grass seed, grasshoppers, &c. When we arrived at the Salt lake, we had but one horse and one mule remaining, which were so feeble & poor that they could scarce carry the little camp equipage which I had along; the balance of my horses I was compelled to eat as they gave out.

The company are now starting, therefore must close my close my [sic] communication

Yours respectfully,
Jedediah S. Smith
of the firm of
Smith, Jackson & Sublette

IV.

[*To General William Clark*]

A brief sketch of accidents, misfortunes, and depredations committed by Indians, &c. on the firm of Smith, Jackson & Sublette, Indian traders on the East & west side of the Rocky Mountains, since July 1826 to the present [December?] 24th 1829.

Mr. Smith one of said firm, departed on the 13th July 1827, with a party of Eighteen men and two Indian women, completely equipped for two years, and bound for the relief of a party which had been left by him near the bay of St. Francisco; after which it was his intention to continue the business of the firm more northwardly so far as he supposed to be the U. States territory. He proceeded on S & S E. until he passed the Utaw Indians with whom he had concluded a treaty the year before; he also passed the Sampatch and Piules [Paiutes], living on the west border of the sand plains and in the vicinity of the Collerodo. His course was S. & S. W. leading down the Colleredo until he came to the Muchabes Indians, whom he found apparently friendly as usual; —he remained with them three days, trading of them occasionally some articles of their country produce such as beans, wheat, corn, dried pumkins and melons. After the trade and intercourse with those

Indians was over, Mr. Smith and his party in attempting to cross the river on rafts, was attacked by those Indians and completely defeated with a loss of 10 men and 2 women (taken prisoners) the property all taken or destroyed.

The loss of all papers and journals prevents Mr. Smith from giving precise dates; it happened in August 1827.—Then as no other alternative was left, and in a country destitute of provisions and water, he was obliged to make for the first Spanish settlements (California,) in the vicinity of St. Gabriel, which he accomplished in 9½ days including nights, across the sand plains, and destitute of almost every necessary of life. Here he procured some few necessaries to enable him to proceed to his party before mentioned, made his reports by letter to the nearest place of civil intercourse; left two men, one by his request, and the other on account of a wound which he received in the attack; then with the remaining 7 he pushed on northwardly, joined his party, but in a very unpleasant situation, their supplies were almost entirely exhausted and he without any to assist them. Then as it was his last and only resource to try once more the hospitality of the Californias, he remained with his party two days, procured two Indian guides, and arrived at the mission of St. Joseph in three days. He then made known his situation and wants, requested permission to pass through the province to the Governor's residence (then in Montera) which is 100 miles distant; but instead of complying with his request, he was immediately conveyed to a dirty hovel which they called a guard house, his horses seized and taken away, and only allowed the privilege of writing to the Captain of the Upper Province.

Several days elapsed before any provisions were made for his living, except occasional invitations from an old overseer, when a Lieutenant arrived. After conversing with him, he soon found he was to be tried as an intruder on their rights. This news confounded Mr. Smith very considerably, as he had entered their province the first time in distress also and without molestation; the Lieutenant told him he must be under the necessity of seeing the Governor, but before he left him his situation was much altered for the better.

After the Lieutenant's departure, he was detained 10 or 12 days longer, when he received a polite note from the Governor to pay him a visit. Then he was stript of his arms, and accordingly complied and started well guarded by four soldiers. The third day at 11 o'clock at night, he arrived in Montera, where the Governor lived, and was immediately conveyed to the Callibozo without any refreshment whatever, where he remained until 11 o'clock next day, when a messenger arrived stating the Governor was then ready to receive him. He was conveyed to his dwelling, and met at the door by the Governor who invited him to partake of some refreshment, which he readily accepted. Mr. Smith soon found he could not have a perfect understanding with the Governor for want of a proper interpreter. However, he obtained liberty of the limits of the town, and harbor and of boarding with an American gentleman (Capt. Cooper) from Boston. Next day an interpreter was found by the name of Mr. Hartwell [Hartnell] an English gentleman, to whom Mr. Smith is under many obligations for his kindness and liberality towards him. But yet he could not find out what his future fate was to be; the Governor would sometimes say Mr. Smith must go to Mexico,—at other times Mr. S. & party must be sent off by water—again he would say send fetch in the party here, and continued in this Equivocating manner for several days.—then about the 3rd or 4th Novr. when four American gentlemen masters of vessels took the responsibility on themselves, and appointed Capt. Cooper Agent for the U. States, in order to settle this matter in some shape or manner. Then Capt. Cooper became accountable for the conduct of Mr. S. & party. The treaty was finally concluded on—the party sent for and brought in. Mr S. was then allowed the privilege of purchasing such articles as he stood in need of, to further his Expedition; he also learned while at this place, that after his first excursion through that country, that the Governor had instructed the Muchaba Indians not to let any more Americans pass through the country on any conditions whatever;—to this advice, Mr. S. leaves the entire cause of his defeat, —it undoubtedly was, for any man acquainted with the savage and hostile habits of Indians, cannot judge the matter otherwise. Mr. S. well knows the two Indian guides which led him first to St. Gabriel were immediately, imprisoned, but luckily for one he died in prison and escaped Spanish cruelty; the other was sentenced to death, but reprieved by the priest. Thos. Virgin, one of the party which was left on acct of his wound, was taken to St. Diego, about 250 miles south of St. Gabriel, and there imprisoned and without half sustenance. Mr. S. by frequent application to the Governor had him released and sent on to join the party.

Mr. Smith finding his party weak, knowing he had a great many more hostile tribes to pass, endeavoured to strengthen his party by engaging more Men; found several willing to engage, both Americans & English, but would not be allowed permission to Engage them. He then traded for some articles, such as horses, mules, arms, ammunition, and other necessaries, merely to enable him to return back from whence he came.

Then Mr. Smith went on to visit his party; found them in St. Francisco in a very deplorable state, and would have suffered immensely for want of victuals and clothing, was it not for the timely assistance of Mr Vermont [Virmond], a German gentleman who happened to be trading on the coast, to whom Mr. Smith is under many obligations.

After the conclusion of the treaty between Capt Cooper and the Governor, Mr. S. was allowed two months time to make all necessary preparations to leave the Spanish provinces,—so by very expeditious movements he had himself prepared at the appointed time and very near the boundary line; but on account of the lack of a boat to cross the Bonadventure (which is very large) and only one particular route destined for him to pass, so he took his own leave and left the province by another route, where he knew he could cross the river without their assistance. Mr. Smith being Experienced and well acquainted with Spanish generosity was unwilling to risque himself and property longer than the limited time for fear of further trouble.

Mr. Smith's party was then 21 men strong (though soon after two men deserted) with sufficient supplies to have lasted him back to the Little Lake. He moved on slowly up the Bonadventure, which runs generally N. N. W. and passing numerous tribes of Indians some of which were hostile, he continued on this route still moving very slowly, (and at the same time passing the winter) until the 18th April 1828, when by Examination and frequent trials he found it impossible to cross a range of mountains which lay to the East.

We [He] then struck of[f] N. W. leaving the Bonadventure running N. E. and coming out of a large range of mountains impassable until he came to the sea coast, then travelling along the coast crossing many large streams running into the ocean, on all of which were many tribes of Indians, some of which were hostile and many friendly, until he came to the Umpquah river which is a little more than 100 miles south of the mouth of the Columbia.—Here the Indians were in possession of some articles of trade, and appeared acquainted with whites.

On the 14th July, Mr. Smith had left the Encampment in order to search out a road, the country being very swampy in the low lands and woody in the mountains, and on his arrival at or near the Encampment, he and others which were with him, were fired on by a party of Indians, but fortunately made their Escape; the Camp and property was all in possession of the Indians, 15 of the men killed, one only made his Escape, (a black [*i.e.*, A. Black].) The Indians who made the attack were very numerous; they entered the encampment and massacred the men with their knives, axes, &c. Mr. Smith then made his way to Fort Vancouver, one of the Hudson Bay Co[s] trading posts situated on the N. side of the Columbia river, about 90 miles from the mouth, where he found Mr. Black who had escaped the massacre of the Indians. Mr. Smith acknowledges he has been very kindly and hospitably received by the gentlemen superintending at this post, and by their assistance and Indian influence he recovered the greatest part of the furs, and some horses, mercdze, &c. Mr. Smith remained there untill the 12th March, when he ascended the Columbus [Columbia], and passing several trading posts until he came to the Kettle Falls Fort Caldwell [Colvile]; from there he proceeded on, passing the Flathead trading post on the Flathead river, until he joined one of his partners (D. E. Jackson) in the Colanais [Kutenai] country; from there he proceeded and joined Mr W. L. Sublette, on the 5th August 1829, at the Tetons on Henry's Fork S. branch Columbia.

Names of Men killed at the Muckhabas as follows viz

David Cunningham, Silas Goble, Francois Deromme, Wm. Campbell, Henry Brown, Gregory Ortago, J. B. Ratelle, Potette Labross (mulatto) Robases, a Canadian half breed, John Relle (a Canadian)

Names of Men Killed at Umpquah.

Thos Virgin, Tousant Marreshall, Joseph Palmer, Joseph Lapoint, Marion (an Indian boy) Harrison G. Rodgers, Martin McCoy, Peter Raney, John Gaiter, John Hannah, Abraham Laplant, Manuel Lazares, Peter Raney, Thos. Daw, Char[ls]. Swift.

Murders committed in the vicinity of the Rocky Mountains since July 1826, on men belonging to the firm S. J. S. in 1827:

Pierre Irrequois, by the Black feet

1828. Joseph Coty, by the Black feet; Francois Bouldeau, by the Blackfeet; J. Johnson, A. Godair, P. W. Sublette, F. Rashotte, J. B. Joundreau by the Blackfeet.

1828 By the Snakes or Shoshong, Wm. Bell, James Scott. J. O'Hara, Ephraim Logan

1829. By the Blackfeet—Peter Spoon, Ezekiel Abel, Philip Adam, Luke Lariour

Horses and Mules taken by force and stolen by different tribes is 480
Value of Merchdz. taken $10000; Beaver fur 1500[lb]; Camp Equipage & traps $1000

Now in hope our fellow citizens will take it into consideration after taking a view of the above statement, to assist and more safely protect their fellow citizens in this country than they have done; but until British interlopers are dismissed from off our territory, Americans will never be respected or acknowledged as patrons by Indians on the west side of the Rocky Mountains. Further, the British influence is gaining ground every day, which our losses and sad disasters can easily show and account for. While they pass unmolested throughout all our territories from N. to S. and Even from the Hudson's bay to the mouth of the Columbia. But we, for no other reasons than because we are Americans, are tormented and annoyed by Every tribes.

Smith, Jackson & Sublette Indian traders
on the East & West of the R. Mountains.

[*Three supplementary statements follow, evidently furnished in 1830:*]

Amount of Property lost by the firm of Smith, Jackson & Soublette, from depredations of different tribes of Indians from July 1826 to July 1830.

480 head of horses, at the lowest mountain price $60 per head	$28,000.
Gross amount of Goods lost	10,000.
Traps and Camp Equipage lost	1,000.
Beaver furs taken from us by Indians	4,500.
	$43,500.

This statement will rather fall short than overgo the real amount of our losses from depredations of Indians.

Smith, Jackson & Sublette.

The number of men in our employ for the last four years has varied from to 120 men.

Smith, Jackson & Sublette.

[*Memorandum by General Clark:*
Average 100 packs Beaver per ann. 5 years
Cap. Employed about 30,000 pr. ann.]

Deaths of men caused by accidents and other causes not chargeable to Indians.

In 1825 Marshall was lost in the Willow valley near the Salt Lake.
" " A woman, a half breed died a natural death on Hams fork
" 1823 Holly Wheeler died from wounds received from a bear.
" 1822 [1823]. Mike Fink shot Carpenter—Talbot soon after shot Fink, and not long after was himself drowned at the Tetons.

" 1824 Thomas, a half breed, was killed by Williams, on the waters of Bear river, west of the mountains

" 1828. Bray was killed by a blow from the hand of Mr. Tullock.

Among our parties in the mountains, sickness and natural deaths are almost unknown.

Smith, Jackson & Sublette.

V.

[*To the Secretary of War*]

St. Louis, October 29, 1830.

Sir: The business commenced by General Ashley some years ago, of taking furs from the United States territory beyond the Rocky mountains, has since been continued by Jedediah S. Smith, David E. Jackson, and William L. Sublette, under the firm of Smith, Jackson, and Sublette. They commenced busines[s] in 1826, and have since continued it; and have made observations and gained information which they think it important to communicate to the Government. The number of men they have employed has usually been from eighty to one hundred and eighty; and with these, divided into parties, they have traversed every part of the country west of the Rocky mountains, from the peninsula of California to the mouth of the Columbia river. Pack-horses, or rather mules, were at first used; but in the beginning of the present year, it was determined to try wagons; and in the month of April last, on the 10th day of the month, a caravan of ten wagons, drawn by five mules each, and two dearborns, drawn by one mule each, set out from St. Louis. We have eighty-one men in company, all mounted on mules; and these were exclusive of a party left in the mountains. Our route from St. Louis was nearly due west to the western limits of the State; and thence along the Santa Fe trail about forty miles; from which the course was some degrees north of west, across the waters of the Kanzas, and up the Great Platte river, to the Rocky mountains, and to the head of Wind river, where it issues from the mountains. This took us until the 16th of July, and was as far as we wished the wagons to go, as the furs to be brought in were to be collected at this place, which is, or was this year, the great rendezvous of the persons engaged in that business. Here the wagons could easily have crossed the Rocky mountains, it being what is called the *Southern Pass,* had it been desirable for them to do so, which it was not for the reason stated. For our support, at leaving the Missouri settlements,

Names of Persons Killed belonging to the parties of Wm. H. Ashley and Smith, Jackson & Sublette, &c. &c.

Names of leaders	Names of men killed	Total No.	Places where killed	Year	By whom killed
Major Henry	Mayo, Tyo, Laymay, (one not recollected	4	Mouth of Smith's river	1823	Blackfeet
		14	Arickara village	June 1823	Arickaras
same	J. Anderson, A. Neil	2	On the way from the Arickaras to the Yellow Stone	1823	Gros Ventres
	Decharle, Trumble, (2 others names not recollected)	4	On the Yellow Stone	1823	Gros Ventres (supposed)
	Stevenson, Kremer	2	Mouth of Cannon ball river	1824	St. Peters Sioux
Clyman	Name not recollected	1	The Seetskeeder, or head of the Colarada	1825	Blackfeet (supposed)
J. S. Smith	David Cunningham, Silas Goble, Francis Deramme, Wm. Campbell, Boatswain Brown, Gregory Ortaga, John B. Ratelle, Pale, Polite Robiseau	10	On the Colerado	Aug[t] 1827	Amuchabas.
Samuel Tulock	Pinkney W. Sublette, Batiste, Jeandrois Rariet	3	Port Neuff River	1828	Blackfeet
Robert Campbell	Pierre, an Iroquois Indian	1	Head of the Missouri	1827	Blackfeet
Wm. L. Sublette	J. Cote	1	Godairs river	1828	Blackfeet
	Boileau	1	Little Lake	1828	Blackfeet
J. S. Smith	Bell, Logan, J. Scott & J. O'Hara.*		Snake Country	1827 or 1828	Snakes (supposed)

	Thos. Virgin Tousaint Marishall, Joseph Lapoint, Jos. Palmer, Marion, Harrison G. Rodgers, Martin McCoy, Peter Rannee, John Gaither, John Hanna, Abraham Laplant, Emanuel Lazarus, Thomas Daw, Charles Swift, & one other	19	On the Umpquah	July 1828	Umpquahs
	Ezekiel Abel, Peter Spoon, Adam ——— J. Larime†	4	Bad pass of Big Horn	1829	Blackfeet (supposed)
	A. Chapman, E. More	2	Platte river	1824	Arickaras
	Johnson, Godair	2	Bear River	1828	Blackfeet
Missº fur Co.	. . . .	7	Yellow Stone	1823	Blackfeet
French Co.	. . . .	4	Below the Mandans	1823	Rickaras
Prevoux & La Clere	. . . .	7	Waters of Uta Lake	1824	Snakes
	. . . .	1	Weber's fork	1825	Snakes
Missouri fur Cº.	. . . .	2	Platte in the Black hills	1828	Crows, (supposed)
Drips Co.	. . . .	2	Wind River	1829	Blackfeet (supposed)
American fur Co.	. . . .	1	Arickara village	1829	Arickaras
		94			

* The fate of these men is not known, but the conclusion is hardly doubtful. [Footnote in original.]
† Indian report says these (4) men were killed by the Snakes. [Footnote in original.]

until we should get into the buffalo country, we drove twelve head of cattle, beside a milk cow. Eight of these only being required for use before we got to the buffaloes, the others went on to the head of Wind river. We began to fall in with the buffaloes on the Platte, about three hundred and fifty miles from the white settlements; and from that time lived on buffaloes, the quantity being infinitely beyond what we needed. On the fourth of August, the wagons being in the mean time loaded with the furs which had been previously taken, we set out on the return to St. Louis. All the high points of the mountains then in view were white with snow; but the passes and valleys, and all the level country, were green with grass. Our route back was over the same ground nearly as in going out, and we arrived at St. Louis on the 10th of October, bringing back the ten wagons, the dearborns being left behind; four of the oxen and the milk cow were also brought back to the settlements in Missouri, as we did not need them for provision. Our men were all healthy during the whole time: we suffered nothing by the Indians, and had no accident but the death of one man, being buried under a bank of earth that fell in upon him, and another being crippled at the same time. Of the mules, we lost but one by fatigue, and two horses stolen by the Kanzas Indians; the grass being, along the whole route going and coming, sufficient for the support of the horses and mules. The usual weight in the wagons was about one thousand eight hundred pounds. The usual progress of the wagons was from fifteen to twenty-five miles per day. The country being almost all open, level, and prairie, the chief obstructions were ravines and creeks, the banks of which required cutting down, and for this purpose a few pioneers were generally kept ahead of the caravan. This is the first time that wagons ever went to the Rocky mountains; and the ease and safety with which it was done prove the facility of communicating over land with the Pacific ocean. The route from the *Southern Pass,* where the wagons stopped, to the Great Falls of the Columbia, being easier and better than on this side of the mountains, with grass enough for horses and mules, but a scarcity of game for the support of men. One of the undersigned, to wit, Jedediah S. Smith, on his excursion west of the mountains, arrived at the post of the Hudson's Bay Company, called Fort Vancouver, near the mouth of Multnomah river. He arrived there in August, 1828, and left the 12th of March, 1829, and made observations which he deems it material to communicate to the Government. Fort Vancouver is situated on the north side of the Columbia, five miles above the mouth of the Multnomah, in a handsome prairie, and on a second bank about three quarters of a mile from the river. This is the fort as it stood when he arrived there; but a large one, three hundred feet square, about three quarters of a mile lower down, and within two hundred yards of the river, was commenced the spring he came away. Twelve pounders were the heaviest cannon which he saw. The crop of 1828 was seven hundred bushels of wheat; the grain full and plump, and making good flour; fourteen acres of corn, the same number of acres in peas, eight acres of oats, four or five acres of barley, a fine garden, some small apple trees and grape vines. The ensuing spring eighty bushels of seed wheat were sown: about two hundred head of cattle, fifty horses and breeding mares, three hundred head of hogs, fourteen goats, the usual domestic fowls. They have mechanics of various kinds, to wit, blacksmiths, gunsmiths, carpenters, coopers, tinner and baker; a good saw mill on the bank of the river five miles above, a grist mill worked by hand, but intended to work by water. They had built two coasting vessels, one of which was then on a voyage to the Sandwich Islands. No English or white woman was at the fort, but a great number of mixed blood Indian extraction, such as belong to the British fur trading establishments, who were treated as wives, and the families of children taken care of accordingly. So that every thing seemed to combine to prove that this fort was to be a permanent establishment. At Fort Vancouver the goods for the Indian trade are imported from London, and enter the territories of the United States, paying no duties; and from the same point the furs taken on the other side of the mountains are shipped. The annual quantity of these furs could not be exactly ascertained, but Mr. Smith was informed indirectly that they amounted to about thirty thousand beaver skins, besides otter skins and small furs. The beaver skins alone, at the New York prices, would be worth above two hundred and fifty thousand dollars. To obtain these furs, both trapping and trading are resorted to. Various parties, provided with traps, spread over the country south of the Columbia to the neig[h]borhood of the Mexican territory; and in 1824 and 5, they crossed the Rocky mountains, and trapped on the waters of the Missouri river. They do not trap north of latitude 49 degrees, but confine that business to the territory of the United States. Thus this territory, being trapped by both parties, is nearly exhausted of beavers; and unless the British can be stopped, will soon be entirely exhausted, and no place left within the United States where beaver fur in any quantity can be obtained.

The inequality of the convention with Great Britain in 1818 is most glaring and apparent, and its continuance is a great and manifest injury to the United States. The privileges granted by it have enabled the British to take possession of the Columbia river, and spread over the country south of it; while no Americans have ever gone, or can venture to go on the British side. The interest of the United States and her citizens engaged in the fur trade requires that the convention of 1818 should be terminated, and each nation confined to its own territories. By this commercial interest there are other considerations requiring the same result. These are, the influence which the British have already acquired over the Indians in that quarter, and the prospect of a British colony, and a military and naval station on the Columbia. Their influence over the Indians is now decisive. Of this the Americans have constant and striking proofs, in the preference which they give to the British in every particular.

In saying this, it is an act of justice to say, also, that the treatment received by Mr. Smith at Fort Vancouver was kind and hospitable; that, personally, he owes thanks to Governor Simpson and the gentlemen of the Hudson's Bay Company, for the hospitable entertainment which he received from them, and for the efficient and successful aid which they gave him in recovering from the Umquah Indians a quantity of fur and many horses, of which these Indians had robbed him in 1828.

As to the injury which must happen to the United States from the British getting the control of all the Indians beyond the mountains, building and repairing ships in the tide water region of the Columbia, and having a station there for their privateers and vessels of war, is too obvious to need a recapitulation. The object of this communication being to state *facts* to the Government, and to show the facility of crossing the continent to the Great Falls of the Columbia with wagons, the ease of supporting any number of men by driving cattle to supply them where there was no buffalo, and also to show the true nature of the British establishments on the Columbia, and the unequal operation of the convention of 1818.

These *facts* being communicated to the Government, they consider that they have complied with their duty, and rendered an acceptable service to the administration; and respectfully request you, sir, to lay it before President Jackson.

We have the honor to be sir,
Yours, respectfully,
Jedediah S. Smith,
David E. Jackson,
W. L. Sublette.

To the Hon. John H. Eaton, Secretary of War.

APPENDIX B

Personal Letters by Jedediah S. Smith and His Family

I.

[*Solomon A. Simons to Peter Smith, November 22, 1829*]

Dear Brother in law: I would inform you that we received your letter dated St. Louis, Nov. 1st, in which you requested us to write to you concerning the health of the family which is good one. We hope that these few lines may find you enjoying the same blessing. Father Smith has sore eyes. Eunice enjoys good health. We expect Austin in Decr. to be at Astabula. We have had a letter from Ralph Smith stating that he received a letter from Robert Ca[mp]bel[l] of St. Louis stating that he the said Sr. Cambel was appointed administrator by Jedediah S. Smith on his property in case of his death. We have also heard of his defeat at or near the mouth of Columbia River but not the particulars. But as you are at St. Louis you can go to Robert Cambel— and there get information and then send to us at this place. We also received two other letters from you that I did not answer for want of particulars to write. I got the things from Mr. Thompson which you wrote to me. The boots I let Nelson have, the other I kept myself. Paddock is at work at the Sadler trade in Ashtabula with a Mr. Mead for forty dollars per year. Mr. Gaige has turned out to be miserable drunkard. Mr. Thompson is here. We do not know how he did make out with his clocks but I guess not very well for he has been sued and drawn for money since he come back. He is anxious to move to Illinois, but can not sell his property here. Not any other particulars to write. Concerning Thompson's child Alka come back with him and he has gone to work at distilling for Clark Blodgett to learn. He intends to go to Illinois. He speaks highly of that country. I wish you would write me concerning the place, where——Buffom lives and whether it would be best for me to move there or not. We have had a very wet cold fall. A good share of the corn and potatoes are not harvested in this town at this time, but it has been healthy, not many deaths, but some marriages, Mr. S. H. Farrington to Miss Laura Booth.

Peter I would advise you not to go to Mountain. I think it would be too great a risk to run unless you find Diah and then be advised by him as he is acquainted with the way. But unless you can hear from him so that you can depend upon it do not go but be sure to go to Robert Cambel at St. Louis and there make all the inquiry that you can respecting Diah and his property, whether he left any or not with him. One of his partners name is Jackson and the other I think is Sublett and as soon as you ascertain the particulars write to me to let us know the same and if you should find him alive persuade him to come home and if not do not come yourself as soon as you can is the wish of all the connection in this country. We all send our love to you, wishing the best of Heaven's blessings to attend you until death shall close the scene with you, and then a full salvation at the right hand of God Eternally in the Heavens. This from your Brother in law

S. A. *Simons,*

Ashtabula, Ohio,
Nov. 22nd, 1829.

II.

[*Jedediah* S. *Smith to his parents*]

Wind River, East side of the Rocky Mountains, Decr. 24th 1829
Dear Father & Mother
Your unworthy Son once more undertakes to address his Mutch Slighted Parents—

I have several times written, but have received no answer from any of you, since I left home, with the Exception, of Austin & Peter, they state that our Parents, now reside in Erie County, Pennsylvania, & a few other particulars with regard to the Family, but it would give me great satisfaction to hear more fully—it is a long time since I left home & many times I have been ready, to bring my business to a close & endeavor to come home; but have been hindered hitherto—as our business is at present, it would be the height of impolicy to set a time to come Home, however I will endeavor, by the assistance of Divine Providence, to come home as soon as possible, the greatest pleasure I could enjoy, would be to accompany, or be in company, with my friends, but whether I Shall ever be allowed the privelege, God only knows, I feell the need of the wa[t]ch & care of a Christian Church—

you may well Suppose that our Society is of the Roug[h]est kind, Men of good morals seldom enter into business of this kind—I hope you will remember me before a Throne of grace—perhaps you may think it strange that I do not give you some particulars with regard to what is passing in this country but for this, it is, perhaps, better that we wait a meeting——

I wish I could hear from my Parents, & if they please to write, let them write soon & direct their Letters to the care of W^{m}. L. Sublette, St Louis Missouri; Mr Sublette is a Partner of mine, he will be the bearer of this to St Louis & after remaining there about two months, he will return to Join our other Partner (Mr. David, E, Jackson) & my self, in the Mountains, so I wish no time to be lost in writing

May God of his infinite mercy allow me soon to join My Parents, is the Prayer of your undutiful

Son

Jedediah, S. Smith

M*r* Jedediah Smith &
M*rs* Sally Smith
[Addressed:] to Mr. Jedediah Smith
Ashtabula Ashtabula County Ohio
[Postmarked?] Loudonville O Ap^{l} 30th
[Rate:] 18¾

III.

[*Jedediah S. Smith to Ralph Smith*]

Wind River, East side of the Rocky Mountains, Decr 24, 1829
Dear Brother
It is some length of time since I wrote to You, but I think you will excuse me when I tell you I have never received a Letter from you Since I left home, notwithstanding my repeated requests, in my Letters, for an answer—I can not think you have not wrote—they must have miscarried

I last summer, July 16, received 2 letters from Peter, one wrote in March, 1827 & the other in Decr. 1828 & one from Austin wrote in March 1827 those together with what *Gen* Ashley tells me, Viz. that Father had writen, making some inquiry with regard to me, is all the information I have had respecting our Family since I left home——

I have often writen, but my memorandums are not at hand, & I do not recollect the substance of what I wrote, further than I have always been anxious to know of the welfare of my friends & I do assure you that anxiety Still remains—

I feel thankful for this privilege we enjoy of writing to & inquiring of each others welfare both spiritual & temporal; should you receive this please give me (& as Soon as possible (as my partner will be in *St* Louis a short time, & then return to Join me & my other Partner in the Mountains) an explanation of your Silence & a full account of the situation of our Friends—since I left home I have passed throug[h] various vicissitudes of Fortune; I have been fortunate in some respects in others unfortunate—I have passed through the Country from St. Louis, Missouri, to the North Paciffick Ocean, in different ways—through countrys of Barrenness & seldom one of the reverse, many Hostile Tribes of Indians inhabit this Space, and we are under the necessity of keeping a constant wa[t]ch; notwithstanding our vigilenc[e] we some times suffer; in Augt. 1827 ten Men, who were in company with me, lost their lives, by the Amuchabas Indians, on the Colorado River; & in July 1828 fifteen men, who were in Company with me lost their lives, by the Umpquah Indians, on the River of the Same name, it enters the North Paciffic, one hundred miles South of the Mouth of the Columbia—many others have lost their lives in different parts of the Country—My Brother believe me, we have Many dangers to face & many difficulties to encounter, but if I am Spared I am not anxious with regard to difficulties—for particulars you must await a meeting—

When you write do not omit leting me know how Doctr Simons is, David & Titus Liquie–remember me to my Friends; the D*r* & his Sons; I wish as many of them, as may find it convenient, to write, & that soon for the reason before mentioned—I shall write a few lines to Peter & Austin & as Austin writes they are at the Tin & Copper Smith trade I Shall advise them to make them Selves masters of that Valuable Trade

I Shall liquise write to my other friends (I e) so many as I have time to write to.—I Shall only State the Substance of what I have writen, above, & My Brother will, undoubtedly, do me the Favor to forward them—

As it respects my Spiritual welfare, I hardly durst Speak I find myself one of the most ungrateful; unthankful, Creatures imaginable Oh when Shall I be under the care of a Christian Church? I have need of your Prayers, I wish our Society to bear me up before a Throne of Grace—I can not Speak to my friends with regard to my comeing home I have Set So many times, & always found myself unable to perform, that it is better to omit it—Give My Love to My Father, Mother, Brothers, Sisters, Neffiews & Nieces, none excepted,

I remain as ever Your affectionate Brother

Jedediah. S. Smith

M[r] Ralph Smith

Richland County

P S Aside

please turn over & read a few lines

Providence has made me Steward of a Small pittance; & my My Prayer is, that whilst I am allowed the privilege of using it, I may use it without abuse—I will endeavor to forward a little Money, as you will see below & no doubt my Brother will assist me in disposing of it according to my wish, and it must be your particular care that none, who may receive a benefit, knows from where it comes—in none of the rest of my letters will I Speak of my temporal concerns—in the first place my Brother, our Parents must receive of our beneficence, & if Dr Simons is in want I wish him to be helped; I want, if it is in your Power, that you Should place Ira, B. Paddock, and Nelson, at a good English Sc[h]ool—I will pay no attention to Austin, or, Peter, further, than to advise them to make themselves masters of their Trade, as they are now men—I wish you to consult Dr. Simons, on the method of Educating our Brothers, as it is my wish to carry them into some of the higher branches of Education—I feell in hopes I shall be able, when it is needed, to send more Money; you will Consult the Dr., if a live, if not, some other good jud[g]e, & write to me your own ideas, as well as the conclusion of the Dr. on the subject.

I write to *Gen* W[m]. H. Aashley, of *St* Louis, to take Charge of the Money, & get an interchange of Letters with you, & then take the proper method to forward it Securely——My Partner M[r] W[m] L. Sublette takes this Letter to *St* Louis & forwards it—and if any accident has befallen *Gun* Ashley he will appoint another Agent and let you know by Letter—as I before stated Mr. Sublette will remain in S[t] Louis about 2 Months, before he returns to join M[r] Ja[c]kson & myself in the Mountains—The Sum for which you will expect to receive will be Two Thousand & Two hundred dollars—You will do me the favor to keep an ac[t] of the expenditures, if any of our Friends are in a distrest Situation youl please let me know, recollect that we are Brothers! and I Shall not forgive you, if you do not let me know your own Situation—be not too modest——

It is, that I may be able to help those who stand in need, that I face every danger—it is for this, that I traverse the Mountains covered with eternal Snow—it is for this that I pass over the Sandy Plains, in heat of Summer, thirsting for water, and am well pleased if I can find a shade, instead of water, where I may cool my overheated Body—it is for this that I go for days without eating, & am pretty well satisfied if I can gather a few roots, a few Snails, or, much better Satisfied if we can affo[r]d our selves a piece of Horse Flesh, or a fine Roasted Dog, and, most of all, it is for this, that I deprive myself of the privilege of Society & the satisfaction of the Converse of My Friends! but I shall count all this pleasure, if I am at last allowed by the Alwise Ruler the privilege of Joining my Friends—Oh My Brother let us render to him to whoom all things belongs, a proper proportion of what is his due I must tell you, for my part, that I am much behind hand, oh! the perverseness of my wicked heart! I entangle myself altogether too much in the things of time—I must depend entirely upon the Mercy of that being, who is abundant in Goodness & will not cast off any, who call, Sincerely, upon him; again I say, pray for me My Brother—& may he, before whoom not a Sparrow falls, without notice, bring us, in his own good time, Together again—as I said before let no one know of this little money which is to be forwarded, except the one whoom you consult,—let it be the greatest pleasure that we can enjoy, the height of our ambition, now, when our Parents, are in the decline of Life, to smooth the Pillow of their age, & as much as in us lies, take from them all cause of Trouble—but all this advice is quite unnecessary, to one whom I know to be much more ready than myself, to do that which is a part of our duty—

As I do not know where our friends, may now reside, you will please fill out the Superscription

Your Brother

Jedediah S. Smith

P S I concluded after writing, the above, that if M*r* R. Campbell now resides in St. Louis he should be the Agent, instead of *Gen* Ashley, if he is not there it will be as above written *J. S. S.*

[Addressed:] Mr Ralph Smith
State of Ohio
Richland County
Perrys Ville

favored
by Mr
W*m* L. Sublette

IV.

[*Jedediah Smith, Senior, to Peter Smith, February 16, 1830*]

Ever Dear Son: I now sit down to write a few lines to you to inform you that we are all well and hope these few lines may find you enjoying the same blessing. Eunice has gained her health very much. I received a letter from Austin in November. He was coming home this Fall but was taken sick and concluded to come this Summer. He went to New York and purchased goods and meant to come home and peddle on his way so as not to lose anything. They say he is doing well. I want you to stay where you be till Jedediah S. Smith comes in or till you hear something certain about him. My great wish is to see him once more. You can likely get wages there. I don't feel willing you should go after him. My son Peter I hope you will remember you are among strangers where you be now and behave yourself well. Go to Mr. Robert Cambell and find out what you can by him whether Jedediah left any property with him and write on to me as soon as you receive this letter. I wish you well and shall conclude this letter by subscribing myself your Ever Dear father.

Jedediah Smith.

N. B. Your mother sends her love to you
and your Brothers and Sister send their
love to you.

Kingsvill [Ohio] February 16th, 1830.
to Mr. Peter Smith.

V.

[*Jedediah S. Smith to Ralph Smith*]

Blue River—, fork of Kanzas, 30 miles from the Ponnee Villages,
Sept. 10, 1830
Dear Brother

Yours of March 15" to April 3d were duly received, by which I received the mortifying intelligence of the Death of our much loved Mother, I had indulged the pleaseing hope of again Seeing and, perhaps, administering to the necessities of Her to whoom we owe so much //// but he who had an undoubted right, has called and She is gone——

We can See her no more here; therefore, let us prepare against the same Summons must be received by us—

I am Indebted to Doctor Simons for his epistle dated March 15, 1830 and I wish you to exp[r]ess my gratitude in becoming terms of respect—I fear that Dr Simons thinks I only feel bound, where I sign My Name, but, if so, he to whoom I am under so many obligations, is much mistaken........how happy Should I consider My Self if I could *again* be allowed the privilege of spending some time with my much esteemed Friend—I think the D^{r} recollects this excellent precept, "never exchange a *tried* for an *untried* Friend" again "if you have one *Friend* feel, or, think, your Self happy" I hope I have one *Friend*——on My arrival at the Settlements (Should I be so fortunate as to gain that point, I intend writing to Dr Simons——

You recollect, My Brother that you (in Your favor of 3^{d} April) said you would be glad to see me, in S*t* Louis (if I could not come to Wayne)—You will confer a favor upon J. S. S. to come, on receipt of this, as soon as circumstances will permit——

Should You not be able to come in time apply to Tracy & Wahrendorf, we Shall (if permitted by Him who rules) be in St Louis in thirty five or forty days & I Shall (if permitted by the Same Good being remaine there one Month, perhaps more.—Our business is so arranged that I am not under the necessity of visiting the mountains again—Brother I now recollect, that when I came from home I owed $10 to Ransom Clarke, if it is not settled, pray settle it at once, for that Man will think I am not inclined to pay My honest Debts—you have undoubtedly paid to the D^{r} the few dollars that he will receive —no more at present——

Jedediah. S. Smith

P S

Having overtaken this Letter, this 22^{d} of *Septr* (at the Kanzas Fairry, 30 miles from camp Leavensworth, or, rather Cantonment Leavenworth; I adde, we are thus far Safe

J. S. S.

[Addressed:] Mr Ralph Smith
State of Ohio
Favored pr.) Wayne County
Mr. H. Dougherty) Plaine Township
[Postmarked:] Cant. Leavenworth
8. Octr
[Rate:] 25

VI.

[*Jedediah S. Smith to Hugh Campbell*]

St Louis Nov. 24th 1830

Mr Hugh Campbell

Dear friend

On the eighteenth of the present month I received your Epistle, which I perused with a mixture of gratitude and regret—I have great reason to feel thankful to You My Dear Sir, for the trouble you put your Self to on my account—but, with pain did I peruse that part of your Epistle, which Speaks of the ill health of My *much valued Friend*—Oh is it possible I Shall never again See him in the Land of the living? My Prayer to Almighty God, is, that I may again be allowed the Privilege of passing some time in company with my *Friend*—

I have not written directly to Robert, for this reason, I thought Your Letters would be more certain of their place of destination [Ireland], consequently it would be better for us to correspond, as, in the mean time I shall be in pleasant converse with two friends in stead of one.

I have been under the necessity of going forward with a partnership amounting to part of My Capital, but Shall Still, unavoidable accidents excepted, have eight, or, perhaps, ten thousand Dollars, in March, or April next, which Could not be vested in any way to please me so well, as to have it aid both my FRIEND and me.

According to your intimation, and to my great satisfaction I received from Mr Kyle a price Current of Nov. 10th, together with such information as that Gentleman was able to collect, for this I render my grateful acknowledgments, but Since I wrote, We have engaged a Gentleman (Gen. Wm H. Ashley) to take our Furs forward to Philadelphia and N. York and dispose of the Same

With what pleasure would I have embraced the opportunity of comp[l]ying with your friendly invitation of visiting Mrs Hugh Campbell at Richmond? but my business compells me to remain in St. Louis this Winter.

As you mention Mr Keyte, I will tell what I know of that Gentleman, I had not the honor of a personal acquaintance with Mr K. but on my arrival here this fall (as I knew Mr R. C. had been intimate with him) I called on the Gentleman and made inquiry for my friend, I got little, or no satisfaction.

Mr Keyte has now removed from St Louis, near to a Small Town, called Chariton, in this State.

After the perusal of these two Letters, which I have had the pertinacity to write, it is hardly necessary for me to tell you that I am much more in my element, when conversing with the uncivilized Man, or Seting My Beaver Traps, than in writing Epistles.

believe me
Dr. Sir your
Sincere friend and
Hub. Servant
Jedediah. S. Smith

[Addressed:] M*r* Hugh Campbell
Richmond
Va.
[Postmarked:] St. Louis, Mo. Dec 1
[Rate:] 25

VII.

[*Jedediah S. Smith to Ralph Smith*]

St. Louis, Jan. 26th 1831

Dear Brother

Austin arrived here yesterday; Ira came to St. Louis on the twenty third of Decr. last, he had Braught hand tipe and was to have Pulled for Mr Fairbank, but this City and the vicinity had been previously supplied; I was very glad of the meeting, and soon had arrangements made for him to place himself under my control, that he might receive an Education; some difficulty occurred with regard to conveying the Property to Mr F. as the river was froze and the Mail Stage was at this season irregular; he was only hired conditionally; I finally took the responsibility upon myself to engage to forward Mr F's property, so soon as the River opens, and Ira wrote what we had concluded upon, to Mr F. I then went to Jacksonvill, Illinois, where there is a College & left him at that institution; I cannot say that I am altogether pleased with that Seminary but there is a probability of its becomeing verry respectable and I am verry willing to give it a fair trial, as it is not very far off, and I can the more easily correspond and know his situation—

I had expected to hear by Austin something more particular with regard to what the prospect was with regard to the opportunity of the School for B. P. and N. J. for the ensuing Summer, he said something about the College near Mount Vernon but I could make no certain arrangements; however I have now written to the President of that College & on getting an answer from him, as well as from another Seminary to which I have written, I shall be able to come to some conclusion.—Austin said you spoke of an easy conveyance for them to this place, my Brother! This is the last place to which youngsters should be sent; it is possible if no better chance offers that I may want them sent here, as I can place them in the same Seminary with Ira; but as I before Stated I am not altogether pleased with that place. —I am afraid my Dear Brother that You and my friend the Doctor do not council together upon the Subject of Education, consider my Brother, his respectful age he has had the profit of Education as well as experience, & he is the Father of my Beloved Sister, Your Wife, oh! be on the best and most friendly terms, according to the common course of things he must soon be in the wane of life, and between him and my Father we must make no difference, but let us endeavor to ease & comfort them, to pour on Oil & balm into the wounds, made by the relentless hand of Time, the pleasing thought cheeres me to Shed Tears of Joy.—how long will it be ere you and I will be under the necessity of reme[m]bering (if we are allowed the privilege of living) that we were once Young? and let us now set a pattern to our younger Brothers & Children.—It gave me great pleasure to learn that the Children, under the charge of Doctor Simons, were making fine Progress. I am not Surprised at this, for how could it be otherwise with Children placed under so good a Teacher.

Austin had came by Water but the Ice stopped him at the mouth of Ohio, and he brought none of the letters.

At present I shall only write to your self & Doctor Simons, I have reasons for writing to no more. it is certainly verry far from my wish to have too much publicity given to our business.—I expect You to give my love to our Friends generally.—Next My Brother comes the subject for which we live, are we ungrateful to that God in whoom we live, and moove, and have our being, how often ought we on our bended knees to offer up our greatful acknowledgments for the gift of his Dear Son; is it possible that God "So loved the World that he gave his only begotten Son that whosoever believed on him Should not perish, but have everlasting life"

Then let us come forward with faith, nothing doubting and he will most unquestionably hear us—let us be often found in the means and take my word for it we Shall receive a blessing: some, who have made a profession of Christianity & have by their own negligence caused the Spirit to depart think their day of grace is over; but where did they find Such doctrine? I find our Saviour ever entreating & wooing [moving?] us, useing the most endearing language and endeavoring by every means without compelling, for that would at once destroy our free agency), to bring us to him that we may have life, are we doeing our duty, do we regularly and without fail attend to *Prayers* & keep in mind that in due season we shall receive the Crown, if we faint not, oh! let us be engaged & to that end let us take a view of what the Poet says of the unhapy close of life

"How Shocking must thy summons be, oh death!
To him who is at ease in his possessions!
Who counting on long years of pleasure here,
Is quite unfurnished for the world to come!
In that dread moment, how the frantic Soul
Runs round the walls of his clay tenement;
Runs to each corner and Shrieks for help;
But Shrieks in vain! How wishfully She looks
On all She's leaving now no longer hers!

What a dreadful picture is this which we find in the English reader! But another Poet Sings the following lines

Lord, I believe a rest remains
To all thy People known;
A rest, where pure enjoyment reigns,
And thou art loved alone

Well, My Brother, will it be for us if we have faith in those last lines and make use of it in Such a way that it may produce good works—write soon my Brother, & give me any news which You may consider worth conveying. and believe me, as Ever your affectionate Brother

Jedediah S. Smith

[Addressed:] M[r] Ralph Smith
Wayne County
Mohican T. Ship
Ohio
[Postmarked:] St. Louis Mo. Jan. 26
[Rate:] 25

VIII.

[*Jedediah S. Smith to Ralph Smith*]

St. Louis Feb. 28th 1831

Dear Brother

I yesterday received a Letter from our Father, and am happy that he is well, he says, as it is somewhat unhealthy about where you live, he would prefer living at Solomon's; as that is most pleaseing to him, I presume it will comport with your good judgment that we accomodate our Father in this respect.—Father says he wishes to come and visit Your Family in June next; he has a Waggon and Horse but is in want of a little Money; but as the distance is much greater from here than from where you live, and consequently So much greater risque, I thought best to advise you on the Subject.

Our Father Speaks of seeing Paddock and Nelson liquise, which if it can be done, with propriety, should certainly not be disallowed; Sorry are we, that our Father is not adequate to the Task of being his own Agent, and it should be our care to provide a confidential Agent, and that, convenient, no doubt this is already done. Austin said Mr Jones was to act in that capacity.

You may Judge of my wishes by recollecting that when I had but fifty Dollars, I thought it my duty to Send it for the use of my indigent Parents. (it is true they did not receive it, but I think I can not be blamed for that.)—Infinite Wisdom has seen fit to make Some alterations; as it respects our Parents one is no more; our Brothers are now in a different situation; but my Brother this does not relieve me from my duty to my Father; although I do not now give all, yet, I must See that my Father does not want. it should be our desire and wish, to use an aged Father with careful and filial affection, to know and asscertain, even to anticipate what ever is requisite to comfort, health, or reasonable gratification.

I am anxiously awaiting a Letter from Your self and another from the Doctor, in answer to two which I wrote in January, if you have not written, write Soon, I Shall leave an Agent to transact any little business which may be necessary, it will probably be Messrs. Tracy & Wahrendorff, or Gen. Ashley, but on leaveing here, I shall give some particulars and shall instruct my Agent, in case it is thought advisable by Yourself & Dr Simons, for Paddock and Nelson, to come here, to forward them to the proper place; but I am in hopes that your Letters will soon arrive, and then I shall be able at once to conclude what had better be done.—

Austin has been Sick but is no[w] convalescent, Peter is well; I had a Letter from Ira not long since, he was well—

I enclose a letter to Father, I wish you to read and then forward it.

Your Brother
& Servt.
Jedediah S Smith

[Addressed:] Mr Ralph Smith
Wayne County
Plaine Township
Ohio
[Postmarked:] St Louis, Mo. Mar 3
[Rate:] 25

IX.

[*Jedediah S. Smith to A. W. Doniphan*]

Camp near Big Blue morning
of 4th May 1831

Mr Donaphan
Dear Sir

In the hurry of the time I was ob[l]iged to omit even the formality of taking your hand. But now I send you my best wishes for your well-fare. I hope you will succeed in resting

[*Jedediah S. Smith*]

X.

[*Austin Smith to Jedediah Smith, Senior*]

Walnut Creek, on the Arkansas
300 Miles from the Settlements of Mo
Septr 24, 1831—

My Dear Farther

It is [pain]ful at [all] times to com[municate the death] of a friend,—but [when it f]alls to the lot of a son to communicate to a farther the death of a Brother it is more so—Your son Jedediah was killed on the Semerone the 27th of May on his way to Santa fé by the Curmanch Indians, his party was in distress for water, and he had gone alone in search of the above river which he found, when he was attacked by fifteen or twenty of them—they succeeded in alarming his animal not daring to fire on him so long as they kept face to face, so soon as his horse turned they fired, and wounded him in the shoulder he then fired his gun, and killed their head chief it is supposed they then *rushed* upon him, and despatched him—such my farther is the fate of him who you loved—I am convinced that this intelegence will grieve you much, but do not my dear farther take it to heart too sorely the Lord giveth and the Lord ta[keth away——] be his na[me?——] kind who[   ] trusted, and confided, in the Giver of all good and may we not hope, that his religion, was true, and will be rewarded —Come unto me all ye ends of the earth and ye shall be saved—

I left Santa fé the 28 of August and Peter left the following day for Caliafornia, for the purpose of purchasing mules—I do not apprehend any danger in the trip it is often made with 8 or ten men and no defeats or difficulties experienced—

I shall be in Saint Louis about the first of November, when I will write to you more fully, and give you particulars—I am dear farther your son forever

Austin Smith

[Addressed:] M[r] Jedediah Smith
Ashtabula
Ashtabula Co.
Ohio
[Postmarked:] Independence, Mo. October 1st
[Rate:] 25

XI.

[*Austin Smith to Ira G. Smith*]

Walnut Creek on the Arkansas, 300 miles
from Settlements, Septbr. 24th 1831.

Dear Brother.

An opportunity offers itself of writing to you from this point by some gentlemen who are anxious to reach their families.—It is my painful duty to communicate to you the death of our lamented brother Jedediah, he was killed by the Comanche Indians on the 27th May on the Simarone river between Arkansas river and Santa Fé; his company and Soublett's consisting of 74 men, and animals for 22 Waggons was on the point of Starving for the want of water (near four days without any) he took a due South course from the one we were travelling, which was S. W. and Struck the Simarone. The Spanish traders who trade with those Indians informed me, that he saw the Indians before they attacked him, but supposed there could be no possible chance of an escape, he therefore went boldly up, with the hope of making peace with them, but found that his only chance was defence, he killed the head Chief I do suppose that then they rushed upon him like so many blood-hounds; the Spaniards say the Indians numbered from fifteen to twenty. I have his gun and pistols, got from the Indians by the traders. Such my dear brother is the fate of our guardian and protector on this route, him who had gone through so many dangers, so many privations and almost at the time when he had reached the Goal of his enterprise to be thus torn from us is lamentable indeed; but let us not grieve too much, for he confided in a wise and in a powerful being—Peter left Santa Fé on the 29th of A[u]gust in good health for California with a party to purchase mules, they have taken part of our Merchandise.—I wish you would meet me at Saint Louis about the 25th of October, as I shall be there about that time. I shall make calculations to stay in St Louis this winter, when we can have an interchange of sentiments. I will give you further particulars of what we can do with Peter.—Meanwhile, I am dear Brother yours for ever—

Austin Smith

N. B.—The Spanish traders say that the Indians succeeded in alarming the horse he was riding so as to get his back to them, which when effected, they then forced [fired] on him and wounded him in the shoulder; he then faced them and killed the Chief

Austin Smith.

XII.

[The preceding letter is evidently the source for the only account of Jedediah Smith's death printed in the contemporary press; it appeared in the Jacksonville *Illinois Patriot* late in October 1831, and is here derived from the Vandalia *Illinois Intelligencer*, October 29, 1831:]

From the Illinois Patriot.

FATE OF SMITH.—The following melancholy account is taken from a Letter just received in this town, by a brother of the deceased. Mr. Smith was a partner in the firm of Smith, Sublette and Jackson, and has been engaged in carrying on the Fur Trade with the Indians beyond the Rocky Mountains for some time past. The public are indebted to his enterprise for many valuable facts relating to this almost unknown region. The last time his Company returned to St. Louis, they had been peculiarly successful, and had pushed their expedition to within fifty miles of the Pacific Ocean.

"Our much lamented brother, Jedediah Smith, was killed by the Cormuck Indians on Simerone River on the 27th May.—Our teams were about starving for want of water (having none for four days) and brother went in search of some water a due south from the course we were traveling, which was S. W. The Spanish traders trafficking with these Indians told us that they saw brother a short time before the Indians attacked him, and told him there was no hope for escape, so he went boldly up to them in hopes that he could effect a conciliation. The Indians attempted to frighten his horse, so that he would turn from them, which they did, and then fired on him, and wounded him in the shoulder; he faced about and killed their chief, upon which they rushed upon him and massacred him. The Indians numbered about twenty. AUSTIN SMITH.

IRA G. SMITH, Jacksonville."

XIII.

[*Solomon A. Simons to Ralph Smith, October 23, 1831*]

Dear Brother,

Having received a letter from Austin Smith I think it my duty to write to you [and] let you know some of the contents of sd. letter; it is some grievous. Austin states that J. S. Smith was killed by the Indians the 27th day of May, 1831, three hundred miles from the settlements and that he went to the river to get water, was attacked by fifteen or twenty Indians. They did not fire at him so long as they were face to face, but they scart his horse and then wounded him in the shoulder, rushed upon him to despatch him. This is all that he wrote save that he and Peter should be at St. Louis the first of December and then he would write the particulars concerning the death of Brother Jedediah S. Smith.

I carried the letter to Father Smith last Thursday [October 19]. He seemed to be more resigned than I expected. We are all in good health excepting my side is not well, but I can work some.

I have written to Austin to know whether he wants any assistance to settle the estate of J. S. Smith. Now I wish you to write to me whether you shall go to St. Louis this fall. If you think that you shall if you will write to me the time that you will start I will go with you. If you think it best I will come to your House the time you say if you want my company. If you do not go I wish you to write me on the receipt of this, to satisfy father and the rest of us concerning the estate of Jedediah's property; whether he made his will or not. Probably you know more than any of us about it; therefore father wishes to know. So I must end by subscribing myself affectionately, this 23rd of Oct., 1831.

Solomon A. Simons

[Addressed:] M[r] Ralph Smith
Mohican
Wayne County,
Ohio

ACKNOWLEDGMENTS

One does not come to the end of such a book as this without sober reflection on the united effort that has gone into it. My direct obligations go as far back as 1940, and have been mounting ever since.

For anyone who works with fur-trade history, the Rome to which all roads lead is the Missouri Historical Society. Hardly a page of this book is not dependent in some way on the rich archives of this Society, which have been opened to me in two visits to St. Louis and have also been indefatigably worked for me by the Society's officers. My indebtedness here goes back a long way, to the late Stella M. Drumm and to Mrs. Brenda R. Gieseker, and more recently to Mr. Charles van Ravenswaay, Miss Barbara Kell, and Mrs. Frances Biese, all of whom have contributed a great deal to the making of this book. I am, moreover, greatly obligated to the Society for permission to publish documents from its Ashley, Sublette and Chouteau collections, a wonderfully rich depository.

The Library of Congress, especially for its extraordinary wealth of newspaper files, which I have spaded intermittently since 1942, but also for its general collections, likewise has contributed much of the bone and tissue of this book; and for special courtesies I am indebted to Mr. David C. Mearns, Mr. Donald Holmes and Colonel Willard Webb.

The Kansas State Historical Society is a principal source of information about Jedediah Smith, owing to its possession of original letters by Jedediah and his brother and of the so-called William Clark papers, the letterbooks of the St. Louis Superintendency of Indian Affairs, both of which have provided documents for my Appendix. Copies of these furnished me ten years ago by Miss Louise Barry took me a long step forward, and I have since had courteous assistance from Mr. Edgar Langsdorf and Miss Helen McFarland.

Both the staff and the staggering resources of the National Archives have been at my service over a long period; it would require a book in itself to recite all that has been done for me in the National Archives, but I can at any rate express my particular thanks to Mr. Richard G. Wood, Mr. Francis Heppner, Mr. Carl L. Lokke, Mr. M. D. Moody and Mr. Nelson M. Blake.

The resources of the Bancroft Library at the University of California have likewise been mine to command, with cordial aid from Dr. George P. Hammond, Mrs. Eleanor A. Bancroft and Mrs. Helen H. Bretnor, and so also at Yale University where Mr. James T. Babb, Miss Dorothy W. Bridgwater and Mr. Archibald Hanna have extended me every possible help in mining the Coe Collection. At the Henry E. Huntington Library, Mr. Leslie E. Bliss, Miss Haydée Noya and Dr. R. G. Cleland have been my good friends.

Mr. R. A. Reynolds, Secretary of the Hudson's Bay Record Society, made it possible for me to draw on the rich archives of the Hudson's Bay Company in London, and with the Governor and Committee has granted me permission to publish various documents from these archives which enlarge our understanding of Jedediah Smith and of the interrelationships of the British and American fur trade in the Far West.

Senator Clinton P. Anderson of New Mexico enabled me to obtain a microfilm of the Jedediah Smith transcript journal, which he has given to the Friends of the Middle Border, and a photostat of Jedediah Smith's letter to his parents of Dec. 24, 1829, with permission to print this latter document. With equal generosity, Mr. C. Corwith Wagner of St. Louis gave me permission to print Jedediah's letter of Nov. 24, 1830, to Hugh Campbell, which is a distinguished item in his manuscript collection; and Mr. R. N. Williams, II, Director of the Historical Society of Pennsylvania, authorized me to print from that Society's collections another previously unknown Jedediah Smith letter written from San Diego, Dec. 16, 1826. I have already noted a major indebtedness to the Kansas State Historical Society for permission to print all the letters in their Jedediah Smith collection, most of which have never before been published.

Researches for me in Mexico City were generously prosecuted by Dr. Carlos Bosch-Garcia and Mr. Darel McConkey, with the co-operation of Gen. Manuel Torrea and Señor Francisco Cabrera of the Archivo Historico de la Secretaría de Relaciones Exteriores, and special aid from Señor Reyes Bardales and Señora Lucille Carbajal.

The thanks which like most modern scholars I owe to the booksellers of our day I must express in particular to Mr. Fred Rosenstock, Mr. Glen Dawson, Mr. Charles Eberstadt and Mr. Edward Eberstadt, who have made special searches for me or otherwise contributed significant services and information.

What I owe to the labors of Dr. Charles L. Camp is apparent throughout the book. His book on James Clyman, his monographs on George C. Yount and Daniel T. Potts, and his bibliographical labors with Henry R. Wagner in two editions of *The Plains and the Rockies,* have been veritable guides through a wilderness; he also provided me with a copy of the unpublished letterbook of Benjamin O'Fallon and in many other ways has been my good friend.

While the manuscript was in preparation, Dr. A. R. Mortensen of the Utah State Historical Society placed all the facilities of the Society at my disposal, and I am glad to thank both him and the Society. During all this time, too, the interest of Mr. D. Laurance Chambers and Mr. Harrison Platt of Bobbs-Merrill has played an indispensable part in making a reality of the book; I thank them for both their enthusiasm and their patience.

The manuscript was read in its entirety by Mr. Darel McConkey and Miss Madeline Reeder, and their special perspective and detailed suggestions have been very helpful to me. Important also was the cheerful labor of Miss Patricia Tull in reducing a difficult manuscript to order.

Many others I thank for special researches or other aid: my brothers James S. and Robert H. Morgan, my sister Mrs. Ruth M. Barton, Mr. Robert F. Curtis, Mr. Everett D. Graff, Mr. Thomas W. Streeter, Dr. Harrison C. Dale, Mr. John E. Sunder, Mr. Carl

D. W. Hays, Mrs. Naomi Peres, Dr. LeRoy R. Hafen, Miss Caroline Jakeman, Mr. J. S. Holliday, Mr. Merrill J. Mattes, Mr. Burton Harris, Mr. Paul Oehser, Mrs. Margaret Blaker, Dr. Harvey E. Tobie, Miss Priscilla Knuth, Mr. Bernard DeVoto, Dr. A. P. Nasatir, Mr. Russell K. Grater, Mr. Glenn A. Thompson, Mr. Will G. Robinson, Mr. Leland D. Case, Mr. Charles H. P. Copeland, Mr. Charles Kelly, Mr. Perry W. Jenkins, Mrs. Ruth B. Shipley, Mr. Willis H. Young, Miss Margaret Herbert, Miss Dorothy C. Barck, Mrs. Edna Martin Parratt, Miss Frances M. Molera, Mr. Ray Kooyman, Mr. Herbert Fehmel, Miss Henrietta C. Mirell, Miss Vera Maroon, Mrs. F. J. Riera, Dr. Paul C. Phillips, Mr. David Williams, Mr. Mannel Hahn, Miss Gertrude Hassler, Mr. D. C. Ritter, Miss Josephine L. Harper, Mr. T. E. McQuown, Mr. Matthew D. Smith, Miss Lura S. Smith, Miss May Davis, Mr. James Calhoun, Mrs. Charles Thomas Pike, Mr. F. R. Bacon, Mrs. A. J. Sturzenegger, Mr. G. S. Rollins, Miss Caroline Wenzel, Mr. John James, Mrs. Helena B. Stites, Mr. Francis P. Farquhar, Mr. Stephen T. Riley, Mrs. Clyde Porter, Mr. John A. Gault, Mr. Leland J. Prater, Mr. Walter McCausland, Mr. Hartwell Bowsfield, Maj. Gen. William E. Bergin, Miss Jeanette M. Hitchcock, Miss Helen Payne, Mrs. Alene Snow White, Miss Ellen Shaffer, Mr. Andrew Rolle and all those institutional collaborators who to me are nameless, but without whose aid no book like this is ever written.

Special help, finally, has been given me by the New York Public Library, the New-York Historical Society, the California State Library, the California Historical Society, the National Park Service, the U. S. Forest Service, the Bureau of American Ethnology, the Smithsonian Institution, the Department of State, the Oregon Historical Society, the Western Reserve Historical Society, the Provincial Library of Manitoba, the New York Botanical Garden, the Stanford University Library, the Peabody Museum, the Salt Lake City Free Public Library, and the Massachusetts Historical Society.

NOTES

PREFACE

Jedediah Smith's geographical discoveries were first shown on a map by the French cartographer A. H. Brué, *Nouvelle Carte de l'Amerique Septentrionale* (Paris, 1833). Brué's source was literary, an 1828 French translation of Jedediah's letter of July 12, 1827, to General Clark, and his map in consequence has some curious features. Apparently Jedediah's own map was retained by William H. Ashley, who in 1835 furnished from it some notes which were used by Albert Gallatin for his map published next year in Vol. II of the American Antiquarian Society's *Transactions*. Much more important is David Burr's *Map of the United States of North America with some parts of the Adjacent Countries* ("entered according to the Act of Congress July 10th 1839"), which Burr also published in his *American Atlas* of 1839. Burr was Geographer to the House of Representatives from 1832 and doubtless met Ashley while the general was the member from Missouri, 1831-37. Evidently Burr was given access by Ashley to Jedediah's MS. map, and his conception of the Far West must have come directly from Jedediah's map. Since that map has now disappeared, the Burr map is the closest existing approximation of the original. Jedediah's map seems also to have influenced Charles Wilkes's 1845 map of California—but Wilkes, I judge, gained his information from another Jedediah Smith map which remained in Oregon.

Let me spell out my reference to a second lost map by Jedediah. George Gibbs, who visited the Trinity-Klamath country in September 1851 as a member of Col. Redick M'Kee's party, referred with evident knowledge to a "manuscript map of California and Oregon by Jedediah S. Smith, which was, till lately, the best source of information as to this part of the country." Gibbs said that this map had been "recently purchased in Oregon by the Joint Commission of Army and Navy Officers, and is probably now in Washington." (See his journal in H. R. Schoolcraft, *Information . . . [on] the Indian Tribes*, Philadelphia, 1853, vol. III, p. 136.) I have established that the Commission to which Gibbs referred was a Joint Commission of Navy and Engineer Officers sent out to examine the Pacific Coast in 1850. A search in the National Archives disclosed a file of correspondence from the Army and Navy officers who comprised the commission, but no reference to the purchase of Jedediah Smith's map; nor could the map itself be found. Inquiry at the Division of Maps in the Library of Congress failed to turn it up there, either. So various are the Federal archives in Washington, however, that I should not be surprised if the map is finally found. It seems evident to me that this map was prepared by Jedediah Smith while a guest at Fort Vancouver, and that it remained in Oregon until its purchase by the U. S. officers.

Chapter 1. YOUNG MAN OF ENTERPRISE

1. This famous want ad ran in the *Missouri Gazette,* Feb. 13-March 6, 1822; in the *Missouri Republican,* successor to the *Gazette,* March 20-27, 1822; and in the *St. Louis Enquirer,* Feb. 26-March 23, 1822.

2. My account of St. Louis in 1822 is based primarily on John F. Darby, *Personal Recollections* (St. Louis, 1880); Frederic L. Billon, *Annals of St. Louis in its Territorial Days from 1804 to 1821* (St. Louis, 1888); Richard Edwards and M. Hopewell, *Edwards's Great West* (St. Louis, 1860)—this work the more important for including a reprint of John A. Paxton's *St. Louis Directory and Register* of 1821; and on the contemporary St. Louis newspapers.

3. Maurice S. Sullivan, ed., *The Travels of Jedediah Smith* (Santa Ana, 1934), p. 1. This book, containing the surviving portions of Jedediah Smith's journals, is hereafter cited as *Travels.* Jedediah's summary narrative of his experiences of 1822, which I call his "journal," was probably written in the winter of 1830-1831.

4. Loyd Haberly, *Pursuit of the Horizon, A Life of George Catlin* (New York, 1948), pp. 1-12.

5. Information about Jedediah Smith's maternal ancestry is derived from Benjamin Dwight, *The History of the Descendants of Elder John Strong, of Northampton, Mass.* (Albany, 1871), especially pp. 19, 769-772, 858, 892-893. Some revision and extension of this information is published by G. W. Beattie in *Annual Pubs. of the Hist. Soc. of Southern Calif.,* 1926, vol. XIII, part III, pp. 311-314. The genealogical line of the senior Jedediah Smith has been less satisfactorily worked out. The dates of birth of Jedediah and Sally Strong Smith as stated rest on information furnished to me by Miss May Davis of Mt. Pleasant, Iowa,

who is also my authority for the date of the former's death (Dec. 5, 1849—place not established). The exact date of Sally's death is not known, but the letters in my Appendix show that it was between Feb. 16 and April 3, 1830.

Jedediah Smith had not married Sally Strong at the time of the First Census of 1790 and consequently is not listed by name as the head of a household in that census. The original census returns in the National Archives locate the family as follows during Jedediah S. Smith's lifetime: 1800: New York, vol. 5, Chenango County, Jerico Township, p. 758. 1810: New York, vol. 1, Chenango County, Jerico Township, p. 1051. 1820: Ohio, vol. 15, Richland County, Green Township, folio 193. 1830: Ohio, vol. 2, Ashtabula County, Kingsville Township, folio 123. Presumptive evidence that Jedediah was still living in his father's home at the time of the 1820 census is that the males in the household included one aged between sixteen and twenty-five.

A page from a family Bible into which a birth record for the Smith children was copied sometime after 1834 is reproduced in *Travels*, p. 62; the Bible itself is now owned by Mrs. A. J. Sturzenegger of Los Angeles. A similar Bible record is owned by Miss Davis, and in both, Jedediah Strong Smith's birth date is given as Jan. 6, 1799; evidently the date June 24, 1798, given in the anonymous eulogy "Jedediah Strong Smith" (*Illinois Monthly Magazine,* June 1832, pp. 393-398) is mistaken.

Some inferences in my text as to the migrations of the Smith family are based on later census returns in the National Archives which locate Jedediah's brothers, and on a special census of 1852 for California, a copy of which is in the California State Library: 1850: California, vol. 2, Sacramento City, p. 353. 1850: Illinois, vol. 1, Bond County, p. 136. 1860: Iowa, vol. 13, Mahaska County, Oskaloosa Township, p. 83. 1852: California Census, vol. 5, Sacramento, p. 88. James H. Smith, *History of Chenango and Madison Counties* (Syracuse, 1880), p. 165, mentions the elder Jedediah Smith's coming to Jericho with Cyrus Strong "as early as 1795," and the dubious circumstance of his departure. H. S. Knapp, *A History of . . . Ashland County* (Philadelphia, 1863), p. 356, lists Smith as a property holder in Green Township in 1817. A brief account of the Simons family with which the Smiths intermarried is provided by Maurice Sullivan, *Jedediah Smith, Trader and Trailbreaker* (New York, 1936), pp. 6-7.

6. For lack of a firsthand description of Jedediah, some of these details are inferred from the physical appearance of his brothers; his

vision of the West is quoted by an acquaintance who talked to him in March 1831, and wrote the eulogy cited in the previous note, hereafter cited as *Eulogy*, which is reprinted in Edwin L. Sabin, *Kit Carson Days* (New York, 1935), pp. 821-826.

7. The physical description of Ashley is drawn in part from Darby, pp. 220-221, but mostly from Frederic Billon's account of him, quoted in J. T. Scharf, *History of Saint Louis City and County* (Philadelphia, 1883), pp. 196-197. Billon's is a remarkably accurate picture of Ashley's early career in Missouri, very few details at odds with the extant documentary evidence. Statements that Ashley did not come to Missouri till 1808 are incorrect, as is shown by a document of 1805 published in C. E. Carter, ed., *The Territorial Papers of the United States* (Washington, 1948), vol. XIII, p. 140. Many later references to Ashley's career I will not now cite, as I have in preparation a volume of Ashley Papers. For Ashley's having been a witness of Andrew Henry's marriage in 1805, see Walter B. Douglas' notes to Thomas James, *Three Years Among the Indians and Mexicans* (St. Louis, 1916), p. 265.

8. A brief sketch of Henry by Walter B. Douglas is appended to *Three Years*, as cited in Note 7, pp. 265-266. See also Hiram M. Chittenden, *The American Fur Trade of the Far West* (New York, 1936), vol. I, p. 250, and Joshua Pilcher's statement of Dec. 1, 1831, printed in 22nd Cong., 1st Session, *Senate Document 90* (Serial 213), p. 12.

9. For the Missouri Fur Company of this period see Chittenden, vol. I, p. 147, and what is more illuminating, the MS. letterbook of Thomas Hempstead, June 27, 1821-Feb. 12, 1823, in the Coe Collection at Yale. The latter is full of sidelights on the projected operations of the French Company as well as their own, and shows that Ashley and Henry began laying out goods for their expedition as early as Sept. 1821. The French Fur Company, as it is called in this book, and as it was known to rivals and friends during the early 1820s, had various legal names which changed as partners died or were added; it has often been confused in the literature with another "French" outfit organized in 1829 by Papin, Chenie, the Cerrés and others, though by that time the original French Fur Company had become the Western Department of the American Fur Company. The Hempstead letterbook shows that in the summer of 1821 the French Company hoped to have their upriver expedition led by Wilson Price Hunt of Astorian fame. They were slow about their preparations, and it was not until July 19, 1822, that they obtained from William Clark a license to trade with the "Sioux, Poncas, Chyans, Ricaras, Mandans on the Missouri

above the Council Bluffs." This license was dated two days after the one issued to Wm. P. Tilton & S. S. Dudley (the original American partners of the Columbia Fur Company), who were authorized to trade with the Sioux on the St. Peters, and with the Mandans, Minnetarees and Crows "at their village." (Licenses to trade with the Indians, 18th Cong., 1st Sess., *House Document* 7 [Serial 93].) The guiding genius of the Columbia Fur Company was Kenneth McKenzie; for him and the company's formative period see Annie Heloise Abel, ed., *Chardon's Journal at Fort Clark, 1834-1839* (Pierre, 1932), pp. 331-338.

10. Becknell's journal is printed in *Missouri Intelligencer*, April 22, 1823, and reprinted in A. B. Hulbert, ed., *Southwest on the Turquoise Trail* (Denver, 1933), pp. 56-68.

11. Thomas Hempstead, MS. Letterbook, Coe Collection, Yale University.

12. *St. Louis Enquirer*, April 13, 1822. The texts of this and many other newspaper stories hereafter cited are conveniently reprinted in Donald McKay Frost, *Notes on General Ashley, the Overland Trail, and South Pass* (Worcester, 1945), but I have drawn on original files, especially those of the Library of Congress.

13. Hempstead to Pilcher, May 5, 1822, in Hempstead Letterbook, Coe Collection, Yale.

14. These details from *Travels*, p. 1. Moore in 1821 was listed by Paxton's *St. Louis Directory* as deputy clerk of the Circuit Court at St. Louis, and that is about all that is known of him.

15. Walter Blair and Franklin J. Meine, *Mike Fink, King of Mississippi Keelboatmen* (New York, 1933), pp. 43, 215.

16. Jedediah's own account of the upriver voyage being brief and reminiscent, I have borrowed largely from the account of Paul Wilhelm, Duke of Württemberg, who went up the Missouri in 1823 with a French Fur Company keelboat and kept a graphic diary of the experience. From the Stuttgart edition of 1835 this work was translated by William G. Bek in *South Dakota Hist. Colls.*, 1938, vol. XIX, as "First Journey to North America in the Years 1822 to 1824," and I use this translation.

17. *Missouri Intelligencer*, Jan. 22, 1824.

18. *Travels*, pp. 1-2.

19. A brilliant account of the early exploration of the Missouri River is Bernard DeVoto, *The Course of Empire* (Boston, 1952). The more significant documents are printed in another notable book, A. P. Nasatir, *Before Lewis and Clark* (St. Louis, 1952).

20. Jedediah's journal says "about the 4th of June," but the *St. Louis*

Enquirer of June 3 had news of the misfortune "by a gentleman who has just arrived."

21. *Travels,* p. 2.

22. The precise date Cedar Fort or Fort Recovery was established is not known. The latter name supposedly originated in the circumstance that the Missouri Fur Company with this fort regained ground it had lost on the upper Missouri during the War of 1812. There is some reason to believe that the company did not re-establish itself here till 1822, but Joshua Pilcher testified in 1824 that in April 1820 his Company had two trading houses, "one above, and the other a little below, the Big Bend of Missouri." Pilcher, "Answers to Questions," 18th Cong., 1st Sess., *Senate Document 56* (Serial 91), p. 13.

Much more than the date of its establishment has troubled the history of Fort Kiowa. Fort Lookout, Fort Kiowa, and Brazeau's Fort are one and the same. It would appear that Joseph Brazeau was chosen to head the French Company's upriver movement when negotiations with Wilson Price Hunt fell through, and it would also appear that he had the *dit* name "Cayewa," "Keiwars" or "Keewaws," as variously spelled. According to Scharf, pp. 168-169, two brothers, Joseph and Louis Brazeau, came to St. Louis from Kaskaskia prior to 1782; the former died in 1816, aged seventy-four. The latter, "Old Cayewa," had a large family which included three sons, Louis, Jr., Joseph, Jr., and Auguste. The son Joseph was presumably named "Young Cayewa." He was licensed to trade on the Missouri as early as 1811, and on June 23, 1814, was licensed to trade "with the Teton & Yankton Sieux at Cedar Island on the Missouri." Next year he was again licensed to trade "with the Mahas Panis, Ricaras, Yankton & Teton Sieux." (See T. M. Marshall, ed., *The Life and Papers of Frederick Bates* [St. Louis, 1925], vol. II, p. 281; Carter, vol. XV, p. 85; *American State Papers, Indian Affairs,* vol. 2, pp. 201-203; Edgar Wesley, ed., "Diary of James Kennerly," *Mo. Hist. Soc. Colls.,* vol. VI, pp. 71-72.) As he founded Fort Lookout for the French Company, apparently in the fall of 1822, it came to be generally known by his own and his *dit* name; both persisted for a year after his final return to St. Louis. The simultaneous use of these names is shown by a letter written by either Maj. Daniel Ketchum or Maj. A. R. Woolley, dated "Fort Brazeau or Lookout," July 22, 1823, printed in Washington, D. C., *National Intelligencer,* Sept. 18, 1823. "Fort Kiowa" and "Fort Lookout," alternatively used, were names employed by the Atkinson-O'Fallon expedition of 1825, for which see Note 30, Chapter 8.

A degree of confusion concerning the two forts, and especially the identity of what Ashley in a letter of July 19, 1823, called "Fort Brassaux," has been occasioned by a phrase in that letter; Ashley said that Leavenworth "will pass this place today with his command," which has been taken as proof either that Fort Brassaux was identical with Fort Recovery or that Fort Brassaux was a separate establishment intermediate between Recovery and Kiowa; all this signifies, however, is that Ashley expected Leavenworth to continue on up the river July 19 instead of stopping at Fort Recovery as he actually did. The probable location of the two forts, on the basis of historical and archeological research, is discussed by Merrill J. Mattes in *South Dakota Hist. Colls.*, 1949, vol. XXIV, pp. 517-541. There are clear references to these posts in the travel narratives of Prince Paul in 1823 and of Maximilian, Prince of Wied-Neuwied, in 1833.

Brazeau came down the river for the last time in 1824 and died in St. Louis June 12, 1825. The St. Louis *Missouri Advocate,* June 17, 1825, noted that he had been "for many years past, an active and enterprising trader on the Upper Missouri," and that he had left "an amiable wife and several children"; he died after a short but severe indisposition.

23. This description, from the "Journal of the Atkinson-O'Fallon Expedition," *North Dakota Historical Quarterly,* Oct. 1929, vol. IV, pp. 5-56, more especially applies to Fort Kiowa, but all the forts were built to the same pattern.

24. See Ashley's letters of June 4, 1823, cited in Note 18, Chapter 2, and Pilcher to Leavenworth, Dec. 14, 1823, *St. Louis Enquirer,* Dec. 20, 1823

25. Jedediah's laconic account of the Rees and their behavior on the arrival of white traders I have supplemented from H. M. Brackenridge, *Journal of a Voyage up the River Missouri* (Thwaites edition, Cleveland, 1904), pp. 111-132; and from John Bradbury, *Travels in the Interior of North America* (Thwaites edition, Cleveland, 1904), pp. 131-132.

26. See "Journal of the Atkinson-O'Fallon Expedition," p. 41.

27. Among the stragglers picked up was Daniel T. Potts, whose letters dated July 16, 1826, and July 8, 1827, have considerably enlarged our knowledge of mountain history between 1822 and 1827. Originally printed in the *Philadelphia Gazette & Daily Advertiser,* Nov. 14, 1826, and Sept. 27 and Oct. 19, 1827, they have been reprinted with valuable notes by Donald McKay Frost in *Notes on General Ashley,* and by Charles L. Camp in "The D. T. P. Letters," *Essays for Henry R. Wagner* (San Francisco, 1947).

28. Henry did not reach the Yellowstone without some added trials. Joshua Pilcher in 1824 ("Answers," p. 15) said that the Assiniboines committed a robbery on him in August 1822 a little above the Mandan Villages. "Major Henry was on board of his boat, and had a party of men going by land with some forty or fifty horses; they met a large party of those Indians, who, by their address, got possession of the horses and rode them off." The list of claims cited in Note 1, Chapter 4, includes a claim for $1,840.50, representing the value of horses and merchandise lost in this affair.

Chapter 2. THE HUNTERS AND THE HUNTED

1. *Travels,* p. 8.

2. There are two accounts of Weber. One, which appears to have been published about 1906 in the Jackson (Iowa) *Sentinel* or the *Bellevue Leader,* was apparently written by the Captain's son, William A.; this has been reprinted in Camp, "The D. T. P. Letters," pp. 24-25, and somewhat less accurately in James W. Ellis, *History of Jackson County, Iowa* (Chicago, 1910), vol. I, pp. 370-371. A second account, by an old acquaintance of the Captain, J. C. Hughey of Bellevue, Iowa, was printed in *Salt Lake Tribune,* July 4, 1897, p. 31. In the main, the two accounts corroborate each other. Both overstate Weber's importance through describing him as a full partner of Ashley & Henry; both likewise are erroneous in their dates. Weber's presence at Ste. Genevieve as early as July 29, 1807, is shown by Carter, vol. XIV, p. 178; and he was at Mine à Breton in September 1814 (*Life and Papers of Frederick Bates,* vol. II, pp. 278-279).

3. This account of beaver trapping is drawn from a number of sources, but see especially Bernard DeVoto, *Across the Wide Missouri* (Boston, 1947), pp. 156-158; Burton Harris, *John Colter, His Years in the Rockies* (New York, 1952), pp. 45-49; Frances Fuller Victor, *River of the West* (Hartford, 1870), pp. 64-69; Chittenden, vol. II, pp. 809-811.

4. *Travels,* pp. 8-9.

5. How soon and how far up the Missouri the revitalized Missouri Fur Company got after 1820 is too complicated a question for discussion in a note; there are reports of a harvest in furs from the Yellowstone as early as 1822, but the weight of evidence goes to show that Fort Benton was not established on the Big Horn until the fall

of 1822; and Pilcher ("Answers," p. 13) says, "In September, 1822, I visited the Ricaras villages myself, for the first time. I was going to the Mandans and Minnetarees, for the purpose of establishing trading houses for these Indians." At that time he established Fort Vanderburgh at the Mandan towns, and Immell and Jones pushed on from that base to the Yellowstone.

6. *Travels*, pp. 9-10. Potts has a parallel account of this winter camp.

7. Victor, p. 79; *Eulogy;* William Waldo, "Recollections of a Septuagenarian," *Glimpses of the Past,* April-June, 1938, vol. V, p. 87.

8. Blair and Meine, pp. 177-239. To this lively and informative account of Mike Fink I am much indebted, but I give greater weight than they to "Mike Fink, The Last of the Boatmen," *Western Monthly Review,* July, 1829, pp. 15-19, an account which checks up so well that I refer to it when speaking of "the chronicle" of Fink's life.

9. Potts, letter of July 16, 1826.

10. See the sources cited in Note 8, Chapter 3.

11. The account first quoted is that of the *Missouri Republican,* July 9, 1823; the other is cited in Note 8 above.

12. A. P. Nasatir, ed., "The International Significance of the Jones and Immell Massacre and of the Aricara Outbreak in 1823," *Pacific Northwest Quarterly,* Jan., 1939, vol. XXX, pp. 85-86. Mike Fink's grave at the mouth of the Yellowstone is mentioned in A. H. Redfield to A. M. Robinson, Sept. 1, 1858, 35th Congress, 2nd Sess., *Senate Executive Document 1,* (Serial 974), p. 440.

13. From the chronicle cited in Note 8.

14. *Missouri Republican,* March 12, 1823.

15. *Ibid.,* Jan. 22-March 5, 1823; the advertisement also appeared in the *Enquirer* over this time. Ashley evidently overtook his boat at St. Charles or higher up, for a new license to trade with the "Ricaras, Score, Mandans, Milanaua, Black Foot & crow Tribes, within & West of the Rocky Mountains," which was issued by General Clark to "Ashley & Henry" is dated March 12, 1823. The license was for five years, and the amount of capital employed was stated to be $40,000. (National Archives, Office of Indian Affairs, St. Louis Superintendency, Abstract of Licenses Granted to Trade with the Indians.)

16. Charles L. Camp, ed., *James Clyman, American Frontiersman, 1792-1881* (San Francisco, 1928), pp. 13-14.

17. See Ashley's letters cited in the next note, as also Clyman, p. 15; *Missouri Republican,* July 9, 1823; *Missouri Intelligencer,* July 8, 1823;

St. Louis Enquirer, July 12, 1823, Feb. 9, 1824; *National Intelligencer,* Sept. 3, 1823; Pilcher, "Answers," p. 13. *Washington* (D. C.) *Gazette,* Sept. 13, 1824.

18. This information and much of what follows is based on three letters written by Ashley immediately after his defeat, two dated June 4, the other June 7, 1823; they are nearly the same, but each contains minor details not in the others. The first is Ashley's official communication to Leavenworth and O'Fallon; a contemporary copy sent to Washington by Gen. Clark on July 4, 1823, is in National Archives, War Dept., Office of Secretary, Letters Received, C-77 (17), 1823. This was printed in the *St. Louis Enquirer,* July 12, 1823. The second letter was published in the *Missouri Republican,* July 9, 1823, while the third appeared in the *Missouri Intelligencer,* July 8, 1823. The other principal sources are a letter by an unidentified member of Ashley's party dated "Fort Kiowa, ten miles below the Big Bend," June 17, 1823, in *National Intelligencer,* Sept. 3, 1823; a letter by Hugh Glass to the parents of John S. Gardner, written immediately after the battle (original in South Dakota Historical Society; photographically reproduced in John G. Neihardt, *The Splendid Wayfaring* [New York, 1920]); the Clyman narrative, pp. 15-19; and incidental information in the documents pertaining to the subsequent Leavenworth campaign, for which see Note 1, Chapter 3.

19. Ashley implies that he got all the horses he asked for, from forty to fifty, but the Fort Kiowa letter referred to in Note 18 says, "We purchased about 19 horses," which agrees substantially with Clyman's "twenty horses."

20. Although Jedediah's command of the shore party is generally stated as an established fact, it is an inference from the prominence to which he attained immediately after. It is nevertheless a fair inference in view of his newly acquired familiarity with the country, and the role in which he had come down the river from Fort Henry.

21. *Eulogy;* and see also Waldo, p. 82.

22. Ashley's casualties in the Ree defeat have been consistently misstated, even in the sources. In his two letters of June 4 he listed twelve men dead and eleven wounded, but included among the wounded "Reed Gibson, (since dead)." He added that another of the wounded died later, but did not give the man's name. In his letter of June 7 he gave the same list of the dead, and added the name of one James Davis to the list of the wounded. This made fourteen killed, ten wounded. Benjamin O'Fallon, writing Gen. Clark from Fort

Atkinson July 3, mentioned that "Another of Gen. Ashley's wounded men is dead, making 15 men killed, by the A'Rickarees."

23. This detail comes from Hugh Glass's letter cited in Note 18; the prayer has been called the first recorded act of public worship in South Dakota, and it is commemorated by a highly imaginative mural in the South Dakota State Capitol.

24. Waldo, p. 83, is the sole source for this fact.

25. Ashley's letter of June 7 to the *Missouri Intelligencer* was written after the change of camp and is dated "opposite the mouth of the Shegan River"; his letters of June 4 were written "25 miles below the Aurickaree Towns," seventy-five miles higher up the Missouri.

Chapter 3. THE MISSOURI LEGION

1. My account of the campaign against the Arikaras is primarily based on the following sources: (1) 18th Congress, 1st Sess., *Senate Document 1* (Serial 89), Appendix L, pp. 55-108, the documents accompanying the report of the Secretary of War, Nov. 29, 1823. Some but not all of these documents were reprinted in *South Dakota Hist. Colls.*, 1902, vol. I. (2) Leavenworth's final report, dated Fort Atkinson, Oct. 20, 1823; this was apparently received too late for inclusion in *Senate Document 1*, but was printed in *Missouri Intelligencer*, Dec. 2-9, 1823, and again in *South Dakota Hist. Colls.* as above cited. Neither printing is an entirely accurate transcription, and I have used the original MS. in the National Archives, War Department, Adjutant General's Office, Letters Received, 100-L-1823. (3) Benjamin O'Fallon's MS Letterbook, 1823-1829, an important source placed at my disposal by Dr. Charles L. Camp; some of the letters it contains are in the government archives, but others exist only as found in the letterbook. (4) Joshua Pilcher's letters to Leavenworth and O'Fallon, dated Fort Recovery, Aug. 26 and 25, 1823, printed in *Missouri Republican*, Oct. 15, 1823; and his letter to Leavenworth dated St. Louis, Dec. 14, 1823, printed in *St. Louis Enquirer*, Dec. 14, 1823. (5) The Clyman narrative.

June 18 is given as the date of arrival of Ashley's boat in Leavenworth's final report, and in O'Fallon to Gen. Clark, June 23, 1823, (O'Fallon Letterbook, p. 18). Leavenworth's decision to move to Ashley's relief was made the same day. Ashley's letter cited in Note 13 indicates his boat came down in charge of a Mr. Culver.

2. Although it no doubt expressed his feelings, the cynical reflection is not Pilcher's but Angus McDonald's, in a letter to the *Washington Gazette,* Sept. 13, 1824.

3. 18th Cong., 1st Sess., *Senate Document 56* (Serial 91), Joshua Pilcher's "Answers to Questions," pp. 13-14.

4. All this is set forth in O'Fallon to Clark, Jan. 14, 1824, O'Fallon Letterbook, pp. 28-44; the official copy is in National Archives, War Department, Office of Secretary, Letters Received, C-37 (17) 1824.

5. O'Fallon Letterbook, pp. 12-14, 18. O'Fallon dates this address June 19. The forty-three men included five wounded who were "now in the hospital" when O'Fallon wrote Clark on June 23.

6. O'Fallon Letterbook, pp. 16-17; a copy O'Fallon sent Clark is in National Archives, War Department, Office of Secretary, Letters Received, C-77 (17) 1823.

7. Leavenworth's final report. Oct. 20, 1823.

8. O'Fallon to Clark, July 3, 1823 (National Archives, War Department, Office of Secretary, Letters Received, C-77 (17) 1823); William Gordon to Joshua Pilcher, *Senate Document 1* (Serial 89) pp. 69-72; Nasatir, "The International Significance of the Jones and Immell Massacre," p. 85. The names of those lost come from the Smith, Jackson & Sublette casualty list; see p. 345.

As much is said hereafter of the casualty lists of the fur trade, these may be described now. In the fall of 1831 the President called on the Indian agents and superintendents for certain data about the fur trade, to include the number and names of the American citizens who had been killed or robbed while engaged in the fur trade or Santa Fe trade since 1815. John Dougherty compiled such a list on Oct. 24, 1831, and Joshua Pilcher another on Nov. 20, 1831. From these lists William Clark compiled another, adding such data as his office files provided, which included information contained in the Smith, Jackson & Sublette letter of [Dec.] 24, 1829. These three lists Clark sent to Washington, from which a fourth, strictly chronological, list was compiled in the Office of Indian Affairs. The originals of these four lists are now in National Archives, Office of Indian Affairs, St. Louis Superintendency files, while copies of the first three are in the letterbooks of the St. Louis Superintendency in the Kansas State Historical Society, vol. VI, pp. 341-346, 378-381, 383-386. The copy compiled in Washington, with its transcription errors and errors of organization, was published in 22nd Cong., 1st Sess., *Senate Document 90* (Serial 213), pp. 81-86.

9. Very little is known about these deserters. Pilcher's letter of

July 23, 1823, to O'Fallon says that the Immell-Jones party originally consisted of forty-three men and by the spring of 1823 was reduced to thirty, "a part of the men having deserted their wintering post at the Big Horn." (18th Cong., 1st Sess., *Senate Document 1* [Serial 89], pp. 69-72.) Dougherty's casualty list of 1831 recalled the name of only one of four who were killed by Blackfeet, "on the Musselshell," one Santy—spelled by Pilcher *Santa;* Pilcher agrees that the men were lost on the "Muscleshell."

10. I use "Blackfeet" in the sense the mountain men used it, as a generic name for three cognate tribes, the Siksika or Blackfeet proper, the Bloods and the Piegans. It was the two latter tribes American trappers saw chiefly, and of these the Bloods were by far the most bloodthirsty; Piegans could be troublesome, but at times they lived in amity with surrounding tribes. A fourth tribe, the Atsina or Gros Ventres of the Prairies, lived among the Blackfeet and matched them in savagery, but they were a detached branch of the Arapaho, and every few years moved down the Plains to visit them on the Arkansas. The term "Gros Ventres" was also applied to the Hidatsa or Minnetarees, but to avoid confusion, I have called the latter people Minnetarees in this book, a name frequently used by the mountain men of this period.

11. Blackfoot reports of the Immell-Jones massacre, relayed through British sources, have done much to clarify the confused reports of the American survivors; see Dr. Nasatir's article cited in Note 12, Chapter 2. For the contemporary American reports, see Pilcher to O'Fallon, July 23, 1823 (Note 9 above); William Gordon to Sec. of War, Oct. 3, 1831 (22nd Cong., 1st Sess., *Senate Document 90* (Serial 213), pp. 26-27; *Missouri Republican,* July 16, 1823; *Missouri Intelligencer,* Sept. 30, 1823. Pilcher's casualty list of 1831 lists the dead as Immell, Jones, P. Bergy (or Bry), Plaude, Leblac, Lemere and two others, "names not recollected." A "List of Claimants" for losses to Indians in National Archives, Office of Indian Affairs, St. Louis Superintendency, gives the total loss as $13,445. The H. B. Company offered to restore the Immell-Jones furs which its factor on the Saskatchewan had traded from the Blackfeet, but the records do not show whether this restitution was finally made.

12. Atkinson to Gaines, St. Louis, Aug. 15, 1823, supplies most of this information, obtained verbally from (Samuel M.) Smith, who had just reached St. Louis from Ashley's camp (*Senate Document 1,* p. 83). It has been supposed that Henry might have joined Ashley before the end of June, because Maj. Wm. S. Foster wrote Atkinson on

July 8 concerning receipt of a note from Leavenworth dated July 4 which was carried down by two men who "were from Major Henry, and informed that Gen. Ashley was upon an Island, about one hundred miles below the Ricaras Villages" (*ibid.*, p. 62). This, however, was not information; Ashley had been on this island since June 7, and it is likely the men were stragglers from his camp rather than a part of Henry's force.

13. Ashley to Col. John O'Fallon, Fort Brassaux, July 19, 1823, John O'Fallon Collection, Missouri Historical Society. An extract from this letter, which historians have mistakenly supposed to be addressed to John's brother, Benjamin, is printed in *Senate Document 1*, p. 84; the full text is much more illuminating, and identifies the Smith who carried the letter down as one Samuel M. rather than Jedediah as has been commonly believed.

14. Leavenworth to O'Fallon, July 21, 1823, *Senate Document 1*, pp. 68-69.

15. Evidently at the mouth of the Teton. Leavenworth's final report, Oct. 20, 1823.

16. This detail from Clyman, p. 20. The narrative following is chiefly based on Leavenworth's final report, but a number of details are derived from Clyman and from Pilcher's letters cited in Note 1.

17. Both Clyman and Leavenworth describe this spectacle.

18. Pilcher to O'Fallon, Aug. 25, 1823, *Missouri Republican*, Oct. 15, 1823.

19. Reuben Holmes, "The Five Scalps," *Glimpses of the Past*, Jan.-March, 1938, vol. V, pp. 12-18. This striking account of Rose was first published as "Sketch of the Life of 'Chee-ho-carte,' or The Five Scalps," in the *St. Louis Beacon*, Dec. 1, 4, 8 and 15, 1829.

20. There was a long and acrimonious dispute over the number of Ree casualties, and at this distance it is impossible to establish the facts.

21. Pilcher scorned the accusation at the time, but the Ree villages actually had been fired by Angus McDonald and William Gordon of his company. McDonald vigorously defended his action in a letter to the *Washington Gazette*, Sept. 13, 1824.

Chapter 4. SOUTH PASS

1. National Archives, Office of Indian Affairs, St. Louis Superintendency, list of claims certified by Gen. Clark Jan. 12, 1826, for the period 1808-1823. Claim 15 is that of "Henry & Ashley."

2. Apparently it was not until May 1823 that the Columbia Fur Company reached the Mandan Villages from the east, and not until November that William P. Tilton completed the fort; it was garrisoned the first winter by only seven men. See Maximilian, Prince of Wied-Neuwied, *Travels in the Interior of North America* (Thwaites ed., Cleveland, 1905), vol. II, pp. 223-224. Leavenworth's final report of Oct. 20, 1823, says with regard to the Missouri Fur Company, "I have understood that it was not intended after the defeat of . . . Immel & Jones was known, to send the boats of the Missouri Fur Company above their Fort Recovery." As Maximilian notes, the M. F. Company's Fort Vanderburgh was abandoned in the wake of the Immell-Jones massacre. Vanderburgh, Keemle, and Gordon may have descended the river at the same time Henry did; if not then, soon after.

3. Ashley's letters of June 4 had announced his intention of storing his goods "at the first fort below," and the anonymous writer of the Fort Kiowa letter (see Note 18, Chapter 2) tells us that he was placed in charge of these stores. This detail with regard to the whereabouts of Ashley's goods is important, for it supports Clyman's story that Henry accompanied Ashley down to Kiowa. Disregarding questions of transport and supply, historians have assumed that after the Arikara campaign Henry said good-by to Ashley on the Grand River and with no more ado set out for the Yellowstone.

4. In Pilcher's letter to O'Fallon dated Fort Recovery, Aug. 25, he mentions that he returned to his fort five days before; this would have been a maximum effort, and Ashley must have proceeded more slowly. Prince Paul (see Note 16, Chapter 1), who had come up the Missouri in a keelboat, made a farther journey by horseback from Fort Atkinson to Fort Recovery, arriving Aug. 23. The factor at Fort Kiowa learned of his presence in the country and sent Charbonneau down with an invitation to pay the upper fort a visit, and Prince Paul did so on Aug. 26-27. While ascending the river, the Prince had had a great deal to say about news of Ashley's defeat and the events which followed; had Ashley arrived at the fort before he himself left, he most certainly would have noted the circumstance in his journal. It can therefore reasonably be concluded that Ashley and Henry did not reach Kiowa before the afternoon of Aug. 27, and the date of the Mandan attack on Henry given in Leavenworth's letter on p. 103 is either totally in error or a mistake for Sept. 20.

5. All this information from Prince Paul.

6. Clyman, p. 22.

7. Who was in charge of the fort is obscure, possibly J. P. Ca-

banné. Prince Paul on Aug. 26 spoke of the factor as a "native Frenchman," which would scarcely describe Brazeau; and in fact Brazeau was down the river at about this time—in the Chouteau-Papin Collection, Missouri Historical Society, is a letter he wrote B. Berthold dated River of Mahas, Sept. 17, 1823. It may have been two weeks later that he got back to his fort. See also 19th Cong., 1st Sess., *Senate Document 71* (Serial 91).

8. An article by "Solitaire" (John S. Robb), "Major Fitzpatrick, The Discoverer of South Pass," in *St. Louis Weekly Reveille*, March 1, 1847, has an account of the journey west from Fort Kiowa written on the basis of information furnished by Charles Keemle. This gives the total of Jedediah's party as sixteen men. Clyman's figure of eleven, if correct, does not include Edward Rose or the French Fur Company's guide.

9. Clyman mentions all these men by name. A few years later both Branch and Stone were active in the fur trade of the Southwest, and Branch eventually settled in California. In the sometimes informative, sometimes wildly unreliable book by Frank T. Triplett, *Conquering the Wilderness* (St. Louis, 1883), pp. 386-387, Eddie is made to say that he was one of fourteen men who went to the Yellowstone after the Arikara fight, that his party trapped on the Yellowstone till winter, and then wintered with a Crow village. In the spring they made their way to the Pacific slope, and "when out of ammunition, and almost perishing with hunger, they met a party of trappers, belonging to the Hudson's Bay Company, and were by them taken to their post, on the Columbia River." This scarcely describes the experience of any of the parties, but it is possible Eddie switched to Jedediah's company at the winter camp on Wind River.

10. It has been conjectured that Clyman's White Clay Creek is Medicine Creek, but Clyman's description of the river now and later better fits the White River, and the waterless stretch he describes is hardly to be accounted for by the distance between the head of Medicine Creek and the White. I am inclined to think that the *jornada* Clyman describes was through country south of the White River, and that by taking it Jedediah by-passed almost entirely that portion of the South Dakota Badlands now set apart as a national monument. The badlands Clyman pictures lay farther west, beyond the South Fork of the Cheyenne.

11. Jedediah's trail through the southern reaches of the Black Hills cannot be identified in detail, but on the basis of a visit to the area in 1952 Dr. Charles L. Camp has expressed the opinion to me that Jede-

diah and Clyman entered the hills near Buffalo Gap and continued on across them by a nearly west course, the canyon in which they became entangled being either Hell Canyon or another farther west. Donald McKay Frost, p. 38, has theorized that Jedediah crossed the Black Hills much farther north, and that it was the Belle Fourche rather than the South Fork that he fell upon, west of the divide.

12. A discrepancy between Clyman and Solitaire will only be resolved when another account is found. Clyman was a participant, and I have chosen to follow him, but there is a distinct internal logic to the Solitaire narrative. To anticipate my text slightly, Solitaire says, "While on their route, upon one of the tributaries of Powder river, Mr. Smith was attacked and seriously injured by a grizzly bear, and the company were forced to leave him behind, in the care of two men, in a very hostile country. In a few days after their departure, Col. Keemle . . . at the head of another trapping party, fell in with Smith and his companions, and accompanied them to the village of a roving band of Cheyennes, where Fitzpatrick's company again joined Smith, and, taking him along, they proceeded to the Big Horn . . . where they wintered with the Crow nation." This might mean that the three men left with the worn-out horses were Jedediah and his two companions, and that this happened after, not before, the encounter with the grizzly.

13. George W. Ebberts, "A Trapper's Life in the Rocky Mountains & Oregon, from 1829 to 1839," MS. in the Bancroft Library. However, Waldo, p. 86, says that Jedediah "was twice nearly torn to pieces by a grizzly bear."

14. It has not been understood that Keemle and Gordon were following Jedediah's trail west from Fort Kiowa; historians have supposed, in fact, that these Missouri Fur Company men remained on the Yellowstone after the Immell-Jones massacre, though Gordon was an officer in the Missouri Legion. The implications of the Solitaire account quoted in Note 12 are backed up by a letter of Feb. 7, 1824, from Benjamin O'Fallon to James A. Gray, a relative of Keemle: ". . . he [Keemle] not only survived the defeat of [Immell and Jones] . . . but descended the river—Joined the military expedition against the A'rickaras, and when it returned, set out with another trading trapping and hunting company in a more southerly direction than formerly to avoid entirely those hostile Indians." (O'Fallon Letterbook, p. 54.)

15. West of the Black Hills, Jedediah probably went up Beaver Creek, a western affluent of the South Fork of the Cheyenne, and on to the Powder River at present Arvada by a route approximated today

by US 16; beyond this point, as far as the Big Horn, the route was roughly that of US 14, passing through Sheridan to the Tongue River at Ranchester, up over the Big Horns by Granite Pass, and so on to the Big Horn River near present Greybull. This river was then followed up to Dubois in the Wind River Mountains.

16. Robert Lowie, *The Crow Indians* (New York, 1935), p. 4.

17. Potts, letter of July 16, 1826. Potts has confused the historians by referring to the Big Horn Basin in summer; I would judge that he was one of the party who escorted Ashley and his furs to the Big Horn River in the summer of 1825, and that an unrelated observation from this year is mixed into his account of 1824.

18. 22nd Cong., 1st Sess., *Senate Document 90* (Serial 213), pp. 27-28.

19. Michael E. Immell so deposed to a St. Louis court June 25, 1821; *Bulletin of the Missouri Historical Society*, Jan., 1948, vol. IV, pp. 78-79. Immell mentioned that Crow beaver was not seen on the market from 1811 to 1819.

20. See Bernard DeVoto, *Across the Wide Missouri* (Boston, 1947), pp. 123-124; Lowie, pp. 47-61; 19th Cong., 1st Sess., *House Document 117* (Serial 136), p. 11; and a notably interesting contemporary account by Edwin Thompson Denig edited by John C. Ewers, "Of the Crow Nation," in Bureau of American Ethnology Bulletin 151, *Anthropological Papers, Numbers 33-42* (Washington, 1953).

21. Holmes, p. 48; Washington Irving, *The Adventures of Captain Bonneville*, Chapter XXII. Irving's book was first published at Philadelphia in 1837 under the title, *The Rocky Mountains;* so numerous are the editions that for general convenience I cite it by chapter rather than by page number.

22. Stolen from Irving, Chapter XXII; he in turn had this information from Robert Campbell, who picked it up in 1828-1829 or 1833-1834.

23. Solitaire, p. 284.

24. Clyman, p. 42.

25. Philip Ashton Rollins, *The Discovery of the Oregon Trail* (New York, 1935), prints Robert Stuart's journal and related documents. There has been much idle discussion about the discovery of South Pass, as though it were twenty feet rather than twenty miles wide. Throughout history the trail through the pass varied from one year to the next, as the availability of grass and absence of dust suited individual convenience. From the vicinity of Pacific Spring, Stuart veered to the south, hoping to keep out of the way of Crow

horse thieves, and he kept well south of the Sweetwater until he reached it near Devils Gate.

It has been suggested that Andrew Henry's men in 1810 may have learned of the existence of, and even traversed, South Pass, but little evidence and not even a reasoned argument has been set forth in support of this view. Lisa's men from 1807 were well acquainted with the Big Horn and its back country; the name of Wind River was applied before 1811; and where trappers may have gone in moving up the tributaries of the Big Horn is a question so full of possibility that I would hesitate to say that someone may not have got into South Pass from the east before Stuart reached it from the west in October 1812. But all this did not contribute to effective knowledge of South Pass, nor did the reports of Stuart's party printed in the St. Louis *Missouri Gazette*, May 15, 1813.

26. Clyman, p. 32, speaks of leaving the Sweetwater about the last of February, then contradictorily says the party crossed South Pass "in the month of January" and reached the Green River "on the 20th of February." His diary of Aug. 20, 1844, mentions encamping near the Three Crossings—"clos below another Kenyon through which the creek passes and near to whare we encamped in January 1824 at which time we under J. Smith and T Fitzpatrick first traversed the now well known South pass and camp[d] on green river on the 19th of march 11 days of which time we never saw a drop of water except what we thawed from snow." (p. 90.)

27. Frost, p. 40, has argued that Jedediah's party did not traverse South Pass proper (which on pp. 55-56 Mr. Frost admirably describes), but instead "passed along the southern slopes of the Antelope Hills," a route "necessitated by the biting winds which in winter sweep the treeless South Pass plateau." To support this view Mr. Frost offers only the dubious evidence of Clyman's remark that one fourth of the ground on the ridges south of the Sweetwater was entirely bare from the effects of strong west winds which carried the snow over to the east and south sides of the ridges, and he disregards Clyman's thrice-repeated statement that Jedediah Smith's party traversed South Pass. The Antelope Hills, further, do not extend so far west as to have provided a sheltered route into the open expanse of the pass; compare the map, *Part of Central Wyoming*, published by the U. S. Geological and Geographical Survey of the Territories on the basis of surveys of 1877; this is still the best map of South Pass and the contiguous area.

28. Frémont in 1843 mentioned that Spanish explorers had reached

the river about twenty-five years before and given it the name Rio Verde. Nothing more is known about a possible venture of 1818, but Daniel Potts, in his letter of July 16, 1826, speaks of the river "known to us by the name of Seet Kadu, and to Spaniard, by Green River." Ashley's diary of 1825 used the term Shetskedee until he fell in with trappers from Taos, when he was at once converted to the name Green River; see p. 169. The term "Green River" was likewise used by William Huddart and William Becknell, who trapped the river from New Mexico in the fall and winter of 1824-1825; see their published accounts in *Missouri Intelligencer,* April 19 and June 25, 1825. In view of the direction of the Spanish approach, I am convinced that the river was named for the reasons stated in my text; the name stuck because coincidentally the shales which compose its bed in the upper Green River Valley give the water there a pronouncedly green tint.

29. However, this is not the view of Burton Harris' *John Colter,* which sets forth an itinerary for Colter north of the Green-Gros Ventre divide.

30. Clyman, p. 33, says that "Capt Smith with seven men left us," but does not give the number of Fitzpatrick's party. I am disposed to accept Clyman's prior figure of eleven for the present total of the party, for if the four who soon after separated from Jedediah be subtracted, the number remaining is precisely the seven who turned up in Hudson's Bay Company territory late in the summer.

31. So says Irving, Chapter XXII. But Jim Beckwourth (see Note 19, Chapter 11), p. 38, declares that Ashley's party named Horse Creek "in honor of a wild horse we found on its banks" in 1825, and Ashley's diary for April 20, 1825, says, "one of the hunters brought in a horse which he found running at large on the river bottoms."

32. Clyman, pp. 34, 37.

Chapter 5. THE ADVENTURES OF HUGH GLASS—AND OTHERS

1. My account of Glass is based on four principal sources: (1) Charles L. Camp, ed., "The Chronicles of George C. Yount," *Calif. Hist. Quart.,* April 1923, vol. II, pp. 24-33. This narrative Yount claims to have had in part from Glass himself, in part from Glass's companion, Dutton. (2) "The Missouri Trapper," a narrative first published in the Philadelphia *Port-Folio,* March 1825, pp. 214-219, and reprinted in *Missouri Intelligencer,* June 18, 1825; the author of this sketch is

now established to have been Alphonso Wetmore. (3) Philip St. George Cooke, *Scenes and Adventures in the Army* (Philadelphia, 1857), pp. 137-152. I have discovered that this account of Glass was first published as "Some Incidents in the life of Hugh Glass, a hunter of the Missouri River," over the pseudonym "Borderer," in the *St. Louis Beacon,* Dec. 2-9, 1830. (4) Edmund Flagg, "History of a Western Trapper," Du Buque *Iowa News,* Nov. 2, 1839. Mr. Everett D. Graff has established that this previously unknown account was first published in the *Louisville Literary News-letter,* Sept. 7, 1839, Vol. I, pp. 326-327, under the title "Adventures at the headwaters of the Missouri." A short narrative, "Old Glass," published in the *St. Louis Evening Gazette,* March 17, 1840, has no value historically but does serve to illustrate the literary evolution of the legend. Although these sources agree remarkably well on the main features of Glass's story, they are often discordant on small details, and my account is a composite one.

Glass was listed among the wounded in Ashley's letters of June 4 and 7, 1823, and he himself mentions a wound in the thigh in the letter cited in Note 18, Chapter 2. The Wetmore account calls him "an old man," and a letter by Kenneth McKenzie, dated Fort Union, May 5, 1830, in the Chouteau-Papin Collection of the Missouri Historical Society, refers to him respectfully as "old Glass." Stories that Glass was a Pennsylvanian of Scotch-Irish birth are based on a careless reading of the Wetmore narrative.

2. Heretofore the identification of Bridger as the younger of the two men who stayed with Glass has depended on a verbal tradition reported to Chittenden, vol. II, p. 694, but Flagg names him, "Bridges." I have established Fitzgerald's identity through War Department records in the National Archives, which show that John S. Fitzgerald enlisted at Fort Atkinson April 19, 1824, in Brevet Major Daniel Ketchum's Company (Company I) of the Sixth Regiment. The place of his birth is stated to have been Albemarle Co., Va., date not given. At the end of the five-year hitch he was mustered out April 19, 1829, at Jefferson Barracks, St. Louis, being then a private in Company C, his occupation stated as carpenter. Fitzgerald went up the Missouri with the Atkinson-O'Fallon expedition in 1825, and is frequently mentioned in the journal of that expedition.

3. See Leavenworth's letter of Dec. 20, 1823, p. 103, Potts's letter of July 16, 1826; and "Journal of the Atkinson-O'Fallon Expedition," pp. 35-36.

4. The Wetmore narrative says that Glass "continued to crawl

until he reached Fort Kiowa." Yount says he reached "the nearest trading post." Cooke says he was taken by Sioux to "a small trading house . . . at the mouth of the Little Missouri" (that is, Teton or Bad River—where no post then existed, though Joseph Siré traded for the French Company on this river later in the fall). Flagg says that some Sioux took Glass to "the French trading post, Laseau," *i.e.*, Brazeau. All this would strongly indicate that somehow Glass reached Kiowa. But from the circumstance that nothing is said of Glass in the contemporary reports of the massacre of Langevin's party, and from the general tightness of the chronology, I think it possible that Glass fell in with Langevin before he actually got down to Kiowa.

5. Langevin's party provides an important cross-check on Glass's adventures, apart from its own significance in the history of the upper Missouri. A brief sketch of Langevin, including the details about his will, is printed in Stella M. Drumm's notes to John C. Luttig, *Journal of a Fur-Trading Expedition on the Upper Missouri, 1812-1813* (St. Louis, 1920), pp. 156-157. The further history of Langevin's party is set forth in 19th Cong., 1st Sess., *Senate Document 71* (Serial 91), in which are published letters by Brazeau, Leavenworth and R. T. Holliday of the Columbia Fur Company, the latter incorporating Charbonneau's version of the massacre. See also *Missouri Intelligencer,* March 27, 1824; *St. Louis Enquirer,* March 29, June 14, 1824. The site of the massacre was pointed out to Maximilian in 1833 (Maximilian, vol. I, p. 337; vol. II, p. 225), and the affair is duly noted in all the casualty lists, though the number of dead is sometimes erroneously stated. The names of those killed are printed in the Senate Document above. With its other interest, the episode is valuable in filling in a neglected period in Charbonneau's life. He lived in the vicinity of the Mandan Villages until his death sometime between 1839 and 1843.

6. See Holliday's letter of Feb. 16, 1824, cited in Note 5, as also the newspaper accounts there listed, together with Maximilian, vol. II, p. 225, and Abel, p. 333.

7. This information mainly from the Leavenworth letter on p. 103, with additional details from the Potts letter of July 16, 1826. The exact site of Fort Henry is not known; if it occupied the site of Fort Raymond, established by Lisa in 1807, it was in the gore between the Big Horn and the Yellowstone. But Fort Cass, built in 1832 by the American Fur Company, was about three miles below the mouth of the Big Horn, so both Fort Henry and Fort Benton may have been some distance below the confluence.

8. This speech is put in Glass's mouth by Cooke; his final version of 1857 amends somewhat that printed in 1830.

9. *St. Louis Enquirer,* Jan. 13, 1824. I have not found a copy of this letter in the government archives.

10. One of these men must have been Black Harris. I have not certainly established the name of the other; War Department records show that one James Harris was enlisted August 7, 1824, at Fort Atkinson, and after serving the five-year hitch was honorably discharged at Jefferson Barracks as a sergeant. Flagg says that one George Harris was in company with Glass when he was attacked by the grizzly. The misadventures of Fitzgerald's party en route down the Missouri were remembered by James Kipp and recorded in Maximilian, vol. II, p. 225.

11. National Archives, War Department, Adjutant General's Office, L-117 (17) 1824. An abstract of this letter was published in *Missouri Intelligencer,* Jan. 22, 1824. As observed in Note 4, Chapter 4, I think the attack on Henry's party occurred more probably on Sept. 20 than Aug. 20.

12. See Holliday's letter cited in Note 5; Abel, pp. 331-335; Kennerly, p. 55; O'Fallon to Gen. Clark, July 9, 1824; O'Fallon to Gen. Atkinson, July 17, Aug. 13, 1824 (O'Fallon Letterbook, pp. 68-69, 71-72, 96); *Missouri Intelligencer,* March 27, 1824; *St. Louis Enquirer,* March 29, 1824.

13. The date of departure is from the Wetmore account; the narrative is a composite of Wetmore, Flagg and Yount; the names are from Yount, the casualty lists, and *St. Louis Enquirer,* June 7, 1824.

14. The quotation is from the *St. Louis Enquirer,* June 7, 1824, on the authority of "Mr. [Baronet?] Vasquez, just from the Upper Missouri." Dutton and Marsh, having escaped the Rees on the Platte, and having arrived at Council Bluffs, stated "that Major Henry, has built a Fort at the mouth of the Big Horn—that a Mr. Wheeler was killed by a white bear. Captain Smith, with some of the party, had crossed the Mountains."

15. By the Wetmore account, "the lower end of Les Cotes Noirs (the Black Hills)." O'Fallon to Clark, July 9, 1824: "near the Black Hills on the head waters of the North fork of the River Platte" (O'Fallon Letterbook, p. 68). The Laramie Mountains were then called the Black Hills.

16. The date of their arrival is not certain, but the *St. Louis Enquirer* had the news by June 7; see Note 14.

17. This is from Wetmore, and the language may well be Glass's own.

18. Clyman, pp. 34-37.

19. Charles L. Camp has offered this plausible suggestion. However, accounts most nearly contemporaneous say that the name originated in the circumstance that a company bound for the mountains once spent the Fourth of July there. If so, the name may have been fixed on the rock as late as 1829; mountain-bound companies of previous years should have been farther west by July 4.

20. Since Fitzpatrick was back from this trip by Oct. 25, it is scarcely conceivable that he set out later than Sept. 1.

21. O'Fallon to Clark, July 9, 1824 (O'Fallon Letterbook, p. 67); *St. Louis Enquirer*, July 19, 1824. According to O'Fallon, the Rees carried off "4 mules and five horses belonging to our troops and Genl. Ashly, which the Souix had delivered up." With regard to Gordon's robbery by the Crows, see also his report of 1831 in 22nd Cong., 1st Sess., *Senate Document 90* (Serial 213), p. 27.

22. O'Fallon to Atkinson, July 17, 1824 (O'Fallon Letterbook, pp. 72-73).

23. Henry reached Fort Atkinson on or about Aug. 13; O'Fallon sent down by him his letter of that date to Atkinson, but of Henry says only, "Maj[r]. H. will no doubt inform you that the Grovants or Minetaries have most probably killed four of his men." (O'Fallon Letterbook, p. 96.) The names of the four men killed by the Minnetarees are given as Decharle (or Deharte), Trumble (or Tremble), and two others not recollected. Two other men evidently belonging to the Ashley-Henry parties, Stevenson and Kramer, are reported by the casualty lists to have been killed in 1824 by Sioux at the mouth of Cannonball River (that is, near the Mandan towns). No other reference to these men appears in the literature, and it may be that they were free trappers or deserters. See also, in connection with Henry's return, Note 6, Chapter 8.

Chapter 6. THE STAKES OF THE COLUMBIA

1. Frederick Merk, *Fur Trade and Empire* (Cambridge, 1931), pp. 187-188. This book, which prints George Simpson's journal of 1824-1825 and related documents from the Hudson's Bay Company archives, is one of the most significant contributions to the literature yet made; Dr. Merk was the first to work out the international forces

operating in the fur trade of the Far West, and his book has greatly influenced this chapter and the next.

2. Gordon C. Davidson, *The North West Company* (Berkeley, 1918), especially pp. 163-169. Alexander Ross, on whose *The Fur Hunters of the Far West* (London, 1855), vol. I, most accounts of the Company's Pacific operations rest, had no interest in or clear understanding of the larger objectives of the North West Company on the Columbia, and Davidson fills in some of that background.

3. Ross's *Fur Hunters* was long almost the only source, but much new material with regard to Mackenzie's Snake Expeditions has come forth, and a critical restudy of those expeditions is very much in order.

4. See James, *Three Years,* as cited in Note 7, Chapter 1.

5. Thomas M. Marshall, ed., "Journals of Jules De Mun," *Mo. Hist. Soc. Collections,* Feb., June, 1928, vol. V; *American State Papers, Foreign Relations,* vol. 4, pp. 207-213; and *Missouri Gazette,* Sept. 13, 1817.

6. Ross, *Fur Hunters,* vol. I, p. 212. The MS. of Ross's book is in the Coe Collection at Yale; a good many editorial cuts were made before it was set in type, and one of the omitted passages, which would have appeared on p. 276 of the book as published, declares that in no year had the Columbia Department produced more than 14,000 beaver, half of which, "within a fraction," the Snake Country alone produced. For information on the returns from the Columbia down to 1824 see Merk, pp. 65, 173, 174, 195, 210; Davidson, p. 166.

7. Merk, *passim.*

8. *Ibid.,* pp. 184-185.

9. *Ibid.,* pp. 193-194.

10. E. E. Rich, ed., *Peter Skene Ogden's Snake Country Journals 1824-25 and 1825-26* (London, 1950), pp. 40, 229, 231-232; E. E. Rich, ed., *The Letters of John McLoughlin from Fort Vancouver to the Governor and Committee, First Series, 1825-38* (London and Toronto, 1941), p. 296; Frederick Merk, "Snake Country Expedition 1824-25," *Oregon Hist. Quart.,* June 1934, vol. XXXV, p. 108. These latter two references contain letters by Ogden written June 27 and July 10, 1825.

11. I so infer from Ross, *Fur Hunters,* vol. II, p. 21; in May 1824 Ross gave his men the option of going "to Henry's Fork . . . Lewis's River . . . the Blackfeet River . . . and Bear's Lake," only to have Old Pierre say, "We have already been through [that] country . . . and have trapped in that quarter for two years in succession."

12. Spokane House Journal, Sept. 13, 1822 (Hudson's Bay Com-

pany Archives, B.208/a), quoted by permission of the Governor and Committee of the Hudson's Bay Company.

13. Compare the list of deserters in *Ogden's Snake Country Journals,* p. 49n, with Kenneth W. Porter, "Roll of Overland Astorians," *Oregon Hist. Quart.,* June 1933, vol. XXXIII, pp. 103-112.

14. See Prince Paul's account (cited in Note 16, Chapter 1), pp. 362-363, 417; O'Fallon to Pilcher, Aug. 1, 1823 (O'Fallon Letterbook, p. 27). That these were the same Iroquois is shown by a subsequent document in the O'Fallon Letterbook, p. 109: "Pierre Cha-cha-wea-te" is clearly "Pierre Cassawesa" of the Hudson's Bay Company lists.

15. Merk, pp. 192-193.

16. M. Catherine White, ed., *David Thompson's Journals Relating to Montana and Adjacent Regions, 1808-1812* (Missoula, 1950), pp. 234-236.

17. Irrelevant though it may be to this book, the importance of this remark calls for comment. McDonald here refers to the American, "Mr. Courter," whose death on Clarks Fork at the hands of Piegans is reported in David Thompson's journals in February 1810. McDonald must have meant to say "Corta's" rather than "Corta is"; if so, here is evidence of an American fort in the Three Forks country antedating the stockade the Missouri Fur Company built in the spring of 1810 between the Jefferson and the Madison. Courter, who cannot be identified with either John Colter or the Chouteaus, most probably was associated with the mysterious Jeremy Pinch, who penetrated into this country as early as the summer of 1807. "Corta's old Fort" itself may date that far back.

18. Finan McDonald to John George McTavish, April 5, 1824 (Hudson's Bay Company Archives, B.239/c/1), quoted by permission of the Governor and Committee of the Hudson's Bay Company.

19. Ross, *Fur Hunters,* vol. II, pp. 2-5, 50, 54-59. Ross agrees with McDonald's letter quoted in my text that sixty-eight of seventy-five Piegans were killed in this affray. Passing references to the place where the Piegans were burned to death are found in Ross's daily journal of 1824 (published in abridged form in *Oregon Hist. Quart.,* Dec. 1913, vol. XIV, pp. 379-380), and in William Kittson's journal of 1825 (*Ogden's Snake Country Journals,* p. 219). Jim Beckwourth tells a story of Blackfeet being burned to death by himself and other American trappers, which may have been a conversion to his uses of McDonald's famous experience. I use the edition of Beckwourth reprinted with an introduction by Bernard DeVoto: *The Life and Adventures of James P. Beckwourth . . . written from his own Dictation by T. D. Bonner,* first published in 1856 (New York, 1931), p. 80.

20. That Mackenzie trapped the Green River Valley in 1820-1821 I conclude from the fact that on all the later Snake Expeditions not a single allusion is made to Mackenzie's experiences of 1820-1821, though there are many relating to his first two expeditions. A single shred of evidence is that Ashley, in his letter of December 1825 to Gen. Atkinson, commented that the Green River must once have had many beaver, "the major part of which (as I have been informed) were trapped by men in the service of the North West Company some four or five years ago." (Harrison C. Dale, *The Ashley-Smith Explorations and the Discovery of a Central Route to the Pacific, 1822-29* [revised ed., Glendale, 1941]), p. 134.

21. Merk, "Snake Country Expedition," p. 108. Ogden here says, "we reach'd Bear River supposed by M[r] Bourdon who visited it 1818 and subsequently M[r] Finan McDonald who were at its Sources to be the Spanish River or Rio Collorado, but it is not." By "Sources" Ogden may have meant not the actual sources of the Bear in the Uintas but the stream as far down as Cache Valley, though it is possible that McDonald, at least, trapped the Bear in its upper valley above the Great Bend.

22. *Ogden's Snake Country Journals,* p. 58. I do not understand Ogden's allusion to the 1823 expedition's having been attacked here with the loss of five men; so sanguinary an affray would have received attention in McDonald's letter and Ross's narrative. Ogden may have had in mind the experiences of Bourdon's party in 1822—but Bourdon had only two killed and two wounded, by his own account. Is this an erroneous reference to the battle in which Bourdon was lost?

23. The British journals of 1825 show that McDonald recrossed the Salmon River Mountains to the Lemhi Valley by way of Birch Creek. After recrossing Lemhi Pass, he went down the Beaverhead or the Big Hole to the Jefferson and the Missouri, and on as far as Great Falls, when he evidently recrossed the mountains to Clarks Fork by the route Meriwether Lewis used eastbound in 1806. This was one of the two main roads traveled by the Flatheads to the buffalo country.

24. Merk, p. 198.

25. "Journal of Alexander Ross—Snake Country Expedition, 1824," *Oregon Hist. Quart.,* Dec. 1913, vol. XIV, pp. 372, 378.

26. Merk, p. 45.

27. Ross gives a clear account of where the Iroquois went in neither his book nor his journal, but Ogden's journal for April 23, 1825, shows that they got as far west and south as the upper Portneuf River. See p. 141.

28. "Journal of Alexander Ross," p. 385, his entry for Oct. 14, 1824.

29. Although Ogden did not blame him, his letters of 1825 show that Ross started the chain of causation in which the Iroquois were the ultimate sufferers. See Merk, "Snake Country Expedition, 1824-25," p. 113, and compare Ross, *Fur Hunters,* vol. II, pp. 99-101.

30. Ross, *Fur Hunters,* vol. II, pp. 128-129. Ross says that after talking with his Iroquois he "questioned the Americans, who appeared to be shrewd, *well-meaning* men; they confirmed part of the Iroquois' story. Smith, a very intelligent person, and who seemed to be the leading man among them, acknowledged to me that he had received one hundred and five beaver for escorting back the Iroquois. . . ." (The words I italicize appear in Ross's original manuscript, but were stricken out by his London editor.) In his MS. journal Ross wrote on Oct. 15, 1824: "Today I learned that the Worthy Iroquois on meeting with the Americans, traded upwards of 100 Beaver, of which, 40 went forse [sic] horse hire 20 for Amunition 10 for an Old Pistol 35 for Looking Glasses, Buttons, tape Needles, &c. . . ." (H. B. C. Arch. B. 202/a/1, fo. 55 d.)

31. Dale, p. 153.

32. On my map I have had to commit myself to some one route, and have chosen the Bear River variant, but the evidence is not satisfactory one way or the other. To my mind, the chief argument for the route via Jackson Hole is that the Burr map of 1839 shows a Jedediah Smith itinerary into the Hole, which was possible only in the fall of 1824, the fall of 1825 or the spring of 1826.

33. "Journal of Alexander Ross," p. 385.

34. The published version of Ross's journal includes very few entries for the journey to Flathead Post after he was joined by Jedediah Smith. The Hudson's Bay Company has sent me a few additional dates, by which it appears that the combined party crossed Lemhi Pass Oct. 28 and Gibbon Pass Nov. 1, passed the celebrated Ram's Head Nov. 7, and reached Flathead Post Nov. 26, 1824.

35. Ross, *Fur Hunters,* vol. II, pp. 140-141.

36. Finan McDonald to John George McTavish, March 22, 1825, in R. Harvey Fleming, ed., *Minutes of Council Northern Department of Rupert Land 1821-1831* (London and Toronto, 1940), p. 54.

37. T. C. Elliott, "Peter Skene Ogden, Fur Trader," *Oregon Hist. Quart.,* Sept. 1910, vol. XI; *Ogden's Snake Country Journals,* pp. xi-lxxix.

38. Merk, pp. 44-48, 54-57.

Chapter 7. ACTION ON THE FUR FRONTIER

1. "Journal of Alexander Ross," p. 386. The account that follows is from the Flathead Post Journal Ross began to keep on arrival there.

2. This quotation, which does not appear in the abridged version of the journal which has been published, has been furnished me from the MS. by the Hudson's Bay Company, and is printed by permission of the Governor and Committee.

3. *Ogden's Snake Country Journals*, p. lv.

4. *Ibid.*, pp. 2-3.

5. Reason for including Sublette in the party is found in Note 24; also Ashley's accounts in his diary of 1825 include a mention of Sublette as "Smith asst." Eddie's presence in the party depends on the credence that can be given Triplett; see Note 9, Chapter 4. If Black was in the party of 1823, he was in the party now.

6. *Minutes of Council*, p. 443; Ross, *Fur Hunters*, vol. I, *passim*. *Ogden's Snake Country Journals* includes Kittson's journal of 1824-1825, as also a striking map he drew; journal and map provide more information on previous British exploration of the Snake Country than does Ogden's own journal. My account of the march south is based primarily on these journals.

7. Mr. Glenn A. Thompson, U. S. Forest Supervisor at Salmon, Idaho, is of the opinion that Ogden's party crossed over to the Lemhi Valley by Bannock rather than Lemhi Pass. While deferring to Mr. Thompson's knowledge of the terrain, I am disposed to believe that Ogden used Lemhi Pass outbound, Bannock Pass inbound.

8. This is my own interpretation and is at variance with the notes to *Ogden's Snake Country Journals*, which identify "Day's Defile" as Birch Creek, rather than Little Lost River. The Kittson, Ferris and Bonneville maps, and the Arrowsmith map, *British North America*, 1837, perfectly illuminate and are illuminated by the Kittson and Ogden journals on this point.

9. After Ogden reached the Bear, a party he had sent to trap the sources of the Blackfoot returned unsuccessful, and he observed, "it appears that quarter had been trapped by the Americans last Year." (*Ogden's Snake Country Journals*, pp. 40-41.) Although this could be a reference to Weber's party, in view of the fact that Weber was moving down the Bear it does not seem logical that his men

should have left the watershed of that river to trap the sources of another stream.

As noted on p. 173, Ashley in the summer of 1825 recovered no less than forty-five packs of beaver, apparently on the Sweetwater, but these may have been cached by Weber's party rather than by Jedediah's.

10. Compare Note 27, Chapter 6. When he made this journal entry, Ogden was following the Portneuf where it runs south to round the Portneuf Range before turning north to flow into the Snake.

11. This killing doubtless gave name to Thomas Fork of the Bear. Ferris, p. 140, says that the stream, which he calls "Talma's Fork," received its name "from an Iroquois who discovered it." (Contradictorily and implausibly, Ferris also says, p. 52, that the stream was "so named in honour of the great French tragedian," Francis Joseph Talma.) Warren Angus Ferris' *Life in the Rocky Mountains* was first published in the *Western Literary Messenger* in 1842-1843, and was simultaneously reprinted in Denver and Salt Lake City, 1940. I use the former edition, which has a superior introduction and reproduces Ferris' MS. map of the fur country.

12. Potts, letter of July 16, 1826.

13. *Ogden's Snake Country Journals*, pp. 43, 231; Merk, "Snake Country Expedition, 1824-25," p. 109.

14. Ferris, pp. 308-309; *Ogden's Snake Country Journals*, pp. 45, 50, 173; Merk, "Snake Country Expedition, 1824-25," p. 113.

15. *Ogden's Snake Country Journals*, pp. 50, 233.

16. Stella M. Drumm, "Etienne Provost," *Dictionary of American Biography*, vol. XV, pp. 250-251; *American State Papers, Foreign Relations*, vol. IV, pp. 207-213. Controversy has attended the spelling of Provost's name, of which a few variants are Provôt, Provott, Proveau. I follow Miss Drumm, on the basis of her research in the church and court records of St. Louis. The pronunciation was "Provo," the spelling employed for the Utah city that bears his name.

17. O'Fallon Letterbook, p. 25; and see Note 14, Chapter 6. In his letter to Pilcher of this date O'Fallon wrote: "I have given two Iroquois Indians my permission . . . to join your expedition to the mountains, with a view of recovering a squaw and two children, whom the Crow nation of Ind^{ns}. took from them on their passage to this place, and I wish you to be so good as to use your influence in affecting that object." A year later, on July 9, 1824, O'Fallon wrote Clark, "M^{r}. Gordon a Gentleman of the Missouri fur Company arrived here a few days since from the Yellow Stone River, states that on

descending He met with a War party of Crow Ind^{ns}. who unhesitatingly robbed him and took prisoner an Ind^{n}. Woman, whom he had purchased of another band of the Souix Nation, with a view of restoring her to her husband (an Iroquois Ind^{n}. from Canada now at this place) and from whom she had been forcibly taken about twelve months before by a War party of the same tribe, with several children. . . ." (O'Fallon Letterbook, p. 68.) When O'Fallon went up the Missouri in 1825, the recovery of two Iroquois prisoners from the Crows was a major item of business and provoked a celebrated incident; see "Journal of the Atkinson-O'Fallon Expedition," p. 36, and compare Beckwourth, p. 53.

18. The best known of the LeClaires was Antoine, Jr., for whom see Charles Snyder, "Antoine LeClaire, The First Proprietor of Davenport," *Annals of Iowa,* Oct. 1941, Third Series, vol. XXIII, pp. 79-117. Antoine's brother Francois, who was born at St. Joseph, Mich., Nov. 17, 1795, has been regarded as most probably the partner of Provost. Francois, or a person of the same name, was an overland Astorian in 1811-1813, and in 1815 was granted a license to trade with the Indians on the upper Arkansas, so that he might have known Provost as early as 1815. If he actually was Provost's partner, he must have been back in Missouri by the late summer of 1825, for the *Missouri Republican,* Oct. 17, 1825, publishes a notice by Antoine Le Clair, Jr., and Francois Le Clair that they have obtained letters of administration on the estate of Antoine Le Clair, Sr., dated Sept. 7, 1825. Francois was still living in 1830, as shown by the accounts of Thomas Forsythe's Sac and Fox Agency. Yet another LeClerc, possibly Narcisse, was associated with Pilcher in 1823-1824, and others are scattered all over the literature.

19. Ceran St. Vrain, then a novice in the trade, wrote Bernard Pratte on April 27, 1824, from Taos: "After a long and trublesum vioage of five months we have at Length retch this place it is now 37 days Since we arived and we have Sold but verry fue goods & goods is at a verry redused price at present. I am in hopes when the hunters comes in from there hunt that I well Sell out to Provoe & Leclere, if I doe not succeed to Sel out to them and othere hunters, my intenshion is to buy up goo[d] Articles that will Sout the market of Sonora to purchess mulls; but I Shall first doe all I can to mak arragement with Provoe & Leclere to furnish them with goods. Should I succeed thare is no doubt but it will [be] a verry profitable buisness." (Chouteau-Papin Collection, Missouri Historical Society.)

20. See pp. 169-170.

21. Ferris, pp. 308-309; Blanche C. Grant, ed., *Kit Carson's Own*

Story of His Life (Taos, 1925), p. 65. It had been supposed that the massacre of Provost's party occurred on the Provo River, since Ferris located the affair "on a stream flowing into the Big Lake that now bears his name," but when the Ferris map came to light, it developed that he applied the name "Proveau's Fork" to what is now the Jordan River, which literally flows into "the Big Lake," and is much more plausible otherwise, for the Provo River flowed entirely through Ute territory, while the Great Salt Lake Valley historically was a no man's land for Snakes and Utes.

22. This follows from Provost's services to Ashley described in Chapter 8 and explains how it happened, as Ogden observed, that Provost knew nothing of other Americans being in the country down to May 22, 1825 (*Ogden's Snake Country Journals*, p. 50). Sometime this year, either before or after meeting with Ogden, Provost had a man killed by the Snakes on "Webers fork," but the circumstance is recorded only in the casualty lists; nothing is said of it by Ashley or the British diarists.

23. Merk, "Snake Country Expedition, 1824-25," p. 113.

24. This important interpretation follows from a communication by Ashley to the *Missouri Observer & St. Louis Advertiser*, Oct. 31, 1827. Referring to Ogden's Snake expedition of 1825, he said: "Some of the American hunters, who were then, and others who had been, in my employ, went to the British camp, which consisted of about sixty men in the service of the Hudson Bay Company. The circumstance which produced this visit had nearly led to serious consequences. Messrs. Jedediah S. Smith, Wm. L. Sublette and several others of the American party, intelligent young men, of strict veracity, had visited the British camp and reported to their comrades, that the British flag had been repeatedly hoisted during their stay there. The Americans, indignant at such impertinence and understanding, too, that the British camp was within eight miles of them, resolved to proceed to the place and tear down the flag, even at the risk of their lives. Twenty-two of them, with the American flag hoisted, advanced to the spot, but no British flag was to be seen. They made known their business to Mr. Ogden, and protested in threatening language against a recurrence of the same insult offered them; they also required of Mr. Ogden to move his party from that vicinity without delay. Mr. O. first hesitated, calling upon his men for protection, but ultimately finding there would probably be much danger in delay, he lost no time in getting under way, and has kept a respectful distance ever since. At the

time of this occurrence I was descending the Rio Colorado of the West, but shortly after returned and joined the party of American hunters, from whom I received the above account."

Ogden's camp in the canyon of the Weber, which was at present Mountain Green, was six miles by the modern highway above the canyon mouth. In view of this fact and Ashley's statement above, it will be understood why Ogden observed in his letter of July 10, 1825, "it was an unfortunate day Mr. Ross consented to allow the 7 Americans to accompany him to the Flatheads, for it was these fellows that guided and accompanied them to our Camp," though he added erroneously, "the whole party were on their return home to St. Louis and were enduced to return by letters they received from the Iroquois Chiefs." Merk, "Snake Country Expedition, 1824-25," pp. 112-113.

25. My account of the desertion of Ogden's men is based on the Ogden and Kittson journals and Ogden's two letters of June 27 and July 10, 1825.

26. McLoughlin wrote Simpson on Aug. 10, 1825, that the Company would "loose Furs to the amount of about Three thousand pounds" through the desertion of Ogden's men. (Merk, p. 254). McLoughlin evidently included the prospects of the hunt, had Ogden been able to keep his trapping force intact, for the direct loss was only seven hundred skins, worth in London perhaps £1,100 (*Letters of John McLoughlin,* pp. lxxvi, 298). The British generally figured a beaver catch in skins, the Americans in pounds; a beaver skin seems to have averaged about 1.66 pounds. Stories got into circulation later that Ashley was made wealthy by this single transaction with the British deserters; Nathaniel Wyeth wrote in 1833 that Ashley obtained from the deserters "about 130 packs or 13000 lbs. worth at that time about $75000." The accounts Ashley kept at rendezvous in 1825 show that he bought skins from the deserters for three dollars a pound in merchandise, but it cannot be determined how much he marketed them for or what his profit was after deducting transportation and other expenses. Some of the skins he must have acquired from Gardner and other free trappers, not directly.

27. *Ogden's Snake Country Journals,* p. 62; Merk, "Snake Country Expedition, 1824-25," p. 114. I cannot account for so large or indeed any party of Americans in this area at this time; perhaps the tale was idle rumor.

28. *Letters of John McLoughlin,* p. lxiv.

Chapter 8. RENDEZVOUS: 1825

1. Licenses to Trade with the Indians, 19th Cong., 1st Sess., *House Document 118* (Serial 136).

2. Report of Thomas Forsythe, St. Louis, Oct. 24, 1831, 22nd Cong., 1st Sess., *Senate Document 90* (Serial 213), p. 74.

3. *St. Louis Enquirer,* quoted in Little Rock *Arkansas Gazette,* Nov. 16, 1824; see *Niles' Weekly Register,* Dec. 4, 1824, vol. 27, p. 224.

4. James, *Three Years,* pp. 265-266.

5. Kennerly, pp. 77, 78.

6. Ashley Papers, Missouri Historical Society. This letter is the more interesting in the light of one written by William Carr Lane to his wife, St. Louis, Aug. 31, 1824: "The Election is over . . . all as it shd. be, except Ashley's part, & who knows but good may come of that also—Nothing from him upon that subject since your departure, not even a word—Major Henry has returned with a valuable cargo of Fur, & a few of the Hunters—Some have been slain—the balance are west of the Mountains—Henry goes back soon—what influence this return may have upon the affairs of A. I know not—there is much talk about his insolvency—But I believe him solvent & honest. . . ." (*Glimpses of the Past,* July-Sept., 1940, vol. VII, p. 88.)

7. J. P. Cabanné to Pierre Chouteau, Jr., dated Establishment at the Bluffs, Nov. 8, 1824, mentions that the Pawnees had finally got peace; he kept them until the arrival of General Atkinson, who was more humane than O'Fallon and sent them away satisfied. Cabanné also noticed the passage of Ashley, who said he was going to the Columbia River; Cabanné thought Ashley would try to get the exclusive right to hunt there through the influence of Major O'Fallon. (Chouteau-Papin Collection, Missouri Historical Society.)

8. The account of Ashley's expedition which follows is derived from his letter dated December [ ], 1825, to Gen. Henry Atkinson, of which a draft copy is in the Ashley Papers, Missouri Historical Society. I have not succeeded in finding the fair copy sent Atkinson, or the topographical map Ashley enclosed. Atkinson delivered these documents in person to the War Department on Feb. 20, 1826; his covering letter is present in the files (National Archives, War Department, Adjutant General's Office, A 9-1826), but this says merely, "I have the honor to enclose herewith The report of Genl. Ashley of his tour

beyond the Rocky mountains, with a topographical sketch of the country over which he passed. Also a drawing exhibiting the plan of Cant. Barbour [the temporary camp of 1825 at the mouth of the Yellowstone]." These documents cannot be found in the files. The draft copy, with some minor errors of transcription, has been printed by Dale, pp. 115-157; my quotations are from the MS.

9. Ham, like Francis Z. Branch, went to California in 1830-1831 in William Wolfskill's party, and is said to have drowned in the Colorado a little later. H. H. Bancroft, *History of California* (San Francisco, 1885), vol. III, pp. 387, 774.

10. Supplementing Beckwourth's own account of his beginnings, see Ralph P. Bieber's notes to Lewis Garrard, *Wah-To-Yah and the Taos Trail* (Glendale, 1938), pp. 309-310. His name was properly Beckwith, but the sonorous spelling adopted for his *Life and Adventures* serves usefully to distinguish him from other Beckwiths.

11. Edwin James, *Account of An Expedition from Pittsburgh to the Rocky Mountains Performed in the Years 1819, 1820* (Thwaites, ed., Cleveland, 1905), vol. II, pp. 220, 235, 282; vol. III, pp. 58, 226-227. James's MS. journal is in the New York Botanical Garden, New York City; the MS. journal of Capt. John R. Bell, also kept on the Long Expedition, is in the Stanford University library.

12. This MS. diary, acquired by the Missouri Historical Society in 1931, was long supposed to be the diary of William L. Sublette. The true authorship was established in the course of my research for this book. The Missouri Historical Society generously made it available for use here, and hereafter I expect to publish it in full in a documentary collection of Ashley Papers. The diary covers the period March 25-June 27, 1825. There are errors of date in the diary, but for lack of a record with which a cross-check can be made, I use the diary dates as I find them in the MS.

13. See my book, *The Great Salt Lake* (Indianapolis, 1947), pp. 60-64, for a more extended discussion of the semimythical geography of the early West.

14. The name did not persist. It is not clear why the name Henrys Fork should have been applied to this stream, and the name has made for some confusion since there is also a Henrys Fork of the Snake, better known and more justly so called because Andrew Henry had a fort on the latter stream in 1810-1811. If Henrys Fork of the Green was named for Andrew Henry, the name was purely honorary; however, there may have been other men of this name in the mountains;

the stream could even have been called for Henry (Boatswain) Brown, lost in the Mojave Massacre of 1827.

15. This is Ashley Falls, so named because a painted inscription with Ashley's name and the year 1825 was found here by the Powell expedition of 1869.

16. Compare Beckwourth's spacious account, pp. 35-36. The one detail in Beckwourth's narrative which is factually correct is that Ashley was "no swimmer."

17. Little enough is known about the difficulties of the Taos-based trappers in this country; for a summary, see Dale, pp. 151-152. A few more details are provided by "Sketches from the Life of Peg-Leg Smith," *Hutchings' Illustrated California Magazine*, Oct. 1860-March, 1861, vol. V.

18. In his letter to Gen. Atkinson, Ashley said that he explored the Green some fifty miles below the mouth of the Duchesne, but his diary makes it evident that he went only about half that distance, to the vicinity of Minnie Maud Creek.

19. So Beckwourth is right, after all, in saying that Ashley fell in with Provost in the Uinta Basin, and historians who have maligned him may blush a little. The number of Provost's party is variously stated. Ogden's journal for May 23, 1825, has it "a party of 15 men Canadians & Spainards headed by one Provost & Francois one of our deserters." Kittson the same day speaks of "Jack McLoed and Lazard the two Deserters [of 1822] . . . their camp consisting of besides them, 3 Canadians, a Russian, and an old Spaniard . . . under the Command of one Provost." Ogden's letter of June 27, 1825, has it "a party of 25 men, Canadians, Americans and Spanjards" (*Letters of John McLoughlin*, p. 297).

20. See Note 28, Chapter 4.

21. Ashley's route from Green River is accurately known for the first time now that his diary is available. It has been supposed that he went up the Duchesne, rather than the Strawberry, and no details have been known.

22. All Ashley has to say about Jedediah's travels of the winter and spring is: "It appears from Mr Smiths account that there is no scarcity of Buffalo as he penetrated the country. As Mr Smith returned he inclined —— —— west and fell on the waters of the grand lake or Beunaventura, he describes the country in that direction as admitting a free and easy passage and abounding in salt: at one place particularly hundreds of bushels might have been collected from the surface of the earth within a small space, he gave me some speci-

mens which equal in appearance and quality the best Liverpool salt. Mr S also says the Buffalo are very plenty as far as he penetrated the country over it in almost any direction." Dale, p. 154.

23. *Ibid.*, p. 152; Beckwourth, p. 43. It has been understood that Ashley's men moved 20 miles up Henrys Fork, perhaps seeking better grass and a grove of timber, but the sources do not say so. It is possible that the two camps were twenty miles up the Green itself from the mouth of Henrys Fork. Beckwourth here is so busily engaged glorifying Jim Beckwourth that one cannot be sure just what it is he is trying to tell us.

24. Clyman says that his party was doing well "when one day 17 Indians came to us and stayed 3 or 4 days. At last, one night the Indians crept up and killed the man on guard with an ax, and charged on us with two guns a ball passed through my caput that answered for a pillow, but did not touch me. We all sprang up. The Indians flew into the brush, we crawled out into the open ground and made a little breastwork or fort of stone, just about daylight. They tried to get us out from behind it, but didn't succeed. We fired on them, and I think I killed one. We were very much discouraged—being only 3 men in a country full of Indians, and concluded to take Fitzpatricks trail and join him." Clyman also refers to this defeat in his diary of 1844 (Clyman, pp. 44, 225); apparently it happened in the vicinity of present Viola, Wyo., and the name of the man killed was given to LaBarge Creek. Beckwourth has an account of the same action, with the facts blown up to redound to the greater glory of J. Beckwourth (pp. 38-42).

25. Ashley's MS. diary of 1825, Missouri Historical Society.

26. Ogden so observed in his journal on June 11, 1826 (*Ogden's Snake Country Journals*, pp. 182-183).

27. It is not clear whether the 8,829 pounds of beaver included the forty-five packs unearthed from a cache en route east. When Ashley reached the States, the *Missouri Republican* of Oct. 3, 1825, printed a report that he had "from 80 to 100 packs, worth from 40 to $50,000," and on Oct. 10 added that the quantity of beaver "exceeds, in fact," this amount. Chittenden, vol. I, p. 279, quotes a letter from O. N. Bostwick to parties in New York, Oct. 5, 1825, "Gen. Ashley arrived here yesterday with (as rumor says) 100 packs of Rocky Mountain beaver weighing 9,700 pounds. There is no doubt of the fact. It is said to be of fine quality." The weight of a pack varied according to whether it was carried in a boat or by horseback; the former might run from ninety to one hundred pounds, the latter about fifty pounds.

28. L. U. Reavis, *The Life and Military Services of Gen. William Selby Harney* (St. Louis, 1878), p. 68, asserts that in the course of his homeward journey Ashley proposed to the young Capt. Harney, who had come up the Missouri with the Atkinson-O'Fallon expedition, that he go in charge of an outfit Ashley proposed to send to the Yellowstone, Ashley to furnish all the capital, with the profits to be split fifty-fifty, but Harney elected to remain in the Army. If true, Ashley must have envisioned this as a parallel undertaking, for it is unlikely that Jedediah would have gone down from the mountains in the summer of 1825 unless he and Ashley had come to some arrangement about returning.

29. Apparently Ashley lost fifty-three horses. Compare Ogden's journal for Aug. 30, 1825 (*Ogden's Snake Country Journals*, pp. 76-77).

30. Ashley's return with the military forces is noted in both of the known journals, the "Journal of the Atkinson-O'Fallon Expedition" kept by Atkinson's aide-de-camp and published as cited in Note 23, Chapter 1; and the unpublished journal of Stephen W. Kearny in the Missouri Historical Society library. The official report, printed as 19th Cong., 1st Sess., *House Document 117* (Serial 136), has an acknowledgment by Atkinson to "A Mr. Smith, an intelligent young man, who was employed by general Ashley beyond the Rocky Mountains for two years," for information about British trading and trapping west of the mountains.

Chapter 9. PARTNER IN THE FUR TRADE

1. St. Louis *Missouri Advocate,* Oct. 29, 1825. Both the *Advocate* and the *Republican* give the number of men as seventy, but in his letter of Dec. 16, 1826, Jedediah says the party was made up of sixty men; and as appears hereafter, his license to enter the Indian country seems to have named fifty-seven men.

2. See p. 331.

3. Beckwourth's scrambled narrative is never more fascinating than in its bearing on this journey to the mountains. On an earlier page, p. 18, in a context that would seem to be 1824, he tells of arriving in St. Louis and falling in with Ashley, who informed him that he had engaged 120 men who were already en route to the mountains; Ashley declared that Beckwourth was just the man to ride after and overtake them. Jim says he received $800 in gold "to carry to Mr. Fitzpatrick (an agent of General Ashley then stationed in the moun-

tains)," and set out in pursuit of the company on a good horse. Ashley, as Jim adds, "had been recently married, and, feeling some reluctance to tear himself away from the delights of Hymen, he sent me on for the performance of his duties." All this fits in very well with the picture of 1825, though the $800 in gold is doubtless a gilding of the facts. His having been sent on to overtake the company may have suggested the idea of the hazardous express he describes, pp. 58-60, in a context of 1825.

4. Ashley to Gen. A. Macomb, March 1829, 21st Cong., 2nd Sess., *Senate Document* 39 (Serial 203), p. 107.

5. Scharf, vol. I, p. 370, has a sketchy account of Campbell's entrance into the fur trade, and indicates that he was a member of Ashley's party of 1824-1825, which is also Beckwourth's statement. Charles Larpenteur, *Forty Years a Fur Trader* (ed. Elliott Coues; New York, 1898), vol. I, pp. 11-67, shows the regard in which Campbell was held by his men.

6. *San Francisco Evening Bulletin,* Oct. 29, 1858. A letter in the Vasquez Papers, Missouri Historical Society, shows that Vasquez was in St. Louis during the winter of 1824-1825; consequently he must have gone to the mountains with Jedediah Smith in the fall of 1825.

7. *Ogden's Snake Country Journals,* pp. 173, 180.

8. *Ibid.*, p. 146.

9. *Ibid.*, pp. 154-155; "Journal of John Work," *Washington Hist. Quart.*, Jan. 1915, vol. VI, pp. 38, 40-44.

10. In referring to Fitzpatrick through these years, Beckwourth has the Indians calling him Bad Hand, a version of Broken Hand, Withered Hand or Three Fingers, applied to Fitzpatrick in consequence of a crippling accident occasioned by a bursting rifle. However, in the *Jefferson* (Mo.) *Inquirer,* Dec. 25, 1847, is an account picked up from the *St. Louis News-Letter* which describes the accident on the authority of P. A. Sarpy, who was in company with Fitzpatrick at the time, and Sarpy says it happened on the Yellowstone in 1835 during a flight from the Blackfeet.

11. Beckwourth, pp. 62-64. If Jim did participate in this episode, it happened in the spring of 1826; however, the Smith, Jackson & Sublette casualty list gives 1825 as the date of Marshall's death. Ferris, pp. 47-48, whose account I have followed in the main, provides no date.

12. Dale, p. 150.

13. But now I am quoting from a version of his travels given out by Ashley to the *St. Louis Enquirer,* March 11, 1826.

14. Diary of William Marshall Anderson, MS., quoted by courtesy of the owner, Mr. J. S. Holliday of Tucson, Arizona.

15. Communication dated Feb. 16, 1860, *National Intelligencer,* Feb. 25, 1860.

16. Robert Campbell to G. K. Warren, April 4, 1857, *Reports of Explorations and Surveys, to Ascertain the Most Practical and Economical Route for a Railroad from the Mississippi River to the Pacific Ocean* (Washington, 1861), vol. XI, p. 35. Everybody has said that Bridger floated down the Bear to Great Salt Lake in a bullboat, but the sources do not say so. Capt. E. L. Berthoud told Frederick Dellenbaugh (*Frémont and* '49 [New York, 1914] p. 135) that Bridger "dismounted" to get a drink after reaching the lake, and thereby discovered that the water was salt: "Hell, we are on the shore of the Pacific!"

17. *Ogden's Snake Country Journals,* pp. 44, 50, 232-233.

18. There are many scattered references to this "coasting" of the lake; I have followed the account in St. Louis *Missouri Herald,* Nov. 8, 1826. Robert Campbell, in the letter cited in Note 16, recalled that he "went to the Willow or Cache valley in the spring of 1826, and found the party just returned from their exploration of the lake, and recollect their report that it was without any outlet"; four men, he said, made the reconnaissance in "*skin* boats." Other accounts are in Ferris, pp. 69-70; Irving, Chapter XXI; Clyman, pp. 45, 221. Jim Bridger told the Mormons on June 28, 1847, that some of his men had been around the lake in canoes. "They went out hunting and had their horses stolen by the Indians. They then went around the lake in canoes hunting beaver and were three months going around it." (*William Clayton's Journal* [Salt Lake City, 1921], p. 275.) Louis Vasquez, as cited in Note 6, said he "built a boat, and circumnavigated this sheet of brine, for the purpose of finding out definitely whether it was an arm of the sea or not, and thus discovered that it was in reality merely a large inland lake, without an outlet." Black Harris told the Mormons in 1847 "that he had travelled the whole circumference of the Lake, and that there was no outlet to it" (Journal of Orson Pratt, in *L. D. S. Millennial Star,* May 15, 1850, vol. XII, p. 146). Finally, in an undated letter "for the Dallas Herald" written by Warren Ferris probably in the 1850s, for a copy of which I am indebted to Mr. Walter McCausland, it is asserted that the lake was circumnavigated "by Frabb and three others."

19. *Ogden's Snake Country Journals,* pp. 169, 174; and compare Ogden's letter of July 1, 1826, in Merk, *Fur Trade and Empire,* pp. 274-277. The Burr map is nearly conclusive evidence that Jedediah

was at the head of this party, for it shows only his itineraries and Ashley's.

20. The site seems to be established by *Travels*, p. 26; "the Cache" was on the direct line Jedediah traveled in 1827 from the head of Box Elder Canyon to the mouth of Blacksmiths Fork Canyon.

21. *St. Louis Enquirer*, March 11, 1826; the departure is also noted in *Missouri Republican*, March 9, 1826.

22. This is the account cited in Note 13, "New Route to the Pacific Ocean, discovered by Gen. William H. Ashley, during his late Expedition to the Rocky Mountains."

23. I am able to find no contemporary account of LeClerc's death, and no information about it except that provided by John Dougherty's casualty list of 1831. He lists among the casualties of 1825 "Le Clerc" and "1 Not Known, killed on Head Waters Kansa River by Indians not known, employed by selves, engaged in the Mexican trade." If this was Provost's partner and the man was actually killed, it is established that his partner was some other LeClerc than Francois; see Note 18, Chapter 7.

24. See the sources cited in Note 2, Chapter 2.

25. According to Beckwourth, pp. 58, 60, Sublette was left in charge of Ashley's interests in the mountains during the summer and fall of 1825. A biography of William L. Sublette is in preparation by Mr. John E. Sunder at Washington University, St. Louis.

26. Waldo, p. 82, is the sole source for Jackson's participation in the fight with the Rees. Leavenworth's final report of Oct. 20, 1823, definitely gives the name of the Ashley man appointed to a lieutenancy in the Missouri Legion as George C. Jackson; he was perhaps the same George Jackson who between 1815 and 1818 was a justice of the peace and surveyor in Howard County, Mo. (Carter, vol. XV, pp. 85, 188, 190, 278, 371). A G. Jackson is listed in Ashley's accounts in his diary of 1825. I have been able to learn nothing of David E. Jackson's antecedents, and nothing of his life after 1838. The St. Louis *Missouri Argus*, Jan. 13, 1838, reports two actions for debt against Jackson in the circuit court for Franklin County on Nov. 3, 1837, Jackson being required to settle these in Union, Franklin County, in Feb. 1838 or have judgment entered against him and his estate sold to satisfy it. He appears at this time to have been in partnership with one Robert Chapman. A study of Jackson is in progress by a descendant, Mr. Carl D. W. Hays, and this may develop some information about a notably obscure life.

27. Ashley to (B. Pratte & Co.), Oct. 14, 1826, Ashley Papers,

Missouri Historical Society. In a document in the Sublette Papers dated Oct. 13, 1830, Ashley receipts to Smith, Jackson & Sublette for "all accts of any nature whatever (except holding them accountable for their settlement and satisfaction to forty two men who were hired to Ashley & Smith, & transfered to said Smith Jackson & Sublette in the summer of Eighteen hundred & twenty six for which I hold their obligation."

28. Sublette Papers, Missouri Historical Society.

29. *Missouri Republican*, Sept. 21, 1826. This reports his returns at 123 packs. The *Missouri Intelligencer*, Sept. 28, 1826, has it 125. Chittenden, vol. I, p. 279, quotes a letter by O. N. Bostwick of the American Fur Company dated Sept. 21, 1826, "Fortune has again smiled upon . . . General Ashley. He is within a few day's march of this place with 123 packs of beaver. There is no doubt of the truth of this report; It was brought by some men who came from the mountains with him."

Chapter 10. THE SOUTH WEST EXPEDITION

1. The journals of Jedediah's clerk, Harrison G. Rogers, are in the Ashley Papers, Missouri Historical Society. They have been printed, with some inaccuracies in transcription and some liberties in typesetting, in Dale, pp. 194-224, 242-275. There are two journals; the first is a fragment for the period (Nov. 26, 1826)-Jan. 27, 1827; the other a complete journal for the period May 10-July 13, 1828. So abruptly does the first journal begin as to make it seem probable that the diary handed over by Jedediah Smith to the California governor in Dec. 1826—still an object of search in the Mexican archives—was made up of pages removed from this record. While at rendezvous, as early as Aug. 5, 1826, Rogers began to use this first journal as a daybook for recording the issue of supplies to Jedediah's men. Later he wrote diary entries on these same pages, so that the entries have accounts interspersed. I have found these accounts notably illuminating, and they have contributed a good deal to this chapter. For the convenience of students, I cite the Rogers journals in their printed form, but quotations are from the MSS.

2. Potts, letter of July 16, 1826.

3. See Jedediah's letter of Dec. 16, 1826, p. 331

4. On Sept. 14, 1819, Rogers was one of the signers of a petition to the President by "inhabitants of the Howard Land District" (Carter, vol. XV, p. 559).

5. In two letters printed in my Appendix, Jedediah says he set out "with thirteen men," and "with a party of fifteen men." When he reached California, Echeandia wrote to Mexico that Jedediah had come in command of fourteen of his countrymen; and a letter by Capt. W. H. Cunningham written from San Diego in Dec. 1826 speaks of "a party of fourteen men" (Dale, p. 214). Approaching the problem from a different angle: references in the Rogers diary during Dec. 1826 and Jan. 1827 establish the presence in the party of Smith, Rogers, Black, Evans, Ferguson, Gaiter, Gobel, Hanna, Laplant, Lazarus, McCoy, Ranne, Reed and Wilson, a total of fourteen. Rogers' accounts show Reubascan's presence in the party as late as Sept. 22, 1826, but there is no mention of him afterward; however, Rogers' diary of 1828, in listing "Mens names with J. S. Smith," includes John Reubascan, so his continued presence in the party of 1826 has to be assumed. Rogers' accounts show supplies issued to Manuel Eustavan on Aug. 1, 15, 16, 24, 28, 30, Sept. 1, 8, but never afterward; and to Neppasang on Aug. 15, 16, Sept. 1, 22. These two men cannot be fitted into a total of thirteen, fourteen or fifteen, and as they disappear utterly from the record, I assume that they did not go all the way to California. Louis Pombert is mentioned in neither accounts nor diary. Bancroft, vol. IV, p. 782, nevertheless says of him that he was an arrival of 1826, a "Canadian trapper of Jed. Smith's party, who left the party in '27, lived 18 months on Higuera's rancho, and in Apr. '29 at S. Jose, age 28." A search of the records in the Bancroft Library has not developed any allusions to him in the California archives before 1831. Presumably this was the same Louis Pombert who on June 24, 1819, was an American Fur Company boatman at Mackinac (*Wisconsin Hist. Colls.*, 1892, vol. XXII, pp. 154-169). Capt. Howard Stansbury in 1849 learned from Jim Bridger that the tributary of the Weber River now called Lost Creek was known to the mountain men as Pumbar's Fork, which might mean that Pombert was with Provost in 1825. But save for the fact that "Pompare" was a member of Jedediah's party in Jan. 1828, and that he then deserted the company with Reed, this is the sum total of the information.

6. See p. 334.

7. The Beale-Heap party, which entered Utah by the Spanish

Trail in the summer of 1853 and turned south up the Sevier River, saw its valley much as Jedediah must have found it in 1826; they also were brought to a full stop by the impassable canyon of the Sevier. Heap's description of Marysvale Canyon, through which a road was not cut till 1918, makes it apparent why Jedediah turned west up Clear Creek. See Gwinn Harris Heap, *Central Route to the Pacific* (Philadelphia, 1854), pp. 87-88, and compare the Burr map.

8. Jedediah's route, from the time he reached the site of Cove Fort, is followed almost exactly by present US 91. Escalante, coming south through Utah in 1776, veered considerably to the west; the trails of the two explorers separated near Levan, north of the Sevier River, and did not come back together again until they climbed to the Rim of the Great Basin south of Cedar City.

9. This account of the Indians in the Virgin Valley is based on Jedediah's letters of 1826 and 1827 and his summary journal of 1827, with additional details drawn from Thomas D. Brown, Journal of the Southern Indian Mission, typed transcript in the Utah State Historical Society library. The life of these Indians had changed scarcely at all by 1854, when Brown and other Mormon missionaries came to them.

10. The party of Antonio Armijo went down the right bank of the Colorado as far as Vegas Wash in January 1830, and scouts may have penetrated all the way to the Needles area. See LeRoy R. Hafen, "Armijo's Journal," *Huntington Library Quart.*, Nov. 1947, vol. XI, pp. 87-101.

11. "Out of 50 horses which they started with, they brought only 18 in with them; the others having died on the road for want of food and water." Letter of Capt. W. H. Cunningham cited in Note 5. The implication of Jedediah's letter to Gen. Clark is that he followed the river pretty closely, but his journal of 1827 shows that he left it at one place, at least, and had an extraordinarily difficult time descending a canyon to reach it again. See p. 238. Mr. Russell K. Grater, Park Naturalist of the Lake Mead National Recreational Area, suggests to me that Smith might have made his way successfully through Boulder Canyon only to be forced away from the river on reaching Black Canyon. He would have left the river at Willow Beach, going south up a broad wash toward the present Pope Mine, then returned to the river by way of the narrow and rather spectacular canyon that leads from the Pope Mine to the Colorado. Below this point he should have been able to follow the river.

12. Garcés did go on to Oraibe by a route south of the Colorado,

and the trail he took brought him at one point back to the canyon of the Colorado, but he made no attempt to ascend the river along its banks.

13. Descriptions of the Mojaves essentially as Jedediah must have known them are found in Elliott Coues, ed., *On the Trail of a Spanish Pioneer* [Garcés] (New York, 1900), vol. I, pp. 226-235, 308-312; L. Sitgreaves, *Report of an Expedition down the Zuñi and Colorado Rivers* (Washington, 1853), pp. 16-20; Lt. A. W. Whipple's report of 1854 in *Reports of Explorations and Surveys to Ascertain the Most Practicable and Economical Route for a Railroad from the Mississippi River to the Pacific Ocean* (Washington, 1856), vol. III, pp. 112-119; E. W. Beale, *Wagon Road from Fort Defiance to the Colorado River* (Washington, 1858), pp. 74-76; Joseph C. Ives, *Report upon the Colorado River of the West, Explored in 1857 and 1858* (Washington, 1861), pp. 65-91.

14. The route taken by Jedediah west from the Colorado appears to have been nearly the same as that traveled by Lt. Whipple in March 1854; it bent somewhat to the north by way of Paiute Spring, Rock Springs and Marl Spring to Soda Lake, thence up the Mojave River. See Whipple's Map No. 2 in vol. XI of the Pacific Railroad reports. In his letter to Gen. Clark, Jedediah says he traveled "a west course fifteen days over a country of complete barrens," which might describe his journey as far as the San Bernardino Mountains. He left the Colorado Nov. 10, and the Rogers diary shows that by the night of Nov. 16 he had crossed the mountains and reached the San Bernardino Valley.

15. See the discussion in George William Beattie and Helen Pruitt Beattie, *Heritage of the Valley* (Pasadena, 1939), pp. 23-24, 327-329. The trail went up the west fork of the Mojave and Sawpit Canyon, descending Devil Canyon on the other side to the San Bernardino Valley.

16. Dale, p. 194. The "mansion" Rogers describes was located about four miles northeast of Mission San Gabriel, as is shown by Rogers' journal entry for Jan. 18, 1827.

17. This letter has been found in the Mexican archives, and is to be published in the *Mississippi Valley Historical Review*.

18. The alternative suggestion that Jedediah named the Sierra for Mission San Jose is not even remotely plausible. An attractive picture of Father Sánchez is painted in Alfred Robinson, *Life in California* (San Francisco, 1891 ed.), pp. 44-45. See also Zephyrin Engelhardt,

San Gabriel Mission and the Beginnings of Los Angeles (San Gabriel, 1927), pp. 139-154.

19. *Travels,* p. 47; and see p. 339.

20. Rogers says "St. Pedro," clearly a mistake, for he gives the proper distance to Los Angeles and there was nothing at San Pedro worth Jedediah's riding thirty-four miles to see.

21. Cunningham's log for the ship *Courier* is in the Peabody Museum, Salem, Mass., but it has nothing to say about his activities ashore in behalf of Jedediah Smith.

22. See Jedediah's letter of Dec. 16, 1826, p. 332. The letter says Jedediah set out with Cunningham on the tenth, this date being written over "9th," but the Rogers diary shows that ninth was correct.

23. Robinson, pp. 28-31, 262-263; A. Duhaut-Cilly, *Voyage Autour du Monde* (Paris, 1834); extracts translated by Charles Franklin Carter as "Duhaut-Cilly's Account of California in the Years 1827-28," *California Hist. Quart.,* vol. VIII, June 1929, pp. 161-164; Sept. 1929, pp. 217-219.

24. Echeandia to the Minister of War, Dec. 30, 1826, digest copy in Department State Papers, vol. XIX, pp. 37-38, Bancroft Library. With this letter Echeandia enclosed "a diary of events and an itinerary," which have not yet been found in the Mexican archives.

25. I suppose the letter was written this day; Rogers received it Dec. 18 (Dale, pp. 207-208).

26. Department State Papers, vol. II: pp. 19-21, Bancroft Library. The document was signed by Wm. G. Dana, Wm. H. Cunningham, Wm. Henderson, Diego Scott, Thos. M. Robbins and Thos. Shaw; the text is printed in Dale, p. 209.

27. Wilson was discharged Jan. 17 while still at San Gabriel but could not get permission to remain in the country, and rejoined Jedediah on Jan. 25; Rogers says, "we [were] obliged to let him come back to us; he remains with the company but not under pay as yet; I expect he will go on with us." (Dale, p. 223.) It appears from *Travels,* p. 39, that Wilson accompanied the party as far as Tulare Lake, or Chintache Lake, as Jedediah called it, where he was again discharged. When Jackson visited California after Jedediah's death, in 1831-1832, Wilson brought suit for wages allegedly due by Smith, Jackson & Sublette, and won a judgment in the California courts for $100. (Sublette Papers, Missouri Historical Society.)

28. This detail from Echeandia's letter cited in Note 24.

29. Jedediah may have left by Cajon Pass, but it seems more likely

he went the way he came, and that he used Cajon Pass for the first time the following summer. Once across the mountains, he had age-old Indian trails to guide him to the San Joaquin Valley; he left the Mojave River near present Hesperia.

30. Bancroft, vol. II, pp. 43-57; Herbert E. Bolton, "In the South San Joaquin Ahead of Garcés," *California Hist. Quart.*, Sept. 1931, vol. X, pp. 211-219; *On the Trail of a Spanish Pioneer*, vol. I, pp. 265-304.

31. Dale, p. 207.

32. It was long argued by students of Jedediah Smith's trails that he attempted to cross the Sierra by way of Kings River, the "Wimmul-che," as he called it—this on the authority of his letter to Gen. Clark. It will be seen that the letter does not say this; what it does say is that here he began his spring hunt. Jedediah's letter of May 19 to Father Durán speaks of having made "several efforts to cross the mountains," but it seems likely this was language as loose as that in his "Brief Sketch" (see p. 340), which speaks of "frequent trials" at crossing the Sierra in 1828, by no means borne out by his journal. Probably the only serious effort to get over the mountains in the spring of 1827 was by way of the American River.

33. Jedediah's journal for Feb. 20, 1828, notes the circumstance of his having "struck the [American] river on the last Ap^{l}." I assume that the 1,568 pounds of beaver and 10 otter skins he sold next December were taken in the course of his spring hunt. *Travels,* pp. 44, 63.

34. That Jedediah attempted to cross the Sierra by way of the American River seems firmly established; his journal of 1828 and the Burr map agree well on this. His letter to Father Durán would indicate that the attempt was made the first week in May.

35. *Travels,* p. 63.

36. Jedediah appears to have had a brush with the Indians at some point north of the Stanislaus. On May 21, 1827, Ignacio Martínez wrote Echeandia, "in the ranchería of the gentile Muquelemes they were surrounded for battle, but the Americans forming into square bodies killed five gentiles; these seeing they were not our soldiers became appeased." Bancroft Library, Archivo del Arzobispado de San Francisco, MS., part I, p. 33. Jedediah does not directly refer to such a fight, but his journal for Jan. 31, 1828, mentions a visit from Indians "who were so hostile to me the last spring," and he was then in the country of the "Mackalumbrys." Because of the base camp

set up on the Stanislaus in May, the river became known to trappers as Smiths River. See Alice Bay Maloney, *Fur Brigade to the Bonaventura* (San Francisco, 1945), p. 66.

37. Bancroft Library, Archivo del Arzobispado de San Francisco, part V, pp. 27-33. For this and other translations I have relied on Maurice Sullivan, in his notes to Smith's journal and in his *Jedediah Smith, Trader and Trailbreaker.*

38. See p. 333.

39. Martínez to Echeandia, May 21, 1827, Archivo Arzobispado de San Francisco, part II, pp. 30-33; Echeandia to Martínez, May 23, 1827, Departmental Records, vol. V, pp. 124-125, both in the Bancroft Library.

40. Francis P. Farquhar, "Jedediah Smith and the First Crossing of the Sierra Nevada," *Sierra Club Bulletin,* June 1943, vol. XXVIII, pp. 35-52, argues that Jedediah crossed the Sierra not by Sonora Pass, as is now generally supposed, but probably by Ebbetts Pass, some eighteen miles to the northwest, which he would have approached by way of the North Fork of the Stanislaus and Hermit Valley. If he did cross by Sonora or another pass farther south, the two northward-flowing streams he passed would have to be the east and west forks of the Walker.

41. In general terms, this route would have taken him east from Walker Lake between the Gabbs Valley Range and the Pilot Range, around the southern end of the Shoshone Mountains and the Toiyabe Range, and across the Toquima Range near Manhattan. Thence east across the Monitor Range and down Hot Creek to come into the route of US 6 below Black Rock Summit. As does the highway, Jedediah would then have gone northeast, along the base of the Pancake Range and on across Currant Summit, almost as far as Ely. His route would have bent a little south around the Schell Creek Range and north of Wheeler Peak, then turned nearly north along the base of the Snake Range to reach the Utah line in the vicinity of Gandy.

42. This was the water at present Orrs Ranch in Skull Valley. From Thomas Creek at the base of the Deep Creek Range, Jedediah and his companions had turned northeast toward the north end of the Fish Spring Range, the southern reaches of the Salt Desert on their left, and continued across the low Dugway Range into Skull Valley, which lies at the base of the high Stansbury Mountains.

43. This may have been Spring Creek, just inside the present Skull Valley Indian Reservation.

44. Apparently by way of Blacksmiths Fork Canyon.

Chapter 11. RENDEZVOUS: 1827

1. Beckwourth, pp. 62, 71.

2. Nor is it certain that Colter himself saw Yellowstone Lake. His newest biographer, Burton Harris, does not claim more for him than that he saw the South Arm and the Thumb from a distance, having missed the main trail to the lake. The late John G. White of Cleveland, Ohio, argued cogently to W. J. Ghent, in a correspondence of 1926 of which I have copies, that Colter actually saw a composite of Shoshone Lake and Lewis Lake. That Sublette headed the party in which Potts traveled is assumed from the circumstance that the Burr map calls Yellowstone Lake "Soublett Lake," to which it may be added that Potts's movements fit in precisely with Sublette's subsequent known travels.

3. This is the celebrated "Sweet Lake" letter of July 8, 1827, of which Daniel Potts is now established to have been the author. As first published, the letter seems to have been cut in two, half being printed in the *Philadelphia Gazette & Daily Advertiser* of Sept. 27, 1827—this being the part previously known—and the other half in the *Gazette* of Oct. 19, 1827. They have been reprinted as cited in Note 27, Chapter 1.

4. See Chapter 14.

5. A sketch of Harris by Charles L. Camp is published in Clyman, pp. 53-57. My authority for his birthplace is the *St. Louis Democrat*, June 12, 1844. Miller's comment on him is from Marvin Ross, ed., *The West of Alfred Jacob Miller* (Norman, 1951), p. 67. Enough new material on Harris has appeared to justify an extended account of his life.

6. The narrative that follows is on Sublette's own authority. In the course of his excursion to the Rockies in the William Drummond Stewart party of 1843, Sublette told this story to the journalist Matt Field, who noted the details in his diary under date of Aug. 21, 1843. (The diary is now in the Missouri Historical Society library.) On returning to the States, Field wrote two articles on the basis of these notes, "The Death of a Dog" and "A Perilous Winter Journey," which he published in the *New Orleans Daily Picayune*, Dec. 27, 1843, and March 14, 1844. Beckwourth, p. 62, notes the fact of the midwinter journey but misdates it. The reason for the journey is only now documented.

7. I have suggested in Chapter 9 that Jedediah Smith's mountain-

bound party of 1825 was first to travel this road. How Ashley went to and from the mountains in 1826 is not certainly known. Sublette's use of this route, however, is unquestionable, the first of record for travel to or from the mountains.

8. Ashley to (B. Pratte & Co.), Oct. 14, 1826, Ashley Papers, Missouri Historical Society.

9. Chittenden, vol. I, p. 276, who consistently misconceives Provost's relation to Ashley, says that he fell out with the General at the rendezvous of 1826 and "forthwith set out for St. Louis, arriving there ahead of Ashley, and entered into negotiations with Bernard Pratte and Company by which he was to conduct a rival expedition to the mountains in the following year. Ashley, on his arrival, nipped this opposition in the bud by himself offering Bernard Pratte and Company a share in his next expedition to the mountains." Chittenden cites no source, and the Chouteau papers now in the Missouri Historical Society do not show what proposition Provost did make to the French Company. Chittenden clearly did not understand the drift of the proposal Ashley made in this instance.

10. B. Berthold to J. P. Cabanné, Dec. 9, 1826, Chouteau-Papin Collection, Missouri Historical Society.

11. Ashley Papers, Missouri Historical Society.

12. *Ibid.*

13. *Ibid.* The agreement finally arrived at was reached within two days of Sublette's arrival in St. Louis, for the *Missouri Republican*, March 8, 1827, has the following ad: "FOR THE ROCKY MOUNTAINS. W. H. ASHLEY's expedition for the Rocky Mountains will leave St. Louis in a few days. FIFTY competent men may meet with employ in that service if application be immediately made. March 6, 1827."

14. Bruffee as the business agent was paid $800 for his services; Scott as the field captain was paid $2.00 a day for 140 days. This information comes from a fiscal accounting on the men who were employed for the venture, a document now in the Ashley Papers, Missouri Historical Society. This shows that there were forty-four men in the outbound party, thirty-eight inbound, eight having elected to stay in the mountains with Smith, Jackson & Sublette. Robert Evans and one other man joined the inbound party, Evans being paid $51 for his services. In all, the cost in wages for this venture came to $5,061.

15. See Ashley to Macomb, cited in Note 4, Chapter 9.

16. Ashley Papers, Missouri Historical Society.

17. Licenses to Trade with the Indians, 20th Cong., 1st Sess., *Senate Document 96* (Serial 165).

18. Ogden found so few beaver in this country by the fall of 1827 that Jackson may have cleaned out the rivers the previous spring.

19. Potts, second half of letter of July 8, 1827.

20. Ross, *Fur Hunters*, vol. I, p. 227; vol. II, p. 63; and the Kittson map in *Ogden's Snake Country Journals*. The Ferris and Bonneville maps, and Arrowsmith's map of *British North America*, 1837 (on which the better-known Abert or Hood map of Oregon, 1838, is based) are useful for a study of the early history of Bear Lake. Beckwourth's references to Weaver's Lake, which is *not* Great Salt Lake as has been supposed, are on pp. 62, 66 of his book.

21. Potts, first half of letter of July 8, 1827.

22. Beckwourth, pp. 71-73.

23. The mention of Quimanuapa is interesting as perhaps the earliest notice of the chief Warren Ferris calls Conmarrowap, and just as interesting is the Spanish version of the name of the Shoshoni.

24. 25th Cong., 2nd Sess., *House Document 351* (Serial 332), pp. 228-230.

25. These figures are from Nathaniel Wyeth's instructions to Robert Evans, whom he was leaving in charge of Fort Hall in Aug. 1834; see the Fort Hall Account Books, MS., Oregon Historical Society.

26. Thomas Biddle to John Scott, Jan. 1826, printed in *Missouri Republican*, Sept. 14, 1826.

27. See Note 27, Chapter 9.

28. John Dougherty reported in 1831, with respect to the fur trade on the Missouri and its waters, including the Rocky Mountains, "that clerks were paid $500 per year, men $150 per year." These prices may have obtained on the Missouri, but it seems likely higher wages prevailed in the mountains. 22nd Cong., 1st Sess., *Senate Document 90* (Serial 213), p. 53. Even for service on the Missouri, Ashley in 1823 advertised a wage of $200 per year. See p. 50.

29. Dale, pp. 269-270.

30. Potts, both halves of letter of July 8, 1827.

31. This quotation from Ogden's MS. journal has courteously been given to me by the Hudson's Bay Company, and is printed by permission.

32. Account rendered by James Bruffee, Oct. 18, 1827, Ashley Papers, Missouri Historical Society.

33. Sublette Papers, Missouri Historical Society.

34. Ashley to Macomb, cited in Note 4, Chapter 9; Ogden's journal of 1827-1828, see p. 294; J. P. Cabanné to P. Chouteau, Jr., Jan. 6, 1828, Chouteau-Papin Collection, Missouri Historical Society.

Chapter 12. THE CALIFORNIA QUAGMIRE

1. Fort Hall Account Books, Oregon Historical Society.

2. These names are derived from the Smith and Rogers journals and from the two Smith, Jackson & Sublette casualty lists printed on pp. 341, 344-345.

3. *Travels*, pp. 26-27.

4. After crossing over to the Bear, Jedediah may have followed that river up to where Ashley's trail of 1825 reached it from the west, then crossed a low divide to Chalk Creek and gone on down to the Weber. It is a little more probable that in the vicinity of present Evanston he turned up Yellow Creek and so on to the head of Chalk Creek. Once he reached the Weber, he went up it to Kamas Prairie and over to the Provo at the south end of the Prairie, then down the Provo to Utah Valley, where he came back into his trail of 1826.

5. The history of the southwestern fur trade still needs intensive work. R. G. Cleland, *This Reckless Breed of Men* (New York, 1950), is the only summary of the fragmentary monographic literature.

6 Santiago Argüello to Echeandia, San Gabriel, Feb. [Oct.] 8, 1827, Bancroft Library, Department State Papers, vol. II, pp. 35-37, advises that Smith left the San Bernardino Valley Sept. 2. Since in his "Brief Sketch" Jedediah says he was nine and a half days in coming from the Colorado, and his journal adds that he remained in the San Bernardino Valley five days, the date of the Mojave Massacre might have been Aug. 18.

7. No account of the massacre appears in Jedediah Smith's journal, which has a page and a half blank, followed by two missing pages; the only firsthand account therefore is that in the "Brief Sketch"; see p. 338. Peter Skene Ogden's anonymously published *Traits of American Indian Life* (London, 1853), pp. 12-13, has a more or less imaginary version of the massacre.

8. This famous gateway into southern California may have been used by Fages in 1772, and it was certainly traveled by Zalvidea in 1806, but Jedediah's passage through it in 1827 opened a new era in its history. Beattie and Beattie, pp. 328-329.

9. *Travels*, pp. 34-35. Jedediah adds: "The overseer told me that some of the Amuchaba chiefs had been in to the settlement and brought the news of their having defeated a party of Americans, which was no doubt the same of which Francisco spoke. But instead of quar-

reling among themselves the probability is that they were defeated by the indians, separated in two parties in the affray, and traveled different ways." See also the unpublished portion of the Orange Clark MS. on George Yount in the Bancroft Library.

10. The letter by Argüello cited in Note 6 recounts that one Manuel had guided the American from the mouth of the Cajon de Muscupiabe to the Indian village, Atongallavit, on the Mojave River near present Hesperia, and says that Jedediah left Sept. 2.

11. *Travels,* p. 36; and see p. 338.

12. Duhaut-Cilly in *California Hist. Quart.,* Sept. 1929, vol. VIII, p. 238. Alfred Robinson, pp. 85-86, gives a more favorable picture of Father Durán.

13. A recent biography is Susanna Dakin, *The Lives of William Hartnell* (Stanford, 1948).

14. This quotation and the foregoing come from Jedediah's journal. Alfred Robinson, p. 98, relates that Galbraith used to amuse himself by shooting off the heads of blackbirds at twenty paces. Waldo, p. 85, says that the Maine-born Galbraith returned to Missouri in 1832 and died at Independence. He bequeathed "his herculean frame to a physician who had befriended him, and up to the commencement of the late Civil War, his skeleton could be seen in the doctor's office—a fine specimen of a Maine giant."

15. Alice Bay Maloney, "The Richard Campbell Party of 1827," *California Hist. Quart.,* Dec. 1939, vol. XVIII, pp. 347-354.

16. The original instrument, in Spanish and with Jedediah's signature, is in the Bancroft Library, M. G. Vallejo, *Documentos para la historia de California,* vol. XXIX, p. 171. Maurice Sullivan's translation is in *Travels,* p. 172. On Nov. 15, before leaving Monterey, to protect Cooper, Jedediah signed a bond for $30,000 insuring the faithful performance of the bond given the government; this is in the Sublette Papers, Missouri Historical Society, having been brought from California by David E. Jackson in 1832.

17. Vallejo *Documentos,* vol. XXIX, p. 173, Bancroft Library; translated by Sullivan in *Travels,* p. 173.

18. James Wolfe, Journal of a Voyage on Discovery in the Pacific and Beering's Straits on board H. M. S. Blossom, MS, Coe Collection, Yale University, pp. 209-211.

19. Sublette Papers, Missouri Historical Society; this is dated Dec. 27, 1827.

20. Virgin had undergone a characteristic grilling. See Argüello to Echeandia, San Gabriel, Feb. [Oct.] 8, 1827, and Echeandia to Ar-

güello, Monterey, Sept. 14, 1827 (Department State Papers, vol. II, pp. 35-37; vol. V, p. 89), Bancroft Library.

21. 25th Cong., 2nd Sess., *House Document 351* (Serial 332), pp. 246-248. In this exchange of correspondence the American minister, under date of Aug. 20, 1828, sent to the Mexican Secretary of State "a letter very lately received from the said Smith, in which he accounts satisfactorily for his being found within the Mexican territories, and complains of the harsh treatment he had experienced from the authorities of the Californias." The letter was transmitted through Cooper and J. Lenox Kennedy, the American consul at Mazatlán; it has not yet been found in the Mexican archives.

Chapter 13. THE UMPQUA MASSACRE

1. *Travels,* pp. 53, 174-175.

2. *Ibid.,* p. 48.

3. This is Simpson's figure (see Note 1, Chapter 14), pp. 58-59. The total of 315 horses is stated in a letter, William Todd to Edward Ermatinger, York Factory, July 15, 1829, *Washington Hist. Quart.,* July 1907, vol. I, p. 257. Todd had seen Jedediah in California.

4. Those interested in the local details of Jedediah's journey up through California, over to the ocean, and then up the California-Oregon coast should study his journal and that of Rogers. Francis A. Wiley, *Jedediah Smith in the West,* Ph.D. thesis, University of California, 1941, examines the route, and so does H. C. Dale in the revised edition, 1941, of his *Ashley-Smith Explorations.* The Historical Society of Humboldt County has minutely annotated the Rogers diary in *The Quest for Qual-a-wa-loo [Humboldt Bay]* (San Francisco, 1943), pp. 31-74; and Alice Bay Maloney has studied the itinerary from the Oregon line to the Umpqua in "Camp Sites of Jedediah Smith on the Oregon Coast," *Oregon Hist. Quart.,* Sept. 1940, vol. XLI, pp. 304-323.

5. They reached the ocean at Mussel Point, north of Redwood Creek. See *The Quest for Qual-a-wa-loo,* pp. 38-39.

6. This name from the casualty lists; see pp. 341, 345.

7. *Travels,* pp. 123, 125.

8. McLoughlin to the Governor, Deputy Governor and Committee, Fort Vancouver, Aug. 10, 1828, *Letters of John McLoughlin,* pp. 68-70. For the locale, see Lancaster Pollard, "Site of the Smith Massacre July 14, 1828," *Oregon Hist. Quart.,* June 1944, vol. XLV, pp. 133-137.

9. S. A. Clarke, *Pioneer Days of Oregon History* (Portland, 1905), vol. I, p. 216.

10. McLoughlin's letter of Aug. 10, 1828, cited in Note 8. Apparently Jedediah left the coast at present Tillamook, going up the Trask River and descending the Tualatin River to the Willamette.

11. See p. 294.

12. Merk, p. 23.

13. The best biography is Richard Montgomery, *The White Headed Eagle* (New York, 1935), but a new study of McLoughlin is called for in the light of four recent volumes of his letters.

14. Merk, pp. 123-124.

15. *Ibid.*, pp. 254-255.

16. *Ibid.*, p. 283. McLoughlin at the same time improved the rate structure for the engaged men. *Letters of John McLoughlin*, pp. 27-28, 33-35.

17. Merk, p. 291.

18. *Ibid.*, pp. 286-287.

19. See p. 233.

20. See p. 282.

21. Abridged versions of ms. journals of 1826-1827, 1827-1828, and 1828-1829 are published in *Oregon Hist. Quart.*, 1910, vol. XI; eventually these will be published in full by the Hudson's Bay Record Society. His journal of 1829-1830 was lost in a whirlpool in the Columbia River.

22. *Letters of John McLoughlin*, pp. 35-36.

23. Simpson as cited in Note 1, Chapter 14, pp. 152-153.

24. Merk, pp. 294-295.

25. Merk, "Snake Country Expedition, 1824-25," pp. 118-119.

26. Merk, pp. 294-295.

27. *Letters of John McLoughlin*, pp. 65-66.

28. Maloney, *Fur Brigade to the Bonaventura*, p. 104.

29. *Travels*, pp. 112-113.

30. *Ibid.*, pp. 109-111 (H. B. C. Arch. B. 223/6/4, fos. 27 d.-29); reprinted by permission of the Governor and Committee of the Hudson's Bay Company.

Chapter 14. "GOOD, MERCHANTABLE BEAVER FURR"

1. The foregoing account is based on Simpson's report to the Governor and Committee in London, mostly under date of March 1, 1829, but with additions on March 24 and June 5; the dispatch has

been printed in full as *Part of Dispatch from George Simpson Esq*[r] *Governor of Ruperts Land To the Governor & Committee of the Hudson's Bay Company London* (London and Toronto, 1947). I have especially drawn on pp. 30-31, 38-39, 47-72. Some extracts from this document were printed by Sullivan in *Travels,* pp. 143-150.

2. Burt Brown Barker, ed., *Letters of Dr. John McLoughlin Written at Fort Vancouver 1829-1832* (Portland, 1948), p. 78. McLoughlin to Simpson, March 24, 1830, refers to McLeod's arrival from the Umpqua as having been on the morning of Dec. 14, 1828; however, Simpson's letter quoted on p. 285 speaks of Jedediah's furs as having been exposed to every rainstorm from April to Dec. 22, 1828, which would imply a later arrival.

3. McLeod's MS. California journal of 1829-1830 is in the Hudson's Bay Company archives. Alice Bay Maloney published John Work's journal of the California expedition of 1832-1833 as *Fur Brigade to the Bonaventura,* and scattered information about later "Southern expeditions" is found in the three volumes of McLoughlin's letters published by the Hudson's Bay Record Society. The severe criticism McLeod met with on his return from California in 1830 is contained in the letterbook cited in Note 2.

4. The whole text of the letter is printed in Merk, pp. 302-306, and in *Travels,* pp 136-240 from H. B. C. Arch. D. 4/16, fos. 13-16.

5. The letter has previously been printed by Merk and Sullivan, and is now reprinted by permission of the Governor and Committee of the Hudson's Bay Company from *ibid.,* fos. 16d.-17.

6. Apparently Jedediah accepted Simpson's offer immediately, for on Dec. 26, 1828, Simpson wrote the Hudson's Bay Company's agent at Lachine that he had drawn on him at thirty days sight in favor of Messrs. Smith, Jackson & Sibbeth for the sum of £550. 2s. 6d Halifax Currency, to be charged to the Northern Dept. of Rupert's Land "being the amount of Furs & Horses sold to the Honble. Hudson's Bay" and delivered at Fort Vancouver. (Hudson's Bay Company Archives, D.4/16, fo. 17d). On March 9, 1829, Simpson again advised James Keith at Lachine that he had drawn a bill of exchange on him at sight in favor of Messrs. Smith, Jackson & Sublit for the sum of £541. 0s. 6d Halifax Currency, to be "charged in account with the Northern Department Outfit 1828 being the balance of Accounts of Furs and Horses sold to the Honble. Hudson's Bay Company" and delivered at Fort Vancouver. (Hudson's Bay Company Archives, B.134/c/5.) The use of the word "balance" would imply two different transactions, rather than a March correction of a December transaction, yet it is unaccount-

able how enough property could have been turned over by Jedediah on the stated terms to have called for two such payments. The H. B. Company has found for me (in H. B. Ç. Arch. B. 223/d/21a) indications that the first draft was canceled.

7. Simpson, p. 57.

8. *Ibid.*, pp. 67-68.

9. It is not clear how early this news reached Fort Vancouver. Simpson replied on Feb. 18 to a letter by Pilcher, but may have had earlier word of the American visitants.

10. Not much is known about the later life of Black. The last reference I have to him is a document in the Missouri Historical Society archives, an order signed by Kenneth McKenzie at Fort Union, June 30, 1832, on P. Chouteau, Jr., St. Louis, to pay to the order of Mr. Arthur Black fifteen hundred & one dollars for value received in beaver.

11. According to Maloney, *Fur Brigade to the Bonaventura*, p. 105, Turner went immediately back to California with McLeod in Jan. 1829; he again went to California in 1832-1833, and at that time left the Hudson's Bay Company service to join a party under Ewing Young which was trapping the Sacramento.

12. Barker, p. 14. The Hudson's Bay Company searched its archives for me without developing anything further about Leland.

13. The same route was traveled by John Work in August 1826, though after reaching Clarks Fork he went on up the river by canoe. See his journal in *Washington Hist. Quart.*, Jan. 1915, vol. VI, pp. 26-49.

14. Ashley to Thomas H. Benton, Jan. 20, 1829, 20th Cong., 2nd Sess., *Senate Document* 67 (Serial 181), p. 13.

15. Beckwourth, pp. 74-79.

16. See Ogden's journal for Feb. 16, 1828, quoted on p. 294, and compare McLoughlin to Simpson, Fort Vancouver, July 10, 1828 (*Letters of John McLoughlin*, p. 61), from which it appears that fourteen of the deserters appeared at Flathead Post the previous winter. See also Simpson, p. 48.

17. Ashley to Benton, cited in Note 14. See Ferris, p. 103, and compare the Bonneville map. "Joseph Cotty" had been one of Ashley's *engagés* in the expedition of 1827; if this is the same man, he must have gone back to the mountains in the fall of 1827, and this death would be proof of contact between Sublette's party and the supply caravan from the States prior to Sublette's spring hunt of 1828.

18. Ogden's journal of 1827-1828, quoted from the MS. by permission of the Governor and Committee of the Hudson's Bay Company.

19. Ashley to Benton, p. 14. Ogden learned what had happened to Tullock's party on May 10, 1828.

20. *Ibid.*, pp. 14-15. Compare Beckwourth, p. 65.

21. *Travels*, p. 126; and see pp. 341, 344-345.

22. The description of their deaths is Ashley's, in the letter to Benton; Bear River is given as the place in the Smith, Jackson & Sublette casualty list, p. 345.

23. Beckwourth, pp. 66-69; Ashley to Benton, pp. 13-14.

24. See Joshua Pilcher's statement cited in Note 8, Chapter 1.

25. O'Fallon to Pilcher, Aug. 6, 1824 (O'Fallon Letterbook, p. 88).

26. See Licenses to Trade with the Indians, 19th Cong., 1st Sess., *House Document 118* (Serial 136), and 19th Cong., 2nd Sess., *House Document 86* (Serial 152)

27. Pilcher to the Secretary of War, 1830, 21st Cong., 2nd Sess., *Senate Document 39* (Serial 203), pp. 7-8. The casualty lists show that in 1828 J. Pilcher & Co. had two men, Cabanné and Le More, killed by the Crows on "Big River Platte."

28. J. P. Cabanné to P. Chouteau, Jr., Sept. 22, Oct. 14, 1828, both letters dated "Near the Bluffs." Chouteau-Papin Collection, Missouri Historical Society.

29. The casualty lists show the loss in 1829 of Garreau and Mino by the Blackfeet on the Yellowstone, these men employed by "Fontenelle & Drips." There is, however, some ambiguity about the relationship of Fontenelle & Drips to the American Fur Company, down to the mid-'30s, which historians of the fur trade will have to work out.

30. John Work to Edward Ermatinger, Fort Colvile, March 28, 1829, *Frontier and Midland*, Nov. 1933, vol. XIV, p. 67.

31. Simpson, pp. 55-56.

32. Merk, pp. 307-308.

33. Pilcher's statement cited in Note 27, pp. 8-9. Pilcher does not mention the loss of his man in this statement but does include his name in the casualty list he furnished Gen. Clark on Nov. 20, 1831. Purchase of traps from him "in 1828 & 29" is noted in one of the accounts in the Sublette Papers.

34. Sublette's arrival from the mountains is reported in two letters written by James Aull at Lexington to Tracy & Wahrendorff, Sept. 25, Oct. 2, 1828 (Ralph P. Bieber, ed., "Letters of James and Robert Aull," *Missouri Hist. Soc. Colls.*, June 1928, vol. V, pp. 272-273). J. P. Cabanné to P. Chouteau, Jr., Sept. 22, 1828, indicates that he brought in about seventy packs of beaver. See Note 28.

35. Merrill J. Mattes, "Hiram Scott, Fur Trader," *Nebraska History*,

July-Sept., 1945, vol. XXVI, pp. 127-162. Like Mr. Mattes and most other modern scholars, I assume the identity of Hiram Scott with the Scott who gave name to Scotts Bluff.

36. Ferris, pp. 30-31.

37. William Marshall Anderson, MS. Diary, quoted by courtesy of Mr. J. S. Holliday. In a rewritten version of his diary, Anderson speaks angrily of "the canting hypocrite and scoundrel" who deserted Scott. Who, then, was he?

38. Sublette Papers, Missouri Historical Society.

39. Robert Newell, Memorandum of Robert Newell's Travels in the Territory of Missouri, 1829-41, MS. in University of Oregon library. Newell appears to have begun this record in the spring of 1836, and events before that date are discussed reminiscently, but thereafter the MS. sometimes has the character and value of a diary. Newell's recollection that Sublette's company left St. Louis March 7, 1829, and reached rendezvous July 17, 1829, is probably wrong in both instances; Meek's dates of March 17-*ca.* July 1 better fit the probabilities and the scanty records with which a cross-check can be made. The Ebberts MS. in the Bancroft Library appears to agree with Newell as to the number who composed the company, "52 men and two Indians, 54 altogether."

40. Victor, pp. 43-48. A fine biography by Harvey E. Tobie, *No Man Like Joe* (Portland, 1949), critically restudies Meek's whole life, revising and correcting Mrs. Victor in many instances. Dr. Tobie tells me that he is convinced Meek kept a diary in the mountains, a record he did not succeed in locating.

41. On Meek's—or Mrs. Victor's—authority, it has been supposed that Sublette had no idea where Jackson was, but this would appear to be incorrect; it would seem that Jackson sent Fitzpatrick as an express to arrange a rendezvous with Sublette west of the divide. In his diary for Aug. 9, 1834, William Marshall Anderson describes an atmospheric phenomenon Fitzpatrick experienced while "encamped at the forks of Wind river" on June 20, 1829. Since Gov. Simpson specifically said that Fitzpatrick had been Jackson's clerk in the Flathead country the previous winter, it must be supposed that Jackson had sent Fitzpatrick to meet Sublette; he may have set out before Jedediah reached Jackson's camp. After the rendezvous with Sublette, Fitzpatrick evidently set out without delay to meet Jackson, for Jedediah's letter of Dec. 24, 1829, to his brother Ralph speaks of having received family letters written as late as Dec. 1828 (and therefore brought to the mountains by Sublette) on July 16, 1829. Doubtful an authority as

Ebberts may be on other points, he has something interesting to say here: "The year I came [to the mountains], Smith came here [to Oregon] . . . We sent Fitzpatrick on to meet him. Fitzpatrick came on and met Smith, & we came & met him." Ebberts goes on to say that Sublette's party moved on to Pierres Hole by the Three Tetons: "We were lying in Jackson's Hole when the express came back to us at the Three Tetons. We were lying there & Fitzpatrick, he came back to us. . . . Then we moved to them—to Smith's."

42. David L. Brown, *Three Years in the Rocky Mountains,* reprinted from the *Cincinnati Atlas,* Sept. issues of 1845, by Edward Eberstadt & Sons (New York, 1950), p. 12. Brown knew Bridger in the mountains during 1837-1838.

43. Beckwourth, pp. 88-99.

44. Sublette Papers, Missouri Historical Society.

45. See p. 345; and Note 29.

46. Victor, p. 57.

47. Bieber, p. 275: James Aull to Tracy & Wahrendorff, Lexington, Aug. 20, 1829, "Mr. Campbell with one part of Sublets company from Rocky Mountains have just arrived here with 45 Packs of Beaver. . . ." Before leaving the mountains, Campbell was given a draft on Ashley for $3,016, but it is not stated whether this was a settlement for one year's services and beaver catch only. (Sublette Papers.)

48. Newell's date, "August 20," is probably mistaken, like his previously noted dates for 1829; perhaps this should be Aug. 5, as would follow from Jedediah's statement.

49. Simpson, pp. 49, 56.

50. The pressure on the southern fur country is shown by the way Hugh Glass, Pegleg Smith, Milton Sublette and others who had been operating in the south began to appear at the annual rendezvous in the north after 1827.

51. This may have been the area of the present Chico Hot Springs. The Burr map depicts a hot-spring region west, rather than east, of the Yellowstone, probably a mistake.

52. Victor, pp. 73-81.

53. *Ibid.,* p. 81; see also p. 313.

Chapter 15. THE THINGS OF TIME

1. Jedediah S. Smith to Jedediah and Sally Smith, Dec. 24, 1829; see Appendix for this and other letters quoted.

2. Jedediah S. Smith to Ralph Smith, Dec. 24, 1829.

3. Jedediah S. Smith to Ralph Smith, Jan. 26, 1831.

4. *Eulogy* (see Note 5, Chapter 1). Waldo, p. 87, remarks at length "the religious character and the liberality of Jedediah Smith."

5. A tradition preserved by a descendant of Ralph Smith is that Jedediah was in love with Ralph's wife, Louisa Simons, "a very beautiful woman," and for that reason never paid any attention to other women; this may have been so, but there is not the slightest suggestion of any such feeling in Jedediah's letters, nor did he make any special provision for her in his will. Late marriages were characteristic of a number of Jedediah's associates in the fur trade, Sublette and Campbell, for instance, and Jedediah died in his thirty-third year.

6. Jedediah was the only man in the party to whom Harrison Rogers, en route to California in 1826, issued shaving soap; later entries in Rogers' diaries exhibit Jedediah's abstemious ways. See also *Travels*, p. 45.

7. *Eulogy*.

8. Victor, pp. 82-84. Newell also mentions going from the Big Horn to Powder River to remain till spring. The Burr map mistakenly indicates a winter camp on Tongue River—a point beyond which it does not show Jedediah's travels.

9. This is the conjectural route shown on the end-paper map, but it may be that in returning to the Yellowstone Jedediah trapped up the Judith to its sources, then over to the upper Musselshell, and so on back, making a loop rather than a double traverse along a single line of travel.

10. Victor, pp. 88-89. See an allusion to the accident on p. 346. The man killed may have been Glaud Ponto, mentioned in the Ashley and Sublette Papers.

11. Ogden's letter of March 12, 1831, briefly describing this exploration is printed by John Scaglione in *California Hist. Quart.*, June 1949, vol. XXVIII, pp. 121-122.

12. Chittenden, vol. I, pp. 293, 306-307.

13. Licenses to Trade with the Indians, 21st Cong., 2nd Sess., *House Document 41* (Serial 207).

14. William Marshall Anderson, ms. Diary, May 12, 1834; H. C. Dale, ed., "A Fragmentary Journal of William L. Sublette," *Mississippi Valley Hist. Rev.*, June 1919, vol. VI, pp. 99-110: Sublette on May 28, 1843, speaks of "Sublette's Old Trace."

15. See pp. 350, 356.

16. The clearest account of the situation at the Mandans from 1822 to 1826 is Maximilian's, vol. II, pp. 223-224.

17. Abel, pp. 197-199; compare Chittenden, vol. I, pp. 325-328, and John Forsythe's statement of Oct. 24, 1831, in 22nd Cong., 1st Sess., *Senate Document 90* (Serial 213), p. 75.

18. Chittenden, vol. I, pp. 342-343; this and the letter following are not now in the Chouteau Collection.

19. *Ibid.*, p. 330.

20. *Ibid.*, pp. 330-331; vol. II, p. 933. Chittenden quotes from a letter of McKenzie's dated March 15, 1829, "Old Glass came to Fort Floyd last fall."

21. Camp, "The Chronicles of George C. Yount," pp. 24, 30-32.

22. Maximilian, vol. XXII, p. 294; vol. XXIII, p. 197; vol. XXIV, pp. 101-104. A letter from John F. A. Sanford to William Clark, July 26, 1833 (National Archives, Office of Indian Affairs, Mandan Agency files, 1833), mentions that Rose and one Menard were killed with Glass at this time. Johnson Gardner apparently continued a free trapper down to the time Smith, Jackson & Sublette left the mountains; on Aug. 1, 1830, they gave him a note for $1,321.48, evidently the purchase price of his beaver.

23. For the deal with Robidoux see J. P. Cabanné to P. Chouteau, Oct. 14, Dec. 29, 1828 (Chouteau-Papin Collection, Missouri Historical Society). Pilcher's other partner, Charles Bent, went out to Santa Fe in the summer of 1829, and the rest of his life is associated with the history of the Southwest. Some arrangement was made with Fontenelle & Drips at this time, for with Robidoux they took an American Fur Company brigade to the Rockies in 1830. A sketch of Vanderburgh's life is printed by Paul C. Phillips in *Mississippi Valley Hist. Rev.*, Dec. 1943, vol. XXX, pp. 377-394, but does not greatly clarify this period.

24. Kenneth McKenzie to Pierre Chouteau, Fort Tecumseh, July 7, 1829 (Chouteau-Papin Collection, Missouri Historical Society).

25. Kenneth McKenzie to "The Gentleman in charge of Fort Tecumseh," Fort Union, May 5, 1830 (Chouteau-Papin Collection).

26. A member of this party was Warren Angus Ferris; see Note 11, Chapter 7.

27. This information comes from Ashley's receipt (as Smith's executor) of Jan. 5, 1833, in the Sublette Papers, and from an inventory of the assets of Jedediah Smith's estate, File 930, in the St. Louis Probate Court records. While at Santa Fe, on Aug. 23, 1831, Jackson & Sublette gave David Waldo a power of attorney to collect what they

recalled as "upwards of sixteen thousand dollars" at the New Mexico price for beaver, $4.25 per pound; and it has been supposed that this document, which provided against the contingency that Fitzpatrick might make delivery on the furs there instead of in Missouri, set forth the terms of the note given at Wind River in 1830.

28. There is no documentation of such an understanding, but my text sets forth the circumstantial evidence for it.

29. The party may have come in by detachments; the *St. Louis Beacon,* Oct. 7, 1830, announces that "Messrs. Smith and Jackson have just arrived," while the *Missouri Republican* of Oct. 19 and the *Beacon* of Nov. 4 give the date of arrival as Oct. 11.

30. This phrase is from the *Beacon's* brief story of Oct. 7; the quotation following is from the fuller account of Nov. 4.

31. Solomon A. Simons to Peter Smith, Nov. 22, 1829; see p. 349.

32. Sublette Papers, Missouri Historical Society. Jedediah's share of the additional returns, amounting to $17,604.33, was not paid until after his death.

33. The inventory of the assets of Jedediah's estate recites: "It also appears from the receipt of Ralph Smith that said J. S. Smith paid him the said Ralph Fifteen hundred dollars for the purpose of purchasing in the name of said Jedediah a tract of land in the County of Wayne in the State of Ohio—then the property of Maj[r] Tiller."

34. *Ibid.* The Negro man, William, was thirty-eight years old, valued at $400; the woman, Elizabeth, was twenty-one, valued at $325.

35. Jedediah S. Smith to Ralph Smith, Jan. 26, 1831; see p. 359.

36. Jedediah S. Smith to Hugh Campbell, Nov. 24, 1830; see p. 357.

37. See the sketch of Parkman in *Pioneer and General History of Geauga County [Ohio]* (n. p., 1880), pp. 704-705. It is stated that he went to the mountains in 1829 with Sublette, returned to St. Louis in the autumn of 1830, and "was engaged during the winter of 1830-31 in arranging the notes, and making maps of the route through which they had traveled. At the same time he prosecuted the study of the Spanish language, in preparation for a visit to New Mexico, which he had then in contemplation, and which was carried out in the spring of 1831." Parkman became superintendent of a silver mine at Guanajuato, Mexico, and died there in 1873.

On J. J. Warner's authority, it has been supposed that Jedediah intended only to outfit his brothers Peter and Austin for a venture in the Santa Fe trade, and that he himself went along only when the size of the investment at the last moment made this expedient.

("Reminiscences of Early California from 1831 to 1846," *Ann. Pubs. of the Hist. Soc. of So. Calif.*, 1907-1908, p. 177.) It will be noted that Austin Smith did not even arrive in St. Louis till Jan. 25, 1831, which could not have been more than a day or so before Jedediah wrote Ashley for a passport; and he had had some business deal in prospect as far back as November.

38. National Archives, State Department, Passport Letters, Jan. 3-Nov. 15, 1831. The passport is No. 2269 in Passports, vol. 12, Oct. 7, 1829-April 23, 1831. Unfortunately, no physical description is provided.

39. The letter and passport for Sublette are in the two volumes above cited; the passport is No. 2332. The original is in the Sublette Papers, Missouri Historical Society. Jackson may have gone to Santa Fe on Sublette's passport, as the Smith brothers did on Jedediah's.

40. Warner left several versions of his reminiscences; besides that cited in Note 37, there are some nearly identical reminiscences in MS. in the Bancroft Library, and two brief sketches.

41. Photographic copies of this contract and some related documents, including the contemporary copy of Austin Smith's letter to Ira G. Smith, Sept. 24, 1831, have been furnished me through the courtesy of Gen. Manuel Torrea, Director, and Señor Francisco Cabrera of the Archivo Historico de la Secretaría de Relaciones Exteriores in Mexico City. It would appear that these documents were obtained from Ira G. Smith by the Mexican vice consul in St. Louis, and transmitted to Mexico by Francisco Pizarro Martínez, the consul at New Orleans.

42. The number of wagons which made up the company is best described by J. J. Warner in one of his Bancroft Library reminiscences (Cal. MSS. E 65, No. 29). His published reminiscences speak of ten wagons among the twenty-three belonging to "Messrs. Mills & Chadwick" and attribute none to Jedediah's ownership. In his two letters of Sept. 24, 1831, Austin Smith speaks of the whole company as made up of twenty-two wagons and seventy-four men, which probably describes the Smith and the Jackson & Sublette components. The eventual total of eighty-five men would seem to include Fitzpatrick and an *engagé*, who joined up after the journey began.

43. The date is from the *Eulogy*. Warner, p. 177, says he left St. Louis in Jedediah's employ "about the first of April and traveling by land with mule wagons we reached Lexington, Mo., to which point some goods had been shipped. A week or two was spent in Lexington and a day or two at Independence in adding to the means of transportation and in the laying in of stores for the journey. On the 4th of

May, 1831, the camp on the left bank of the Little Blue, where we had remained two or three days making final preparations, was broken up and the party started in its pathless way across the plains for Santa Fe."

44. This will is in the St. Louis Probate Court records, File 930, with the papers governing the administration of Jedediah's estate. The text of the will is printed in *Travels,* pp. 157-158.

45. See Jedediah's note of this date on p. 362, and compare Note 43.

46. Ferris, pp. 124-125. Joe Meek's account of the fall hunt of 1830 is one of the most defective portions of Mrs. Victor's book. What is here said of it rests on Fitzpatrick's own authority, a story published in the *St. Louis Beacon,* May 12, 1831, which mentions his arrival at Lexington "a few days since" from the mountains; but again mine is the interpretation of the considerations that brought Fitzpatrick down to the States.

47. Ira G. Smith, then executor of Jedediah Smith's estate, on April 10, 1834, billed Fitzpatrick for $2,800 plus interest for goods bought by Fitzpatrick from Parkman as Smith's agent at Santa Fe in July 1831. In reply Fitzpatrick asked for a corrected bill, saying, "The agreement was thus Sublette & Jackson to furnish 2/3 J Smith 1/3 but J S. Smith went a little over his proportion"; he added with respect to the interest, "I acknowledge now I took such articles as you could not dispose of in Mexico and articles which you were glad to get rid of." (Sublette Papers, Missouri Historical Society.) The $2,800 indebtedness is noted in the inventory of the assets of Jedediah's estate, stated as $2,850.

48. All this is clearly set forth by Ferris, pp. 124-126. After Jedediah's death, Fitzpatrick was fitted out in just this fashion; his forty men engaged at Taos included young Kit Carson. It was expected that Fitzpatrick would bring the returns of the Rocky Mountain Fur Company back to Taos, but instead he went directly down to the States this fall, returning to the mountains with Sublette in the spring of 1832. This much to straighten out the record on Fitzpatrick, which has got badly confused on his movements between 1830 and 1832.

49. Accounts of Vanderburgh's troubles of 1830, in the shape of letters from the upper Missouri, are published in *Missouri Republican,* March 22, 1831, and *St. Louis Beacon,* March 24, 1831; to these may be added the advices from Fitzpatrick in the *Beacon* for May 12, 1831

50. Josiah Gregg, *Commerce of the Prairies* (Thwaites ed., Cleveland, 1905), vol. I, pp. 218-219, 236. An unpublished letter from William L. Sublette to Ashley, written from Walnut Creek Sept. 24 1831,

which is in private hands in St. Louis, says, "On our Way out to Santafee we lost Mr Minter killed on the pawnee fork we supose by the pawnees it hapened on the 19th of June Mr J. S. Smith was killed on the Cimeron June 27th by the Comanches We met with no other losses by indians & arive in Santafee July 4th." It is evident that Sublette's dates should be May 19 and May 27, or the party could not have reached Santa Fe by July 4.

51. This version is from the *Eulogy;* I think the anonymous eulogist may have obtained his information from Fitzpatrick himself in St. Louis during the winter of 1831-1832. Stories that Jedediah set out alone in search of water are not necessarily contradictory but apply to the last phase of the hunt, after he separated from Fitzpatrick. My version of Jedediah's death is primarily based on Austin Smith's letters of Sept. 24, 1831, and on the account in the *Eulogy.* Others may be found in Gregg, pp. 236-238; Waldo, pp. 86-87, and Warner, pp. 177-178. It is said that when at last Jedediah fired on the Comanche chief, his ball passed through the man's body and killed another behind him; Waldo explains this by saying that the two Indians were riding the same horse.

E. D. Smith, who devoted much study to the problem, wrote J. L. Gillis on May 17, 1915, a letter in the California State Library: "Smith met his death at the hands of a band of twenty Comanchie Indians at a water hole known in my time as Fargo Spring, to the later Santa Fe traders as Wagon Body Spring. Do not confuse this with Wagon Bed Spring just above the confluence of the dry Cimarron with the Cimarron. This water hole was (I use the past tense with knowledge, the Spring is now filled up) on the north side of the Cimarron at the mouth of a canyon which comes down from the north, and is near the west line of Seward county, Kansas."

My final quotation comes from the *Eulogy.*

APPENDIX

The letters printed in my Appendix need not be annotated in detail, but some acknowledgments and other comment are called for.

The letter of Dec. 16, 1826, is from the Joel R. Poinsett Papers, Gilpin Collection, Historical Society of Pennsylvania, and is printed with the permission of that Society. The letter of May 19, 1827, to Father Narciso Durán is not known to exist in the original; I reprint it from the earliest printed text, Edmund Randolph, *Address on the*

History of California, from the Discovery of the Country to the Year 1849 (San Francisco, 1860). An apparently contemporary Spanish translation is copied into the Bancroft Library digest of the Department State Papers, vol. II, pp. 17-19.

The text I have followed for the letter of July 12, 1827, to Gen. Clark is the copy in the letterbooks of the Superintendent of Indian Affairs at St. Louis, now in the Kansas State Historical Society; vol. VI, containing letters dated between Sept. 10, 1830, and April 1, 1832, has Jedediah's letter of July 12, 1827, on pp. 46-49, and his "Brief Sketch" of [Dec.] 24, 1829, immediately following, pp. 49-54. What has become of the originals of these, no one knows. A copy of the letter of July 12, 1827, is in National Archives, Office of Indian Affairs, 1827 Miscellaneous; this is not the original as sometimes stated, and in fact is plainly marked a copy, but I have been unable to learn when the copy was made and sent to Washington; it is a little more imperfect than the Kansas copy. A version of the letter printed in the *Missouri Republican*, Oct. 11, 1827, was freely revised and condensed before publication.

The supplementary statements which follow the "Brief Sketch" in my text were furnished to Gen. Clark by Jedediah after his return to Missouri in the fall of 1830; Clark's report on the fur trade, Nov. 20, 1831, published in 22nd Cong., 1st Sess., *Senate Document 90* (Serial 213), p. 7, acknowledged the valuable assistance given him by this "intelligent, active, enterprising citizen." The Smith, Jackson & Sublette formal casualty list is copied into the Clark letterbook on pp. 297-300.

I have not been able to locate the original of the letter to the Secretary of War, Oct. 29, 1830, or even to establish when and under what circumstances it was received in Washington; my text comes from the printed version in 22nd Cong., 2nd Sess., *Senate Document 39* (Serial 203), pp. 21-23.

The letters by Solomon A. Simons to Peter Smith, Nov. 22, 1829, and by Jedediah Smith, Sr., to Peter Smith, Feb. 16, 1830, are from typewritten copies in the Kansas State Historical Society furnished to E. D. Smith by the late Walter Bacon of Los Angeles, a son-in-law of Peter Smith. Jedediah S. Smith's letter to his parents of Dec. 24, 1829, was purchased from the estate of Maurice Sullivan, together with the Jedediah Smith transcript journal, by Senator Clinton P. Anderson of New Mexico, and by him presented to the Friends of the Middle Border. For safekeeping, it and the journal are temporarily in the custody of the Library of Congress; the letter is printed by permission of Senator Anderson. Jedediah's letters to his brother Ralph, Dec. 24, 1829, Sept. 10, 1830, Jan. 26, 1831, and Feb. 28, 1831, were presented by E. D. Smith, a grandson of Ralph, to the Kansas State Historical Society, with whose permission they are now printed. Jedediah's letter of Nov. 24, 1830, to Hugh Campbell, is owned by Mr. C. Corwith Wagner of St. Louis, and has been made available by him for publication here. The brief note of May 4, 1831, to A. W. Doniphan, not in Jedediah's own hand, comes from one of the flyleaves of the Jedediah Smith transcript journal. (Perhaps I should add that the "transcript journal" is so called because it is a transcript of the fragmentary original, made for Jedediah by Samuel Parkman in St. Louis during the winter of 1830-1831; it was this version Jedediah proposed to publish.)

Austin Smith's letter of Sept. 24, 1831, to his father, was discovered by the late E. D. Smith and presented by him to the Kansas State Historical Society; it was a little worm-eaten when found, and a few words of the text have been lost. Austin's second letter of Sept. 24, 1831, to his brother Ira comes from a copy made in St. Louis in Oct. 1831; see Note 41, Chapter 15. The letter by Solomon A. Simons to Ralph Smith, Oct. 23, 1831, is reprinted from *The Travels of Jedediah Smith,* p. 156; the original is believed to be stored with some papers of the late E. D. Smith preserved by his daughter, Miss Lura S. Smith of Meade, Kansas.

INDEX